Guided Stu...

Surviving Chemistry: One Concept at a Time

A Guided Study Book for High School Chemistry

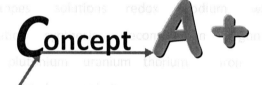

by

Effiong Eyo

Scholastic Publishing

For more information and to order:

www.e3chemistry.com   (877) 224 – 0484

info@e3chemistry.com

Acknowledgement:
Many thanks to Mary Lou Horton for her hard work with the editing of this book.

Dedication:
To my wife, Felicia, and kids, Amaia, Nyssa, Jayden and Aiyden. You are all very special to me. I love you all.

© 2010 by E3 Scholastic Publishing.
All rights reserved. No part of this book may be reproduced or transmitted in any form or by any means, electronic, mechanical, photocopying, recording, or otherwise, without prior written permission of E3 Scholastic Publishing

ISBN-10   0983132909

ISBN-13   978-0-9831329-0-5

Printed in the United States of America

Library of Congress Control Number: 2010943152

Format of this book.

This book is written in sets of concepts. Each numbered set tackles a different chemistry concept. Chemistry books should be studied, not just read. The format of this book allows you to choose and study each concept separated. By doing so, you'll be able to build up your understanding of each concept. The more of these concepts you know, the better your understanding of chemistry as a whole.

I encourage you to focus on one set of concept at a time, study that set until you understand the information of that concept. You can always skip a set of concept if you feel that you know the information related to that concept. This book is written to allow you to choose and focus on the concepts that you are struggling with. Use this book to study for your class test and finals.

There are approximately 25 to 35 review questions at the end of each topic. These questions are state standard exam questions, and are excellent practice for class test and final exams. These questions will test your understanding of concept facts and task associated with each topic. Hundreds more questions for each topic can be found in the workbook (sold separately).

Black and white version

The variation in print color that you will see in this book is due to the fact that this book was written using various color fonts. Some prints may appear darker or lighter than normal depending on the color font that was used.

This book is also available in color paperback print.

Color print version.

This book is available in color paperback print and in downloadable pdf. The colorful nature of the book enhances your visual learning of chemistry: comparisons are clearer and easier to see. Diagrams and graphs stand out more, and convey the concepts better. Explanations and solutions to problems are easier to follow and understand. Best of luck in chemistry.

Workbook.

A great companion to this study book is the workbook, which is sold separately. The workbook contains almost 5000 problems in four sections: Worksheets, multiple choices, constructed responses, and reference tables. Questions in the workbook are also separated into concept sets. This allows you to work on questions related to the same or similar concept. By working on groups of questions related to the same concept, you will test your understanding of that concept. Each concept covered in the study book has at least one set of questions in the workbook.

For more information, visit www.e3chemistry.com

Table of Contents

Topic 1 – Matter and Energy — Pg 1 – 28

- Lesson 1: Types of matter
- Lesson 2: Phases of matter and temperature
    - Temperature conversions
    - Phase change diagrams
- Lesson 3: Heat energy and heat calculations
- Lesson 4: Characteristics of gases and gas law calculations
- Lesson 5: Physical and chemical properties of matter

Topic 2 – The Periodic Table — Pg 31 – 46

- Lesson 1: Arrangement of the Elements
- Lesson 2: Types of elements and their properties
- Lesson 3: Groups of elements and their properties
- Lesson 4: Periodic Trends

Topic 3 – The Atomic Structure — Pg 49 – 72

- Lesson 1: The Historical development of the modern atom
- Lesson 2: The Atomic Structure
- Lesson 3: Electrons location and arrangement
    - Electron configuration
    - Ground and excited state
    - Spectral lines
- Lesson 4: Valance electrons and ions

Topic 4 - Chemical Bonding — Pg 73 – 96

- Lesson 1: Chemical bonding and stability of atoms
- Lesson 2: Chemical bonding and energy
- Lesson 3: Types of bonding between atoms (intramolecular forces)
    - Metallic bonds
    - Ionic bonds
    - Covalent bonds
- Lesson 4: Types of substances and their properties
- Lesson 5: Lewis electron-dot diagrams and bonding
- Lesson 6: Bonding between molecules (intermolecular forces)

Topic 5 - Chemical formulas and equations — Pg 97 – 120

- Lesson 1: Interpretation (qualitative and quantitative) of chemical formulas
- Lesson 2: Types of chemical formulas
- Lesson 3: Writing and naming chemical formulas
- Lesson 4: Chemical equations: Types of equations and balancing equations

Copyright © 2010 E3 Scholastic Publishing. All Rights Reserved.

Table of Contents

Topic 6 - Mole calculations : Mathematics of formulas and equations   Pg 121 – 138

Lesson 1: Mole interpretation in formulas
        Mole of atoms
        Gram formula mass
        Percent composition
        Percent composition of hydrates
        Molecular formulas from mass and empirical formula
Lesson 2: Mole interpretation in equations
        Mole – mole problems
        Volume – Volume problems
        Mass – mass problems

Topic 7 – Solutions   Pg 139 – 164

Lesson 1: Properties of solutions
Lesson 2: Solubility factors
Lesson 3: Descriptions of solution and the solubility curves
Lesson 4: Expression of concentration of solutions
        Molarity calculations
        Parts per million calculations
Lesson 5: Vapor pressure
Lesson 6: Effect of solutes on physical properties of water

Topic 8 - Acids, bases and salts   Pg 165 – 188

Lesson 1: Definitions of acids and bases
        By theories
        By relative ions concentrations
        By pH values
        By changes on indicators
Lesson 2: Reactions of acids and bases
        Metal – acid reaction
        Neutralization reaction
        Titration
Lesson 3: Salts
Lesson 4: Electrolytes
Lesson 5: Formulas and names of acids and bases

Topic 9 - Kinetics and Equilibrium   Pg 189 – 222

Lesson 1: Kinetics: Rate of reactions
Lesson 2: Energy and chemical reactions
        Potential energy diagrams
Lesson 3: Entropy
Lesson 4: Equilibrium
        Physical equilibrium
        Chemical equilibrium (Le Chatelier's principle)

Table of Contents

Topic 10 - Organic Chemistry   Pg 223 – 260

Lesson 1: Characteristics of carbon and organic compounds

Lesson 2: Classes of organic compounds

    Hydrocarbons

    Functional groups compounds

Lesson 3: Isomers

Lesson 4: Drawing and naming organic compounds

Lesson 5: Organic reactions

Topic 11 – Redox and Electrochemistry   Pg 261 – 288

Lesson 1: Oxidation numbers

Lesson 2: Oxidation and reduction (redox) reactions

Lesson 3: Electrochemistry

    Voltaic cells

    Electrolytic cells

Lesson 4: Spontaneous reactions

Topic 12 - Nuclear chemistry   Pg 289 – 316

Lesson 1: Nuclear transmutations

    Natural transmutation: Alpha decay, Beta decay, positron emission

    Artificial transmutation

Lesson 2: Nuclear energy

    Fission

    Fusion

Lesson 3: Half-life and half-life calculations

Reference Tables   R-1 – R-12

Glossary   G-1 – G14

Index   I-1 – I-8

Topic 1 - Matter and Energy

Topic outline

In this topic, you will learn the following concepts:

- Types of matter and their characteristics
- Phases of matter and their characteristics
- Phase changes and relationship to energy
- Physical and chemical properties
- Temperature
- Heat energy
- Properties of gases
- Physical and chemical changes
- Temperature conversions
- Heat energy calculations
- Gas law calculations

Lesson 1: Types of matter

Introduction

Chemistry is the study of matter: Its composition, structures, properties, changes it undergoes, and energy accompanying these changes.

Matter is anything that has mass and takes up space. Matter, in another word, is "stuff."
Matter can be grouped and classified as pure substances or mixtures.

In this lesson, you will learn about different types of matter and its characteristics. You will also learn to recognize different types of matter by chemical symbols and diagrams.

1. Pure substances: Definitions, facts and examples

Concept Facts: Study to remember characteristics of pure substances listed below.

A Pure substance is a type of matter in which every sample has:
- Definite and fixed (same percent) composition
- Same unique sets of properties
- *Elements* and *Compounds* are classified as pure substances

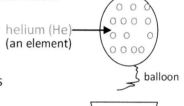

Examples of some common pure substances:

Elements	*Compounds*
Na (sodium)	H_2O (water)
Al (aluminum)	CO_2 (carbon dioxide)
H_2 (hydrogen)	NH_3 (ammonia)
He (helium)	$C_6H_{12}O_6$ (sugar)

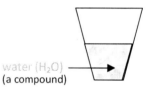

Helium and water are both classified as pure substances.

2. Elements: Definitions, facts and examples

Concept Facts: Study to remember characteristics of elements listed below.

An Element is a pure substance that:
- Is composed (made up) of identical atoms with the same atomic number
- CANNOT be decomposed (broken down) into simpler substances neither by physical nor by chemical methods

Examples of some elements:
Mg (Magnesium) Br_2 (Bromine)   Au (gold)

Helium, an element, is composed of helium atoms.

Helium cannot be broken down into any simpler substances because it is an element.

There are more than 100 known elements.
Elements' names and symbols can be found on the Periodic Table of the Elements.

LOOKING AHEAD ⟹ **Topic 2 - Periodic Table**, you will learn more about the elements.

Copyright © 2010 E3 Scholastic Publishing All Rights Reserved.

Topic 1 - Matter and Energy

3. Compounds: Definitions and facts

Concept Facts: Study to remember characteristics of compounds listed below.

A Compound is a pure substance:
. Composed of two or more different elements chemically combined
. That has a definite composition (fixed ratio) of atoms in all samples
. CAN BE decomposed into simpler substances by chemical methods
. Has the same unique set of properties in all of its samples
  NOTE: Properties of a compound are different from those of the elements which it is composed.

Law of definite proportion states: The types of atoms in a compound exist in fixed ratio

Examples of some common compounds:
H_2O (Water) CO_2 (Carbon Dioxide)
NH_3 (Ammonia) $NaCl$ (Sodium Chloride)

Below are similarities and differences between compounds and elements
Concept Facts: Study to remember these comparisons.

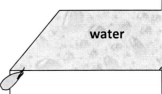

H_2O (water), a compound, is composed of two different atoms chemically combined.

H_2O can be chemically broken down (decomposed) to its components (H and O)

Compounds are similar to elements in that:
.Both are pure substances
.Both always have homogeneous properties
.Both have fixed and definite compositions in all samples

Compounds are different from elements in that :
.Compounds can be broken down (decomposed) by chemical means
   Elements cannot be broken down.

4. Why are oxygen and water considered pure substances? Comparison of samples

Oxygen sample collected from
Saint **M**ary **P**rimary **S**chool
D4 Camp, Cross River State, Nigeria

Oxygen sample collected from
Our **L**ady of **L**ourdes HS
Poughkeepsie, NY, USA

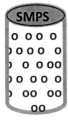

55°C	*Melting/freezing temperature*	55°C
90°C	*Boiling temperature*	90°C
8 protons 8 electrons	*Compositions of oxygen atom*	8 protons 8 electrons

Both oxygen samples **chemically react** with H to make H_2O (water)

Water sample collected from
Saint **M**ary **P**rimary **S**chool
D4 Camp, Cross River State, Nigeria

Water sample collected from
Our **L**ady of **L**ourdes HS
Poughkeepsie, NY, USA

0°C	*Melting/freezing temperature*	0°C
100°C	*Boiling temperature*	100°C
2 H 1 O	*Compositions of a water molecule*	2 H 1 O

Both water samples **chemically react vigorously** with sodium.

Oxygen and water **are both pure substances** because a sample from one place has exact same sets of properties, compositions and reactivity as a sample taken from another place.

Topic 1 - Matter and Energy

5. Mixtures: Definitions and Facts

Concept Fact: Study to remember characteristics of mixtures listed below:

A Mixture is a type of matter:
- Composed of two or more substances that are *physically* combined
- That has varying ratio of composition from one sample to another sample
- CAN BE physically separated into its components
- Retains properties of its components

Examples of some common mixtures
Salt water	NaCl (aq)
Sugar solution	$C_6H_{12}O_6$ (aq)
Hydrochloric acid solution	HCl (aq)
Soil, concrete, and air.	

Similarities and differences between mixtures and compounds are given below.

Concept Facts: Study to remember these comparisons.

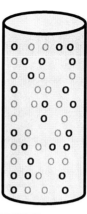

Oxygen and helium gas mixture

Mixtures are similar to compounds in that:
- Both are composed (made of) of two or more different substances
- Both can be separated into their components

Mixtures are different from compounds in that:
- Components of a mixture are *physically* combined, composition varies
  - In compounds, they are *chemically* combined; composition is definite (same)
- Components of a mixture are separated by *physical methods*
  - In compounds, they are separated by *chemical methods*
- Mixtures can be classified either as homogenous or heterogeneous
  - Compounds can only be homogenous

6. Homogeneous and Heterogeneous Mixtures: Definitions and facts

Homogeneous mixtures:
A mixture is classified as a homogeneous mixture if:
- The components of the mixture are uniformly and evenly mixed throughout
- Samples taken within the same mixture have the same composition

- Aqueous solutions are homogeneous mixtures made with water.

Examples of some aqueous solutions:
Salt water - A scoop of salt in a glass of water makes aqueous solution (homogenous mixture) of water

L⊙⊙KING AHEAD ⟹ **Topic 7 - Solutions.** You will learn more about aqueous solutions.

Heterogeneous mixtures:
A mixture is classified as a heterogeneous mixture if:
- The components of the mixture are not uniformly mixed throughout
- Samples taken within the same mixture have different compositions

Examples of heterogeneous mixtures:
Concrete, soil, sand mixed with salt.

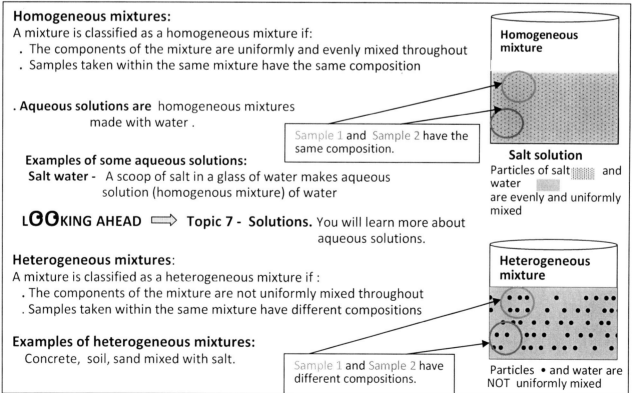

Sample 1 and Sample 2 have the same composition.

Salt solution
Particles of salt and water are evenly and uniformly mixed

Sample 1 and Sample 2 have different compositions.

Heterogeneous mixture
Particles • and water are NOT uniformly mixed

Copyright © 2010 E3 Scholastic Publishing All Rights Reserved.

Topic 1 - Matter and Energy

7   Classification of matter diagram

Below is a flow diagram summarizing classes of matter.

Concept fact: Study to remember the different classes of matter.

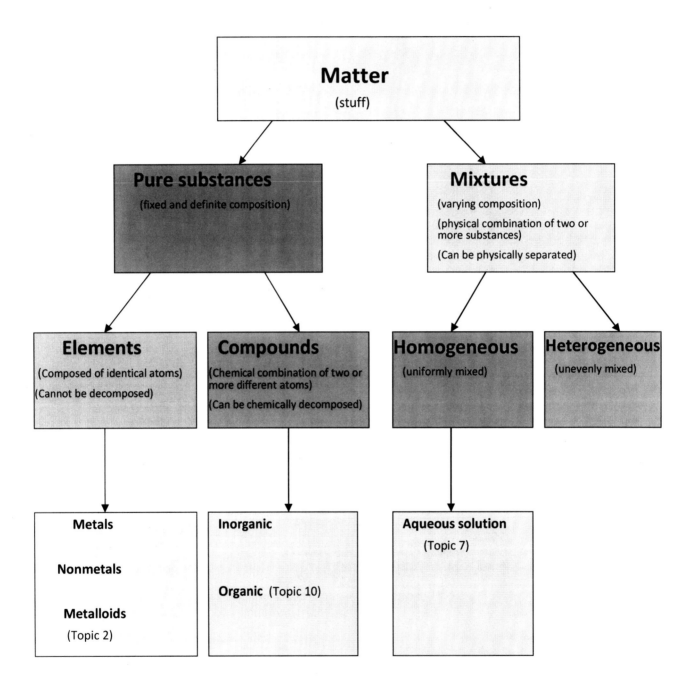

Topic 1 - Matter and Energy

8. Chemical Symbols of matter: Recognizing chemical symbols of matter

Chemical symbols are used to show the compositions of elements, compounds and mixtures.

Examples:
$Au(s)$ is the chemical symbol for gold, an element.
$H_2O\ (l)$ is the chemical symbol for water, a compound.
$C_6H_{12}O_6(aq)$ is the chemical symbol for sugar water, a mixture.

Concept Task: Be able to determine which chemical symbol represents an element, a compound, and a mixture.

Pure substances
To determine formula or name of a pure substance:
To determine a formula that has fixed or definite composition

LOOK for a name or a symbol of an element or a compound

Elements
To determine formula or name of an element:
To determine which substance CANNOT be decomposed:
To determine which substance is composed of atoms with the same atomic number.

LOOK for a name or symbol that can be found on the Periodic Table
LOOK for a symbol written with one capital letter only

Compounds
To determine formula or name of a compound
To determine which substance CAN BE decomposed by chemical method:

LOOK for name or symbol containing two or more different elements (or with two or more capital letters)

Binary compounds
To determine formula or name of a binary compound

LOOK for a name or a symbol containing JUST TWO different elements.
Formulas of binary compounds contains TWO capital letters

NOTE: (s), (l), or (g) may be written next to a chemical symbol of show the phase (solid, liquid, or gas) of the pure substance (compound and element).

Mixtures
To determine symbol of a homogeneous mixture
To determine symbol of matter whose composition can vary

LOOK for symbol containing (aq)

Example 1

Which set of formulas contains only of pure substances?

1) $Ca(s)$ and $CaCl_2(aq)$
2) $NH_3(g)$ and $NH_3(aq)$
3) $Cl_2(g)$ and $NaCl(s)$
4) $NaOH(aq)$ and $H_2O\ (l)$

Answer: Choice 3 because $Cl_2(g)$ is an element and $NaCl(s)$ is a compound.

Example 2:

Which substance cannot be decomposed into simpler substances?

1) Water   3) Lithium
2) Carbon monoxide 4) Ethanol

Answer: Choice 3 Because Lithium an element (See Periodic Table), and elements cannot be decomposed.

Example 3:

Which set of substances can only be decomposed by chemical methods?

1) $H_2O_2(l)$ and $KClO_3(s)$
2) $Na(s)$ and $NaCl(aq)$
3) $N_2(g)$ and $NO_3(g)$
4) $CH_4(g)$ and $CO_2(aq)$

Answer: Choice 1 because both H_2O_2 and $KClO_3$ are composed of two or more elements, and therefore are compounds. Compounds CAN BE decomposed by chemical methods.

NOTE: H_2O_2 is a binary compound?

Example 4:

Which of the followings represents a homogeneous mixture?

1) $NH_3(aq)$ 3) $Br_2(l)$
2) $MgSO_4(s)$ 4) $Ar\ (g)$

Answer: Choice 1 because (aq) always indicates a mixture

Topic 1 - Matter and Energy

9. Diagrams of matter: Recognizing diagram representations of matter

Diagrams can also be used to show compositions of elements, compounds and mixtures. Examples are given below.

Concept Task: Be able to recognize a diagram that shows an element, a compound or a mixture. Study the examples below to learn how to recognize diagrams of elements, compounds and mixtures.

Given the following symbols:

Atom X	Atom Y
○	●

Element   To determine if a diagram is showing composition of an element

LOOK for a diagram containing only of identical atoms (or shapes).

Below, examples of element X and Y

   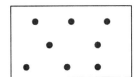

Diatomic element X   Monatomic element Y

Compound   To determine if a diagram is showing compositions of a compound

LOOK for a diagram containing two different atoms touching. Each unit MUST BE identical to others in the box

Below, examples of compounds from atom X and Y

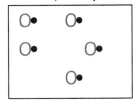   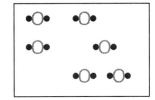

Compound composed of   Compound composed of
one atom X and one atom Y   two atoms Y and one atom X

(Five identical units of ○●) (Six identical units ●○●)

Mixture   To determine if a diagram is showing composition of a mixture

LOOK for a diagram showing a mixture of different atoms and /or compounds. The different substances should NOT be touching

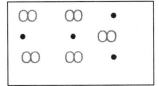   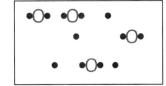

A Mixture of diatomic element X   A mixture of compound XY
and monatomic element Y   and atom Y

6   Copyright © 2010 E3 Scholastic Publishing. All Rights Reserved.

Topic 1 - Matter and Energy

10. Separation of mixtures: Definitions, facts and examples.

Substances making up a mixture can be separated by various physical methods.

Recall that substances making up a mixture are physically combined. Since they are physically combined, substances in a mixture retain their individual physical properties. Physical properties of each substance makes it possible to separate one substance from the others in a mixture. The method of separation depends on the physical characteristics of the substances in the mixture.

For example: Consider a heterogeneous mixture of iron and salt.

  One physical property of iron is its ability to attract a magnet.

  A magnet can be use to separate the substances by removing iron from the mixture, and leaving behind the salt.

Below are three common separation techniques that can be used to separate components of a mixture.

Pouring (Decantation)
Decantation is a process of pouring off a top layer of a mixture while leaving materials at the bottom of the container.
When oil and water are mixed together, layers of oil and water form because oil and water are immiscible (do not mix) liquids. The top layer of oil can be slowly poured off. The bottom layer of water will be left behind in the container.

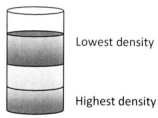

A mixture of three immiscible liquids separates into layers. Each layer of liquid can be separated from the others by pouring.

Distillation/Boiling/Evaporation
Distillation is a process of separating a homogeneous mixture (solutions) in which the components of the mixture have different boiling points. In a salt solution, the salt particles are homogeneously mixed with the water. Distillation process can be used to separate water from the salt in this mixture. During distillation, the mixture is heated in a glass container that is connected to series of tubes. When the temperature of the mixture reaches the boiling point of water, water will evaporate out of the mixture and into a condenser tube. Once cooled, the steam in the condenser tube will condense to water, and is collected. Once all of the water is boiled (evaporated) off from the mixture, the salt part of the mixture is left behind in the container.

Filtration
Filtration is a process that is used to separate a liquid mixture composed of substances with different particle sizes.
A filter is an equipment containing holes that allow particles of a mixture that are smaller than the holes to pass through, while particles that are bigger than the holes are kept in the filter. A mixture of salt water and sand can be separated with a filter. The aqueous phase of the mixture contains molecules of water and particles of salt, which are smaller than the holes of a filter. During filtration the aqueous components (salt and water) will go through the filter. The sand will stay on the filter because the sand particles are larger than the holes of the filter paper.

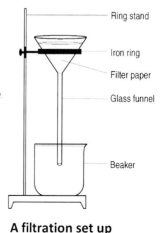

A filtration set up

Topic 1 - Matter and Energy

Lesson 2 – Phases of matter

Introduction

There are three phases of matter: solid, liquid, and gas. The fourth phase of matter, plasma, is not commonly discussed in high school chemistry.

The nature of a substance determines the phase in which the substance will exist under normal conditions. For example, gold will always be a solid at room temperature (23°C). At the same room temperature, water will always exists as a liquid, and oxygen will always exist as a gas.

Most substances can change from one phase to another. The nature of a substance also determines conditions needed for the substance to change from one phase to another.

In this lesson, you will learn about the three phases of matter. You will also learn phase changes of matter, and relationship to temperature and energy.

11. Phases of matter: Definitions, facts, and diagram representations

The notes below define and summarize characteristics of substances in the different phases.
To the right are diagrams showing particles arrangements in each phase.

Concept Fact: Study to remember the facts below, and note the differences between the diagrams.

Solid: A substance in the solid phase has:
. Definite volume and definite shape
. Particles arranged orderly in a *"regular geometric pattern"*
. Particles vibrating around a fixed point
. Particles with strong attractive force to one another
. Particles that cannot be easily compressed (incompressible)

Orderly and regular geometric arrangement of particles in **solid** phase

Liquid: A substance in the liquid phase has:
. Definite volume, but no definite shape (It takes the shape of its container)
. Particles that are less orderly arranged than those in solid phase
. Particles with weaker attractive forces than those in sold phase.
. Particles that flow over each
. Particles that cannot be easily compressed (incompressible)

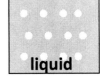

Gas: A substance in the gas phase has:
. No definite volume and no definite shape (it takes volume and shape of its container)
. Particles far less orderly arranged (most random)
. Particles that move fast and freely throughout the space of the container
. Particles with very weak attractive force to each other
. Particles that can be easily compressed (compressible)

12. Phases of matter: Symbol representations of substances in different phases

When a formula of a substance is given, the phase in which the substance exists is often indicated, in parenthesis, next to the formula. Examples are given below.

Concept Task: Be able to interpret formula in different phases

Example formulas	Interpretation
$H_2O(s)$	Water in **solid** phase
$Br_2(l)$	Bromine in *liquid* phase
$NH_3(g)$	Ammonia in *gas* phase
$KCl(aq)$	Aqueous solution of potassium chloride.
	OR
	A mixture of potassium chloride

Example 5:
Which of the following substances have particles that are arranged in regular geometric pattern?

1) Al(s) 3) $CCl_4(l)$
2) Ar(g) 4) $NH_3(aq)$

Answer: Choice 1: Because Al(s) is a solid, and particle of a solid are arranged in regular geometric pattern.

Topic 1 - Matter and Energy

13. Phase changes: Phase change definitions and equations

During a phase change, a substance changes its form (or state) without changing its chemical composition. Therefore, a phase change is a physical change. Any substance can change from one phase to another given the right conditions of temperature and/or pressure. Most substances require a large change in temperature to go through one phase change. Water is one of only a few chemical substances that can change through all three phases within a narrow range of temperature.

Below are six phase changes you need to know.

Concept Fact: Study to remember their definitions, and note example equation for each.

Fusion (also known as **melting**) is a change from *solid* to *liquid*. $H_2O(s) \longrightarrow H_2O(l)$

Freezing is a change of phase from *liquid* to *solid* $H_2O(l) \longrightarrow H_2O(s)$

Evaporation is a change of phase from *liquid* to *gas* $C_2H_5OH(l) \longrightarrow C_2H_5OH(g)$

Condensation is a change of phase from *gas* to *liquid* $C_2H_5OH(g) \longrightarrow C_2HOH(l)$

Sublimation is a change of phase from *solid* to *gas* $CO_2(s) \longrightarrow CO_2(g)$

Deposition is a change of phase from *gas* to *solid* $CO_2(g) \longrightarrow CO_2(s)$

NOTE: $CO_2(s)$, solid carbon dioxide (also known as dry ice), and $I_2(s)$, solid iodine are two chemicals substances that readily sublime at room temperature. Most substances do not sublime.

14. Phase change and energy: Definitions and facts

Phase changes defined above occur when a substance had absorbed or released enough heat energy to rearrange its particles (atoms or molecule) from one phase to another. Some phase changes require a release of heat by the substance, while other phase changes require the substance to absorb heat.

Below are two heat related terms and how they relate to phase changes.

Concept Fact: Study to remember them

Endothermic describes a process that absorbs heat.

Fusion, evaporation and sublimation are endothermic phase changes.

Exothermic describes a process that releases heat.

Freezing, condensation and deposition are exothermic phase changes.

Below is a summary diagram of phase changes their relationship to heat energy.

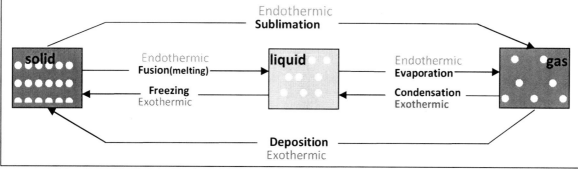

Topic 1 - Matter and Energy

15. Phase change and energy: Relating phase change equation to heat energy

Concept Task: Be able to determine which phase change is exothermic (heat released) and which phase change is endothermic (heat absorbed).

Example questions are given below.

Example 6.

Which phase change equation is exothermic?

1) $N_2(l) \longrightarrow N_2(g)$
2) $Hg(s) \longrightarrow Hg(l)$
3) $CH_4(g) \longrightarrow CH_4(l)$
4) $I_2(s) \longrightarrow I_2(g)$

Answer: Choice 3: Equation is showing condensation.
Condensation requires a release of heat (exothermic).

Example 7

Heat will be absorbed by a substance as it changes from

1) Solid to gas
2) Liquid to solid
3) Gas to solid
4) Gas to liquid

Answer: Choice 1: This is sublimation, and sublimation is an endothermic phase change.

16. Temperature: Definitions and facts

Below, definition and facts related to temperature are given.

Concept Fact: Study to remember the following terms and facts.

Temperature is a measure of the average kinetic energy of particles in matter.

Kinetic energy is energy due to movements of particles in a substance.
. The higher the temperature of a substance, the greater its kinetic energy
. As temperature increases, the average kinetic energy increases

Thermometer is an equipment that is used for measuring temperature.

Two units of measuring temperature are: Degree Celsius (°C) and Kelvin (K).

The mathematical relationship between Celsius and Kelvin is given by the equation:

$$K = °C + 273$$ See Reference Table T

According to this equation, the Kevin temperature value is always 273 higher than the same temperature value in Celsius.

Two fixed reference points are needed to create a thermometer scale:
The *freezing point (0°C, 273K)* and the **boiling point (100°C, 373K)** *of water* are often used as the two reference points in creating a thermometer scale.

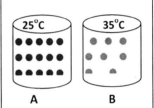

Since particles • in B are at a higher temperature, • will be moving faster (higher kinetic energy) than particles • in A

Important temperature points

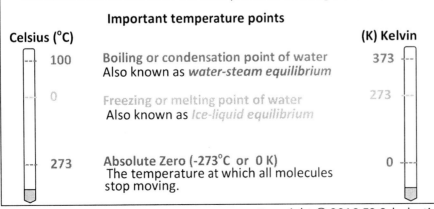

Celsius (°C)

- 100 — Boiling or condensation point of water
  Also known as *water-steam equilibrium* — 373 (K) Kelvin

- 0 — Freezing or melting point of water
  Also known as *Ice-liquid equilibrium* — 273

- 273 — Absolute Zero (-273°C or 0 K)
  The temperature at which all molecules stop moving. — 0

A graph showing a direct relationship between temperature and kinetic energy

Topic 1 - Matter and Energy

17. Temperature: Determining substance with higher or lower kinetic energy

Concept Task: Be able to determine which temperature has the highest or lowest kinetic energy.

To determine which substance has:

Highest kinetic energy: **LOOK** for the Highest temperature
Lowest Kinetic energy: **LOOK** for the Lowest temperature

Example 8:
Which substance will contain particles with the highest average kinetic energy

1) NO (g) at 40°C
2) N_2O(g) at 30°C
3) NO_2g) at 45°C
4) N_2O_3(g) at 35°C

Answer: Choice 3. It is the choice with the highest temperature

NOTE: Type of substance does not matter.

Example 9:
Which container contains water molecules with the lowest average kinetic energy?

40°C   50°C   60°C   70°C

1)   2)   3)   4)

Answer: Choice 1: Because it is at the lowest temperature:
NOTE: Amount of the substance in the containers does not matter.

Example 10:
Which change in temperature is accompanied by greatest increase in average kinetic energy of a substance?

1) -20°C to 15°C
2) 15°C to -20°C
3) -35°C to 30°C
4) 30°C to -35°C

Before choosing:
Consider: For kinetic energy to increase, temperature must be increasing.
Consider choices 1 and 3 because these two show increase in temperature.
To find the greatest increase, choose the choice with a greater difference in temperature.

Answer: Choice 3. The difference between -35 and 30 is 65. In choice 1, the difference is only 35.

18. Temperature conversion: Be able to change a temperature from one unit to another

Concept Task: When a temperature is given in one unit (°C or K) be able to convert it to a different unit.

To Convert temperature from one unit to another,

Use the equation: $K = °C + 273$

SEE Reference Table T for equation

Example 11:
Which Celsius temperature is equivalent to +20 K?

1) -253   3) +253
2) -293   4) +293

Before choosing
Write equation: $K = °C + 273$
Substitute 20 for K: $20 = °C + 273$
Solve for °C $°C = -253$

Answer: Choice 1

Topic 1 - Matter and Energy

19. Phase change diagrams: Understanding phase change diagrams

A phase change diagram is a diagram that shows the relationship between temperature and phase changes of a substance over a period of time as the substance is heating or cooling.

The heating and cooling of a substance experiment can be conducted in a laboratory to see the change in temperature of that substance over time. The data of time and temperature from the experiment can be collected, plotted, and graphed to generate a phase change diagram.

The unique thing about all phase change data and diagrams is that temperature of the substance changes only at certain times. The temperature remains constant at other times even though heat is continuously being added to (or removed from) the substance at a constant rate. Your ability to explain this phenomenon depends on your understanding of the relationship between heat, temperature, kinetic energy, potential energy, and particles arrangement of a substance in different phases.

There are Two Phase Change Diagrams.

Concept Fact: Study to remember information related to these two curves.

The heating curve:
. Shows a change of a substance starting with the substance as a solid
. Shows temperature change of a substance as heat is absorbed (endothermic process)

The cooling curve:
. Shows a change of a substance starting with the substance as a gas
. Shows temperature change of a substance as heat is released (exothermic process)

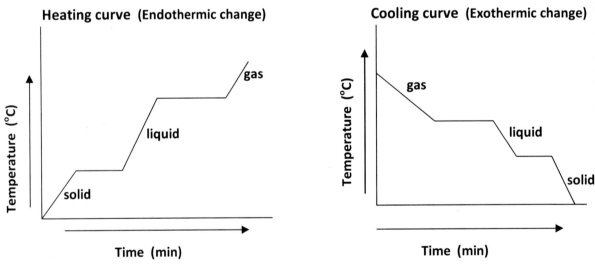

Understanding a phase change diagram can help you determine the following information about a substance:
. Freezing, melting, and boiling points of a substance
. When potential and kinetic energy are changing or remaining constant
. When a substance is in one phase: solid, liquid, or gas phase
. When a substance is in two phases: solid/liquid or liquid/gas mix
. The total time a substance stays in any phase.
. The total time it takes for a substance to go through any of the phase change

The notes on the next section will show you how to determine the above information from any given phase change diagram. Follow the examples given when interpreting other phase change diagrams.

Topic 1 - Matter and Energy

20. Phase change diagrams: Identify freezing, melting and boiling points, and other segments

Concept Task: Be able to identify segments and interpret heating and cooling curves. Follow and study interpretations given below for the heating and the cooling curves.

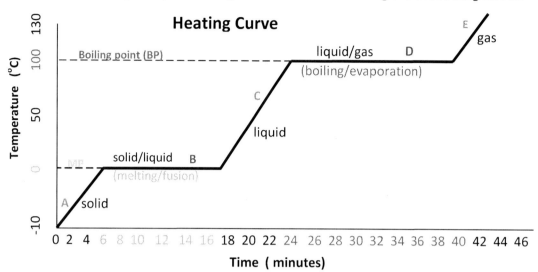

Some important information about the above heating curve.

Melting point / freezing point/ solid - liquid equilibrium occurs at :	0°C
Boiling point / condensation point/ liquid-gas equilibrium occurs at :	100°C
kinetic energy increases / potential energy remains constant during segments:	A, C, and E
The substance exists in one phase during segments:	A, C, and E
Potential energy increases / kinetic energy remains constant during segment:	B and D
The substance exists in two phases during segments:	B and D
Total time the substance goes through boiling (from 24 to 40 minutes) :	16 minutes

The substance is likely water because solid water(ice) melts at 0°C **and boils at 100°C**

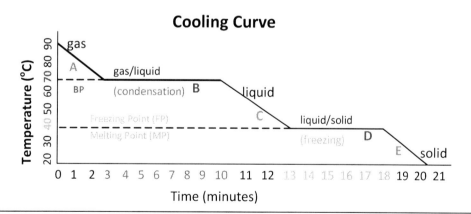

Some important information about the cooling curve above:

Melting point / freezing point/ solid - liquid equilibrium occurs at :	40°C
Boiling point / condensation point/ liquid gas-equilibrium occurs at :	70°C
kinetic energy decreases / potential energy remains constant during segments:	A, C, and E
Potential energy decreases / kinetic energy remains constant during segment:	B and D
Total time for substance to freeze (from 13 to 18 minutes) :	5 minutes

The substance is not water because the freezing **and boiling points are different from those of water.**

Topic 1 - Matter and Energy

Lesson 3 – Heat energy and heat calculations

Introduction

Heat is a form of energy that can flow (or transfer) from one object to another.
Direction of heat flow depends on the temperature difference.
Heat will always flow from an area or object of a higher temperature to an area or object of a lower temperature.
During chemical and physical changes, heat energy is either absorbed or released. The amount of heat energy absorbed or released can be determined using various methods. One of those methods (and the most convenience) is to take the temperature of a reaction before and after a change, and use the temperature difference in a heat equation. When other factors are known about a substance, the amount of heat absorbed or released can be calculated using a heat equation.
In this lesson, you will learn about heat and its relationship to temperature. You will also learn how to use heat equations to calculate the heat absorbed or released during temperature and phase changes.

21. Heat: Definitions and facts

Heat is a form of energy that can flow from high to low temperature area.

Below are some important information related to heat energy.

Concept Facts: Study to remember them.

Joules and **calories** are the two most common units for measuring heat.
Calorimeter is a device used in measuring heat during physical or chemical changes.

Exothermic describes a process that **releases** (emits or loses) heat.
  As an object or a substance releases heat, its temperature decreases.

Endothermic describes a process that **absorbs** (gains) heat.
  As an object or a substance absorbs heat, its temperature increases.

Direction of heat flow

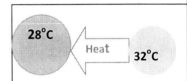

Lower temp   Higher temp

Heat will always flow from high temperature to lower temperature.

22. Relating heat to temperature: Determining direction of heat flow

Concept Task: Be able to determine and the describe direction of heat flow.

Example 12.

Object A and object B are placed next to each other. If object B is at $12°C$, heat will flow from object A to object B when the temperature of object A is at

1) $6°C$ 2) $10°C$ 3) $12°C$ 4) $15°C$

Answer: Choice 4. Heat will ONLY flow from A to B if the temperature of A is higher. $15°C$ is the correct choice because it is higher than $12°C$.

Example 13:
Given the diagrams

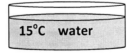

Which correctly describes the heat flow when the metal object is dropped into the water?

1) Heat will flow from the metal to water, and the water temperature will decrease
2) Heat will flow from the metal to water, and the water temperature will increase
3) Heat will flow from water to the metal, and the water temperature will decrease
4) Heat will flow from water to the metal, and the water temperature will increase

Answer: Choice 2. Heat will flow from the metal to the water because the metal has a higher temperature than the water.
As heat flows to the water, its temperature increases. The metal temperature will decrease.

Topic 1 - Matter and Energy

23. Heat calculations: Understanding heat equations and heat constants

The amount of heat absorbed or released by a substance can be calculated using heat equations. There are three heat equations, and each heat equation contains a heat constant. The heat equations and the heat constants for water are given on the Reference Tables.

Reference Table B: Heat constant for water

Heat of fusion (Hf)	334 J/g
Heat of Vaporization (Hv)	2260 J/g
Specific Heat Capacity of $H_2O(l)$ (C)	4.18 J/g·°C

Reference Table T: Heat equations

Heat(q)	$q = mC\Delta T$
	$q = mH_f$
	$q = mH_v$

The notes below explain more about the heat constant and the heat equation, as well as when to use each heat equation.

24. Specific heat capacity: Understanding heat equation during temperature change

A substance can change from one temperature to another by either absorbing or releasing heat.
If heat is absorbed, the temperature of the substance will increase.
If heat is released, the temperature of the substance will decrease.

$$\text{Heat} = m \times C \times \Delta T$$

If the specific heat capacity and the mass of a substance are known, the amount of heat absorbed or released by the substance to change from one temperature to another can be calculated using the equation below:

$$\text{Heat} = m \times C \times \Delta T$$

m	= mass of substance (g)
C	= specific heat capacity (J/g·°C)
ΔT	= difference in temperature (°C)
(ΔT	= High temp - Low temp)

Specific heat capacity (C) of a substance is the amount of heat needed to change the temperature of a 1 gram sample of a substance by just 1°C.

Specific heat capacity (C) for water = 4.18 J/g·°C   **See Reference Table B**

This value (4.18 J/g·°C) for water can be interpreted in the following ways:

It takes 4.18 Joules (J) of heat energy to change the temperature of a one gram (g) sample of water by just one degree Celsius (°C).
Or
A one gram sample of water must absorb (or release) 4.18 Joules of heat energy to change its temperature by just one Celsius degree (°C)

In heat equations, the specific heat capacity (C) serves as a conversion factor that allows you to calculate the amount of heat absorbed (or released) by any given amount (grams) of a substance to change from any given temperature to another.

NOTE: Specific heat capacity for other substances are different from that of water.

Topic 1 - Matter and Energy

25. Heat of fusion: Understanding heat equation during melting and freezing

A substance can change between the solid and the liquid phase by absorbing or releasing heat.
If heat is absorbed by a solid, the substance will change to its liquid state. This is called fusion (or melting).
If heat is released by a liquid, the substance will change to its solid state. This is called freezing.

If the heat of fusion and the mass of a substance are known, the amount of heat absorbed or released by the substance to melt or freeze can be calculated using the heat equation below:

$$\text{Heat} = m \times H_f$$

m = mass of solid or liquid (g)
H_f = Heat of fusion (J/g)

Heat of fusion (H_f) of a substance is the amount of heat needed to melt or freeze a one gram sample of the substance.

Heat of fusion of water = 334 J/g

See Reference Table B

Interpretation:
It takes 334 Joules of heat to melt or freeze a one gram sample of water (at a constant melting point).

In the equation above, the heat of fusion (H_f) serves as a conversion factor that allows you to calculate the amount of heat being absorbed (or released) by any given amount (gram) of a substance to melt or freeze.

Concept Fact: For any substance, the heat of fusion is always lower than the heat of vaporization.

26. Heat of vaporization: Understanding heat equation during boiling and condensing phase changes.

A substance can change between the liquid and the gas phase by absorbing or releasing heat.
If heat is absorbed by a liquid, it will change to its gaseous state. This is called boiling (or vaporization).
If heat is released by a gas, it will change to its liquid state. This is called condensation.

If the heat of vaporization (H_v) and the mass (g) of a substance are known, the amount of heat absorbed or released by the substance to change between the liquid and the gas states can be calculated using the heat equation below:

$$\text{Heat} = m \times H_v$$

m = mass of solid or liquid (g)
H_v = Heat of vaporization (J/g)

Heat of vaporization (H_v) of a substance is the amount of heat needed to change a one gram sample of the substance between the liquid and the gas phase at constant boiling temperature.

Heat of vaporization of water = 2260 J/g

See Reference Table B

Interpretation: (2260 J/g) for water can be interpreted as such:
It takes 2260 Joules of heat to vaporize or condense a one gram sample of water (at a constant boiling point).

In the equation above, the heat of vaporization (H_f) serves as a conversion factor that allows you to calculate the amount of heat being absorbed (or released) by any given amount (gram) of a substance to vaporize or condense.

Concept Fact: For any substance, the heat of vaporization is always Higher than the heat of fusion.

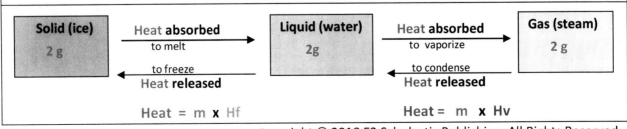

Topic 1 - Matter and Energy

27. Heat calculations: Solving for heat in heat calculation problems.

Concept Task: Be able to use heat equation to set up and calculate heat absorbed or released by a substance.

As mentioned earlier, one of the most important steps in solving a heat problem is to choose the correct heat equation. Once the correct equation is chosen, solving heat problem becomes a matter of plugging in the right numbers into the equation and calculating your setup. Your set up and calculation must all be correct to get the right heat value for the problem given.

Which heat equation to choose? Below are example key words and phrases in heat questions that indicate which of the three heat equations you should choose. Example heat problem for each equation, and step-by-step instruction of solving are given on the right. Study both sides to learn how to solve heat problems.

A. Heat equation for temperature change

$$\text{Heat} = m \times C \times \Delta T$$

Choose this equation for heat questions that have any of the following key words or phrases.
- Changes temperature from...
- Two different temperatures given
- A change in temperature is given

Example 14:
How much heat is released by a 3 gram sample of water to change its temperature from 15°C to 10°C?

Step 1. Identify the known and unknown
  Known: **Unknown**
  Mass (g) = 3   Heat = ?
  ΔT (°C) = 15 – 10 = 5
  C (J/g·°C) = 4.18 (for water – Table B)

Step 2. Choose and write down equation to use
  Heat = m × C × ΔT

Step 3. Substitute known into equation & solve
  Heat = m × C × ΔT
  Heat = 3 × 4.18 × 5 = **62.7 Joules**

B. Heat equation for fusion phase change

$$\text{Heat} = m \times H_f$$

Choose this equation for heat questions that have any of the following key words or phrases.
- To melt or to freeze
- Changes from solid to liquid
- Changes from liquid to solid
- At constant temperature of 0°C

Example 15:
What is the number of joules needed to melt a 6 g sample of ice to water at 0°C?

Step 1. Identify the known and the unknown.
  Known   **Unknown**
  Mass (g) = 6   Heat = ?
  Hf (J/g) = 334 *(for water – Table B)*

Step 2: Choose and write down equation to use:
  Heat = m × Hf

Step 3: Substitute known into equation & solve
  Heat = m × Hf
  Heat = 6 × 334 = **2004 J**

C. Heat equation for evaporation phase change

$$\text{Heat} = m \times H_v$$

Choose this equation for heat questions that have any of the following key words or phrases.
- To evaporate or vaporize
- To boil, to condense
- To change from liquid to gas
- To change from gas to liquid
- At constant temperature of 100°C

Example 16:
Liquid ammonia has a heat of vaporization of 1.35 KJ/g. How many kilojoules of heat are needed to evaporate a 5 gram sample of ammonia at its boiling point?

Step 1: Identify the known and the unknown
  Known   **Unknown**
  Mass (g) = 5   Heat = ?
  Hv (KJ/g) = 1.35 (for ammonia)

Step 2: Choose and write down equation to use

Step 3: Substitute known into equation & solve
  Heat = m × Hv
  Heat = 5 × 1.35 = **6.75 KJ**

Topic 1 - Matter and Energy

28. Heat problems: Solving for other unknowns in heat problems

Concept Task: Be able to set up for and calculate other unknowns in a heat problem.

On the previous pages, the example heat problems only deal with calculating the amount of heat absorbed or released by the substance. You should also be able to calculate other factors of a heat equation. In a question, the amount of heat will be given and you may be asked to calculate mass, heat of fusion, heat of vaporization or even temperature change of the substance. To set up and calculate for the unknown, you must choose the correct heat equation. Once the known numbers are put into the correct equation, solving for the unknown becomes simple algebra.

Below are example problems in which factors other than heat are calculated.
Note: The example problems are given as multiple choice type questions.
  Study each problem to learn how to solve for other factors in heat equations.

Example 17. Solving for ΔT in temperature change problem:
What will be the temperature change of 5 gram sample of water that had absorbed 200 joules of heat?

  1) $40°C$ 2) $1000°C$ 3) $4.8°C$ 4) $20.9°C$

Before choosing:
Identify Known and unknowns:

Known:
mass = 5 g
Heat = 200 J
C = 4.18 J/g·°C

Unknown:
ΔT = ?

Choose equation and write it down: Heat = m × C × ΔT
Set up and solve for ΔT 200 = 10 × 4.18 × ΔT
    $\dfrac{200}{41.8}$ = $\dfrac{(41.8)\Delta T}{41.8}$

Answer: Choice 3 $4.8°C = \Delta T$

Example 18: Solving for heat of fusion (Hf) in a phase change problem:
What is the heat of fusion of an unknown solid if 4800 Joules of heat is required to completely melt a 10 gram sample of this solid?

  1) 334 J/g 2) 480 J/g 3) 48000 4) 3340 J/g

Before choosing:
Identify known and unknowns:

Known:
Mass = 10 g
Heat = 4800 joules

Unknown:
Hf = heat of fusion = ?

Choose equation and write it down: Heat = m × Hf
Set-up and solve for Hf   4800 = 10 × Hf
    $\dfrac{4800}{10}$ = $\dfrac{10(Hf)}{10}$

Answer: Choice 2   480 J/g = Hf

Topic 1 - Matter and Energy

Lesson 4 – Characteristics of gases and gas law calculations

Introduction

Behavior of gases is influenced by three key factors: volume(space), pressure and temperature. The relationships between these three factors are the basis for gas laws and gas theories. These laws and theories attempt to explain how gases behave.

In this lesson you will learn about the kinetic molecular theories, the gas laws, and gas law calculations

29. Behavior of gases: The Kinetic molecular theory of ideal Gas: Definitions and facts

The kinetic molecular theory of an ideal gas is a model that is often used to explain the behavior of gases.

Concept Task: Study to remember the following facts related to ideal gas theory and real gases.

I. **An ideal gas** is a theoretical (or assumed) gas that has all properties summarized below.

Summary of Kinetic Molecular Theory of an ideal gas. Study to remember them.
- Gas is composed of individual particles
- Distances between gas particles are far apart
- Gas particles are in continuous, random, straight-line motion
- When two particles of a gas collide, energy is transferred from one particle to another
- Particles of gases have no attraction to each other
- Individual gas particle has no volume (negligible or insignificant)

II. **A real gas** is a gas that we know to exist.

Examples of real gases: *oxygen, carbon dioxide, hydrogen, helium etc.*

Since the kinetic molecular theory (summarized above) applies mainly to an ideal gas, the model cannot be used to predict exact behavior of real gases. Therefore, real gases deviate from (do not behave exactly as) an ideal gas.

III. **Why Real gases behave differently from ideal gas?**
- Real gas particles do attract each other   (Ideal gas particles are assumed to have no attraction)
- Real gas particles do have volume   (Ideal gas is assumed to have no volume)

IV. **Types of gases that behave most like an ideal gas:**
Real gases with small molecular mass behave most like an ideal gas.

Hydrogen (H) and **Helium (He),** the two smallest real gases by mass, will behave most like an ideal gas than all other real gases.

V. **Temperature and Pressure conditions that** real gases behaves most and least like an ideal gas:

Real gases behave most like an ideal gas under conditions of :

High temperature **and** Low pressure

Example: Helium, a real gas, will behave most like an ideal gas at:

300 K **and** 1 atm. THAN AT 273 K **and** 2 atm

Real gases behave least like an ideal gas under conditions of:

Low temperature **and** High pressure

Example: Hydrogen, a real gas, will behave least like an ideal gas at:

273 K **and** 2 atm THAN AT 300 K **and** 1 atm.

Topic 1 - Matter and Energy

30. Deviation from ideal gas: Determining which gas behaves most like an ideal gas

Concept Task: Be able to determine which gas will behave most like (or least like) an ideal gas.

To determine which gas will :

Behave most like an ideal gas:
   LOOK for the gas with the smallest mass

Behave least like an ideal gas:
   LOOK for the gas with the greatest mass

NOTE: Mass of gases can be determined from information on the Periodic table. Just look on the Periodic Table for the elements symbols given as choices, and compare their masses.

Concept Task: Be able to determine conditions of temperature (°C or K) and / or pressure (atm or KPa) in which a gas will behave most like or least like an ideal gas.

To determine conditions in which a real gas will:

Behave most like an ideal gas:
   LOOK for Highest temperature and Lowest pressure

Behave least like an ideal gas:
   LOOK for Lowest temperature and Highest pressure

Example 19.

According to the Periodic Table, which of the following gases will behave least like an ideal gas?

1) Ar   2) Ne   3) Xe   4) Kr

Before choosing:

Find and note the mass of each element from the periodic table:

Ar: 40 g   Xe: 131 g
Ne: 20 g   Kr: 84 g

Answer: *Choice 3.* Because Xe has the greatest mass, it will behave least like an ideal gas.

Example 20.

Under which conditions of temperature and pressure would oxygen behave most like an ideal gas?

1) 25°C and 100 kPa
2) 35°C and 100 kPa
3) 25°C and 80 kPa
4) 35°C and 80 kPa

Answer: *Choice 4.* This choice contains the highest temp (35°C) and lowest pressure (80 kPa) of all the choices given. Gases behave most like ideal gas at the highest temperature and lowest pressure.

31. Pressure, volume, temperature: Definitions, facts, and units

Concept facts: Study to remember the followings about the three factors that influence gas behaviors.

Pressure
Pressure of gas is a measure of how much force is put on a gas in a closed container.
   Units: atmosphere (atm) or Kilopascal (kPa)   *1 atm = 101.3 kPa*

Volume
Volume of a gas is a measure of the space a confined gas occupies (takes up).
Volume of a gas is the space (or volume) of the container the gas is placed.
   Units: milliliters (ml) or liters (L)   *1 L = 1000 ml*

Temperature
Temperature of a gas is a measure of the average kinetic energy of the gas particles.
As temperature increases, the gas particles moves faster, and their average kinetic energy increases.
   Units: degree Celsius (°C) or Kelvin (K)   *K = °C + 273*

The relationships between these three factors of a confined gas are discussed in the next few pages.

Topic 1 - Matter and Energy

32. Avogadro's law (hypothesis): Definitions, facts and example problems

Concept Fact: study to remember.
Avogadro's law states that: Under the same conditions of temperature and pressure:
   Equal volume of different gases contain **equal number of molecules (particles)**.

Container A contains helium gas and container B contains oxygen gas.
NOTE that both containers have the same volume (2L), and are at the same temperature and pressure.

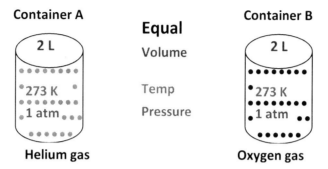

If the number of helium gas molecules are counted in Container A and the number of oxygen gas molecules are counted in container B, you will find that:
The number of molecules of helium in A **is the same** as the number of molecules of oxygen in B.

Concept Task: Be able to determine which gas sample has the same number of molecules as a gas given in the question.

To determine which gas sample has the same number of molecules as a gas given in the question

   LOOK for a gas that has the same volume (L or mL)

Concept Task: Be able to determine which two gases have the same number of molecules

To determine which two gas samples contain the same number of molecules
   LOOK for two gas samples with **same** temperature and pressure

Example 21:
At STP, a 1.0 L sample of $H_2(g)$ would have the same number of gas molecules as

1) 2.0 L of Ne   3) 0.5 L of He
2) 1.0 L of CO   4) 3.0 L of N_2

Answer: **Choice 2.** Because CO has the same volume (1.0 L) as the volume in the question.

Example 22:
The table below gives the temperature and pressure of four different gas samples, each in a 1.5 L container:

Gas sample	Temperature (K)	Pressure (atm)
SO_2	200	1.5
Ar	300	3.0
N_2	200	1.5
O_2	300	1.5

Which two gas samples contain the same number of molecules?

1) Ar and O_2 3) SO_2 and Ar
2) Ar and N_2 4) SO_2 and N_2

Answer: **Choice 4** because both SO_2 and N_2 gases have the same volume, temperature and pressure

Copyright © 2010 E3 Scholastic Publishing All Rights Reserved.

Topic 1 - Matter and Energy

33. Boyle's law: Volume – Pressure relationship at constant temperature: Facts and equation

Boyle's law describes the relationship between pressure of a gas and its volume at a constant temperature.

Concept Fact: Study to remember the following relationships:

At a constant temperature, the *volume* of a confined gas *is inversely proportional* to the *pressure* of the gas.

This fact can be expressed in a few different ways:

As pressure decreases on a gas, the volume occupied by the gas increases.
. If pressure on a gas is cut in half, the volume of the gas will double

As pressure increases on a gas, the volume occupied by the gas decreases.
. If pressure on a gas is doubled, the volume of the gas will be cut in half
(see diagram to the right)

Boyle's law equation (below) can be used to calculate the new volume of a gas when pressure on the gas is changed at constant temperature:

$$P_1 V_1 = P_2 V_1$$

P_1 = Initial pressure (atm or KPa)
P_2 = New pressure (atm of kPa)
V_1 = Initial volume (ml or L)
V_2 = New volume (ml or L)

According to Boyle's law:

At constant temperature, the product of the new pressure (P_2) and volume (V_2) will always be equal to the product of the initial pressure (P_1) and volume (V_1).

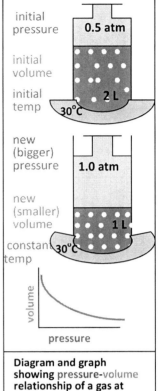

Diagram and graph showing pressure-volume relationship of a gas at constant temperature.

34. Charles' law: Volume – Temperature relationship at constant pressure: Facts and equation

Charles's law describes the relationship between volume of a gas and its Kelvin temperature at a constant pressure.

Concept Facts: Study to remember the following relationships.

At a constant pressure, the *volume* of a confined gas *is directly proportional* to its *Kelvin temperature.*

This statement can be expressed in a few different ways:

As temperature is increased on a gas, the volume of will also increase.
. If temperature of a gas is doubled, the volume of will also double

As temperature of a gas is decreased, volume of the gas will also decrease.
. If temperature of a gas is cut in half, the volume will also be cut in half
(see diagram to the right)

Charles' law equation (below) can be used to calculate the new volume of a gas when temperature of the gas is changed at constant pressure.

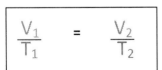

T_1 = Initial Kelvin temperature (K)
T_2 = New Kelvin temperature (K)
V_1 = Initial volume (ml or L)
V_2 = New volume (ml or L)

According to Charles' law:

At constant pressure, the ratio of new volume (V_2) and Kelvin temperature (T_2) will always be equal to ratio of initial volume (V_1) to Kelvin temperature (T_1).

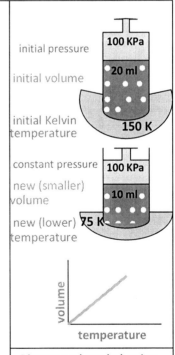

Diagram and graph showing temperature – volume relationship of a gas at constant pressure

Topic 1 - Matter and Energy

35. Gay-Lussac's law: Pressure – Temperature relationship at constant volume: Facts & equation

Gay-Lussac's law describes the relationship between pressure of a gas to its Kelvin temperature at a constant volume.

Concept Facts: Study to remember the following facts:

At constant volume, the *pressure* of a confined gas is *directly proportional to* its Kelvin temperature.

This statement can be expressed in a few different ways:

As temperature of a gas is decreased, pressure of the gas will also decrease
. If temperature of a gas is cut in half, pressure will also be cut in half

. As temperature is increased on a gas, pressure of the gas will also increase
. If temperature of a gas is doubled, pressure of the gas will also double.
(See diagram to the right)

The Gay-Lussac's law equation below can be used to calculate the new pressure of a gas when temperature of the gas is changed at constant volume.

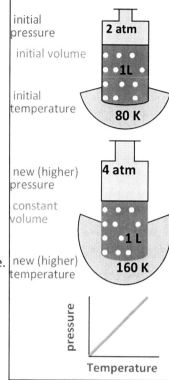

Diagram and graph showing temperature-pressure relationship of a gas at constant volume

$$\frac{P_1}{T_1} = \frac{P_2}{T_2}$$

T_1 = Initial Kelvin temperature (K)
T_2 = New Kelvin temperature (K)
P_1 = Initial pressure (atm or kPa)
P_2 = New pressure (atm or kPa)

According to Gay-Lussac's law:
At constant volume, the ratio of new pressure (P_2) to temperature (T_2) will always be equal to the ratio of initial pressure (P_1) to temperature (T_1).

36. Combined gas law: Pressure, volume and temperature relationship.

The combined gas law describes the relationship between all three factors: volume, pressure, and temperature: In the combined gas law, the only constant is the mass of the gas.

The combined gas law equation below is a combination of Boyle's, Charles', and Gay-Lussac's law equations:

$$\frac{P_1 V_1}{T_1} = \frac{P_2 V_2}{T_2}$$

NOTE: In all gas law problems, mass (or number of particles) of the gas is constant.

Combined Gas Law Equation: See Reference Table T

The combined gas law equation is all that is needed to solve any gas law problem.
On the next page, you will learn how to use the combined gas law equation to solve all gas law problems.

37. STP: Standard Temperature and Pressure

STP stands for: Standard Temperature and Pressure

REFERENCE TABLE A: STP values

Standard Temperature: 273 K or 0°C
Standard Pressure: 1 atm or 101.3 kPa

In some gas law problems, the temperature and pressure of the gas may be given at STP.
When a gas is said to be at STP in a gas law problem, substitute these values into your gas law equation as needed. Be sure the unit of STP you choose is the same as the other unit in the given question.

NOTE: Always use Kelvin temperature **in all gas law calculations.**

Topic 1 - Matter and Energy

38. Pressure conversion: Converting pressure between atm and kPa

Concept Task: Be able to convert the unit of pressure from atm to kPa (and vice versa) using the relationship below.

$$1 \text{ atm} = 101.3 \text{ kPa}$$

atm : atmospheric pressure
kPa : kilopascal pressure

Example 23:

What pressure, in kPa, is equivalent to 1.7 atm?

Step 1: Write out the known conversion: 1 atm = 101.3 kPa
Step 2: Set up proportion   1.7 atm = X
Set 3: Cross-multiply to get   X (1) = 1.7 (101.3)
                                         X = 172. 2 kPa (is the same pressure as 1.7 atm)

Example 24.

What is the pressure of 65 kPa in atm?

Step 1: Write out the known conversion: 1 atm = 101.3 kPa
Step 2: Set up proportion   X = 65 kPa
Step 3: Cross multiply to get   X(101.3) = 65 (1)
Step 4: Divide both sides by 101.3   101.3   101.3
                                          X = 0.64 atm (is the same pressure as 65 KPa)

39. Gas law problem at constant temperature: Example problem

Concept Task: Be able to solve gas law problems at constant temperature

Example 25:

At a constant temperature, what will be the new of volume of a 20 L sample of oxygen gas if its pressure is changed from 2.5 atm to 5.0 atm?

1) 5.0 L   2) 10 L   3) 20 L   4) 40 L

Before choosing a choice:

Step 1: Identify factors in the question:

Known:
V_1 = 20 L
P_1 = 2.5 atm
P_2 = 5.0 atm

Unknown (solve for)
V_2 = X

Step 2: Write down combined gas law equation: $\dfrac{P_1 V_1}{T_1} = \dfrac{P_2 V_2}{T_2}$

Step 3: Eliminate T (because temperature is constant): $P_1 V_1 = P_2 V_2$
Step 4: Set up problem by plugging in factors: (2.5)(20) = (5) X
Step 5: Solve by: Multiplying out $\dfrac{50}{5} = \dfrac{5X}{5}$
        Divide both sides by 5
        Answer   10 L = X

Choose: Choice 2

As you can see, the new volume calculated (10 L) is half the initial volume (20 L).
This makes sense because the new pressure(5 atm) is doubled the initial pressure (2.5 atm).
RECALL : At constant temperature, when pressure is doubled, volume will be half.

Topic 1 - Matter and Energy

40. Gas law problem at constant Pressure: Example problem

Concept Task: Be able to solve gas law problems at constant pressure.

Example 26:
The volume of a confined gas is 25 ml at 280 K. At what temperature would the gas volume be 75 ml if the pressure is held constant?

1) 140 K   2) 280 K   3) 560 K   4) 840 K

Before choosing a choice:

Step 1: Identify factors in the question:
$V_1 = 25$ ml $T_1 = 280$ K
$V_2 = 75$ ml $T_2 = X$ (unknown)

Step 2: Write down the combined gas law equation:
$$\frac{P_1 V_1}{T_1} = \frac{P_2 V_2}{T_2}$$

Step 3: Eliminate P (because Pressure is constant):
$$\frac{V_1}{T_1} = \frac{V_1}{T_2}$$

Step 4: Set up problem by plugging in factors:
$$\frac{25}{280} = \frac{75}{X}$$

Step 5: Solve by: Cross-multiplying
Divide both sides by 25
$$\frac{25X}{25} = \frac{21000}{25}$$

Answer $X = 840$ K $= T_2$

Choose: Choice 4

As you can see, the new calculated temperature (840 K) is three times the initial temperature (280 K). This makes sense because the new volume (75 ml) is also three times the initial volume (25 ml).
RECALL: At constant pressure, the volume is directly proportional to Kelvin temperature.
That is to say, if volume is tripled, the temperature is also tripled.

41. Gas law problem at constant volume: Example problem

Concept Task 18: Be able to solve gas law problems at constant volume.

Example 27. NOTE: this problem is not a multiple choice problem
Pressure on a gas changes from 20 kPa to 50 kPa when the temperature of the gas is changed to 30°C. If volume was held constant, show set up, and calculate the initial temperature of the gas?

Step 1: Identify all factors in question:
$P_1 = 20$ kPa $T_1 = $ unknown
$P_2 = 50$ kPa $T_2 = 30$°C (must be in Kelvin)
                                            $T_2 = 30 + 273 = 300$ K

Step 2: Write down combined gas law equation:
$$\frac{P_1 V_1}{T_1} = \frac{P_2 V_2}{T_2}$$

Step 3: Eliminate V (Because volume is constant):
$$\frac{P_1}{T_1} = \frac{P_2}{T_2}$$

Step 4: Set up for T_1 by: Cross multiply factors $P_2 T_1 = P_1 T_2$

Divide both sides by P_2 $T_1 = \dfrac{P_1 T_2}{P_2}$

Step 5: Substitute factors and solve for T_1 $T_1 = \dfrac{(20)(300)}{50}$

Answer $T_1 = 120$ K

Topic 1 - Matter and Energy

42. Combined gas law problem: Example problem

Concept Task: Be able to solve gas law problems at STP.

Example 28.   NOTE that is not a multiple choice problem

Hydrogen gas has a volume of 100 mL at STP. If temperature and pressure are changed to 0.5 atm and 546 K respectively, what will be the new volume of the gas?

Step 1: Identify all factors in the question:

$V_1 = 100$ mL $V_2 = X$

STP $\begin{cases} T_1 = 273 \text{ K} \\ P_1 = 1 \text{ atm} \end{cases}$ $T_2 = 546$ K $P_2 = 0.5$ atm

Step 2: Write out combined gas law equation:
(no constant, do not eliminate any factor)

$$\frac{P_1 V_1}{T_1} = \frac{P_2 V_2}{T_2}$$

Step 3: Substitute numbers into equation:

$$\frac{(1)(100)}{273} = \frac{(0.5)(X)}{546}$$

Step 4: Solve by: Cross – multiplying to get: $(1)(100)(546) = (273)(0.5) X$

Multiply out to get: $\dfrac{54600}{136.5} = \dfrac{(136.5) X}{136.5}$

Divide both sides by 136.5

Answer: $400 \text{ mL} = X$

(This is V_2)

43. Gas laws: Summary table

Below, a table summarizing the relationships between pressure, volume, and temperature of a gas. You can use this table for a quick studying, and comparisons of the three factors.

	Constant Temperature	Constant Pressure	Constant Volume
Pressure	↑ ↓	↙	↑ ↓
Volume	↓ ↑	↑ ↓	↙
Temperature	↙	↑ ↓	↑ ↓

NOTE: Mass of gas is always constant.

Topic 1 – Matter and Energy

Lesson 5 – Physical and chemical properties and changes

Introduction

> **Properties** are set of characteristics that can be used to identify and classify matter. Two types of properties of matter are physical and chemical properties.
>
> In this lesson, you will learn the differences between physical and chemical properties, as well as the differences between the physical and chemical changes of matter.

44. Physical and chemical properties: Definitions, facts and examples

Concept Facts: Study to know the difference between physical and chemical properties.

Physical property is a characteristic of a substance that can be observed or measured without changing the chemical composition of the substance.

Examples: Color, shape, size, texture, luster, malleability, ductile, conductivity

Melting point, boiling point, and density

State (phase), solubility (does it dissolve?), Compressible (can it be compressed ?)

Differences in physical properties of substances make it possible to separate one substance from another in a mixture.

Chemical property is a characteristic of a substance ability to interact with (or change) into other substances.

Examples: It burns, it combusts, it decomposes, it reacts with, it combines with.

Physical and chemical properties of some common substances

Substance	Physical properties				Chemical properties
	Color	Phase At (STP)	Melting Point (°C)	Boiling Point (°C)	
Oxygen	Colorless	Gas	-218	-183	Reacts with Hydrogen to form water
Hydrogen	Colorless	Gas	14	20	Reacts with Oxygen to form water
Water	Clear	Liquid	0	100	Chemical decomposes to hydrogen and oxygen
Gold	Yellow	Solid	1064	2856	Combines with oxygen to form gold oxide

45. Physical and chemical changes: definitions, facts, and examples

Physical change is a change of a substance from one form to another without changing its chemical compositions.

Examples: Phase change

Size change

Dissolving

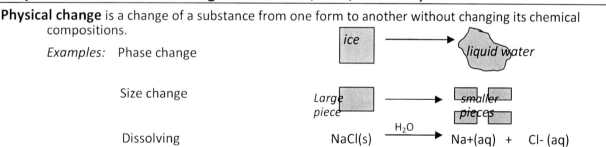

Chemical changes is a change in compositions of one substance to those of other substances.
Chemical reaction is a means by which chemical changes occurs.
  Types of chemical reactions: Synthesis, decomposition, single and double replacements.

LOOKING Ahead ⇨ **Topic 5 – Formulas and Equation:** You will learn more about these reactions.

Topic 1 – Matter and Energy

Check-A-list

Concept Terms

Below is a list of vocabulary terms from Topic 1. You should know the definition and facts related to each term.

Put a check in the box [V] next to each term if you know its definition and other facts related to the term.

[ ] Matter
[ ] Pure substance
[ ] Element
[ ] Compound
[ ] Mixture
[ ] Homogeneous mixture
[ ] Heterogeneous mixture
[ ] Law of definite composition
[ ] Filtration
[ ] Distillation
[ ] Solid
[ ] Liquid
[ ] Gas
[ ] Fusion
[ ] Condensation
[ ] Evaporation
[ ] Sublimation
[ ] Deposition
[ ] Exothermic
[ ] Endothermic
[ ] Temperature
[ ] Chemical change
[ ] Kinetic energy
[ ] Potential energy

[ ] Phase change diagram
[ ] Ice/liquid equilibrium
[ ] Liquid/steam equilibrium
[ ] Absolute Zero
[ ] Heat
[ ] Joules
[ ] Specific heat capacity
[ ] Heat of fusion
[ ] Heat of vaporization
[ ] Calorimeter
[ ] Kinetic molecular theory
[ ] Ideal gas
[ ] Avogadro's law
[ ] Boyle's law
[ ] Charles law
[ ] Gay – Lussac's law
[ ] Physical property
[ ] Chemical property
[ ] Physical change

Concept Tasks

Below is a list of concept tasks from Topic 1. You should know how to solve problems and answer questions related to each concept task.

Put a check in the box [V] next to a concept task when you know how to solve problems and answer questions related to it.

[ ] Recognizing chemical symbol of elements, compounds, and mixtures
[ ] Recognizing diagram representation of elements, compounds, and mixtures
[ ] Recognizing chemical symbol representation of substances in different phases
[ ] Recognizing phase change equation
[ ] Determining substance with highest and lowest kinetic energy based on temperature
[ ] Temperature conversion between Kelvin and Celsius units
[ ] Interpreting phase change diagrams (heating and cooling curves)
[ ] Determining direction of heat flow based on temperatures of two objects
[ ] Heat calculation during temperature and phase changes
[ ] Determining gases that behave most or least like an ideal gas
[ ] Determining temperature and pressure that a gas behaves most or least like an ideal gas
[ ] Determining gases that contain equal number of molecules
[ ] Pressure conversion between atm and kPa units
[ ] Gas law calculations at constant temperature
[ ] Gas law calculations at constant pressure
[ ] Gas law calculation at constant volume
[ ] Combined gas law calculation
[ ] Determining physical and chemical properties of a substance
[ ] Determining physical and chemical changes of a substance

If you don't have a check next to a concept task, look it up or ask your teacher.

Topic 1 – Matter and Energy

Concept Fact Review Questions

1. Which of these terms refers to matter that could be heterogeneous?
    1) Element
    2) Compound
    3) Mixture
    4) Solution

2. One similarity between all mixtures and compounds is that both
    1) Are heterogeneous
    2) Are homogeneous
    3) Combine in definite ratio
    4) Consist of two or more substances

3. Which correctly describe particles of substances in the gas phase?
    1) Particles are arranged in regular geometric pattern and are far apart
    2) Particles are in fixed rigid position and are close together
    3) Particles are moving freely in a straight path
    4) Particles are move freely and are close together.

4. When a substance evaporates, it is changing from
    1) Liquid to gas
    2) Gas to liquid
    3) Solid to gas
    4) Gas to solid

5. Energy that is stored in chemical substances is called
    1) Potential energy
    2) Activation energy
    3) Kinetic energy
    4) Ionization energy

6. The specific heat capacity of water is 4.18 J/°C.g . Adding 4.18 Joules of heat to a 1 gram sample of water will cause the water to
    1) Change from solid to liquid
    2) Change from liquid to solid
    3) Change its temperature 1 degree Celsius
    4) Change its temperature 4.18 degree Celsius

7. Real gases differ from an ideal gas because the molecules of real gases have
    1) Some volume and no attraction for each other
    2) Some attraction and some attraction for each other
    3) No volume and no attraction for each other
    4) No volume and some attraction for each other

8. Under which two conditions do real gases behave most like (deviate least from) an ideal gas?
    1) High pressure and low temperature
    2) Low pressure and high temperature
    3) High pressure and high temperature
    4) Low pressure and low temperature

9. At constant pressure, the volume of a confined gas varies
    1) Directly with the Kelvin temperature
    2) Indirectly with the Kelvin temperature
    3) Directly with the mass of the gas
    4) Indirectly with the mass of the gas

10. Under which conditions would a volume of a given sample of a gas decrease?
    1) Decrease pressure and increase temperature
    2) Decrease pressure and decrease temperature
    3) Increase pressure and decrease temperature
    4) Increase pressure and increase temperature

Topic 1 – Matter and Energy

Concept Task Review Questions

11. When sample X is passed through a filter a white residue, Y, remains on the filter paper and a clear liquid, Z, passes through. When liquid Z is vaporized, another white residue remains. Sample X is best classified as
    1) An element
    2) A compound
    3) A heterogeneous mixture
    4) A homogeneous mixture

12. **Given diagrams A, B, and C below: Answer questions 5 - 7 based on the diagrams.**

    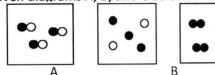

    ● = particle X
    ○ = particle Y

    Which diagrams or diagrams can be classified as pure substances?
    1) A and B
    2) A and C
    3) B and C
    4) B, only

13. Which phase change correctly shows the release of heat to the surrounding?
    1) $NH_3(l) \rightarrow NH_3(g)$
    2) $CO_2(s) \rightarrow CO_2(g)$
    3) $NaCl(s) \rightarrow NaCl(l)$
    4) $H_2O(g) \rightarrow H_2O(l)$

14. The graph below represents the relationship between temperature and time as heat is added at a constant rate to a substance, starting when the substance is a solid below its melting point

    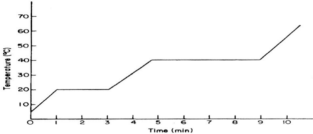

    During which time period (in minutes) is the substance average kinetic energy remains the same?
    1) 0 – 1
    2) 1 – 3
    3) 3 - 5
    4) 9 – 10

15. Molecules of which substance have the lowest average kinetic energy?
    1) $NO(g)$ at $20°C$
    2) $NO_2(g)$ at $-30°C$
    3) NO_2 at 35 K
    4) N_2O_3 at 110 K

16. At STP, the difference between the boiling point and the freezing point of water in Kelvin scale is
    1) 373
    2) 273
    3) 180
    4) 100

17. How much heat is needed to change a 5.0 gram sample of water from $65°C$ to $75°C$?
    1) 210 J
    2) 14 J
    3) 21 J
    4) 43

18. A real gas will behave most like an ideal gas under which conditions of temperature and pressure?
    1) $0°C$ and 1 atm
    2) $0°C$ and 2 atm
    3) $273°C$ and 1 atm
    4) $273°C$ and 2 atm

19. A 2.0 L sample of $O_2(g)$ at STP had its volume changed to 1.5 L. If the temperature of the gas was held constant, what is the new pressure of the gas in kilopascal?
    1) 3.0 kPa
    2) 152 kPa
    3) 101.3 kPa
    4) 135 kPa

20. A gas occupies a volume of 6 L at 3 atm and $70°C$. Which setup is correct for calculating the new volume of the gas if the temperature is changed to $150°C$ and the pressure is dropped to 1.0 atm?
    1) $6 \times \dfrac{3 \times 150}{1 \times 70}$
    2) $6 \times \dfrac{3 \times 80}{1 \times 150}$
    3) $6 \times \dfrac{3 \times 423}{1 \times 343}$
    4) $6 \times \dfrac{3 \times 343}{1 \times 423}$

Topic 1 – Matter and Energy

Constructive Response Questions

	Show work here
21. Calculate the heat released when 25.0 grams of water freezes at 0°C? Show all work. Record your answer with appropriate unit.	21.
22. What is the total amount of heat energy, in joules, absorbed when the temperature of a 31.0 gram sample of water increases from 24.0°C to 36.0°C?	22.
23. What is the volume of 2.12 L in millimeters?	23.

Base your answer to questions 24 through 26 on the information and diagrams below.

Cylinder A contains 22.0 grams of $CO_2(g)$ and Cylinder B contains $N_2(g)$. The volumes, pressures, and temperatures of the two gases are indicated under each cylinder.

A
CO_2
V = 12.3 L
P = 1.0 atm
T = 300. K

B
N_2
V = 12.3 L
P = 1.0 atm
T = 300. K

24. How does the number molecules of $CO_2(g)$ in cylinder A compares to the number of molecules of $N_2(g)$ in container B. Your answer must include both $CO_2(g)$ and $N_2(g)$.

24.   Show work here

25. The temperature of $CO_2(g)$ is increased to 450. K and the volume of cylinder A remains constant. Show a correct numerical setup for calculating the new pressure of $CO_2(g)$ in cylinder A.

25.

26. Calculate the new pressure of $CO_2(g)$ in cylinder A based on your setup.

26.

Copyright © 2010 E3 Scholastic Publishing. All Rights Reserved.

Topic 2 – The Periodic Table

Topic outline

In this topic, you will learn the following concepts:

. Arrangements of the elements
. Types of elements and their properties
. Groups of elements and their properties
. Periodic trends
. Allotropes

Lesson 1 – Arrangement of the Elements

Introduction:

The modern Periodic Table contains all known elements that are arranged in order of increasing atomic number.

There are more than 100 known elements. Most of the elements are naturally occurring, while others have been artificially produced. Important information about the elements can be found in the box of each element on the Periodic Table.

In this lesson, you will learn about the different arrangements of the elements, and important facts about the Periodic Table.

1. Properties of the Modern Periodic Table: Facts about the table

The followings are important facts about the table that you should know.

Concept Facts: Study to remember the following about the Periodic Table.
. Elements are arranged in order of increasing atomic numbers
. Chemical properties of the elements are periodic functions of their atomic numbers
. The elements on the Periodic Table can be categorized as metals, nonmetals, or metalloids
. More than two thirds (majority) of the elements are metals
. The Periodic Table contains elements that are in all three phases (solid, liquid, and gas) at STP
. The majority of the elements exist as solids
. Only two (mercury and bromine) are liquids
. A few elements are gases

The following information can be found in the box of each element.

   LOOK on the Periodic Table for these two elements: Oxygen and Gold
   NOTE all the information you can get from the box of each element.

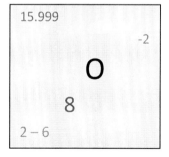

Mass number
Selected Oxidation states (charge)
Element's symbol
Atomic number
Electron configuration

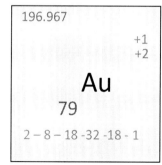

Information listed in the box of each element can tell you a lot about the atomic structure of that element.

LOOKING AHEAD ⇒ Topic 3 - The atomic structure. You will learn to relate information on the Periodic Table to the atomic structure.

Topic 2 - The Periodic Table

2. Groups and Periods: Definitions and facts

The elements are placed in **Groups** and **Periods**. Every element has a Group number and a Period number.

For example: Element phosphorous (P) is in Group 15, Period 3.

LOOK on the **Periodic Table** to confirm this fact.

Concept Facts: Study to remember the following facts related to Group.

Groups are the vertical arrangements of the elements.
. Elements in the same group have the same number of valance electrons and have similar chemical properties.
. There are 18 Groups on the Periodic Table of the Elements

The Group names are listed below.

Group 1 :	Alkali metals
Group 2 :	Alkaline earth metals
Group 3 – 12:	Transition metals
Group 17:	Halogens
Group 18:	Noble (Inert) gases

Periods are the horizontal rows of the Periodic Table.
. Elements in the same Period have the same number of occupied electron shells
. There are seven (7) periods on the Periodic Table of the Elements

Periodic Law: The properties of the elements are periodic function of their atomic numbers.
In other words, by arranging the elements in order of increasing atomic numbers, as a new period of elements is forming, the properties of the elements in previous period are repeated.

3. Groups and Periods: Determining elements with same characteristics

Concept Task: Be able to determine element with similar chemical characteristics

To determine elements with similar chemical properties:

LOOK for elements that belong in the same group (vertical column).

Concept Task: Be able to determine elements with the same number of occupied electron shells.

To determine elements with same occupied electron shells:

LOOK for elements belonging in the same Period (Horizontal rows)

Example 1

Which of these elements has similar chemical properties as iodine?

1) Xe 2) Te 3) Br 4) Se

Answer: Choice 3
Because Br (bromine) is in the same Group (vertical column) as iodine (I).

Example 2

Which two elements have the same number of occupied electron shells?

1) Mg and Be 3) Mg and O
2) Mg and Al 4) Mg and Ca

Answer : Choice 2
Because Both Mg and Al are in the same Period (Horizontal row)

Topic 2 - The Periodic Table

Lesson 2 – Types of elements and their Properties

Introduction

There are three general categories of elements: metal, nonmetals, and metalloids.

The location of an element on the Periodic Table can be used to determine if it is a metal, nonmetal, or metalloid.

Elements belonging in each category have a set of physical and chemical properties that can be used to distinguish these elements apart from elements in other categories.

In this lesson, you will learn of the three different types of elements, their location on the Periodic Table, and their properties.

4. The three types of elements: Location of metals, metalloids, and nonmetals

A table showing elements that are metals, metalloids, and nonmetal

H																	He
Li	Be		metals		metalloids		nonmetals					B	C	N	O	F	Ne
Na	Mg											Al	Si	P	S	Cl	Ar
K	Ca	Sc	Ti	V	Cr	Mn	Fe	Co	Ni	Cu	Zn	Ga	Ge	As	Se	Br	Kr
Rb	Sr	Y	Zr	Nb	Mo	Tc	Ru	Rh	Pd	Ag	Cd	In	Sn	Sb	Te	I	Xe
Cs	Ba	Lu	Hf	Ta	W	Re	Os	Ir	Pt	Au	Hg	Tl	Pb	Bi	Po	At	Rn
Fr	Ra	Lr	Rf	Db	Sg	Bh	Hs	Mt	Ds	Uuu	Uub		Uuq				
		La	Ce	Pr	Nd	Pm	Sm	Eu	Gd	Tb	Dy	Ho	Er	Tm	Yb		
		Ac	Th	Pa	U	Np	Pu	Am	Cm	Bk	Cf	Es	Fm	Md	No		

5. Physical Properties of elements: Definitions and facts of properties of the elements

There are several physical properties that can be used to describe and identify the elements.

The following is a list of physical properties and their definitions.

Concept Facts: Study and to remember these properties.

Malleable describes how easily a solid can be hammered into a thin sheet.

Ductile describes well a solid can be drawn into a thin wire.

Brittle describes how easily a solid can be broken or shattered into pieces when struck by an object.

Luster describes the shininess of a substance.

Conductivity describes the ability to conduct heat or electricity.

Electronegativity describes atom's ability to attract electrons from another atom during bonding.

Ionization energy describes an element's ability to lose its most loosely bound valance electrons.

Atomic radius describes the size of an atom of an element.

Density describes the mass to volume ratio of an element

LOOK on Reference Table S to find and compare electronegativity, ionization energy, atomic radius, and density values of the elements.

Topic 2 - The Periodic Table

6. Metal: Properties, definitions, and facts

Metal elements can be found to the left of the Periodic Table.
All elements in Group 1 – 12 (except hydrogen) are classified as metals.
The rest of the metal elements are found spread out in Groups 13, 14 and 15.
The majority (about 75%) of the elements are metals.

Iron (Fe)

Below are some general properties that are characteristics of metals.

Concept Facts: Study to remember these properties.
. Almost all metals are solids. The exception is mercury (Hg), which is a liquid
. Solid metals are malleable, ductile, and have luster
. Metals tend to have high (good) conductivity due to their mobile valance electrons
. Metals tend to have low electronegativity values (because they do not attract electrons easily)
. Metals tend to have low ionization energy values (because they lose their electrons easily)
. Metals generally lose electrons and form positive ions
. Radius (size) of a metal atom generally decreases as it loses electrons and form a positive ion
. The size of a positive (+) metal ion is always smaller than the size of the neutral atom

7. Metalloid: Properties, definitions, and facts

Metalloids are the seven elements located between the metals and the nonmetals.
Metalloid elements are located on the Periodic Table along the thick zigzag line.

Below are some generally properties that are characteristics of metalloids.

Concept Facts: Study to remember these properties.
. Metalloids tend to have properties of both the metals and of the nonmetals
. Metalloids properties are more like those of metals, and less like nonmetals
. Metalloids exist only as solids at STP.

Tellurium (Te)

8. Nonmetals: Properties, definitions and facts

Nonmetal elements are located to the right of the Periodic Table.

All elements in Groups 17 and 18 are classified as nonmetals. The rest of the nonmetals can be found in Group 14, 15, and 16. Hydrogen is also a nonmetal.

Below are some general properties that characterized the nonmetals.

Concept Facts: Study to remember these properties.

Sulfur (S)

. Nonmetals are found in all three phases: solid, liquid, and gas.
. Most nonmetals exist as molecular gases and solids. Bromine is the only liquid nonmetal
. Solid nonmetals are generally brittle and dull (lack luster, not shiny)
. Nonmetals have low (poor) electrical and heat conductivity
. Nonmetals tend to have high electronegativity values (because they attract or gain electrons easily)
. Nonmetals tend to have high ionization values (because they do not lose electrons readily)
. Nonmetals generally gain electrons and form negative ions
. Radius of a nonmetal atom generally increases as it gains electrons and forms a negative ion
. The size of the negative nonmetal ion is always bigger than its neutral atom

Topic 2 - The Periodic Table

9. Types of elements: Summary of properties of metals, metals, and nonmetals

	Phases at STP	Physical properties	Conductivity	Electrone-gativity	Ionization energy	In bonding	Common ion	Ionic size (radius)
Metals	Solid Liquid	Malleable Luster Ductile	High	Low	Low	Lose electrons	+ (positive)	Smaller than atom
Nonmetals	Solid Liquid Gases	Brittle Dull	Low	High	High	Gain electrons	- (negative)	Bigger than atom
Metalloids	Solid only	Properties of metals and nonmetals	Low	-	-	Lose electrons	+ (positive)	Smaller than atom

10. Types of element: Identifying element as metal, nonmetal, or metalloid

Concept Task: Be able to classify an element as a metal, metalloid, or a nonmetal.

To determine which element is a metal, nonmetal, or metalloid:

Locate the elements on the Periodic Table.
Be sure to know the boundary separating metals from metalloids, and metalloids from nonmetal.

Concept Task: Be able to identify an element base on properties.

To determine which element has properties described in questions:

Determine if properties given describe metals, nonmetals or metalloids
Once you have correctly determine the type of element choose a choice of element that is of that type.

Concept Task: Be able to determine properties of a a given element's name or symbol

To determine properties of a given element in a question:

Determine what type of element (metal, nonmetal, or metalloid) is given.
Choose properties related to the type of element you've determined.

Example 3
Which of these elements is metalloid?
1) Gallium   3) Phosphorous
2) Germanium   4) Tin

Answer: Choice 2
Find Ge on the Periodic Table and note its location.

Example 4
Which element is brittle and a non conducting solid?
1) S   2) Ne   3) Ni   4) Hg

Before choosing:
Relate properties to type of element:
- *Brittle* and *non conductivity* are properties of nonmetallic solid.

Answer: Choice 1 because Sulfur (S) is a nonmetal solid

Example 5.
Which properties best describes the element mercury?
1) It has luster
2) It is brittle
3) It has a high electronegativity value
4) It a poor electrical conductor

Before choosing:
Determine what type of element is mercury
Mercury is a metallic element

Answer: Choice 1 because metals have luster
All other (wrong) choices are properties of nonmetals.

Topic 2 - The Periodic Table

Lesson 3 – Groups name and their properties

Introduction

An element is in a certain group based on its chemical properties. Elements with similar chemical properties are in the same group.

In this lesson, you will learn more about group names, and the general properties that characterized members of each group.

11. The Periodic Table of the Elements

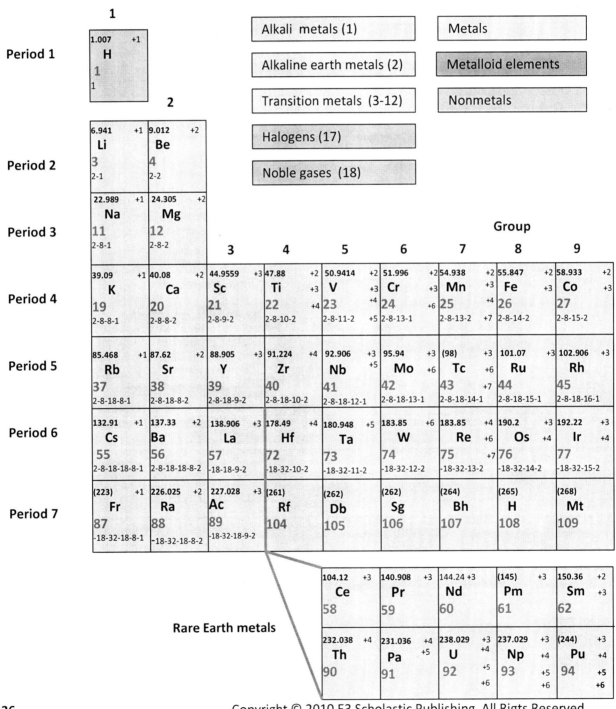

Topic 2 - The Periodic Table

Key / Legend box:
- Atomic mass: 30.973
- Element's symbol: P
- Atomic number: 15
- Electron configuration: 2 – 8 – 5
- Selected oxidation states: -3, +3, +5

	18
	4.002 0 **He** 2 2 — Period 1

Periodic Table

	13	14	15	16	17	
	10.81 +3 **B** 5 2-3	12.011 -4 **C** +2 6 +4 2-4	14.006 -3 **N** +2 +3 7 +4 +5 2-5	15.999 -2 **O** 8 2-6	18.998 -1 **F** 9 2-7	20.179 0 **Ne** 10 2-8 — Period 2
	26.981 +3 **Al** 13 2-8-3	28.085 -4 **Si** +2 14 +4 2-8-4	30.973 -3 **P** +3 15 +5 2-8-5	32.06 -2 **S** +4 16 +6 2-8-6	35.453 -1 +1 +3 **Cl** +5 +7 17 2-8-7	39.948 0 **Ar** 18 2-8-8 — Period 3

10	11	12							
58.69 +2 **Ni** +3 28 2-8-16-2	63.546 +1 **Cu** +2 29 2-8-18-1	65.39 +2 **Zn** 30 2-8-18-2	69.72 +3 **Ga** 31 2-8-18-3	72.59 -4 **Ge** +2 32 +4 2-8-18-4	74.921 -3 **As** +2 33 +4 2-8-18-5	78.96 -2 **Se** +4 34 +6 2-8-18-6	79.904 -1 **Br** +1 35 +5 2-8-18-7	83.80 0 **Kr** +2 36 2-8-18-8 — Period 4
106.42 +2 **Pd** +4 46 2-8-18-18	107.868 +1 **Ag** 47 2-8-18-18-1	112.41 +2 **Cd** 48 2-8-18-18-2	114.82 +3 **In** 49 2-8-18-18-3	118.71 +2 **Sn** +4 50 2-8-18-18-4	121.75 -3 **Sb** +3 51 +5 2-8-18-18-5	127.60 -2 **Te** +4 52 +6 2-8-18-18-6	126.905 -1 +1 **I** +5 +7 53 2-8-18-18-7	131.29 0 +2 **Xe** +4 +6 54 2-8-18-18-8 — Period 5
195.08 +2 **Pt** +4 78 -18-32-17-1	196.967 +1 **Au** +3 79 -18-32-18-1	200.59 +1 **Hg** +2 80 -18-32-18-2	204.383 +3 **Ti** 81 -18-32-18-3	207.2 +2 **Pb** +4 82 -18-32-18-4	208.980 +3 **Bi** +5 83 -18-32-18-5	(209) +2 **Po** +4 84 -18-32-18-6	(210) +2 **At** +4 85 -18-32-18-7	(222) 0 **Rn** 56 -18-32-18-8 — Period 6
(269) **Unn** 	(272) **Uuu** 111	(277) **UUb** 112		(285) **Uuq** 114					Period 7

Lanthanoid Series

| 151.96 +2
Eu +3
63 | 157.25 +3
Gd
64 | 158.925 +3
Tb
65 | 162.50 +3
Dy
66 | 164.930 +3
Ho
67 | 167.26 +3
Er
68 | 168.934 +3
Tm
69 | 173.04 +2
Yb +3
70 | 174.967 +3
Lu
71 |

Actinoid Series

| (243) +3 +4
Am +5 +6
95 | (247) +3
Cm
96 | (247) +3
Bk
97 | (251) +3
Cf
98 | (252)
Es
99 | (257)
Fm
100 | (258)
Md
101 | (259)
No
102 | (260)
Lr
103 |

Copyright © 2010 E3 Scholastic Publishing. All Rights Reserved

Topic 2 - The Periodic Table

12. Group 1 Alkali Metals: Facts and properties of the alkali metals

Alkali metals are elements in **Group 1** of the Periodic Table.

Members include Lithium, sodium, potassium, rubidium, cesium and francium.

Hydrogen is NOT an alkali metal, even though it is often placed in Group 1.

Properties (characteristics) of the alkali metals are listed below.

Concept Facts: Study to remember these properties.

- One valance electron
- Positive one (1+) ion from losing their one valance electron
- Very low electronegativity and very low ionization energy values.
- Found in nature as compounds (not as free elements) due to high reactivity
- Are obtained from electrolytic reduction of fused salts (NaCl, KBr..etc)
- If **X** represents a **Group 1** atom and **Y** represents a **Group 17** halogen atom
    - **XY** is the general formula of a Group 1 atom bonding with a Group 17 atom
    - **X$_2$O** is the general formula of a Group 1 atom bonding with **O** (to form an oxide)
- **Francium** is the most reactive metal in Group 1, and of all metals
- All alkali metal exist as solids at room temperature

H 1	
Group 1 Alkali	**Group 2**
Li 3	
Na 11	
K 19	
Rb 37	
Cs 55	
Fr 87	

13. Group 2 - Alkaline Earth Metals : Facts and properties of alkaline earth

Alkaline Earth Metals are elements in **Group 2** of the Periodic Table.

Members include beryllium, magnesium, calcium, strontium, barium, and radium.

Properties (characteristics) of alkaline earth metals are listed below.

Concept Facts: Study to remember these properties.

- Two (2) valence electrons
- Form positive two charge (+2) ion by losing two valance electrons
- Found in nature as compounds, not as free element, due to high reactivity.
- Are obtained from fused salts compounds (MgCl$_2$, CaBr$_2$..etc)
- If   represents a   atom and Y represents a Group 17 halogen atom.
    - Y$_2$ is the general formula of a   atom bonding with a Group 17 atom
    -      O is the general formula of a   atom bonding with an O (to form an oxide)
- All alkaline earth metals exist only as solids at room temperature

Group 1	Group 2 Alkaline Earth
	Be 4
	Mg 12
	Ca 12
	Sr 38
	Ba 56
	Ra 88

Topic 2 - The Periodic Table

14. Group 3 – 12 Transition metals: Properties and facts of the transition elements

Transition metals are the elements in Groups 3 – 13 of the Periodic Table
Properties of these elements vary widely. However, a few unique properties can be observed among them.
Properties (characteristics) of transition metals are listed below.

Concept Facts: Study to remember these properties.

. They tend to form multiple oxidation numbers
. They can lose electrons in two or more different sublevels of their atoms
. Their ions usually form colorful compounds
    $CuCl_2$ – is a bluish color compound
    $FeCl_2$ - is an orange color compound

Transition metals

3	4	5	6	7	8	9	10	11	12
Sc	Ti	V	Cr	Mn	Fe	Co	Ni	Cu	Zn
Y	Zr	Nb	Mo	Tc	Ru	Rh	Pd	Ag	Cd
La	Hf	Ta	W	Re	Os	Ir	Pt	Au	Hg
Ac	Rf	Db	Sg	Bh	Hs	Mt	Uun	Uuu	Uub

15. Group 17 Halogens: Properties and facts of the halogens

Halogens are elements in Group 17 of the Periodic Table.
Members include fluorine, chlorine, bromine, and iodine

Properties (characteristics) of halogens are listed below.

Concept Facts: Study to remember these properties.

. Exists as a diatomic (two-atom) elements; (F_2, Cl_2, Br_2)
. Seven (7) valance electrons
. Very high electronegativity and ionization energy values
. Form negative one (-1) ion from gaining one electron to fill their valance shell
. F and Cl are obtained from their fused salt (NaF, NaCl..etc)
. If Y is a Group 17 halogen
    XY is the general formula of a Group 17 atom bonding with a Group 1 X atom
    MY_2 is the general formula of a Group 17 atom bonding with a Group 2 M atom
. The only group containing elements in all three phases at room temperature:
    Gases (Fluorine and Chlorine) Liquid (Bromine) Solid (Iodine)
. Fluorine is the most reactive of the group, and the most reactive nonmetal overall
. Astatine (At) in this group is a radioactive element and behaves quiet
    differently from the other four elements.

Group 17 Halogens
F 9
Cl 17
Br 35
I 53
At 85

Topic 2 - The Periodic Table

16. Group 18 - Noble (inert) gases: Properties and facts of the noble gases

Noble gases are elements in Group 18 of the Periodic Table.
Members include helium, neon, argon, krypton, xenon, and radon
Properties (characteristics) of noble gases are listed below.

Concept Facts: Study to remember these properties.

- Each exists as a monatomic (one - atom) nonpolar molecule (Ne, He, Kr...)
- All are gases are at standard temperature and pressure (STP)
- They all have full valance shell with eight electrons
    (Exception: Helium is full with only two electrons)
- They neither gain nor lose electrons due to their full valance shells
- They are very stable and are nonreactive (do not form too many compounds)
- Argon (Ar) and Xenon (Xe) have been found to produce a few stable compounds with fluorine.
    Ex. XeF_4 (xenon tetrafluoride)

Group 17	Group 18 Noble gases
	He 2
	Ne 10
	Ar 18
	Kr 36
	Xe 54
	Rn 86

17. Groups and Groups Properties: Summary Table

Concept Fasts: Study to learn properties of elements within each Group.

Group number	Group name	Types of elements	Phases (at STP)	Valance electrons (during bonding)	Common oxidation number (charge)	Chemical bonding (general formula)
1	Alkali metals	Metal	Solids (all)	1 (lose)	+1	XY with halogens (17) X_2O with oxygen (16)
2	Alkaline earth	Metal	Solids (all)	2 (lose)	+2	MY_2 with halogens (17) MO with oxygen (16))
3-12	Transition metals	Metal	Liquid (Hg) Solids (the rest)	(lose)	Multiple + charges	Varies (forms colorful compounds)
13	-	Metalloid Metal	Solids (all)	3 (lose)	+3	LY_3 with halogens (17) L_2O_3 with oxygen (16)
14	-	Nonmetal Metalloid Metal	Solids (all)	4 (some share) (some lose)	vary	-
15	-	Nonmetal Metalloid Metal	Gas (N) Solids (the rest)	5 (gain or share)	-3	-
16	Oxygen group	Nonmetal Metalloid	Gas (O) Solids (the rest)	6 (gain or share)	-2	X_2O with alkali metals (1) MO with alkaline earth (2)
17	Halogens (Diatomic)	Nonmetal	Gases (F and Cl) Liquid (Br) Solid (I)	7 (gain or share)	-1	XY with alkali metals (1) MY with alkaline earths (2)
18	Noble gases (Monatomic)	Nonmetal	Gases (all)	8 (neither)	0	Forms very few compound. XeF_4 is the most common.

Topic 2 - The Periodic Table

18. Groups and Group properties: Relating properties to Group

Concept Task: Be able to relate element's name to a given property.
Study each example question below, and note the explanations for each correct choice.

Example 6:

Which element exist as a diatomic molecule?

1) Mg   2) Fe   3) Br   4) He

Answer: Choice 3. Br is a halogen. Halogens exist as diatomic molecules

Example 7:

Which element is likely to gain electron during bonding?

1) S   2) Cr   3) Ne   4) Na

Answer: Choice 1. S (sulfur) is a nonmetal. Nonmetals are likely to gain electrons.

Example 8:

An unknown element Z bonds with oxygen to produce an oxide with a general formula of ZO. Element Z is likely

1) Potassium   2) Beryllium   3) Aluminum   4) Ar

Answer: Choice 2: Oxygen combines with Group 2 alkaline earth in a 1:1 ratio (ZO). (See summary Table)
Beryllium (Be) is a Group 2 alkaline earth metal. (See Periodic Table)

Example 9:

Which is likely a colorful compound?

1) KCl   2) $MnCl_2$ 3) $AlCl_3$ 4) $SrCl_2$

Answer: Choice 2. Transition metals form colorful compounds. Mn (in $MnCl_2$) is a transition metal.

Lesson 3. Periodic Trends

Introduction

Periodic trends refer to patterns of properties that exist as elements are considered from one end of the table to the other.

Trend in atomic number is a good example (and the most obvious) of a periodic trend found on the Periodic Table.

It is easy to see that as elements are considered one after the other from:

Left to **Right** across a Period: Atomic number of the elements increases

Bottom to **Top** up a Group: Atomic number of the elements decreases

Many other trends exist on the periodic table even though they are not so obvious.
In this lesson, you will learn of the following trends.

Trends in atomic and ionic radius (size).
Trends in metallic and nonmetallic properties.
Trends in electronegativity and ionization energy.

Topic 2 - The Periodic Table

19. Trends in atomic size (atomic radius): Definitions and facts

Atomic radius is defined as half the distance between two nuclei of the same atom when they are joined together.
Atomic radius measurements give a good approximation of the size of each atom.

The general trend in atomic size found on the Periodic Table is as follows:
Concept Facts: Study to remember the following trends.

LOOK on Reference Table S for atomic radius of the elements.

Top to Bottom down a **group**: *Atomic size increases due to an increase in the number of electron shells.*

Example: Consider these atomic diagrams of the first three elements in Group 1 from **top** to **bottom**.

H — One electron shell : Smallest (size) radius

Li — Two electron shells

Na — Three electron shells : Largest (size) radius

electron shells

Note: Each additional electron shell makes the atom below bigger than the element above it.

Left to Right across a **Period**: *Atomic size (radius) decreases due to increase in nuclear charge*

Example: Consider the atomic diagrams of the first three elements in Period 2 from **left** to **right**

Li (3+)   Be (4+)   B (5+)

Smallest nuclear charge
Biggest radius (size)

Greatest nuclear charge
Smallest radius (size)

NOTE: The increase in positive nuclear charge (atomic number) allows the negative electron shells to be attracted closer to the nucleus. This increased attraction allows an atom on the right to be smaller when compared to the atom to its left.

20. Trend in atomic size: Determining an element with the largest or smallest atomic size

Concept Task: Be able to determine element with the largest or the smallest radius (size):
Use reference Table S to determine the atomic radius of each element given as choices:

You can also determine the answer based on the trend by considering the position of each element on the Periodic Table.

Largest atomic size: Farthest Left and farthest down
Smallest atomic size: Farthest Right and farthest up

Example 10

Which of the following elements has the largest atomic radius?

1) K   2) Ca   3) Al   4) Na

Answer: Choice 1 because K, on the Periodic Table, is the *farthest left* and the *farthest down* of all the four elements.

42 Copyright © 2010 E3 Scholastic Publishing. All Rigts Reserved.

Topic 2 - The Periodic Table

21. Trends in metallic and nonmetallic properties: Facts

Elements on the bottom left of the table have more metallic properties, but less nonmetallic properties. Elements on the top right (excluding noble gases) have more nonmetallic and less metallic properties.

Trends in metallic and nonmetallic properties can be summarized as follows.
Concept Facts: Study to remember the following trends.

Top to **Bottom** down a **Group**: Metallic properties increase AND Nonmetallic properties decrease
LEFT to **Right** across a **Period**: Metallic properties decrease AND Nonmetallic properties increase

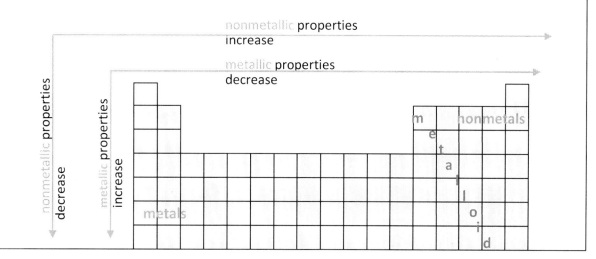

22. Trend in metallic and nonmetallic properties: Determining which element is more metallic or less metallic (or nonmetallic)

Concept Task: Be able to determine which element has the most (or least) metallic or nonmetallic properties

To determine which element from the given choices has:
Greatest (most) metallic characteristics
   OR
Least nonmetallic characteristics:
 . **Consider** the location of each element on the Periodic Table
 . **Choose** the element farthest left and/or closest to bottom

To determine which element given has the
Least metallic properties
   OR
Greatest (most) nonmetallic properties
 . **Consider** the location of each element on the Periodic Table
 . **Choose** the element farthest right and/or closest to the top

Example 11
Which of the following element has the most metallic characteristics?

1) In   2) Ga   3) Sn   4) Ge

Answer: Choice 1

On the Periodic Table, **In** (of the four choices given) is the element farthest left and closest to the bottom.

Example 12
Which of these elements has the most nonmetallic properties?

1) I   2) Te   3) Po   4) At

Answer: Choice 1

because, on the Periodic Table, I is the farthest right and farthest up of the four choices given.

(Look on the Periodic Table for location of each element)

Copyright © 2010 E3 Scholastic Publishing. All Rights Reserved

Topic 2 - The Periodic Table

23. Trends in electronegativity and ionization energy: Definitions and facts

Electronegativity defines an atom's ability to attract (gain) electrons from another atom during chemical bonding. The value of the electronegativity assigned to each element is relative to one another.

Fluorine (F) is assigned the highest electronegativity value of 4.

Cesium (Cs) and Francium (Fr) are assigned the lowest value of 0.7.

This means that of all the elements, fluorine has the greatest tendency to attract (gain) electrons. Cesium and francium have the least ability (tendency) to attract electrons during bonding.

Ionization energy refers to the amount of energy needed to remove the most loosely bound electrons from an atom. Ionization energy of an atom measures the tendency of (how likely) the atom is to lose electrons. The lower the ionization energy of an atom, the easier it for that atom to lose its most loosely bound valance electron (and form a positive ion).

The alkali metals in Group 1 tend to have the lowest ionization energy. Since group 1 alkali elements only have one valance electron, they are willing to lose its one electron and form a more stable ionic configuration.

The noble gases have the highest ionization energy values since these elements already have full valance shell and are unwilling to lose any of its electrons.

LOOK on Reference Table S for electronegativity and ionization energy values for the elements.

The general trends in electronegativity and ionization energy are as follows.

Concept Facts: Study to remember the following trends.

Top to **Bottom** down a **Group**: Electronegativity (tendency to gain or attract electrons) decreases.

Ionization energy (tendency to lose electrons) decreases

Left to **Right** across a **Period**: Electronegativity increases

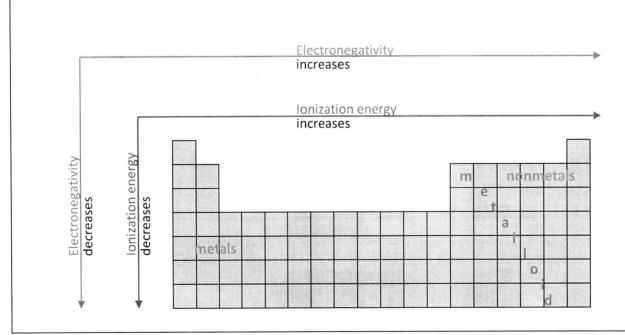

Topic 2 - The Periodic Table

24. Trend in ionization and electronegativity energy:
Determining element with greatest or least tendency

Concept Task: Be able to determine an element that has the greatest or least tendency to attract electrons.

To Determine which element has:

Greatest attraction for electrons (Most likely to gain)
  Choose elements with the HIGHEST electronegativity value

Least attraction for electrons (Least likely to gain)
  Choose element with the LOWEST electronegativity value

USE Reference Table S to locate electronegativity values

Example 13
Which of these elements is most likely to attract electrons from another atom during chemical bonding?
1) Fe   2) P   3) Al   4) Fr

Before choosing:
Use **Reference Table S** to find and note electronegativity value of each atom.

Fe	P	Al	Fr
1.8	2.2	1.6	0.7

Answer: Choice 2 because phosphorous has the highest electronegativity value of the four atoms.

Concept Task: Be able to determine which element has the greatest or the least tendency to lose electrons.

To determine which element has:

Greatest tendency to lose electrons
  Choose elements with the LOWEST ionization energy value

Least tendency to lose electrons
  Choose element with the HIGHEST ionization energy value

USE Reference Table S to locate ionization energy values

Example 14
Which of the following elements has greatest tendency to lose its valance electrons?
1) Be   2) S   3) Ne   4) Ca

Before choosing:
Use **Reference table S** to find and note the ionization energy value for each choice of atom.

Be	S	Ne	Ca
900	1000	2081	590

Answer: Choice 4 because calcium has the lowest ionization energy value. Therefore, it will lose its electrons the easiest.

25. Allotropes: Definitions, facts, and examples

Allotropes refer to two or more different molecular forms of the same element in the solid state.
Allotropes of the same element have different molecular structures.
  . **Differences in molecular structures** give allotropes of the same element different physical properties (color, shape, density, mass) AND different chemical properties (reactivity).

Examples of some common allotropes: Study to remember them

  Oxygen allotropes: Air (O_2) and Ozone (O_3)
      O_2 and O_3, although both considered oxygen, have different molecular, structures and different chemical and physical properties.

  Carbon allotropes: Diamond, graphite, and buckminsterfullerene
      Although all three are element carbon, diamond, graphite, and fullerene have different molecular structures and different chemical and physical characteristics.

Topic 2 – The Periodic Table of Elements

Check-A-list

Concept Terms

Below is a list of vocabulary terms from Topic 2. You should know the definition and facts related to each term.

Put a check in the box [V] next to each term if you know its definition and other facts related to the term.

- [ ] Periodic aw
- [ ] Group
- [ ] Period
- [ ] Metal
- [ ] Nonmetal
- [ ] Metalloid
- [ ] Alkali metal
- [ ] Alkaline Earth metal
- [ ] Transition element
- [ ] Halogen
- [ ] Noble gas
- [ ] Malleable
- [ ] Luster
- [ ] Brittleness
- [ ] Dull
- [ ] Ionization energy
- [ ] Electronegativity
- [ ] Atomic radius
- [ ] Conductivity
- [ ] Properties of metals
- [ ] Properties of nonmetals
- [ ] Properties of metalloids
- [ ] Properties of Group 1 alkali metals
- [ ] Properties of Group 2 alkaline earth metals
- [ ] Properties of Group 3 – 12 transition metals
- [ ] Properties of Group 17 halogens
- [ ] Properties of Group 18 noble gases
- [ ] Trend in metallic and nonmetallic properties
- [ ] Trend in atomic size or radius
- [ ] Trend in ionization energy
- [ ] Trend in electronegativity

If you don't have a check next to a term, look it up or ask your teacher.

Concept Task:

Below is a list of concept tasks from Topic 2. You should know how to solve problems and answer questions related to each concept task.

Put a check in the box [V] next to a concept task when you know how to solve problems and answer questions related to it.

- [ ] Determining elements with the same characteristics
- [ ] Identifying an element as a metal, metalloid, or nonmetal
- [ ] Determining element's name or symbol based on given properties
- [ ] Determining property or properties of a given elements name or symbol
- [ ] identifying an element based on the Group it is located
- [ ] Relating elements name or symbol to group properties
- [ ] Determining element with the largest or smallest atomic radius
- [ ] Determining element that has the most or least metallic properties
- [ ] Determining element that has the most or least nonmetallic properties
- [ ] Determining element with greatest or least tendency to attract electrons
- [ ] Determining element with greatest or least tendency to lose electrons

If you don't have a check next to a concept task, look it up or ask your teacher.

Topic 2 – The Periodic Table of Elements

Concept Fact Review Questions

1. The observed regularities in the properties of the elements are periodic functions of their
   1) Atomic numbers
   2) Atomic mass
   3) Oxidation state
   4) Reactivity

2. The similarities in chemical properties of elements within the same group is due to similarity in
   1) Number of electron shells
   2) Number of neutrons electrons
   3) Number of protons
   4) Number of valance electrons

3. Group 18 elements on the periodic table are called
   1) Transition metals
   2) Halogens
   3) Alkaline earth
   4) Noble gases

4. Electronegativity values of the elements measure the elements' ability to
   1) Lose electrons
   2) Attract electrons
   3) Carry heat
   4) Carry electricity

5. During chemical bonding, atoms of metallic elements tend to
   1) Gain electrons and form negative ions
   2) Gain electrons and form positive ions
   3) Lose electrons and form negative ions
   4) Lose electrons and form positive ions

6. When a halide salt is formed between a halogen Y and a Group 2 element M, the general formula of the halide will be
   1) MY_{17}
   2) MY
   3) M_2Y
   4) MY_2

7. Which halogen is correctly paired with the phase it exists as at STP?
   1) Br is a liquid
   2) F is a solid
   3) I is a gas
   4) Cl is a liquid

8. As the elements in Group 1 of the Periodic Table are considered in order of increasing atomic number, the atomic radius of each successive element increases. This is primarily due to an increase in the number of
   1) Neutrons in the nucleus
   2) Unpaired electrons
   3) Valance electrons
   4) Electrons shells

9. When elements within Period 3 are considered in order of decreasing atomic number, ionization energy of each successive element generally
   1) Increases due to increase in atomic size
   2) Increase due to decrease in atomic size
   3) Decrease due to increase in atomic size
   4) Decrease due to decrease in atomic size

10. Which set of characteristics of is true of elements in Group 2 of the Periodic Table?
    1) They all have two energy level and share different chemical characteristics
    2) They all have two energy level and share similar chemical characteristics
    3) They all have two valance electrons and share similar chemical properties
    4) They all have two valance electrons and share different chemical properties

Topic 2 – The Periodic Table of Elements

Concept Task Review Questions

11. Elements strontium and beryllium both form a bond with fluorine with similar chemical formula. The similarity in their formulas is due to
    1) Strontium and beryllium having the same number of kernel electrons
    2) Strontium and beryllium having the same number of valance electrons
    3) Strontium and beryllium having the same number of protons
    4) Strontium and beryllium having the same molecular structure

12. The element Antimony is a
    1) Metal   2) Nonmetal   3) Metalloid   4) Halogen

13. Which of these elements in Period 2 is likely to form a negative ion?
    1) Oxygen   2) Boron   3) Ne   4) Li

14. Which of these characteristics best describes the element sulfur at STP?
    1) It is brittle   2) It is malleable   3) It has luster   4) It is ductile

15. Which of these elements has high thermal and electrical conductivity?
    1) Iodine   2) Carbon   3) Phosphorous   4) Iron

16. Which element is an alkali metal?
    1) H   2) Li   3) Al   4) Mg

17. Chlorine will bond with which metallic element to form a colorful compound?
    1) Aluminum   2) Sodium   3) Strontium   4) Manganese

18. According to the Periodic Table, which sequence correctly places the elements in order of increasing atomic size?
    1) Na -----> Li ------> H -----> K
    2) Ba -----> Sr -----> Sr -----> Ca
    3) Te -----> Sb -------> Sn ------> In
    4) H ------> He -------> Li ------> Be

19. Which of these elements has stronger metallic characteristics than Aluminum?
    1) He   2) Mg   3) Ga   4) Si

20. Which element has a greater tendency to attract electron than phosphorous?
    1) Silicon   2) Arsenic   3) Boron   4) Sulfur

21. Which of these Period 2 elements has the greatest tendency to lose its most loosely bound valance electrons?
    1) Li   2) Be   3) B   4) C

T 2Q

Topic 2 – The Periodic Table of Elements

Constructed Response Questions

Base your answer to questions 22 through 25 on the information below.

A metal, M, was obtained from compound in a rock sample. Experiments have determined that the element is a member of Group 2 on the Periodic Table of the Elements.

Write answers here.

22. What is the phase of element M at STP?

22.

23. Explain, in terms of electrons, why element M is a good conductor of electricity.

23.

24. Explain why the radius of a positive ion of element M is smaller than the radius of an atom of element M.

24.

25. Using the element symbol M for the element, write the chemical formula for the compound that forms when element M reacts with Iodine?

25.

The table below shows the electronegativity of selected elements of the Periodic Table.

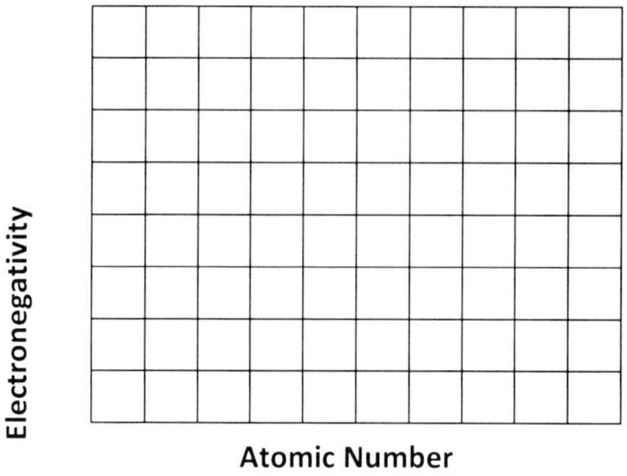

Element	Atomic Number	Electronegativity
Beryllium	4	1.6
Boron	5	2.0
Carbon	6	2.6
Fluorine	9	4.0
Lithium	3	1.0
Oxygen	8	3.4

Electronegativity

Atomic Number

26. On the grid set up a scale for electronegativity on the y-axis. Plot the data by drawing a best-fit line.

Write answers here.

27. Using the graph, predict the electronegativity of Nitrogen.

27. _____

28. For these elements, state the trend in electronegativity in terms of atomic number.

28.

Copyright © 2010 E3 Scholastic Publishing. All Rights Reserved

Topic 3 – The Atomic structure

Topic outline

In this topic, you will learn about:

. The historical development of the modern atom

. The subatomic particles; protons, electrons, neutrons

. Atomic number, mass number and atomic mass

. Isotopes and isotopes symbols

. Electrons shells and electron arrangement

. Ground and excited state of atom

. Bright-line spectra

. Valance electrons, neutral atoms and ions

Lesson 1 - The historical development of the modern atom

Introduction:

The atom is the most basic unit of matter. Since atoms are very small and cannot be seen with the most sophisticated equipment, several scientists, for thousands of years have proposed different models of atoms to help explain the nature and behavior of matter.

In this lesson, you will learn about these historical scientists, their experiments and their proposed models of atom.

1. Historical development of atom: Definitions and facts

Concept Facts: Study to remember the following about the development of the modern atom.

. **Many scientists** over many years have contributed to the development of the modern atomic model.

. ***The wave mechanical-model*** is the current and the most widely accepted model of the atom.

The wave-mechanical model of an atom is summarized below.

. Each atom has small dense positive nucleus

. Electrons are found outside the nucleus in a region called an **orbital**.

. **An Orbital** is the most probable location of finding an electron with certain energy in an atom.

Below are the historical scientists and their proposed models of the atom starting with the earliest. Description of model and key feature for each model are given below the atom.

Concept Facts: Study to remember the order of atomic model starting with the earliest model.

John Dalton (Earliest model)	J.J. Thompson	Earnest Rutherford	Neil Bohr	Current model
			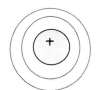	
Hard-sphere model (cannonball) .No internal structure	**Plum-pudding model** .Electrons and positive charges disperse throughout the atom.	**Empty-space model** (Nuclear model) .Small dense positive nucleus . Electrons revolve around the nucleus	**Bohr's model** (Planetary) . Electrons in specific orbit . Orbits have fixed energy .Orbits create electron shells	**Wave-mechanical** (electron cloud) .Electrons in orbital . **Orbital** is area electron is likely to be found

Topic 3 – The Atomic structure

2. Historical scientific experiments: Earnest Rutherford Gold Foil experiment

Earnest Rutherford conducted an experiment that led him to proposed the empty space theory of an atom

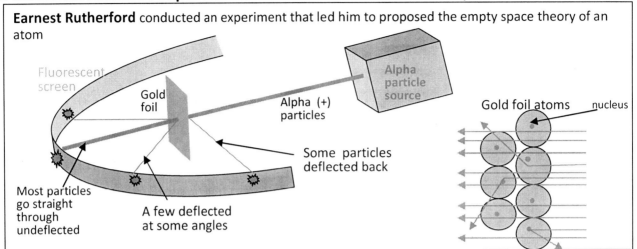

Concept Facts: Study to remember the following about the Gold Foil experiment

The set up:

Equipment was set up to shoot alpha particles at a gold foil.

.An Alpha particle is a **positively** charge helium nuclei.

A Fluorescent screen was set around the foil

. The Screen was to detect the path of the particles once they had hit the gold foil

Rutherford's atom

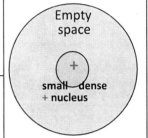

Results:	Conclusions:
Most of the alpha particles went straight through the foil undeflected.	Atom is mostly empty space
A few of the particles were deflected back or hit the screen at different angles.	The center of the atom is dense positive, and very small
This means that the positive alpha particles had encountered an area in the atom that is small, dense and positive (the nucleus).	**Remember:** Like charges (in this case, two positives: + alpha and + nucleus) will repel.

3. Historical scientific experiment: J.J. Thompson cathode ray experiment

J.J. Thompson conducted experiment that led him to discover the electron.

Concept Facts: study the followings

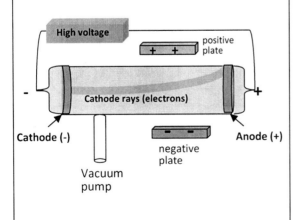

The Set up:

A tube with a metal disk at each end was set up to trace a beam from electrical source. The metals were connected to an electrical source in this experiment.

Anode: The Metal disk that becomes + charge

Cathode: The Metal disk that becomes – charge.

Results: A beam of light (ray) travel from the cathode end to the anode end of the tube.

When electrically charged + and - plates were brought near the tube, the beam (ray) is deflected toward (attracted) the positive plate. The beam was repelled by the negative plate.

Conclusion: The beam (ray) is negatively charge (electron)

Copyright © 2010 E3 Scholastic Publishing. All Rights Reserved.

Topic 3 – The atomic Structure

Lesson 2 – The atomic structure

Introduction

An atom may be the smallest unit of matter, but it is composed of other smaller units of particles. These particles are called the subatomic particles.

In this lesson, you will learn more about the modern atom and the subatomic particles. You will also learn about the relationships between subatomic particles, atomic numbers, and mass numbers.

4. The atom: Definitions and fact

The atom is the basic unit of matter.

Atom is composed of three **subatomic particles**: Protons, electrons and neutrons

NOTE: The only atom with no neutron is an atom of hydrogen with a mass of 1.

Concept Facts: Study to remember the followings about the atom.

- Atom is mostly empty space
- Atoms have small dense positive core (nucleus), and negative electron cloud surrounding the nucleus
- Elements are composed of atoms with the same atomic number
- Atoms of the same element are similar.
- Atoms of different elements are different

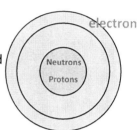

5. The nucleus: Definitions and facts

The nucleus is the center (core) of an atom.

Concept Facts: Study to remember the followings about the nucleus

- The nucleus contains protons (+) and neutrons (no charge)
- Overall charge of the nucleus is positive (+) due to the protons
- Compared to the entire atom, the nucleus is very small BUT very dense.
- Most of atom's mass is due to the mass of the nucleus

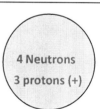

6. Protons: Definitions and facts

Protons are positively charge subatomic particles found in the nucleus of an atom.

Concept Facts: Study to remember the followings about protons

- A proton has a mass of 1 atomic mass unit (amu) and a +1 charge
- A proton is about 1836 times more massive (heavier) than an electron
- Protons are located inside the nucleus
- The number of protons is the same as the atomic number of the element
- All atoms of the same element must have the same number of protons
- The number of protons in the nucleus is also the nuclear charge of the element

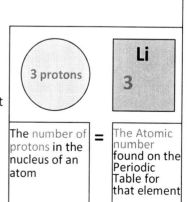

Copyright © 2010 E3 Scholastic Publishing. All Rights Reserved.

Topic 3 – The Atomic structure

7. Electrons: Definitions and facts

Electrons are negatively charged subatomic particles found in orbital outside the nucleus of an atom.

Concept Facts: Study to remember the followings about electrons

. An electron has insignificant mass (zero) and a -1 charge.
. An electron has a mass that is $1/1836^{th}$ that of a proton (or neutron).
. An electron is found in **orbital** outside the nucleus
. Electron arrangements in an atom determines the chemical properties of the elements
. Number of electrons is always equal to the number of protons in a a neutral atom

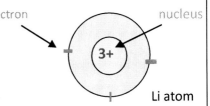
Li atom

In a Li atom, the number of electrons (3 e-) is equal to the number of protons (3+).

In all neutral atoms, there are equal numbers of electrons to protons.

8. Neutrons: Definitions and facts

Neutrons are neutral (no charge) subatomic particles located inside the nucleus of an atom.

Concept Facts: Study to remember the followings about neutrons

. A neutrons has a mass of 1 amu and a zero charge
. A neutron has the same mass (1 amu) as a proton
. Neutrons are located in the nucleus along with protons
. Atoms of the same element differ in their number of neutrons

A Lithium nucleus   A different Lithium nucleus

Nuclei from two different atoms of Lithium have the same number of protons but different numbers of neutrons.

9. The subatomic particles: Summary Table

Protons, electrons and neutrons are different in mass, charge, and location in an atom.

The table below summarizes information about all three particles.

NOTE: Some information on this Table can be found on **Reference Table O.**

Subatomic particle	Symbol	Mass	Charge	Location
Protons	$^{1}_{+1}p$	1	+1	Nucleus
Neutrons	$^{1}_{0}n$	1	0	Nucleus
Electrons	$^{0}_{-1}e$	0	-1	Orbital (outside the nucleus)

Topic 3 – The Atomic Structure

10. Atomic number: Definitions and facts

The **atomic number** of an element identifies each element.

Concept Facts: Study to remember the followings about atomic number

. Atomic number of an element is **equal** to the number of protons.
. All atoms of the same element have the same atomic number and the same number of protons.
. The atomic number can be found on the Periodic Table
. Elements on the Periodic Table are arranged in order of increasing atomic number

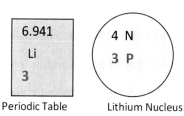

Periodic Table | Lithium Nucleus

Lithium (Li) has atomic number of 3.
Nucleus of all Li atoms contains 3 protons.
No other atom can have 3 protons in their nucleus BUT Li atoms

11. Nucleons: Definitions and facts

Nucleons are particle in the nucleus of an atom (Protons and neutrons)

Concept Facts: Study to remember the followings about nucleons

. Nucleons account for the total mass of an atom
. The total number of nucleons in an atom is equal to the sum of protons **plus** neutrons

The Total number of nucleons for this Li atom is 7 (3 P + 4 N = 7)	The total number of nucleons of this Li atom is 8 (3 P + 5 N = 8)

12. Mass number: Definitions and facts

Mass number identifies different isotopes of the same element.

Concept Facts: Study to remember the followings about mass number

. Atoms of the same element differ by their mass numbers
. The mass number is equal to the number of protons **plus** neutrons
. The mass number shows the total number of nucleons

Two different nuclei of Li atoms

The mass number of this Li atom is 7 (3 + 4 = 7 amu)	The mass number of this Li atom is 8 (3 + 5 = 8 amu)

Copyright © 2010 E3 Scholastic Publishing. All Rights Reserved.

Topic 3 – The Atomic Structure

13. Relating one particle to another in neutral atoms:

Determining number of one particle from number of other particles.

Concept Task: Be able to determine and compare number of subatomic particles.

Summary of relation between the atomic particles is given below.
Study to remember them. Also, note the example problem for each relationship.

For neutral atoms only

Number of protons
- = The atomic number of the element
- = Number of electrons
- = Number of nuclear charge
- = Number of nucleon – neutrons
- = Mass number – number of neutrons

Example 1
A neutral atom contains 12 neutrons and 11 electrons. The number of protons in this atom is
1) 1   2) 11   3) 12   4) 23
Answer: Choice 2

Number of electrons
- = The atomic number of the element
- = Number of protons
- = Number of nuclear charge
- = Mass number – number of neutrons

Example 2
What is the number of electrons in a neutral atom of Fluorine?
1) 9   2) 19   3) 10   4) 28
Answer: Choice 1

Number of neutrons
- = Mass number – number of protons
- = Mass number – atomic number
- = Mass number – number of electrons
- = Nucleons – number of proton

Example 3
The number of neutrons in a neutral atom with a mass number of 86 and 37 electrons is
1) 86   2) 37   3) 123   4) 49
Answer: Choice 4

Atomic number
- = Number of protons
- = Number of electrons
- = Number of nuclear charge
- = Mass number – number neutrons

Example 4
What is the atomic number of a neutral element whose atoms contain 60 neutrons and 47 electrons?
1) 13   2) 47   3) 60   4) 107
Answer: Choice 2

Mass number
- = Number of protons + Neutrons
- = Number of electrons + Neutrons
- = Nuclear charge + Neutrons
- = Number of nucleons

Example question 5:
What is the mass number of an atom that contains 19 protons, 18 electrons, and 20 neutrons?
1) 19   2) 38   3) 39   4) 58
Answer: Choice 3

Number of nucleons
- = Mass number
- = Number of protons + Neutrons
- = Number of electrons + Neutrons
- = Nuclear charge + Neutrons

Example question 6:
How many nucleons are there in an atom with a nuclear charge of +20 and 23 neutrons?
1) 58   2) 20   3) 3   4) 43
Answer: Choice 4

Nuclear charge
- = Number of protons
- = Atomic number
- = Mass number - neutrons

Topic 3 - The Atomic

14. Isotopes: Definition and facts

Isotopes are atoms of the same element with the same number of protons but different number of neutrons.

There are few different atoms of the element Lithium. All atoms of Lithium contain the same number of protons in their nucleus. The difference between these atoms is in the number of neutrons.

Since all Lithium atoms have the same number of protons (3), they all have the same atomic number of 3. Since they have different number of neutrons, they each have a different mass number.

These different atoms of Lithium are referred to as isotopes of Lithium.

Isotopes of the same element must have:

. **Different** mass numbers (nucleons)

. **Different** number of neutrons

. **Same** atomic number

. **Same** number of protons (Nuclear charge)

. **Same** number of electrons

. **Same** chemical reactivity

Symbols showing two isotopes of Lithium

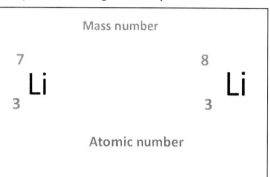

Mass number

$^{7}_{3}Li$ $^{8}_{3}Li$

Atomic number

15. Isotope symbols: Different notation to represent isotopes of same element

Different isotopes of an element have different mass numbers. Therefore, the mass number of an isotope is written next to the element's name (or symbol) to distinguish it from the other isotopes.

Example: Lithium – 7 and Lithium – 8 are two isotopes of lithium.

The 7 and the 8 are the mass numbers of these two lithium isotopes.

There are other notations that are also used to represent isotopes of elements.

Below are different ways of representing the two Lithium isotopes.

When studying the notations below:

. **Pay attention** to how Lithium-7 and Lithium-8 are similar, and also how the are different in each notation.

. **Also** pay attention to how all four notations of the same isotope are related

Element – mass number (isotope's name)	*Lithium – 7*	*Lithium – 8*
Symbol – mass number notation:	*Li – 7*	*Li – 8*
Common isotope notation:	$^{7}_{3}Li$	$^{8}_{3}Li$
Nucleus symbol notation:	(4 n, 3 p)	(5 n, 3 p)

Topic 3: The Atomic Structure

16. Isotope symbols: Determining symbols that are isotopes of the same element

Concept Task: Be able to determine or recognize two symbols that are isotopes of the same element.

To determine which two symbols are isotopes of the same element.

LOOK for two symbols that have:
- **Differen**t mass # (Top number)
- **Same Chemical symbol**
- **Same** Atomic # (bottom #) and same symbol

NOTE: The bottom number must be the correct atomic number for the element.

To determine which two nucleus notations are isotopes of the same element:

LOOK for nucleus symbols that contain:
- **Same** number of protons (p)
- **Different** number of neutrons (n)

NOTE: If name or symbol of an element is given in the question, the number of protons **must match** the atomic number of the element

---

Example 7
Which two notations represent isotopes of the same element?

1) $^{40}_{19}K$ and $^{40}_{20}Ca$ 3) $^{23}_{11}Na$ and $^{24}_{12}Na$

2) $^{20}_{10}Ne$ and $^{22}_{10}Ne$ 4) $^{16}_{8}O$ and $^{17}_{8}N$

Answer: Choice 2. Both notations have:
- *Top numbers* that are different and
- *Bottom Numbers* that are the same

NOTE: The bottom number, 10, is also a correct atomic number for Ne (neon)

Example 8
Which symbol could represent an isotope of element iron?

1) $^{55}_{55}X$ 2) $^{26}_{55}X$ 3) $^{55}_{26}X$ 4) $^{26}_{8}X$

Answer: Choice 3: The bottom number (26) is the atomic number of iron (Fe).

Example 9
Which two nuclei are isotopes of the element phosphorous?

1) (15 P, 16 n) and (16 p, 15 n)

2) (15 p, 15 n) and (16 p, 16n)

3) (15 p, 15 n) and (15 p, 16 n)

4) (31 p, 15 n) and (15 p, 31 n)

Answer: Choice 3. The element in question is phosphorous, so the number of protons in both nuclei MUST BE 15 **(The atomic number for phosphorous).**
Choice 3 is correct because both nuclei have the same protons (15 p) BUT different neutrons (15 n and 16n)

Topic 3 - The Atomic Structure

17. Isotope symbols: Determining and comparing particles in isotope symbols

In any given isotope notation, you should be able to determine the following information.
. Mass number, number of nucleons, and the sum of protons and neutrons
. Atomic number, number of protons, nuclear charge, and number of electrons
. Number of neutrons

When two isotope symbols are given, you can determine and compare the number of particles between them.
Below, an isotope of sulfur and an isotope of phosphorous are given.

As you study the information below:
Note the differences and similarities in the number of particles between the two isotopes.

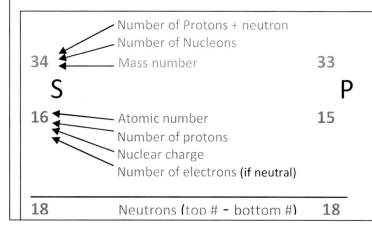

According to information from the isotope symbols, the following comparisons can be made:

^{34}S has **more** nucleons than ^{33}P

$^{33}_{15}$P has one **fewer** proton than $^{34}_{16}$S

^{34}S has a **greater** nuclear charge than ^{33}P

P-33 has the **same** number of **neutrons** as S-34

18. Isotope symbols: Determining and comparison number of particles in isotope symbols

Concept Tasks: Be able to determine the number of subatomic particles from a given isotope notation.
Be able to compare the number of subatomic particles of two given isotope symbols.

To correctly determine and compare number of particles in isotope symbols, you must know where to look isotope symbols. (see above notes)
The use of your Periodic Table is also recommended.

Example 10

What is the total number of protons and neutrons in the nuclide $^{80}_{35}$Br

1) 35   2) 80   3) 45   4) 115

Answer: Choice 2. Top number (80) is the mass number.
Mass number = Protons + neutrons

Example 11

The nucleus of the atom ^{107}Ag contains

1) 60 neutrons and has a nuclear charge of +47
2) 60 electrons and has a nuclear charge of +47
3) 47 neutrons and has a nuclear charge of +107
4) 47 electrons and has a nuclear charge of +107

Answer: Choice 1. Ag has atomic number of 47.
+47 Nuclear charge = atomic number 47
60 neutrons = 107 − 47

Example 12

Which nuclide contains the greatest number of neutrons?
1) ^{207}Pb   2) ^{84}Kr   3) ^{207}Ti   4) ^{208}Bi

Before choosing:
Determine atomic number (bottom #) for each.
Subtract bottom from top to get # of neutrons
$^{207}_{82}$Pb $^{84}_{36}$Kr $^{207}_{81}$Ti $^{208}_{83}$Bi

Neutrons = 125   48   126   125

Answer: Choice 3.

Example 13

Which nuclide contains 20 protons?
1) Ca-40   3) B-10
2) Ne-20   4) He-5

Answer: Choice 1. Ca has an atomic number of 20
20 protons = atomic number 20

Topic 3 - The Atomic Structure

19. Atomic mass unit: Definition and fact

Atomic mass unit (amu) is a unit for measuring mass of atoms based on carbon – 12.

$$1\ \text{amu} = \frac{1}{12}^{\text{th}} \text{ the mass of } ^{12}C$$

Interpretation:

Hydrogen – **1** has a mass that is $1/12^{th}$ the mass of ^{12}C

Lithium – **6** has a mass that is $6/12^{th}$ or half the mass of ^{12}C

Magnesium – **24** has a mass that is $24/12^{th}$ or 2 times the mass of ^{12}C

20. Atomic mass: Definition and facts

Atomic mass of an element is the average mass of all the naturally occurring stable isotopes of an element.

Atomic mass is based on the masses of the stable isotopes and their percent in a sample.

To get a better understanding of what this means, read the explanation below.

Natural sample of an element consists of a mix of two or more isotopes (different atoms). Usually, there is a lot of one isotope, and very little of the others.

Consider the natural sample of chlorine: The sample will contain mainly of two chlorine isotopes: Chlorine with a mass of 35 (Cl-35) and chlorine with a mass of 37 (Cl-37). In this natural sample of chlorine, the relative percentages (abundance) of these isotopes will be approximately 75% of Cl-35 and 25% of Cl-37. That means there will more chlorine atoms with mass of 35 amu than atoms with the mass of 37 amu.

The atomic mass of Chlorine given on the Periodic Table is the average mass of these two isotopes.

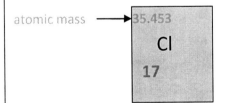

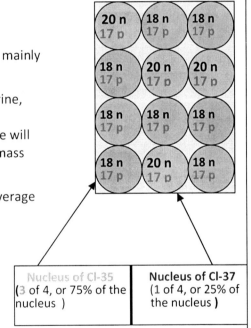

| Nucleus of Cl-35 (3 of 4, or 75% of the nucleus) | Nucleus of Cl-37 (1 of 4, or 25% of the nucleus) |

Although the atomic mass of an element can be found on the Periodic Table, student are often asked to calculate the atomic mass from given percentages and mass numbers of its isotopes.

On the next page, you will see examples of how average atomic mass of elements are calculated. Follow the steps in these examples when you are asked to calculate atomic mass for any element.

Topic 3 – The Atomic Structure

21. Average atomic mass: How to calculate average atomic mass

Concept Task: Be able to calculate average atomic mass of an element given the mass numbers and percent abundance of its isotopes.

Three examples are given below to show you how to calculate or determine the average atomic mass of an element.

Study the steps in each example to how to calculate atomic mass of elements.

Example 14
A natural sample of chlorine contains 75% of ^{35}Cl and 25% of ^{37}Cl. Calculate the atomic mass of chlorine?

	Step 1 (Change % to decimal)	Step 2 (multiply by mass #)	step 3 (Find products)	step 4 (add products to get mass)
75% of ^{35}Cl	.75	x 35	= 26.25	+ = 35.5 amu
25% of ^{37}Cl	.25	x 37	= 9.25	

Example 15
A sample of unknown element X contains the following isotopes:
80% of ^{64}X, 15% of ^{65}X, and 5% of ^{66}X.

What is the average atomic mass of element X?

	Step 1 (Change % to decimal)	Step 2 (multiply by mass #)	step 3 (Find products)	Step 4 (add products to get mass)
80% of ^{64}X	.80	x 64	= 51.2	+
15% of ^{65}X	.15	x 65	= 9.75	= 64.25 amu
5% of ^{66}X	.05	x 66	= 3.3	+

In each of the two examples, **NOTE** how the average atomic mass calculated is closer to the mass of the isotope with the highest percentage.
In example 14: 35.5 amu is closer to mass of Cl-35. The higher percentage (75%) isotope is Cl-35
In example 15. 64.25 amu is closer to the mass of ^{64}X. The higher percentage (80%) isotope is ^{64}X

Mathematically speaking, this makes sense and will always be the case. Example question 3 below, and similar questions, can be answered using the same logical thinking.

Example 16
Two isotopes of elements X have average atomic mass of 54 amu. What are the relative percentages of these two isotopes of element X?
1) 80% of ^{50}X and 20% of ^{55}X
2) 20% of ^{50}X and 80% of ^{55}X
3) 50% of ^{50}X and 50% of ^{55}X
4) 75% of ^{50}X and 25% of ^{55}X

You can choose without doing the math:
  Consider the choice in which the mass with the higher percentage is a mass that is closest to 54 amu
  Answer: Choice 2 : The percentages in this choice will average out to be 54 amu. The choice also makes sense because the higher percentage has a mass of 55. The average atomic mass of 54 is closer to 55.

Topic 3 – The Atomic Structure

22. Isotope of hydrogen:

The element hydrogen has three main isotopes: protium, deuterium, and tritium

As with all isotopes, these three isotopes of hydrogen differ in number of neutrons (and also in mass number.)

Names, symbol notations and nuclear diagram of these isotopes are shown below.

	Isotopes of hydrogen		
	Protium	**Deuterium**	**Tritium**
Name – mass	Hydrogen-1 (H-1)	Hydrogen-2 (H-2)	Hydrogen-3 (H-3)
Isotope symbol	$^{1}_{1}H$	$^{2}_{1}H$	$^{3}_{1}H$
Mass number	1	2	3
Protons (atomic number)	1	1	1
Neutrons	0	1	2
Nucleus diagram	1 p 0 n	1 p 1 n	1 p 2 n

Protium
Hydrogen-1 atom has the most basic atomic structure of all atoms. It is composed of 1 proton, 1 electron, and no neutron. It is the only atom without a neutron in its nucleus. When H-1 loses its only electron, the Hydrogen ion (H+) that forms is just a proton.
A sample of hydrogen is composed almost entirely (about 99.9%) of protium (H-1). Only trace amounts of deuterium (H-2) and tritium (H-3) would be found in a natural sample of hydrogen. The H-1 is the main hydrogen found in water molecules ($^{1}H_2O$).

Deuterium.
Water may also be composed of molecules of $^{2}H_2O$. This is called **heavy water** because the molecules are composed of deuterium atoms, a heavier hydrogen atom isotope. Heavy water is commonly used in nuclear power plants to cool down the reactors.

Tritium
Tritium's main application is also in nuclear reaction. It is the most commonly used reactant in nuclear fusion.

LOOKING AHEAD ⇒ **Topic 12-Nuclear chemistry:** You will learn about nuclear fusion.

Topic 3 – The Atomic Structure

Lesson 3 – Electrons location and arrangement

Introduction

According to the wave-mechanical model of atoms, electrons are found in orbital outside the nucleus.
Orbital describes the area (or region) in space outside the nucleus where an electron is likely to be found.
The orbital an electron occupies depends on the energy of the electron. While one electron of an atom has enough energy to occupy an orbital far from the nucleus, another electron of that same atom may have just enough energy to occupy a region closer to the nucleus. The result is a formation of energy levels (or electron shells) around the nucleus of the atom.
The Bohr's atomic model is often used to show arrangement of electrons in electron shells (energy levels) of an atom. Each electron shell in Bohr's atomic model corresponds to the amount of energy the electrons occupying that shell have.
The arrangement of electrons in atoms is complex. In this lesson, you will learn the basic and simplified arrangement of electrons in electron shells. You will also learn of electron transition (movement) from one level to another, and the production of spectrum of colors.

23. Electron shells: Definitions and facts

Electron shells refer to the energy levels in which electrons of an atom occupied.
The following are facts about electron shells of atoms:

Concept Facts: Study to remember the followings about electron shells

. An atom may have one or more electron shells.
. The electron shell (1st) closest to the nucleus always contains electrons with least amount of energy
. The electron shell farthest from the nucleus contains electrons with the most amount of energy
. On the Periodic Table, the Period (horizontal row) number indicates the total number of electron shells in the atoms of elements.
. The electrons configurations found in the box of each element shows the arrangement of electrons in these electrons shells

A Bohr's atomic model (shell diagram) can be drawn to show electrons in the electrons shells of an atom. Below, Bohr's atomic models for three atoms are drawn using information from the Periodic Table.

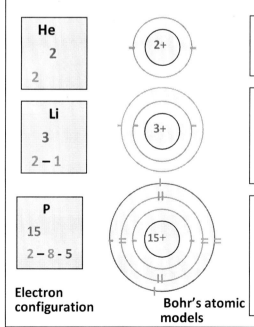

Electron configuration   Bohr's atomic models

According to the electron configuration, a Helium atom has all its electrons in **ONE** electron shell:
  1st shell: 2 electrons

According to the electron configuration, a Lithium atom has all its electrons in **TWO** electrons shells:
  1st shell: 2 electrons (electrons with lowest amount of energy)
  2nd shell : 1 electron (electron with the greatest amount of energy)

According to the electron configuration, a phosphorous atom has all its electrons in **THREE** electron shells:
  1st shell: 2 electrons (electrons with the least amount of energy)
  2nd shell : 8 electrons (electrons with a little more energy)
  3rd shell : 5 electrons (electrons with the most amount of energy)

Topic 3 – The Atomic Structure

24. Electron shell: Determining number of electron shells in an atom or configuration

Concept Task: Be able to determine number of electron shells in an atom or a configuration.

The notes below show you how to make these determinations. Also, study the example questions to right.

To determine number of electron shells in a given element

Locate the element on the Periodic Table.
  The Period (horizontal row) in which the element is found is also the number of electron shells of that element

  Ex: Chlorine is in Period 3. It has a total of 3 electron shells containing electrons.

To determine number of electron shells from a given electron configuration

Count the numbers in the configuration.
  Total numbers counted is the number of electron shells in the configuration

  Ex. In the configuration **2 – 8 – 8 – 1**
  There are four electron shells.

Example 17
How many electron shells containing electrons are found in an atom of calcium?
1) 2   2) 4   3) 20   4) 40

Answer: Choice 2 because Calcium is in Period 4.

Example 18
The total number of electron shells in the configuration 2 – 8 – 1 is
1) 1   2) 2   3) 3   4) 8

Answer: Choice 3 because the configuration contains 3 numbers

25. Electron shells: Determining electron shell with most or least energy electrons

Concept Task: Be able to determine the electron shell of a given atom or configuration containing electrons with the highest or lowest energy.

If an element is given, **Locate** its electron configuration on the Periodic Table, and consider the followings:

The first shell: Always contains electrons with **lowest energy**

The last shell: contains electrons with the **highest energy**

Example:

$$2 - 8 - 8 - 1$$
$$1^{st} \quad 2^{nd} \quad 3^{rd} \quad 4^{th}$$
ELECTRON   SHELLS

4th shell is the last shell. It contains electrons with the highest energy

Example 19
In which electron shell would an electron with the most energy be found in an atom of cesium?
1) 2   2) 8   3) 18   4) 6

Before choosing:
LOOK on Periodic Table for Cs (atomic # 55)
LOOK at its electron configuration: It has six electron shells.

Answer: Choice 4: The last shell (the 6th) contains electrons with the most energy

Example 20
In the electron configuration
$$2 - 8 - 3 - 1$$
Which shell contains electrons with the greatest energy?
1) 1st 2) 2nd 3) 3rd 4) 4th

Answer: Choice 4: The configuration has 4 shells. Highest energy electrons are found in the last shell (the 4th)

Topic 3 – The Atomic Structure

26. Electron configuration: Determining number of electrons in electron shells

Concept Task: Be able to determine the number of electron in any given electron shell of an atom or configuration

To determine number of electrons in each electron shell

Ex. $\underset{1^{st}}{2} - \underset{2^{nd}}{8} - \underset{3^{rd}}{8} - \underset{4^{th}}{1}$

To determine total number of electrons in a configuration:
  Add up all the numbers in the configuration
  $2 + 8 + 8 + 1 = $ **19 total electrons**

Example 21
How many electrons are in the fourth electron shell of an Iodine atom?
1) 17   2) 18   3) 8   4) 53
Answer: Choice 2 because iodine configuration is 2-8-18-18-7

Example 22
The total number of electrons in the configuration $2 - 8 - 17 - 2$ is
1) 4   2) 2   3) 29   4) 11
Answer: Choice 3 because the sum of all the numbers is 29.

27. Electron shells: Determining maximum number of electrons in any electron shell

Each electron shell has a maximum number of electrons that can occupy that shell. A full understanding of this concept requires lessons on quantum number. This concept will not be discussed. However, you still can determine the maximum number of electrons that can occupy different electron shells.

Concept Task: Be able to determine maximum number of electrons in any electron shell

You can determine maximum electrons in any electron shell using a very simple formula.

If **n** represents the electron shell in question:
For example: n = 1 means 1st shell, n = 3 means 3rd shell...etc

Maximum number of electrons in a shell $= 2(n^2)$

  Square the electron shell number then multiply the result by 2

Example 23
What is the maximum number of electrons that can occupy the first and the third shells of an atom?
First shell: n = 1
  $2(n^2) = 2(1^2) = 2(1) =$ **2**
  2 electrons max in 1st

Third shell: n = 3
  $2(n^2) = 2(3^2) = 2(9) =$ **18**
  18 electrons max in 3rd

28. Electron configurations: Determining atom or configuration with partially or completely filled shell

An electron shell is completely filled if it has the maximum number of electrons according to the equation $2(n)^2$.

Concept Task: Be able to determine an atom with a Partially or completely filled electron shell

To do this:
  .Determine maximum electrons $(2n^2)$ for the electron shell in the question.

  . Make a comparison to number of electrons that the atom in the question actually has in that shell.

Use configuration on Periodic Table to make comparison

Example 24
Which element has an incomplete 4th electron shell?
1) Hg   2) Rn   3) Cs   4) W
Before choosing:
Determine maximum electrons in the 4th shell:
  $2n^2: 2(4)^2 = 32$.
LOOK on Periodic Table for electron configurations of Hg, Rn, Cs, and W
Choose the element that does not have 32 (electrons) in the 4th shell of its configuration.
Answer: Choice 3. Cs only has 18 if the 4th shell

Topic 3 – The Atomic Structure

29. Ground state, Excited state and Spectral lines: Definitions and facts

An atom is most stable when its electrons occupy the lowest available electron shell. When this is the case, the atom is said to be in the ground state. When one or more electrons of an atom occupy a higher energy level than they should, the atom is said to be in the excited state. Electron configurations given for all the elements on the Periodic Table are of atoms in the ground state. This means that each configuration on the Periodic Table shows electrons of the atom filling from the lowest to the highest electron shells.

Below are definitions and facts related to ground and excited state atoms and spectral lines

Concept Facts: Study to remember the followings

Ground state:

When an atom is in the ground state:

. Electron configuration is the same as given on the Periodic Table

. Electrons are filled in order from lowest to highest shell

. The energy of the atom is at its lowest

. The atom is most stable

. An electron in a ground state atom must absorb energy to go from a lower level to a higher level.

. As an electron of a ground state atom absorbed energy and moves to the excited state, the energy of the electron and of the atom increases

Ground state configuration for nitrogen.

Same as on the Periodic Table

Excited state:

When an atom is in the excited state:

. Electron configuration is different from that of the Periodic Table for that atom

. The energy of the atom is at its highest

. The atom is unstable

. An electron in the excited state atom releases energy to return from the higher level to lower level

. As an electron in the excited state atom releases energy to return to the ground state, the energy of the electron and of the atom decreases.

. Spectrum of colors are produced when excited electrons released energy and return to the ground state.

Quanta is a discrete (specific) amount of energy absorbed or released by an electron to go from one level to another.

Excited state configuration for nitrogen.

Different from that of the Periodic Table.

NOTE: total number of electrons is still 7

Spectral lines:

Spectral lines **are band of colors** produced when excited electron returns from high (excited) to low (ground) state

.Spectral lines are produced from energy released by excited electrons as they returned to the ground state

.Spectral lines are viewed through a spectroscope.

.Spectral lines are called "fingerprints' of the elements because each element has its own unique patterns (wavelength of colors)

Spectral lines (bright-line spectra)

Topic 3 – The Atomic Structure

30. Spectral lines: Determining which electron transition will produce spectral lines

Concept Task: Be able to determine which electron transition will produce spectral lines.

RECALL that spectral lines are produced ONLY when an electron from an excited state (High level) returns to the ground state (Low level).

Study the notes below to help you answer questions on electron transitions between two shells.

Electron transition from:

Low to higher shell :
Ex: 5th shell to 6th shell
. Energy is absorbed (gained) by the electron
. Energy of the atom increases

High to Lower shell:
Ex: 6th shell to 5th shell
. Energy is released (emitted) by the electron
. Produced bright line spectrum of colors
. Energy of the atom to decreases

NOTE:
The greater the difference between the two electron shells, the more energy is absorbed or released.

Example 25
As an electron moves from 3rd electron shell to the 4th electron shell, the energy of the atom
1) Increases as the electron absorbs energy
2) Increases as the electron releases energy
3) Decreases as the electron absorbs energy
4) Decreases as the electron releases energy

Answer: Choice 1. The transition is from a lower (3rd) to a higher (4th) shell.

Example 26
Electron transition between which two electron shells will produce bright line spectrum of colors?
1) 2nd to 3rd 3) 1st to 4th
2) 3rd to 4th 4) 2nd to 1st

Answer: Choice 4 because spectrum of colors are only produced when electron goes from a higher (2nd) to a lower (1st) shell.

Example 27
As an electron in an atom moves between electron shells, which transition would cause the electron to absorb the most energy?
1) 1st to 2nd 3) 2nd to 4th
2) 2nd to 1st 4) 4th to 2nd

Answer: Choice 3. Energy is absorbed when electron goes from low to high level. Although choice 1 is also from low to high, **Choice 3** has a greater difference between the two shells.

31. Excited and Ground State: Determining configuration for ground and excited state atom

Concept Task: Be able to determine which electron configuration is of an atom in the ground or excited state.

To determine which configuration is of an atom in the:
Ground state:
  LOOK for a configuration that is the same as on the Periodic Table for that atom:

Excited state
  LOOK for a configuration that has the same total number of electrons as of the element given, BUT, different arrangement as on the Periodic Table

Examples:
2 – 8 – 5 is the **Ground state** configuration for phosphorous
2 – 7 – 6 is an **Excited state** configuration for phosphorous

Example 28
Which is an excited state electron configuration for a neutral atom with 16 protons and 18 neutrons?

1) 2-8-5-1   3) 2-8-6-2
2) 2-8-8   4) 2-8-6

Correct: Choice 1. An atom with 16 protons is sulfur. The atom also has 16 electrons since it is neutral. **Choice 1** has a total of 16 electrons. But the electrons are arranged differently from the ground state configuration that is given on the Periodic Table for sulfur.

Topic 3 – The Atomic Structure

32. Flame test and spectral chart: Definition and facts

Flame test is a lab procedure in which compounds of metallic ions are heated to produce unique flame colors.
. The flame color produced is due to the excited electrons in the metal atoms returning from high (excited) state to low (ground) state.
. The flame color produced can be used to identify which metal ion is in a compound.
. However, since two or more metallic ions can produce the same color flame, flame test results are not very reliable
. Colored flame produced during flame tests can be viewed through a spectroscope

A Spectroscope is equipment that can separate a light into colors (spectrum of colors) that the light is composed of.

Bright-line spectra chart shows band of colors at different wavelength that are produced by the elements.
Below, bright-line spectra for hydrogen, lithium, sodium and potassium is shown.
Bright line spectra of an unknown substance was compared to those of H, Li, Na and K. Substances in the unknown can be identified by matching the lines in the unknown to the lines for H, Li, Na and K.

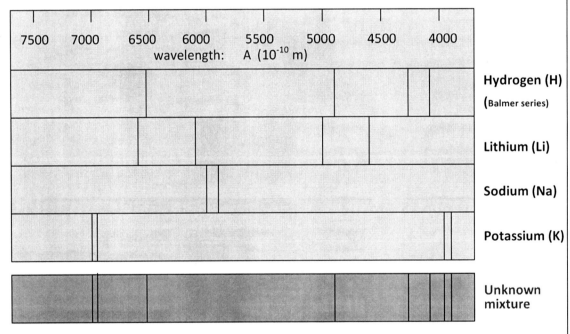

Concept Task: Be able to interpret spectral lines chart

Example 29
Which elements are in the unknown substance?
  1) H and Na   2) K and Li   3) H and K   4) K and Na
Answer: Choice 3. The lines in the unknown match those of K and H only. (See Chart)

Example 30:
Which element produce bright line spectra with the following wavelengths:
  6600×10^{-10} A, 6100×10^{-10} A, 5000×10^{-10} A and 4600×10^{-10} A
  1) H   2) Li   3) Na   4) K
Answer: Choice 2: Wavelengths given match those of Li (See the Chart)

Topic 3 – The Atomic Structure

Lesson 4 – Valance electrons and ions

Introduction:

Most atoms (with the exception of the noble gases) are unstable because they have incomplete valance (outermost) electron shells. For this reason, most atoms need to lose, gain or share electrons to fill their valance shell so they can become stable. When an atom loses or gains electrons, it forms an ion.

LOOKING AHEAD ⟹ **Topic 4: Chemical bonding.** You will learn more about the role of valance electrons in chemical bonding.

In this lesson, you will learn about valance electrons, neutral atoms and ions.

33. Valance electrons: Definition and facts

Valance electrons are electrons in the outermost electron shell of an atom.
Valance shell of an atom is the last (outermost) shell that contain electron.

RECALL: Elements in the same Group (vertical column) of the Periodic Table have the same number of valance electrons, and similar chemical reactivity.

Concept Task: Be able to determine the number of valance for any atom or configuration

In any electron configuration, the last number is always the number of valance electrons.

P
15
2 – 8 – 5

LOOK on the Periodic Table for Phosphorous:
The configuration for phosphorous is : 2 – 8 – 5
The last number is 5.
Phosphorous has 5 valance electrons in its valance (the third) shell.

34. Ions (charged atom) and Neutral atoms: Definitions and facts

A neutral atom may lose its entire valance electron to form a new valance shell that is completely filled.
A neutral atom may also gain electron(s) to fill its valance shell with electrons.
Ions are formed when a neutral atom loses or gains electrons.
For most atoms, a completely filled valance shell must have eight (8) electrons.
  NOTE: H and He need only two (2) to fill their valance shell.

Below, definitions and facts related to neutral atoms and ions

Concept Facts: Study to remember them

	Symbols of neutral atoms and ions
Neutral atom . A neutral atom has equal number of protons and electrons . The electron configurations given on the Periodic Table are for neutral atoms of the elements	**Na** a neutral sodium atom **S** a neutral sulfur atom
Ion . An ion is a charged atom with unequal number of protons to electrons . An ion is formed when an atom loses or gains electrons	
A Positive ion is a charged atom containing LESS electrons (-) than protons (+) . A positive ion is formed when a neutral atom loses one or more electrons . Metals and metalloids tend to lose electrons and form positive ions	**Na$^+$** a positive sodium ion
A negative ion is a charged atom containing MORE electrons (-) than protons (+) . A negative ion is formed when a neutral atom gains one or more electrons . Nonmetals tend to gain electrons and form negative ions	**S^{2-}** a negative sulfide ion

Topic 3 – The Atomic Structure

35. Ion vs. neutral atom: Comparing atomic diagram

When electrons are lost or gained by a neutral atom, the ion formed will be different in many ways from the neutral atom. Number of electrons, electron configuration, properties, and size of the ion will all be different from the neutral atom.

The following note summarizes the comparison between positive and negative ions to their parent neutral atom.

Concept Facts: Study to learn these comparisons.

How is a positive ion compares to its neutral (metallic) atom?
When a neutral atom (usually a metal or metalloid) loses its valance electron(s):
- The positive ion has FEWER electrons than the neutral atom it was formed from
- The positive ion electron configuration has one less electron shell than the neutral atom
- As a neutral atom loses electrons, its size (atomic radius) decreases
- Ionic radius (size) of a positive ion is always smaller than the atomic radius of the neutral atom
- The positive ion has a different chemical reactivity than the neutral atom

Below, Bohr's diagrams showing size comparison of a neutral Na atom to Na⁺ ion.

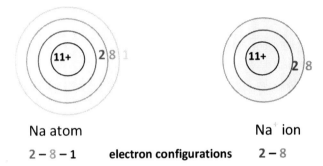

Na atom   Na⁺ ion

2 – 8 – 1   electron configurations   2 – 8

How is a negative ion compares to its neutral (nonmetallic) atom?
When a neutral atom (usually a nonmetal) gains electron to fill its valance shell (s):
- The negative ion has MORE electrons than its parent neutral atom
- The negative ion's electron configuration has the same number of electron shell as the neutral atom
- As the neutral atom gains electrons, its size (atomic radius) increases
- Ionic radius (size) of a negative ion is always larger than the atomic radius of the neutral atom
- The negative ion has a different chemical reactivity than the neutral atom

Below, Bohr's diagrams showing size comparison of a neutral S atom to S²⁻ ion

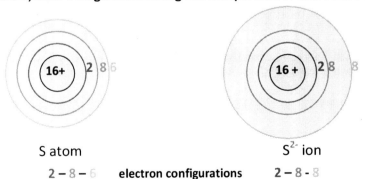

S atom   S²⁻ ion

2 – 8 – 6   electron configurations   2 – 8 – 8

NOTE: Electron configuration of an ion is similar to that of the nearest Group 18 Noble gas element.

Sulfur is Atomic # 16

Argon, atomic # 18, is the closest noble gas to Sulfur.

The configuration of sulfur ion (2 – 8 – 8) is the same as that of Argon. (See Periodic Table to confirm)

Topic 3 – The Atomic Structure

36. Ions: Determining and comparing number of particles and size of ions to neutral atom

Concept Task: Be able to determine differences and /or similarities in the number of particles between an ion and a neutral atom.

Study the information below.

To determine difference in electrons:
Consider the following comparisons.

A Positive ion **always has** FEWER electrons **than the neutral atom**
The difference in number of electrons is equal to the value of the charge.

Ex.   Na$^+$ ion has 1 LESS electron than neutral Na atom

A Negative ion **always has** MORE electrons **than the neutral atom**
The difference in number of electrons is equal to the value of charge.

Ex.   S^{2-} ion has 2 MORE electrons than neutral S atom

NOTE: Both the ion and the neutral atom always have the **SAME number of protons**

Study example multiple choice questions below.
NOTE: In questions, PAY ATTENTION to what is being compared to what.

Example 31
Compare to Na, Na$^+$ has
1) 1 more protons   2) 1 fewer protons   3) 1 more electrons   4) 1 fewer electrons

Answer: Choice 4   (see sodium atom and ion diagrams on the last page)

Example 32
How does the size of Na atom compares to Na$^+$?
1) Na is bigger than Na$^+$ because Na has fewer electrons
2) Na is bigger than Na$^+$ because Na has more electrons
3) Na is smaller than Na$^+$ because Na has fewer electrons
4) Na is smaller than Na$^+$ because Na has more electrons

Correct: Choice 2.   (see sulfur atom and ion diagrams on the last page)

Example 33
Compare to S^{2-}, S has
1) 2 more protons   2) 2 fewer protons   3) 2 more electrons   4) 2 fewer electrons

Answer: Choice 4   (see sulfur atom and ion diagrams on the last page)

Example 34
How does the size of S^{2-} ion compares to S?
1) S^{2-} is bigger than S because S^{2-} has more electrons
2) S^{2-} is bigger than S because S^{2-} has less electrons
3) S^{2-} is smaller than S because S^{2-} has more electrons
4) S^{2-} is smaller than S because S^{2-} has less electrons

Answer: Choice 1   (see sulfur atom and ion diagrams on the last page)

Copyright © 2010 E3 Scholastic Publishing. All Rights Reserved.

Topic 3 – The Atomic Structure

37. Ions: Determining number of particles in an ion

Concept Task: Be able to determine the number of electrons and/or protons of an ion.

These can be done by logically thinking the problem through. If necessary, you can use the following relationships:

To determine the number of electrons in any ion:

Number of electrons = Atomic number − charge
= Number of protons − charge

Concept Task: Be able to determine the correct charge of an atom from number of protons and electrons.

Again, think it through or use the following relationships

To determine the charge of an ion:

Charge = number of protons - number of electrons
= nuclear charge   - number of electrons

Example 35
How many electrons are in Cu^{2+} ion?
1) 2   2) 27   3) 31   4) 29

Before choosing, think it through OR Use equation given on your left.
NOTE : Atomic number of Cu is 29
# of Electron = atomic # - charge
# of Electron = 29 - (+2) = **27**
Answer: Choice 2

Example 36
What is the charge of an atom with 19 electrons, 20 neutrons, and a nuclear charge of +17?
1) -2   2) +1   3) +2   4) -3

Before choosing, think it through OR Use equation given on your left
Charge = nuclear charge - # of electrons
Charge = 17 - 19 = **-2**

Answer: Choice 1

38. Ion: Determining electron configuration for ions

Concept Task: Be able to determine electron configuration of a positive or a negative ion.

RECALL: An atom loses or gains electrons to become an ion. Ions, therefore, always have a different number of electrons and different electron configurations from that of the original atom.

NOTE: *The number of electrons and the electron configuration of an ion is usually the same as that of the closest Group 18 (noble gas) atom.*

To determine the correct electron configuration for an ion:
  Locate the element of the ion given in the question on the Periodic Table.
  Find a Group 18 element whose atomic number is closest to that of the element.
   OR
  Determine number of electrons in the ion.
  Locate the element with an atomic number equal to the number of electrons you determined
  Choose the electron configuration of that element

LOOKING Ahead ⟹ **Topic 4: Chemical Bonding:** You Will learn more about the configurations of bonded atoms.

Example 37
Which is correct electron configuration for Ca^{2+}?
1) 2-8-2   3) 2-8-8
2) 2-8   4) 2-6-1-1

Answer: Choice 3. Ca is closest to Ar. Its ion, Ca^{2+}, configuration is similar to that of Ar.

Example 38
The electron configuration for As^{3-} is
1) 2 – 8 – 18 – 5   3) 2 – 8 – 17 – 6
2) 2 – 8 – 18 – 8   4) 2 – 8 – 18 – 5 – 3

Answer: Choice 2. As^{3-} has 36 electrons. Its configuration is similar to Kr (Atomic number 36).

Topic 3 – The Atomic Structure

Check-A-list

Concept Terms

Below is a list of vocabulary terms from Topic 3. You should know the definition and facts related to each term.

Put a check in the box [v] next to each term if you know its definition and other facts related to the term.

[ ] Atom
[ ] Hard sphere model
[ ] Plum-pudding model
[ ] Empty space model
[ ] Bohr's atomic model
[ ] Wave mechanical model
[ ] Gold foil experiment
[ ] Cathode ray experiment
[ ] Orbital
[ ] Nucleus
[ ] Neutron
[ ] Proton
[ ] Electron
[ ] Nucleon

[ ] Nuclear charge
[ ] Atomic number
[ ] Mass number
[ ] Atomic mass
[ ] Atomic mass unit
[ ] Isotope
[ ] Electron shell
[ ] Electron configuration
[ ] Ground state
[ ] Excited state
[ ] Flame test
[ ] Spectral lines (bright line spectrum)
[ ] Balmer series

[ ] Valance electron
[ ] neutral atom
[ ] Ion
[ ] Positive ion
[ ] Negative ion
[ ] Ionic configuration
[ ] Ionic radius

If you don't have a check next to a term, look it up or ask your teacher.

Concept Tasks

Below is a list of concept tasks from Topic 3. You should know how to solve problems and answer questions related to each concept task.

Put a check in the box [v] next to a concept task when you know how to solve problems and answer questions related to it.

[ ] Determining and comparing number of one subatomic particle to another
[ ] Determining or recognizing which two symbols are of isotopes of the same element
[ ] Determine number of subatomic particles from a given isotope notation
[ ] Comparing number of subatomic particles of two given isotope symbols
[ ] Calculating average atomic mass from mass numbers and percentages of isotopes
[ ] Drawing Bohr's atomic model from electron configuration
[ ] Determine number of electron shells in an atom or a configuration
[ ] Determining the electron shell containing electrons with highest or lowest energy.
[ ] Determining number (or total number) of electrons in any electron shell of an atom or configuration
[ ] Determining electron transition between electron shells that will produce spectral lines
[ ] Interpreting electron transition between electron shells
[ ] Determining and interpreting electron configuration in ground or excited state.
[ ] Interpreting spectral lines chart
[ ] Determining and comparing number particles between an ion and the neutral atom.
[ ] Determining number of electrons and/or protons of an ion.
[ ] Determining the correct charge of an atom from number of protons and electrons
[ ] Determining and interpreting ionic configuration

If you don't have a check next to a concept task, look it up or ask your teacher.

Topic 3 – The Atomic Structure

Concept Fact Review Questions

1. Which group of atomic models is listed in order from the earliest to the most recent?
   1) Hard-sphere model, wave-mechanical model, electron-shell model
   2) Hard-sphere model, electron-shell model, wave mechanical model
   3) Electron-shell model, wave-mechanical model, hard-sphere model
   4) Electron-shell model, hard-sphere model, wave-mechanical model

2. Subatomic particles can usually pass undeflected through an atom because the volume of an atom is composed mainly by
   1) Uncharged nucleus
   2) Unoccupied space
   3) Neutrons only
   4) Protons only

3. What is the charge and mass of an electron?
   1) Charge of +1 and a mass of 1 amu
   2) Charge of -1 and a mass of 1 amu
   3) Charge of +1 and a mass of 1/1836 amu
   4) Charge of -1 and a mass of 1/1836 amu

4. The mass of a proton is approximately
   1) 1/2000 times the mass of a neutron and a unit positive charge
   2) 1/2000 times the mass of a neutron and a unit negative charge
   3) 2000 times the mass of an electron and a unit positive charge
   4) 2000 times the mass of an electron and a unit negative charge

5. The number of neutrons in the nucleus of an atom can be determined by
   1) Adding the mass number to the atomic number of the atom
   2) Adding the mass number to the number of electrons of the atom
   3) Subtracting the atomic number from the mass number of the atom
   4) Subtracting the mass number from the atomic number of the atom

6. Isotopes are atoms that have the same number of protons but a different
   1) Atomic number   2) Number of neutron   3) Nuclear number   4) Positron

7. When an electron in excited atom returns to a lower energy state, the energy emitted can result in the production of
   1) Alpha particle
   2) Protons
   3) Isotopes
   4) Spectral lines

8. An atom that has a negative charge must have
   1) Greater number of protons than electrons
   2) Equal number of protons to electrons
   3) Greater number of electrons to protons
   4) Equal number of electrons and neutrons

9. A positive ion is formed when a neutral atom
   1) Loses electrons
   2) Loses protons
   3) Gains electrons
   4) Gains electrons

10. The atomic mass of an element is defined as the weighted average mass of that elements'
    1) Most abundant isotope
    2) Least abundant isotope
    3) Naturally occurring isotope
    4) Radioactive isotope

Copyright © 2010 E3 Scholastic Publishing. All Rights Reserved.

Topic 3 – The Atomic Structure

Concept Task Practice Questions

11. A particle of an atom contains 26 protons, 23 electrons, and 56 neutrons. What will be the correct atomic number for this particle?
    1) 26 2) 23 3) 56 4) 33

12. An atom with 21 neutrons and 40 nucleons has
    1) A nuclear charge of +19
    2) A nuclear charge of +40
    3) A mass number of 61
    4) A mass number of 19

13. Which element could have a mass number of 86 atomic mass unit and 49 neutrons in its nucleus?
    1) In 2) Rb 3) Rn 4) Au

14. Atom X has 16 protons, 18 electrons, and 17 neutrons. Which element is atom X?
    1) S 2) Ge 3) In 4) Cl

15. Which pair of atoms are isotopes of the same element X?
    1) $^{226}_{91}X$ and $^{226}_{91}X$ 2) $^{226}_{91}X$ and $^{227}_{91}X$ 3) $^{227}_{91}X$ and $^{227}_{90}X$ 4) $^{226}_{90}X$ and $^{227}_{91}X$

16. Which atom is an isotope of Oxygen?
    1) $^{14}_{7}N$ 2) $^{16}_{8}N$ 3) $^{14}_{7}O$ 4) $^{17}_{8}O$

17. What is the total number of nucleons in the nuclide $^{65}_{30}Zn$?
    1) 65 2) 30 3) 35 4) 95

18. In which pair of atoms do the nuclei contain the same number of neutrons?
    1) Calcium-40 and Calcium-42
    2) Chlorine-35 and Sulfur-34
    3) Bromine – 83 and Krypton - 83
    4) Iodine – 127 and Bromine – 80

19. Which is a ground state electron configuration of an atom in the fourth electron shell?
    1) 2 – 8 – 4 2) 2 – 8 – 18 – 4 3) 2 – 8 – 18 – 18 – 4 4) 2 – 4

20. The total number of electrons found in the configuration of a neutral chromium atom is
    1) 24 2) 6 3) 13 4) 1

21. The highest amount of energy will be emitted by an electron when it moves from
    1) 4th to 1st electron shell
    2) 1st to 4th electron shell
    3) 1st to 5th electron shell
    4) 5th to 4th electron shell

22. What is the total number of electrons in a Cr^{3+} ion?
    1) 3 2) 21 3) 24 4) 27

Topic 3 – The Atomic Structure

Constructed Response Practice Questions

Base your answers to questions 23 through 25 on the information below.

In the modern model of the atom, each atom is composed of three major subatomic (or fundamental) particles.

Write your answers here.

23. Name the subatomic particles contained in the nucleus.   23.

24. State the charge associated with each type of subatomic particle contained in the nucleus of the atom.   24.

25. What is the sign of the net charge of the nucleus?   25.

Base your answers to questions 26 through 28 on the data table below, which shows three isotopes of neon.

Isotope	Atomic Mass (atomic mass units)	Percent Natural Abundance
^{20}Ne	19.99	90.9 %
^{21}Ne	20.99	0.3 %
^{22}Ne	21.99	8.8 %

Write your answers here.

26. Based on the atomic mass and the natural abundances shown in the data table show a correct numerical set-up for calculating the average atomic mass of neon.   26

27. Based on natural abundances, the average atomic mass of neon is closest to which whole number?   27.

28. In terms of atomic particles, state one difference between these three isotopes of neon.   28.

Topic 4 – Chemical Bonding

Topic outline

In this topic, you will learn the following concepts:

. Chemical bonds and stability of atoms   . Molecular substances and molecular polarity

. Chemical bonding and energy   . Intermolecular forces

. Types of chemical bond between atoms   . Types of substances and their properties

Lesson 1: Chemical bonding Stability of atoms

Introduction

Chemical bonding is the simultaneous attraction of two positive nuclei to negative electrons.
Chemical bonding is said to be the "glue" that holds particles (atoms, ions, molecules) together in matter.
When atoms bond they become much more stable than when they are in their free states. Since most atoms do not have a full valance shell, they are unstable. In other for these atoms to attain a full valance shell and be stable, they must bond with other atoms.
In this lesson, you will learn how and why atoms bond.

1. Chemical bonding and stability: How and why atoms bond

Atoms bond so they can attain a full valance shell and become stable.
Octet of electrons is when an atom has a full valance (outermost) shell with 8 electrons
   NOTE: Not every atom needs eight (8) valance electrons to be stable.

An atom can get a full and stable valance shell configuration by :
   A) **Transferring** or **Accepting electrons** (ionic bonding)
      or
   B) **Sharing electrons** (covalent bonding)

RECALL that noble gas atoms have full valance shell configurations and they are very stable.
. The electron configuration of a bonded atom is similar to that of the nearest noble gas (Group 18) atom
. Therefore, an atom is more stable when it is bonded to other atoms than when it is by itself

2. Chemical bonding and atom stability: Determining the Noble gas atom a bonded atom resembles

Concept Task: Be able to determine which noble gas element an atom (or atoms) in a bond resembles.	**Example 1** *When a sulfur atom bonds with sodium atoms to form the compound Na_2S, the configuration of sulfur atom is similar to which element?* 1) Na 2) O 3) Ne 4) Ar **Answer: Choice 4:** Because the closest noble gas to sulfur (atomic number 16) is Argon (atomic number 18)

To determine which element a bonded atom resembles
 	
  Locate the element in question on the Table and note its atomic number.
 	
  Choose a Group 18 atom that is closest (in atomic number) to the element in the question.
 	
  ⬅ **LOOKING Back: Topic 3- Atomic Structure**
  You had learn about Configurations of ions.
	Example 2
	The electron configuration of Sr and H ions in the formula SrH_2 are similar to those of elements
	   1) Kr and He 3) Ar and Ne
	   2) Rb and He 4) Ca and Li
	Answer: Choice 1. On the Periodic Table:
	The closest Group 18 atom to Sr (# 38) is Kr (# 36).
	The closest Group 18 atom to H (# 1) is He (# 2)

Topic 4 – Chemical Bonding

Lesson 2 – Chemical bonding and energy

Introduction

All chemical substances contain a certain amount of potential energy.

Potential energy is stored in the bonds holding particles of substances together.

The amount of potential energy depends on *composition and structure* of a substance.

In this lesson, you will learn about the relationship between bonding and energy.

3. Bond formation and energy. Definitions and facts

Bond formation between two atoms is an exothermic process.

RECALL that exothermic describes a process that releases heat energy.

When two atoms come together to form a bond, heat energy is always released. Since energy is released, the energy of the atoms decreases. The atoms are now more stable than they were before bonding.

Summary of bond formation and energy

Concept Facts: Study to remember these facts

. Bond formation is exothermic (heat energy released)

. As energy is released during bond formation:
 - Potential energy of the atoms decreases
 - Stability of the atoms increases
 - Stability of the chemical system increases

Concept Task: Be able to recognize bond formation or exothermic equation

$$H + Cl \longrightarrow H - Cl + Energy$$

A Chemical bond **forms** between H and Cl atom. The bonded H and Cl atoms are more stable than the free H and Cl atoms on the left.

Energy released in exothermic or bond formation equation is always written to the **RIGHT** of the arrow.

4. Bond breaking and energy: Definition and facts

Bond breaking is an endothermic process.

RECALL that endothermic describes a process that absorbs heat energy.

When a bond between atoms of a substance is to be broken, energy is always absorbed. Since energy is absorbed, the energy of the atoms increases. The atoms (separated) are now less stable than when they were bonded together.

Summary of bond breaking and energy.

Concept Facts: Study to remember these facts

. Bond formation is endothermic (heat energy absorbed)

. As energy is absorbed during bond breaking:
 - Potential Energy of the atoms increases
 - Stability of the atoms decreases
 - Stability of the chemical system decrease

Concept Task: Be able to recognize bond breaking or endothermic equation.

$$H - Cl + Energy \longrightarrow H + Cl$$

A chemical bond to be broken

Energy absorbed in endothermic or bond breaking equation is always written to the **LEFT** of the arrow.

Topic 4 – Chemical Bonding

Lesson 3 – Types of bonding between atoms

Introduction:

Intramolecular forces describe bonds that hold atoms together to create molecules and compounds.

Bonding between atoms is a result of the atoms competing for electrons to get full valance shells.

Bonding between atoms can occur by two atoms sharing electrons to form covalent bonds, or by atoms transferring and accepting electrons to form ionic bonds.

In this lesson, you will learn about the different types of bonding between atoms.

5. Ionic bond: Definitions, facts and examples

Ionic bond describes the force holding charged particles together in ionic compounds.

The followings are facts related to ionic bonding.

Concept Facts: Study to remember these facts related to ionic bonding.

. Ionic bond is formed by the *transfer of electron(s)* from a metal to a nonmetal
. The metal atom always loses (or transfers) electron to become a positive ion
. The nonmetal atom always gains (or accepts) electron to become a negative ion
. Ionic bond is formed by the electrostatic attraction between the positive metal ion and the negative nonmetal ion.
. Electronegativity difference between the nonmetal and the metal atom in ionic bonds is usually 1.7 or greater

Example of substances containing ionic bonds:

NaCl	CaF$_2$	Fe$_2$O$_3$
sodium chloride	calcium fluoride	iron oxide

NOTE: Each formula above consists of a metal atom and a nonmetal atom.

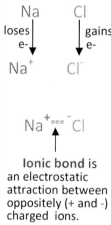

Ionic bond is an electrostatic attraction between oppositely (+ and -) charged ions.

6. Covalent bond: Definitions, facts and examples

Covalent bond describes the force holding atoms of nonmetals together in covalent and molecular substances.

Facts related to covalent bonding are summarized below.

Concept Facts: Study to remember these facts

. Covalent bonding occurs between two nonmetal atoms that are sharing electrons
. Electronegativity difference between the two nonmetals in a covalent bond is usually less than 1.7

Example of substances containing covalent bonds.

H$_2$O   CO$_2$ SiC   H$_2$ O$_2$ C   NH$_4^+$

NOTE: Each formula above consists only of nonmetal atoms.

There are four types of covalent bonding: Polar, nonpolar, coordinate, and network solid

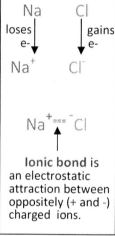

A Covalent bond forms between H and Cl atoms.
A (–) between two nonmetal atoms represents two (a pair) shared electrons.

Topic 4 – Chemical Bonding

7. Polar covalent bond: Definitions, facts and examples

Polar covalent bond is formed by the unequal sharing of electrons between two different nonmetal atoms.

Facts related to polar covalent bonding is summarized below.

Concept Facts: Study to remember these facts

- Sharing of electrons in polar covalent bond is unequal
- Electronegativity difference between the different nonmetal atoms is greater than 0 but less than 1.7

Example of substances containing Polar Covalent Bond

H_2O	HCl	NH_3
water	hydrogen chloride	ammonia

(**NOTE** how each formula consists only of two different nonmetal elements)

Unequal sharing of electrons in polar covalent bonding

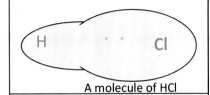

A molecule of HCl

Electrons (..) shared by H and Cl are located closer to the Cl atom. This represents unequal sharing of electrons.

Later, you will learn why electrons are closer to the Cl atom than the H atom.

8. Nonpolar covalent bond: Definitions, facts and examples

Nonpolar covalent bond is formed by equal sharing of electrons between two of the same nonmetals atoms.

Facts related to nonpolar covalent bond is summarized below.

Concept Facts: Study to remember these facts

- Sharing of electrons in nonpolar covalent bond is equal
- Electronegativity difference is zero
- Nonpolar bond is commonly found in Diatomic (two-atom) molecules

Example of substances containing nonpolar covalent bond

H_2	N_2
Hydrogen	Nitrogen

Equal sharing of electrons in nonpolar covalent bonding

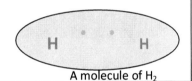

A molecule of H_2

The electrons (..) shared by both H atoms are equal distant from both atoms. This represents equal sharing.

Later, you will learn how electrons are shared equally between two of the same atoms.

(**NOTE** how each formula consists of the same nonmetal element)

9. Network solid covalent bond: Definitions and examples

Network covalent bond is formed between nonmetal atoms in network solid compounds.
Compounds formed by network bonding cannot exist as a discrete individual molecule.

Example of network solid compounds.

(These are the **only three** you need to know: Study and remember them)

C	SiO_2	SiC	
(Diamond)	(Silicon dioxide)	(Silicon Carbide)	Diamond

Topic 4 – Chemical Bonding

10. Coordinate covalent bond: Definitions and examples

Coordinate covalent bond is formed when both shared electrons are provided by ONLY one of the atoms.
. This bond is formed when an H+ (hydrogen ion), which does not have an electron, bonds with a molecule such as NH_3 (ammonia) or H_2O (water).
. NH_3 and H_2O molecules have a lone pair (two unbonded) electrons that they can share with a H+ (hydrogen ion, proton) that doesn't have any electron.

Two (all you need to know) **formulas containing a coordinate covalent bond**

NH_4^+ (ammonium ion)   *forms from* NH_3 *(ammonia) and* H^+ *(hydrogen ion)*

H_3O^+ (hydronium ion)   *forms from* H_2O *(water) and* H^+ *(hydrogen ion)*

11. Metallic bond: Definitions and facts

Concept Facts: Study to remember these facts about metallic bonding.

Metallic bonding is a force that holds metal atoms together in metallic substances.
. Metallic bonding is described as positive ions *"immersed in sea of mobile Valance electrons"*
. Mobile electrons allows for high electrical conductivity in metals

Examples of formulas containing metallic bonds:

Ca (calcium)   **Au** (Gold)   **Fe** (iron)

(**NOTE** that substances containing metallic bonds are metallic elements)

12. Bond types: A summary table. Concept facts: *Use this table for quick studying and comparisons*

Bond Type	Type of elements involve in bonding	Bond description	Electronegativity difference	Type of substances containing bond	Example formula containing bond
Metallic	metal atoms of the same element	positive ions in sea of electrons	----------	metallic substances	Ag, K
Ionic	metal - Nonmetal	transfer of electrons	1.7 or greater	ionic substances	NaCl, Li_2O
Covalent	nonmetals only	sharing of electrons	less than 1.7	molecular substances	HCl
Polar covalent	Two different nonmetals	unequal sharing	greater than 0 but less than 1.7	polar and nonpolar substances	H_2O, CH_4
Nonpolar covalent	same nonmetal (or nonmetal atoms with the same electronegativity)	equal sharing of electrons	zero (0)	diatomic nonpolar substances	H_2, O_2
Coordinate Covalent	two different nonmetals	One atom provides both shared electrons	----------	polyatomic ions	NH_4^+, H_3O^+
Network solid covalent	nonmetals only	No discrete particles	----------	network solids	C, SiC, SiO_2

Topic 4 – Chemical Bonding

13. Types of bonding: Determining type of bonding between atoms

Concept Task: When a bond is given, be able to determine a formula or compound containing that bond.

To determine formula containing:

Ionic bond (transferring of electrons)
   LOOK for a formula or name containing
      a Metal and a Nonmetal

Covalent bond (sharing of electrons)
   LOOK for a formula or name containing
      only nonmetal atoms

Polar covalent bonds (unequal sharing of electrons)
   LOOK for a formula or name containing
      two different nonmetals

Nonpolar covalent bonds (equal sharing of electrons)
   LOOK for a diatomic formula (two of the same nonmetals)

Metallic bond (positive ions in sea of mobile electrons)
   LOOK for a symbol of a:
      metallic element

Both Ionic and covalent bonds
   LOOK for a formula containing
      at least three different elements.

When studying this page BE SURE you KNOW where the metals and nonmetals are on Periodic Table.

Example 3

Which formula contains *ionic* bonds?

1) ClO_2 2) SO_2 3) Li_2S 4) HI

Answer: Choice 3 (Li is a metal, S is a nonmetal)

Example 4

In which compound would the atoms form a bond by *sharing* their electrons?

1) CS_2 2) CaS 3) AgI 4) Hg

Answer: Choice 1 (C and S are both nonmetals)

Example 5

Which two atoms are held together by a *polar covalent* bond?

1) H – H   3) Al – H
2) H – O   4) Al – O

Answer: Choice 2 (H and O are two different nonmetals)

Example 6

In which substance do the atoms *share electrons equally* to form a bond?

1) SiC   2) Ag   3) NH_3 4) Br_2

Answer: Choice 4 (two of same nonmetal)

Example 7

Metallic bonding will form between the atoms of which substance?

1) Nickel   3) Carbon
2) Sodium chloride 4) Hydrogen

Answer: Choice 1 (Nickel is a metal)

Example 8

Which compound contains both *ionic and covalent* bonds?

1) Mg_3N_2 3) H_2O_2
2) $NaClO_3$ 4) O_2

Answer: Choice 2 (Three different atoms; Na Cl O)

Topic 4 – Chemical Bonding

Lesson 4 – Types of substances and their properties

Introduction

In the last lesson, you learned the different bond types found between atoms of different substances. For the most part, the bond name and the type of substances containing that bond are usually the same.

For examples:
1. Ionic substances contain atoms held together by ionic bonds.
2. Metallic substances contain atoms held together by metallic bonds.
3. Network solid substances contain atoms held together by network solid bonds.
4. Molecular (Covalent) substances contain atoms held together by covalent bond
5. Polar molecular substances contain atoms held together by polar covalent bonds.
6. Nonpolar substances are the only substance which this is not always the case.
   A **FEW** nonpolar substances contain atoms held together by nonpolar bonds.
   BUT MOST nonpolar substances contain atoms held together by polar covalent bonds
   This exception will be explained later in this lesson.

In this lesson, you will first learn of the four types of substances and their properties.

Later, you will learn the relationship between bond polarity, molecular symmetry, molecular shape, and molecular polarity (polar and nonpolar molecules).

14. Types of substance and their properties: Summary and facts: Concept facts

Types of substance	Phase at room temperature	Physical Properties (characteristics)		
		Melting point	**Conductivity**	**Solubility** (in water)
Metallic	Solid (except Hg - liquid)	Very High	Good (High) (in Solid and Liquid phases)	NO (insoluble)
Ionic	Solid only	High	Good (High) (in Liquid and Aqueous phases)	Yes (soluble)
Molecular	solid, liquid, gas	Low	Poor (low) (in all phases)	Yes (slightly soluble)
Network solid	Solid only	Extremely high	Very poor (in all phases)	NO (Insoluble)

More information about each type of substance are discussed in the next few page.

15. Example of the four types of substances and their melting points

Below, solid forms of the four types of substances mentioned in the above table are given.
NOTE the huge differences in temperatures at which each solid will melt at STP.

Type of substance	*Molecular* substance	Ionic substance	Metallic substance	Network solid
Example solid:	Ice (H_2O)	Salt (NaCl)	Gold (Au)	Diamond (C)
Melting point	0°C	801°C	1065°C	3550°C

Topic 4 – Chemical Bonding

16. Metallic substances and their properties: Facts and examples

Metallic substances are metallic elements.
. Metallic substances contain atoms held together by metallic bonding
. Metallic substances normally exist as solid at room temperature
. Mercury (Hg) is the only liquid metallic element

Gold (Au)
Atoms of gold, a metallic substance, are held together by metallic bonds.

Example of some metallic substances:
Ca (calcium)   Ni (nickel)

Metallic solid substances tend to have these properties

Concept Facts: Study to remember these metallic properties
. High melting points (highly stable)
. Hard solid
. Insoluble in water
. High (good) electrical conductivity (as solids and liquids)

Electrical conductivity is due to mobile valance electrons

Concept Task: Be able to determine a formula of a metallic substance.

Example 9
Which is a metallic substance?
1) C   2) H_2 3) Sn   4) F

Answer: Choice 3. Sn (tin) is a metallic element.

17. Ionic substances and their properties: Facts and examples

Ionic substances are compounds formed by positive and negative ions.
The positive ion in ionic compounds is usually that of a metallic element.
Exceptions are ionic compounds formed by NH_4^+ (ammonium ion).

salt

The negative ion in ionic compounds is usually that of a nonmetal element or a polyatomic ion.
Reference Table E lists some common polyatomic ions.

Below, two categories of ionic substances are given

I. Binary ionic compounds containing ONLY ionic bonds
. A formula of a compound from this category usually contains two different elements (one metal and one nonmetal)
Examples: NaCl (sodium chloride) Al_2O_3 (aluminum oxide)

Concept Task: Be able to recognize formulas and names of binary ionic compounds

II. Ionic compounds containing BOTH ionic bond and covalent bond
. A formula of a compound from this category usually contains three or more different elements
. A formula of this group of ionic compounds always has a polyatomic ion
Examples: $MgSO_4$ (magnesium sulfate) NH_4Cl (ammonium chloride)

Concept Task: Be able to recognize formulas and names of ionic compounds containing both ionic and covalent bonds.

Ionic solid substances tend to have the following properties:

Concept Facts: Study to remember these ionic compounds properties
. High melting points (stable, and require high heat to decompose).
. High or Good electrical conductivity (ONLY as liquids and aqueous)
. Most are hard solids   . Most are very soluble in water

Electrical conductivity of ionic substances is due to mobile ions produced when the substance is dissolved in water to make a solution.

Example 10
Which is a binary ionic compound?
1) CaS   3) CO_2
2) $CaSO_4$ 4) CH_4

Answer: Choice 1
This formula contains two different elements; a metal (Ca) and a nonmetal (S).

Example 11
Which compound contains both ionic and covalent bonds?
1) $AlCl_3$ 3) C_2H_6
2) NO_3 4) KNO_3

Answer: Choice 4.
KNO_3 formula contains three different elements (K, N, and O).
The formula also contains a positive metal ion (K^+) bonded to a negative polyatomic ion (NO_3^-).

Topic 4 – Chemical Bonding

18. Molecular (covalent) substances and their properties: Facts and examples

Molecular (covalent) substances are substances that contain molecules.
A molecule is the smallest discrete unit of a molecular substance.
A molecule is usually a group of nonmetal atoms covalently bonded.
Molecular substances are found in all three phases: solid, liquid, or gas
Molecular substances can be polar or nonpolar depending on the charge distribution within the molecule. **(SEE NEXT PAGE for explanations.)**

Examples of some common molecular substances.
   H_2O (water)   Ne (neon) CO_2 (carbon dioxide) H_2 (Hydrogen)

Concept Task: Be able to recognize molecular substances by formulas and names.

Molecular solids substances tend to have these properties:

Concept Facts: Study to remember these molecular compounds properties
   . Low melting points (when compared to metallic or ionic substance)
   . Low (Poor) electrical conductivity (in all phases)
   . Solids are usually soft and brittle   . Some are slightly soluble in water

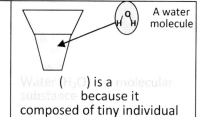
A water molecule

Water (H_2O) is a molecular substance because it composed of tiny individual water molecules.

Example 12
Which is a molecular compound?
1) K_2O 3) Li_2SO_4
2) CH_4 4) Hg
Answer: Choice 2
This formula is composed only of nonmetal (C and H) atoms

19. Properties of substances: Determining formula of substances based on properties

Concept Task: Be able to determine formula or name of a substance with a given set of properties.

To determine formula or name of a substance from properties given in a question:

DETERMINE if properties describe metallic, ionic, or molecular

CHOOSE a formula that represents that type of substance that you had determined.
         (See example 13 on the right)

Concept Task: Be able to determine properties of a given name or formula of a substance

To determine correct set of properties of a name or formula of a substance:

DETERMINE if the formula is of metallic, ionic, or molecular

CHOOSE properties which belong to the type of substance you had determined.
         (See example 14 on the right)

Example 13
Which substance has a high melting point and conducts electricity when it is dissolved in water?
1) $KNO_3(s)$ 3) $CO_2(s)$
2) $C_6H_{12}O_6(s)$ 4) $I_2(s)$
Before choosing:
  DETERMINE type of substance.
   .High melting point and electrical conductivity when dissolved in water are properties of **ionic substances.**
Answer: Choice 1: Because KNO_3 is an ionic compound. KNO_3 is ionic formula because it contains a metal.

Example 14
Which set of properties best describes I_2 (iodine) solid?
1) High conductivity and high melting point
2) High conductivity and low melting point
3) Low conductivity and high melting point
4) Low conductivity and low melting point

DETERMINE type of substance:
  I_2 is molecular (formula I_2 is composed only of nonmetal atoms)
Answer: Choice 4 because these are properties of molecular substances.

Topic 4 – Chemical Bonding

20. Bond and molecular polarity of molecular substances: The difference is symmetry

A molecular substance can be classified as nonpolar or polar based on the symmetry of its molecules.

Concept Facts: Study to remember these relationship between symmetry and molecular polarity

Nonpolar substances contain symmetrical nonpolar molecules.
  Most nonpolar molecules are formed by polar covalently bonded atoms that are symmetrically arranged.
  A few nonpolar molecules are formed by nonpolar covalently bonded atoms that are symmetrically arranged.

Polar substances contain asymmetrical polar molecules.
  All polar molecules are formed by polar covalently bonded atoms that are asymmetrically arranged.

Concept Task: Be able to determine if a molecule or structure is symmetrical or asymmetrical

Symmetrical (nonpolar) structures

$$H - H \qquad\qquad F - \underset{F}{\overset{F}{C}} - F$$

Asymmetrical (polar) structures

$$H - F \qquad\qquad \underset{H\quad\quad H}{\overset{O}{\diagup\ \diagdown}}$$

21. Nonpolar substances: Definitions, facts and examples

Nonpolar substances contain molecules have symmetrical structure.
A molecule has a symmetrical structure when charges are EVENLY distributed within the molecule.
Even charge distribution means that a molecule does not have any positive or negative poles. (nonpolar means no poles) . Nonpoplar molecules can be formed by polar and nonpolar covalently bonded atoms.

Concept Task: Be able to determine formulas of nonpolar molecules or substances

Follow notes and examples for the three categories of nonpolar molecules below.

Nonpolar molecules containing nonpolar covalent bonds (all the diatomic elements)
  The atoms of these molecules share electrons equally to form nonpolar bonds.
  The structures of these molecules are symmetrical and linear.
  Below are examples of nonpolar molecules containing nonpolar bonds

Hydrogen	Chlorine	Nitrogen
H_2	Cl_2	N_2
H – H	Cl – Cl	N ≡ N

Nonpolar molecules containing Polar covalent bonds
  The atoms of these molecules share electrons unequally to form polar bonds. Since bonding in these molecules are unequal and polar, one of the elements has a positive charge and the other element has a negative charge. However, since the atoms of the molecules are symmetrically arranged, the positive and the negative charges will be evenly distributed within the molecules, thereby cancelling each other out. The net charge on the molecules due to this symmetrical arrangement is zero, therefore, the molecule is nonpolar.
  Below are examples of nonpolar molecules containing polar covalent bonds
  NOTE how is shape is symmetrical, while the bond is polar (between two different nonmetals)

Methane	Carbon dioxide	Carbon tetrachloride
CH_4	CO_2	CCl_4
$H-\underset{H}{\overset{H}{C}}-H$	O = C = O	$Cl-\underset{Cl}{\overset{Cl}{C}}-Cl$

Nonpolar monatomic elements (Group 18 elements)
  (All group 18 Noble gases belong to this category of nonpolar molecules)
  Ex. Neon (Ne)   Argon (Ar)

Topic 4 – Chemical Bonding

22. Polar substances: Definitions, facts, and examples

Polar substances contain molecules that have asymmetrical structure.
A molecule has an asymmetrical structure when charges are unevenly distributed within the molecule.
Uneven charge distribution makes one atom of a molecule positive (+) and the other atom negative (-).
(polar means two poles, + and -).

Polar (dipole) molecules can only be formed by polar covalently bonded atoms

Concept Task: Be able to determine formulas of polar molecules or substances
      Study the notes and the examples given below.

Examples of some common polar substances

Hydrogen chloride	Water	Ammonia
HCl	H₂O	NH₃
H – Cl	O with H, H below	H – N – H with H below

Positive and negative ends of polar molecules.

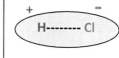

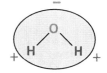

In a polar molecule : Due to uneven electron sharing, one atom appears
to be more negative (-) and the other atom appears to be more positive (+)

(SEE DIAGRAMS TO THE RIGHT)

Concept Task: Be able to determine negative (-) and positive (+) atoms
      of a polar molecule.

To determine the negative (-) atom: Choose the higher electronegativity atom

To determine the positive (+) atom: Choose the lower electronegativity atom

Use Reference Table S to determine and compare electronegativity values of two atoms

23. Molecular structures and shapes: Definitions and facts

Structure and shape of a molecular substance are very important because they determine several properties of the substance. For example, most properties of water would be different if water did not have is bent structure.

When nonmetal atoms bond, the arrangement of the atoms generates one of many different molecular shapes.

The four molecular shapes you need to know are listed below.
      Given are example molecular structures to show each shape.
      The name and formula of each molecular structure are also given.

Concept Facts: Study to remember these molecular shapes.

Linear	Tetrahedral	Angular (bent)	Pyramidal	*molecular shapes*
O = O	H–C–H (with H above and below)	O with H, H	H – N – H with H below	*molecular structures*
O₂	CH₄	H₂O	NH₃	*molecular formulas*
oxygen	methane	water	ammonia	*substances names*

Copyright © 2010 E3 Scholastic Publishing. All Rights Reserved.

Topic 4 – Chemical bonding

24. Bond polarity, Molecular polarity, Molecular symmetry, Molecular shapes: Summary

Below is a table summarizing bond and molecular polarity, as well as symmetry and molecular shapes.

Concepts	Explanations	Depends on	Types	Description	Examples
Bond polarity	Describes polarity (+ and – charges) of a covalent bond between two atoms	Depends largely on the type of atoms or their electronegativity difference	Polar bond	A bond that produces + and - ends on bonded atoms. Found between two different nonmetals	C – H P – Cl
			Nonpolar bond	A bond that does not produce + and – ends on the bonded atoms. Found between two of the same nonmetal atoms	H – H O = O
Molecular polarity	Describes the overall polarity (+ and – charges) of a molecule	Depends largely on the symmetry and charge distributions on a molecule	Polar molecule	Asymmetrical structure. Uneven + and – charge distributions	HF H_2O H – F O with H, H
			Nonpolar molecule	Symmetrical structure. Even + and – charge distributions	Cl_2 CH_4 Cl – Cl H-C-H with H, H
Molecular symmetry	Describes the overall arrangement of atoms to make a molecule	Depends largely on the nature or type of atoms and the number of each atom of the molecule	Symmetrical molecules	Arrangement of atoms is evenly distributed	Br – Br H-C-H with H, H
			Asymmetrical molecules	Arrangement of atoms is unevenly distributed	H- Cl H-N-H with H
Molecular shapes	Describes structural shapes of molecules due to arrangements of its atoms	Depends on several factors including types of and number of atoms, as well as shared and unshared electrons	Linear		H-Cl O=C=O
			Tetrahedral		Cl-C-Cl with Cl, Cl
			Angular		S with H, H
			Pyramidal		H-N-H with H

Topic 4 – Chemical Bonding

25. Degree of bond and molecular polarity: Using electronegativity difference

Bond polarity refers to how ionic, polar, or covalent is a bond between two atoms.

Molecular polarity refers to how polar is a molecule of a substance.

A compound may contain a bond that has more ionic or more covalent characteristics than a bond between atoms of another compound. Some molecules also have more polar characteristics than others do. The degree of bond and molecular polarity of substances depends largely on the electronegativity difference between the two atoms in the formula of the substance.

RECALL: Electronegativity measures atoms ability to attract (pull) electron from another atom during chemical bonding.

To calculate electronegativity difference between two atoms in a bond:

Step 1 : Get electronegativity values for both elements in the formula **(Use Reference Table S)**

Step 2: Calculate electronegativity difference

Electronegativity difference = High electronegativity – Low electronegativity

To determine which formula is most or least ionic or polar: Consider the scale below.

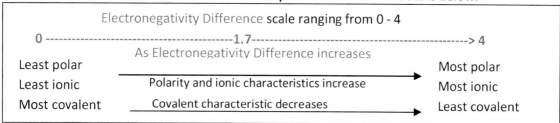

According to above scale:

The smaller the difference in electronegativity, the more covalent, the less ionic and the less polar the substance.

The larger the difference in electronegativity, the less covalent, the more ionic, and the more polar the substance.

26. Degree of bond and molecular polarity. Determining which formula is most or least ionic or polar

Concept Task: Be able to determine which formula is most or least ionic, covalent or polar.

To determine:

Most ionic, Most polar, or Least Covalent: **LOOK** for *Highest* electronegativity difference :

Least Ionic, Least polar, or Most Covalent : **LOOK** for *Lowest* electronegativity difference :

Below, three formulas are given. The formula with most and least are chosen based on the electronegativity difference. Study this example to learn to do the same.

Given the formulas:	LiCl	KCl	FrCl
Get electronegativity values for the elements **(Use Table S)**	Cl = 3.2 Li = 1.0	Cl = 3.2 K = 0.8	Cl = 3.2 Fr = 0.7
Do electronegativity difference	2.2	2.4	2.5
NOTE Lowest and highest difference	(Lowest difference)		(Highest difference)
Determine most and least based on differences	**LiCl :** Least ionic Least polar Most covalent		**FrCl :** Most ionic Most polar Least covalent

Topic 4 – Chemical bonding

Lesson 5 – Lewis electron-dot symbols and bonding

Introduction

RECALL that valance electrons are electrons in the outermost electron shell of an atom.
Valance electrons are the electrons that are involve in chemical bonding.
During ionic bonding, valance electrons are lost by a metal to form a positive ion, and are gained by a nonmetal to form a negative ion.
During covalent bonding, nonmetal atoms share their valance electrons.

In this lesson, you will learn how to show different bond types using Lewis electron-dot diagrams.

27. Lewis Electron – Dot diagram: Recognizing Lewis dot symbol for neutral atoms and ions

Lewis electron- dot diagram is a notation that shows symbol of an atom and dots equal to the number of valance electrons.
Lewis electron-dot diagrams can be drawn for neutral atoms, ions and compounds.
You will first learn to draw and recognize Lewis electron-dot diagrams for neutral atoms and ions.
Later, you will learn how to draw and recognize Lewis electron-dot dot diagrams for ionic and covalent compounds.

Below, notes on Lewis electron-dot diagrams for neutral atoms and ions.
To the right are examples Lewis electron-dot diagrams.
Concept Tasks: Study to learn how to draw and recognize Lewis electron-dot diagrams for neutral atoms and ions.

Neutral atom
Lewis dot diagram shows the **symbol** of the atom and dots equal to number of valance electrons in the atom's electron configuration.
See examples to the right

Sodium (Na) atom	Phosphorous (P) atom
2 – 8 – 1	2 – 8 – 5
Na • (Valance e-)	•P:

Positive ion
Lewis dot-diagram for a positive ion is the same as the symbol of the positive ion.
See examples to the right.

Sodium (Na$^+$) ion	Boron (B^{3+}) ion
2 – 8	2
Na$^+$ or [Na]$^+$	B^{3+} or [B]$^{3+}$

Negative ion
Lewis electron dot diagram for a negative ion must show the symbol of the ion and 8 dots.

NOTE: A negative hydrogen ion (H$^-$) is the only exception with just 2 dots.
See examples to the right.

Phosphide (P^{3-}) ion	Hydride (H$^-$) ion
2 – 8 – 8	2
:P:$^{3-}$ or [:P:]$^{3-}$	H: or [H:]$^-$

NOTE: If a name of an ion is given. For example: Calcium ion or bromine ion. You can find the correct ion on the Periodic Table. **LOOK** on the Period Table for Ca (atomic number 20) and Br (atomic number 35).

Ca^{2+} is always the correct symbol for a calcium ion.
Ca^{2+} is also the Lewis electron-dot diagram for a calcium ion.

Br$^-$ (Br^{1-}) is always the correct symbol for a bromide ion.
:Br: is the Lewis electron-dot diagram for a bromide ion.

Topic 4 – Chemical bonding

28. Lewis electron-dot for ionic compounds: Recognizing Lewis dot for ionic compounds

RECALL that ionic compounds are composed of positive (+) and negative ions (-) ions.

Also **RECALL** that the positive ion is formed by a metal transferring (losing) its valance electrons to a nonmetal. The nonmetal accepts (or gain) the electrons to form a negative ion.

Lewis electron-dot diagram for ionic formula must show the Lewis electron-dot symbols for both the positive and negative ions of the ionic compound.

A CORRECT Lewis electron-dot symbol for a given ionic formula must CORRECTLY show the followings:

CORRECT positive ion symbol of the formula.

CORRECT negative ion symbol of the formula.

CORRECT number of dots around the negative ion of the formula.

CORRECT number of each ion in the formula.

If any of these is incorrect, the Lewis diagram for the ionic formula will also be incorrect.

In the next set of notes, you are shown two different methods of drawing Lewis electron-dot diagrams for some ionic formulas.

29. Lewis electron-dot diagram for ionic compound: Drawing diagram from ion symbols

Concept Tasks: Be able to draw, show or recognize Lewis electron-dot diagrams for ionic compounds.

Below, three ionic formulas are given. Two methods of showing their dot diagrams are given. Study the steps in both methods to learn how to do the same for other ionic compounds.

Method 1: Drawing Lewis electron-dot diagram for ionic compounds using Lewis electron-dot of the ions. This method works best when a chemical formula of an ionic compound is given.

Ionic formula (given in question)	step 1 Write symbols of (+) and (-) ions in the formula (Use Periodic Table)	step 2 write Lewis dot for the (+) and (-) ions (see Set 27 if necessary)	step 3 Complete the Lewis diagram for the formula (Show number of each ion)
NaCl	Na$^+$ Cl$^-$	Na$^+$:Cl̈:$^-$	Na$^+$:Cl̈:$^-$
CaBr$_2$	Ca^{2+} Br$^-$	Ca^{2+} :B̈r̈:$^-$	Ca^{2+} 2 [:B̈r̈:]$^-$
K$_2$O	K$^+$ O^{2-}	K$^+$:Ö:$^{2-}$	2K$^+$:Ö:$^{2-}$

Method 2: Drawing Lewis electron-dot diagram for ionic compounds by showing transfer of electrons. This method works well when a name of ionic compound is given.

Below, names of ionic compounds are given. Steps show how to get the correct Lewis dot diagrams by showing transfer of electrons.

	step 1 Draw Lewis dot for atoms	step 2 Show electron transfer	step 3 Show ions to complete diagrams
Sodium chloride	Na× ·C̈l̈:	Na × → ·C̈l̈:	Na$^+$ ×C̈l̈:$^-$
Calcium bromide	Ca ××	·B̈r̈:	Ca ×× → ·B̈r̈: ↘ ·B̈r̈:	Ca^{2+} ×B̈r̈:$^-$ ×B̈r̈:$^-$

Topic 4 – Chemical bonding

30. Lewis electron-dot symbols for covalent bonding and molecules

RECALL that covalent bonding and covalent molecules are formed by the sharing of valance electrons by nonmetal atoms.

Each pair of electrons (2 electrons) shared between two atoms forms one (single) covalent bond.

Lewis electron-dot diagrams for covalently bonded atoms (a molecule) must show the sharing of electrons by the nonmetal atoms.

A CORRECT Lewis electron-dot diagram for a molecular formula must show the followings:

CORRECT **symbols and number of the nonmetal** atoms

CORRECT number of shared electrons between the atoms

CORRECT number of valance electrons around each atom

If any of these are incorrect, the Lewis electron-dot diagram for the molecule is also incorrect.

In the next set of notes, you will learn how to draw and recognize Lewis electron-dot diagrams for molecular formulas.

31. Lewis electron-dot diagrams for diatomic molecules: Drawing correct diagrams

Concept Task: Be able to draw, show or recognize Lewis electron-dot diagrams for diatomic molecules.

Below, four diatomic formulas are given. The step below shows how to draw their Lewis dot diagrams.

Given the formulas	H_2	Br_2	O_2	N_2
Step 1: Draw symbols for both atoms.	H H	Br Br	O O	N N

Step 2: VERY IMPORTANT step: Determine how many electrons MUST be put between the two atoms. These are the electrons that are shared between the two atoms. These are the electrons that formed the covalent bond between the two atoms. The correct number of electrons MUST be placed between the two atoms. Incorrect number of electrons between the two atoms will result in the wrong bond type for the formula, and an incorrect Lewis dot diagram for the formula.

To determine how many electrons to be place between the atoms, figure out how many electrons each atom needs to have a full valance shell. Put these electrons in the middle next to each atom in the formula.

For example: Hydrogen has 1 valance electron. It needs 1 more electron for a full valance shell. 1 dot is placed in the middle next to each H atom.

Oxygen has 6 valance electrons. It needs 2 more electrons for a full valance shell. 2 dots are placed in the middle next to each O atom.

	H · ˣ H	Br · ˣ Br	O :ˣˣ O	N :ˣˣˣ N
Step 3: Complete each Lewis diagram. Around each atom, add enough **dots** (. or x)so the total number of **dots** is equal to the number of valance electrons for that atom.	H · ˣH	:Br· ˣBrˣ	Ö :ˣˣ Ö	:N :ˣˣˣ N:
	H — H	:Br — Br:	O = O	:N ≡ N:

Topic 4 - Chemical bonding

32. Lewis electron-dot diagrams: Lewis diagrams for common molecular substances

Concept Task: Be able to draw, show, or recognize Lewis electron-diagrams for molecular substances. Below, you will see examples Lewis electron-dot diagrams for some common molecular substances.

Polar substances (note how these diagrams have asymmetrical shapes)

Molecular name	Molecular formula	Lewis electron-dot diagrams
Hydrogen chloride	HCl	
Water	H_2O	
Ammonia	NH_3	

Nonpolar substances (note how these diagrams have symmetrical shapes)

Molecular name	Molecular formula	Lewis electron-dot diagrams
Chlorine	Cl_2	
Carbon dioxide	CO_2	
Methane	CH_4	
Carbon tetrachloride	CCl_4	

Topic 4 - Chemical bonding

33. Lewis electron-dot diagrams: Example multiple choice questions

Concept Task: Be able to recognize the correct Lewis electron-dot diagram for neutral atoms, ions, and compounds.

Example 15
Which Lewis electron-dot notation is correct for a calcium atom?

1) Ca: 2) :Ca: 3) :Ca: 4) [Ca]$^{2+}$

Answer: choice 1:

Example 16
Which is a correct electron-dot symbol for a Strontium ion?

1) [Sr:]$^{2+}$ 2) [:Sr:]$^{2+}$ 3) [:Sr:]$^{2+}$ (with dots above)   4) [Sr]$^{2+}$

Answer: Choice 4

Example 17
Which electron-dot diagram is correct for a fluoride ion, F$^-$?

1) [:F̈:]$^-$ 2) [:F̈:]$^-$ (with dots below)   3) [F·]$^-$ 4) [F]$^-$

Answer: Choice 2.

Example 18
Which is the correct Lewis electron-dot diagram for strontium bromide?

1) Sr$^+$:Br:$^-$ 2) :Sr:$^{2+}$ Br$^-$ 3) Sr^{2+} [:Br:]$^-$ 4) Sr^{2+} 2[:Br:]$^-$

Answer: Choice 4:

Example 19
Which Lewis diagram is correct for a molecule of fluorine, F$_2$?

1) :F̈::F̈:   2) :F̈:F̈:   3) ·F̈:F̈:   4) F : F

Answer: Choice 2. Each fluorine atom has 8 dots around it

Topic 4 – Chemical Bonding

Lesson 6 – Intermolecular forces

Introduction:

Intermolecular forces are forces that exist between molecules in molecular substances.
Intermolecular forces hold molecules of molecular substances together in a liquid or solid state (phase).
Intermolecular forces exist in molecular substances because of unequal charge distribution within the molecules.
Intermolecular forces are generally weaker than the intramolecular forces (bonding between atoms).

In this lesson, you will learn the relationship between intermolecular forces and certain physical properties (vapor pressure, boiling and melting points) of molecular substances.

34. Properties of molecular substances and intermolecular forces: Facts

Certain physical properties of molecular substances depend on the strength of the intermolecular force holding the molecules together.

Concept Facts: Study to remember these facts

These properties include:
  Melting point, boiling point and vapor pressure.

The stronger the strength of intermolecular force:
  The higher the melting and boiling points of the substance
  The lower the vapor pressure of the substance.

The strength of intermolecular forces holding molecules together depend on the following three factors:
  The polarity of the molecules
  The phase of the substance
  The size of the molecules

35. Bonding in water:

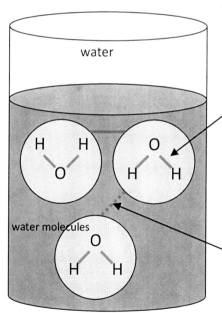

Two types of bonding exist in water and all molecular substances:
Intramolecular **and** intermolecular **bonding**

Intramolecular (polar covalent bonding)
  . Holds the atoms of O and H together to make water molecules
  . Chemical properties (or reactions) of water require the breaking of this bond
  . Stronger bond than the intermolecular bond

Intermolecular (hydrogen bonding)
  . Holds the molecules together in solid and liquid phases
  . Physical properties (such as vapor pressure, boiling and melting points) depend on the strength of this bond
  . Weaker bond than the intramolecular bond

Topic 4 – Chemical Bonding

36. Molecular polarity and intermolecular forces: Facts and examples

The strength of intermolecular forces in molecular substances varies depending on the polarity of the molecules.

In general, intermolecular forces are stronger in polar substances than in nonpolar substances.

In other words, molecules of polar substances are held more strongly and tightly to each other than molecules of nonpolar substances.

For this reason, polar substances usually have higher melting and boiling point, but a lower vapor pressure in comparison to nonpolar substances.

Below is a comparison of boiling point between two substances.

Note that one substance is polar and the other is nonpolar.

Molecular substances	Relative strength of intermolecular force	Relative boiling and melting point
CH_4 (nonpolar)	Weaker	Lower (-161°C)
H_2O (polar)	Stronger	Higher (100°C)

Concept Task: Be able to determine which molecular substance (by formula) has the highest or lowest Boiling Point (BP).

For Lowest BP:
LOOK for a formula of a nonpolar substance

For Highest BP:
LOOK for a formula of a polar substance

37. Phases of substances and intermolecular forces: Facts and examples

The strength of intermolecular forces of a substance will vary depending on the phase of the substance.

In general, intermolecular forces are stronger between molecules of a substance in the solid phase. The force is weaker when the substance is in the gas phase.

In other words, molecules of substances in a solid phase are held more tightly together than molecules of substances in the gas phase. Molecules in solid phase are usually closer together because of their strong intermolecular force.

For this reason, substances with high intermolecular forces may exist as a solid, while similar substances, under same conditions, may exist as a liquid or gas. This relationship between strength of intermolecular and phase is best seen among the halogens.

RECALL that halogens are elements in Group 17 of the Periodic Table.

ALSO RECALL that Cl_2 and F_2 are gases, Br_2 is a liquid, and I_2 is a solid at standard conditions.

Iodine exists as a solid and Chlorine and Fluorine exist as gases because the intermolecular forces in Iodine are stronger when compared to the intermolecular forces in Chlorine and Fluorine.

Below is a comparison among the halogens. NOTE the relationship between the phase in which each halogen exist at STP and the strength of intermolecular forces.

Halogen	Phase at STP	Relative Strength of intermolecular forces
F_2 and Cl_2	Gas	Weaker
Br_2	Liquid	A little stronger
I_2	Solid	Much stronger

Concept Facts:
At STP, Iodine is a solid and fluorine is a gas because iodine has stronger intermolecular forces when compared to fluorine.

Topic 4 – Chemical Bonding

38. Size of molecule and intermolecular forces: Facts and examples

The **strength of intermolecular** forces among similar nonpolar substances varies depending on the size of their molecules. In general, intermolecular forces are stronger in a nonpolar substance with large molecular mass than in similar substances with a smaller molecular mass.

In other words, molecules of a nonpolar substance with a large molecular mass are held more strongly and tighter together when compared to molecule of a similar substance with a smaller molecular mass.

For this reason, the boiling and melting points of nonpolar substances with large molecular mass are usually higher than those of similar substances with smaller molecular masses.

Concept Task: Be able to determine which nonpolar substance has the highest or lowest boiling point (BP)

See examples below

For Lowest BP: Determine and choose a substance with the smallest mass.

For Highest BP: Determine and choose a substance with the biggest mass.

Below, three groups of similar nonpolar substances are given. Note the relationship between the size of these molecules to their strength of intermolecular forces and their boiling points.

Similar nonpolar substances					
Halogens	*Noble gases*	*Hydrocarbons*	*Size of molecule*	*Intermolecular Strength*	*Relative Boiling point*
F_2	He	CH_4	Smallest	Weakest	Lowest
Cl_2	Ne	C_2H_6			
Br_2	Ar	C_3H_8	Biggest	Strongest	Highest

39. Hydrogen Bonding: Definition, fact and example

Hydrogen bonding is a type of intermolecular force that exists in certain polar substances.

It is important to note that among similar polar substances, the degree of polarity varies. This is to say, when similar polar substances are compared, one is always going to be more polar than the other. Because of these differences in polarity, the strength of intermolecular forces also varies among similar polar substances.

Concept Facts: Study to remember the followings on hydrogen bonding

Hydrogen bonding **is a strong intermolecular force that is** said to exist in the following three substances:

H_2O (water) , NH_3 (ammonia) and HF (hydrogen fluoride).

When H_2O is compared to a similar substance (such as H_2S), H_2O will always have a stronger intermolecular force (hydrogen bonding) than H_2S, which has a weaker intermolecular force.

As a result, the *boiling point and the melting point of H_2O will always be higher than that of H_2S*.

The same can be said of NH_3 and HF when they are compared to similar substances (PH_3 and HCl respectively).

Hydrogen bonding exists in these three substances (H_2O, NH_3 and HF) but not in similar substances because:

The hydrogen atom in each formula is bonded to an atom (O, N, or F) which has a **small radius** and **high electronegativity.**

This combination of small radius and high electronegativity allows the molecules of H_2O, NH_3 and HF to be highly polar (more polar) in comparison to similar substances.

Topic 4 – Chemical Bonding

Check-A-list

Concept Terms

Below is a list of vocabulary terms from Topic 4. You should know the definition and facts related to each term.

Put a check in the box [√] next to each term if you know its definition and other facts related to the term.

[ ] Chemical bonding
[ ] Octet of electrons
[ ] Potential energy
[ ] Exothermic
[ ] Endothermic
[ ] Intramolecular forces
[ ] Electronegativity
[ ] Electronegativity difference an bonding
[ ] Ionic bond
[ ] Covalent bond
[ ] Polar covalent bond
[ ] Nonpolar covalent bond
[ ] Network solid covalent bond
[ ] Coordinate covalent bond
[ ] Metallic bond

[ ] Ionic substance
[ ] Molecular (covalent) substance
[ ] Metallic substance
[ ] Properties of metallic substance
[ ] Properties of ionic substances
[ ] Properties of molecular substances
[ ] Properties of network solids
[ ] Bond polarity
[ ] Molecular polarity
[ ] Molecular symmetry
[ ] Molecular shapes
[ ] Polar molecule
[ ] Nonpolar molecule
[ ] Lewis electron-dot diagram
[ ] Intermolecular forces
[ ] Hydrogen bonding

If you do not have a check next to a term, look it up or ask your teacher.

Concept Tasks

Below is a list of concept tasks from Topic 4. You should know how to solve problems and answer questions related to each concept task.

Put a check in the box [√] next a concept task if you know how to solve problems and answer questions related to it.

[ ] Determining which noble gas element an atom (or atoms) in a bond resembles
[ ] Recognizing and interpreting bond formation or exothermic reaction equation
[ ] Recognizing and interpreting bond breaking or endothermic reaction equation
[ ] Determining which formula contains a given bond type
[ ] Recognizing and determining formulas and names of metallic substances
[ ] Recognizing and determining formulas and names of ionic substances
[ ] Recognizing and determining formulas or names of binary compounds
[ ] Recognizing formulas or names of substances containing both ionic and covalent bond
[ ] Recognizing and determining formulas and names of molecular substances
[ ] Determining formula or name of a substance with a given set of properties
[ ] Determining properties given of formula or name of a substance
[ ] Determining molecular symmetry of a formula or structure
[ ] Recognizing molecular shapes of a formula
[ ] Determining formula or name of nonpolar substance (or molecule)
[ ] Determining formula or name of polar substance (or molecule)
[ ] Determining which formula is most or least ionic, covalent or polar
[ ] Drawing and recognizing Lewis electron-dot diagrams for neutral atom
[ ] Drawing and recognizing Lewis electron-dot diagrams for positive ions
[ ] Drawing and recognizing Lewis electron-dot diagrams for negative ions
[ ] Drawing and recognizing Lewis electron-dot diagrams for ionic compounds
[ ] Drawing and recognizing Lewis electron-dot diagrams for diatomic molecules
[ ] Drawing and recognizing Lewis electron-dot diagrams molecular substances
[ ] Determining which molecular substance (by formula) has the highest or lowest Boiling Point (BP)
[ ] Determining which nonpolar substances has the highest or lowest Boiling Point (BP).
[ ] Determining and recognizing formulas and names of substances with hydrogen bonding

If you do not have a check next to a concept task, look it up or ask your teacher.

Topic 4 – Chemical Bonding

Concept Fact Review Questions

1. Atoms bond due to the interaction between
   1) Protons and neutrons
   2) Protons and electrons
   3) Neutrons and electrons
   4) Neutrons and positrons

2. The breaking of a bond of a chemical substance is
   1) Exothermic, which absorbs energy
   2) Exothermic, which releases energy
   3) Endothermic, which absorbs energy
   4) Endothermic, which releases energy

3. The amount of potential energy in chemical bonds of substances depends on
   1) The composition of the chemical substances only
   2) The structure of the chemical substances only
   3) Both the composition and the structure of chemical substances
   4) Neither the composition nor the structure of chemical substances

4. In ionic bonding, electrons are
   1) Always shared between a metal and a nonmetal atom
   2) Always shared between two different nonmetals atoms
   3) Always transferred from a metal atom to a nonmetal atom
   4) Always transferred from a nonmetal atom to a metal atom

5. Covalent bonding occurs when electrons are
   1) Transferred from a metallic atom to a nonmetallic atom
   2) Transferred from a nonmetallic atom to a metallic atom
   3) Shared between metallic atoms
   4) Shared between nonmetallic atoms

6. The ability to conduct electricity in the solid state is a characteristic of metallic substances. This characteristics is best explained by the presence of
   1) High ionization energy
   2) High electronegativity
   3) Mobile protons
   4) Mobile electrons

7. Two nonmetal atoms of the same element share electrons equally. The resulting molecule is
   1) Polar, only
   2) Nonpolar, only
   3) Either polar or nonpolar
   4) Neither polar nor nonpolar

8. Which best describes the shape and charge distribution in polar molecules?
   1) Asymmetrical shape with equal charge distribution
   2) Asymmetrical shape with unequal charge distribution
   3) Symmetrical shape with equal charge distribution
   4) Symmetrical shape with unequal charge distribution

9. Which characteristic is a property of molecular substances?
   1) Good heat conductivity
   2) Good electrical conductivity
   3) Low melting point
   4) High melting point

10. Hydrogen bonding is formed between molecules when the molecules contain a hydrogen atom that is covalently bonded to an atom that has
    1) Small atomic radius and low electronegativity
    2) Large atomic radius and low electronegativity
    3) Small atomic radius and high electronegativity
    4) Large atomic radius and low electronegativity

Topic 4 – Chemical Bonding

Concept Task Review Questions

11. A bond between which two atoms would produce ions with electron configurations similar to those of Kr and Ne respectively?
    1) Li and Cl
    2) K and Cl
    3) Al and Br
    4) Sr and F

12. Atom X and atom Y bond to form a compound. The electron configuration of X in the bond is 2 – 8 – 8. The electron configuration of Y in the compound is 2 – 8. Which two atoms could be X and Y?
    1) X could be magnesium and Y could be sulfur
    2) X could be magnesium and Y could be oxygen
    3) X could be calcium and Y could be sulfur
    4) X could be calcium and Y could be oxygen

13. In the balanced equation
    $$HCl \longrightarrow H_2 + Cl_2$$
    Which is correct of the process talking place as bonds are broken and formed?
    1) The breaking of H–Cl bond is exothermic
    2) The breaking of H–Cl bond is exothermic
    3) The forming of H–H bond is exothermic
    4) The forming of Cl–Cl bond is endothermic

14. Atoms in which compound are held together by ionic bonds?
    1) CH_4
    2) $AlCl_3$
    3) H_2O
    4) NH_3

15. Which formula contains nonpolar covalent bonds?
    1) NH_3
    2) H_2O
    3) O_2
    4) NaCl

16. The atoms of which substance are held together by a metallic bond?
    1) $H_2(g)$
    2) H_2O (l)
    3) SiC(s)
    4) Fe(s)

17. Which compound contains both ionic and covalent bonds?
    1) Ammonia
    2) Lithium sulfate
    3) Methane
    4) Potassium chloride

18. The C – Cl bond in CCl_4 is best described as
    1) Ionic, because electrons are transferred
    2) Ionic, because electrons are shared
    3) Covalent, because electrons are transferred
    4) Covalent, because electrons are shared

19. Which structural formula represents a polar molecule?
    1) H – H
    2) Na – H
    3) H – Br
    4) O = O

20. Which pair of atoms forms a bond that is the least covalent?
    1) Ba and I
    2) Br and Cl
    3) K and Cl
    4) Li and I

21. An atom of nitrogen is most stable when it bonds with
    1) One sodium atom
    2) One magnesium atom
    3) One aluminum atom
    4) One calcium atom

22. Based on bond type, which compound has the highest melting point?
    1) CH_3OH
    2) C_6H_{14}
    3) CuCl
    4) CCl_4

23. Which of the followings has the lowest boiling point?
    1) He
    2) Xe
    3) Ne
    4) Kr

24. Which electron-dot symbol represents a nonpolar molecule?
    1) H:C̈:Cl̈: with H above and H below
    2) H:Ö: with H below
    3) H:C̈:H with H above and H below
    4) H:Ö: with H below

Topic 4 – Chemical Bonding

Constructed Response Questions

Base your answers to questions 17 through 20 on your knowledge of chemical bonding and on the Lewis electron-dot diagrams of H_2S, CO_2, and F_2 below.

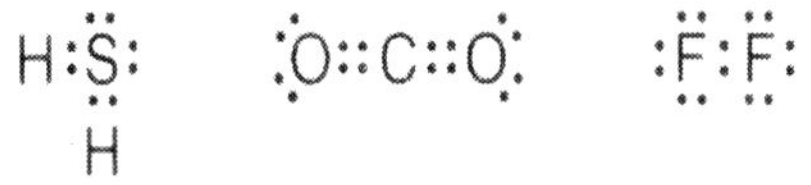

$$H:\ddot{S}: \quad\quad :\ddot{O}::C::\ddot{O}: \quad\quad :\ddot{F}:\ddot{F}:$$
$$H$$

25. Which atom, when bonded as shown, has the same electrons configuration as an atom of argon?

    25. _____

26. Explain, in terms of structure and/or distribution of charge, why CO_2 is a nonpolar molecule?

    26. _____

27. Explain, in terms of electronegativity, why a C = O bond in CO_2 is more polar than F – F bond in F_2?

    27. _____

28. What is the total number of covalent bond in molecule of CO_2?

    28. _____

29. What is the shape and molecular polarity of H_2S?

    29. Shape:

    Molecular Polarity:

Copyright © 2010 E3 Scholastic Publishing. All Rights Reserved.

Topic 5 – Chemical formulas and equations

Topic outline

In this topic, you will learn about the following concepts:

. Interpretation of chemical formulas
. Types of chemical formulas
. Writing chemical formulas
. Naming chemical formulas
. Chemical equations
. Types of chemical equations
. Balancing chemical equations

Lesson 1 – Interpretation of chemical formulas

Introduction

Chemical formulas are used to represent the composition of elements and compounds (Pure substances).
A chemical formula expresses the *qualitative* and *quantitative* composition of a substance.
Qualitative information of a formula shows the type of atoms (or ions) that makes up a substance.
Quantitative information of a formula shows how many of each atom (or ion) is in the formula.
The number of each atom in a formula is usually shown with a subscript.
A subscript in a chemical formulas is the whole number written on the bottom right of each atom in a formula.

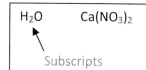

Example of some common chemical formulas :

$NaCl$ (sodium chloride) CO_2 (carbon dioxide) H_2O (water) H_2 (hydrogen)

Each of these formulas shows both qualitative and quantitative composition of the substance.

In this topic, you will learn how to interpret chemical formulas by determining their qualitative and quantitative compositions.

1. Qualitative and quantitative compositions: Counting atoms in formulas

One way to express the qualitative and quantitative composition of a substance is to determine the number of each element in the formula.

This can be done by counting how many of each element (or atom) is shown in the formula.

Three types of compound formulas that you will commonly see are listed below.

For each type, example formula, number of each atom and the total number of atoms in the formula are also given.

Concept Task: Be able to count atoms in different types of formulas.

Study examples below learn how to count atoms in formulas

Type of formula	Example formula	Number of each atom	Total number of atoms
Simple formula	H_2SO_4	2 H atoms 1 S atom 4 O atoms	**Three** different atoms. 7 total atoms
Formula with parenthesis	$(NH_4)_2O$	2 N atom (2 x 1) 8 H atoms (4 x2) 1 O atom	**Three** different atoms. 11 total atoms
Formula of hydrates	$CuSO_4 \cdot 5H_2O$	1 Cu atom 1 S atom 9 O atoms (4 + 5) 10 H atoms (5 x 2)	**Four** different atoms. 21 total atoms

Topic 5 – Chemical formulas and equations

2. Qualitative and quantitative composition: Ratio of ions in ionic compound formulas

Another way of expressing the qualitative and quantitative composition of different substances is to determine the ratio of ions in the formula.

RECALL that ionic compounds are composed of positive and negative ions.

The qualitative and quantitative composition of ionic compounds can also be expressed by the number of each ion in the formula.

Three types of ionic compound formulas that you will commonly see are listed on the table below.

For each type, example formula, ions in the formula, and ratio of these ions are given.

Concept Task: Be able to determine ratio of ions in ionic compounds

Study this information to learn how to determine ratio of ions in ionic formulas.

Type of formula	Example formula	Ions in formula		Ratio of ions in formula
Binary ionic formula	$CaCl_2$ calcium chloride	Ca^{2+} calcium ion	Cl^- chlorine ion	1 Ca^{2+} : 2 Cl^-
Ionic formula of polyatomic ion (with parenthesis)	$Al_2(SO_4)_3$ aluminum sulfate	Al^{3+} aluminum ion	SO_4^{2-} sulfate ion	2 Al^{3+} : 3 SO_4^{2-}
Ionic formula of polyatomic ion (without parenthesis)	KNO_3 potassium nitrate	K^+ potassium ion	NO_3^- nitrate ion	1 K^+ : 1 NO_3^-

Use Table E to confirm symbols and names of polyatomic ions.
Use the **Periodic Table** to confirm charge and symbol of an ion of an element.

3. Qualitative and quantitative composition: Determining number of atoms (or ions) in formulas

Concept Task: Be able to determine number of atoms or total number of atoms in a formula

Example 1

How many hydrogen atoms are found in the hydrate $(NH_4)_3PO_4 \cdot 5H_2O$?

1) 12   2) 19   3) 22   4) 14

Answer: Choice 3: In the formula $(NH_4)_3PO_4 \cdot 5H_2O$?

There are: 12 H + 10 = **22 H atoms**

Example 2

What is the total number of atoms in one formula unit of $Ca(ClO_3)_2$?

1) 3   2) 7   3) 2   4) 9

Answer: Choice 4: In the formula $Ca(ClO_3)_2$ There are: 1 Ca   2 Cl   6 O.

Total number of all atoms   = 1 + 2 + 6 = **9 total atoms**

Concept Task: Be able to determine ratio of ions in ionic compounds

Example 3

In the formula $(NH_4)_2CO_3$, what is the ratio of ammonium to carbonate ion?

1) 2 : 3   2) 2 : 1   3) 8 : 3   4) 3 : 6

Answer: Choice 2: In the formula; $(NH_4)_2 CO_3$

There are: 2 NH_4 : 1 CO_3

Topic 5 – Chemical formulas and equations

Lesson 2 – Types of chemical formula

Introduction:
There are three types of chemical formulas that are used to show the compositions of a substance.
In this lesson, you will learn about molecular formula, empirical formula, and structural formula.

4. Types of formulas: Definitions and facts

A molecular formula is a formula showing the true composition of a known substance.

Examples: H_2O is a molecular formula for water.
C_3H_8 is a molecular formula for a compound known as propane.

An empirical formula is a formula in which the elements are in the smallest whole-number ratio.
CH_4, H_2O, $CaCl_2$ are all formulas in the empirical form.
Subscripts of these formulas cannot be reduced into any simpler ratio.

Some molecular formulas can be reduced to empirical formulas.
C_2H_6 can be reduced to CH_3
N_2O_4 can be reduced to NO_2
Some molecular formulas are already in the empirical forms.
H_2O is both a molecular formula and an empirical formula

A structural formula is a formula showing how atoms of a substance are bonded together.
Below, examples of structural formulas to two molecular formulas are given.

Molecular C_2H_6 (ethane) H_2O (water)

Structural
$$\begin{array}{c} H \quad H \\ | \quad\; | \\ H-C-C-H \\ | \quad\; | \\ H \quad H \end{array} \qquad \begin{array}{c} O \\ / \; \backslash \\ H \quad\; H \end{array}$$

5. Empirical formula: Determining which formula is in the empirical form

Concept Task: Be able to recognize empirical formulas	**Example 4**
	Which is an empirical formula?
	  1) C_2H_4 3) Ca_3P_2
	  2) $C_6H_{12}O_6$ 4) C_4H_6
	Answer: Choice 3. The ratio 3 : 2 in Ca_3P_2 cannot be reduced any further. In the other three formulas, subscripts of atoms are reducible.

To determine which formula is an empirical formula:
LOOK for a formula in which the subscripts are in the lowest whole number ratio
	Example 5
	Which compound has the same empirical and molecular formula?
	  1) C_2H_6 3) N_2O
	  2) H_2O_2 4) $C_6H_{12}O_6$
	Answer: Choice 3. The answer to this type of question is always the formula that is in the empirical form. N_2O is an empirical formula.

Copyright © 2010 E3 Scholastic Publishing. All Rights Reserved.

Topic 5 – Chemical formulas and equations

6. Empirical and molecular formulas: Determining empirical formula from molecular formula

Concept Task: Be able to reduce a molecular formula to an empirical formula.

This can be done by reducing all the subscripts in the molecular formula by the greatest common factor.

To determine the correct empirical formula for a given molecular formula

Find the Greatest Common Factor (GCF) between all subscripts in the formula.

Reduce (by dividing) each subscript by the GCF you had determined.

LOOK for a choice that reflects these reductions by GCF.

Below, three molecular formulas are reduced by GCF to get the correct empirical formula.

Study these examples to learn how to determine empirical formula from a molecular formula.

Molecular Formula	C_4H_{10}	$C_6H_{12}O_6$	NO_2
Find GCF	2	6	1
Divide subscripts by GCF to get			
Empirical formula	C_2H_5	CH_2O	NO_2

Example 6

Which is the empirical formula for C_3H_6?

1) CH_3 3) C_2H_3
2) CH_2 4) C_3H_6

Answer: Choice 2 :

Molecular formula: C_3H_6

GCF :   3

Divide to get empirical: CH_2

Example 7

Which molecular formula could have the empirical formula of C_2H_4O?

1) CH_2O 3) $C_2H_4O_2$
2) $C_4H_8O_4$ 4) $C_4H_8O_2$

Correct: Choice 4:

The formula $C_4H_8O_2$ can be reduced to C_2H_4O (GCF of 2)

Topic 5 – Chemical formulas and equations

Lesson 3 – Writing and naming chemical formulas

Introduction

A chemical formula is correctly written for a known substance when both the qualitative and quantitative information of the formula are both correct. This to say that:
. The element (or ion) symbols in the formula must all be correct for the substance it represented
. The subscripts of the elements (or ions) must also be correctly represented in the formula

Compounds formula MUST be neutral: This is to say:
The sum of positive and negative charges in the formula is equal to Zero. (equalization of charges)

Corrects subscripts in a formula allow charges to balance out and produce a formula that is neutral.

A chemical name is correctly written for a given formula when all of the followings are correctly represented in the name:
. Atoms and/or ions in the formula are named correctly
. Name ending, if necessary, is applied correctly
. Roman numeral, if necessary, is correctly used
. Prefixes, if necessary, are used correctly

In this lesson, you will learn how to write correct chemical formulas and names of compounds in different categories of substances.

A. Writing formulas

7. Chemical formulas: What to expect on multiple choice questions

On multiple choice questions, you will be given a chemical name, and be asked to choose its correct formula. Formulas of the four choices that you will get usually look very similar. One formula may be different from the others by only the subscripts, or by the presence (or absence) of just one atom. To further explain what this means, take a look at the table below.

The Table below shows:
In the left column, names of three chemical substances that could be given in a question.
In the middle column, the correct formula to each name.
In the right columns, three wrong choices on a multiple choice test
NOTE how these formulas look very similar to the correct formula.

Given name in question	Correct formula choice	Possible wrong formulas given as choices		
Aluminum chloride	$AlCl_3$	Al_3Cl	$AlCl$	$AlClO_3$
Magnesium sulfate	$MgSO_4$	MgS	$Mg_2(SO_4)_2$	$MgSO_2$
Copper (II) Fluoride	CuF_2	Cu_2F	Cu_2F_2	CuF

Because all four choices look very similar, you will need to take the time to figure out for sure which of the choices is the correct formula.

In this section of lesson 3, you will learn step-by-step process of determining (or writing) the correct formula when a name of compound is given.

The use of the Periodic Table and Reference Table E, is highly recommended in formula writing.

Topic 5 – Chemical formulas and equations

When a name of a substance is given, and you are asked to determine its correct formula, you will not be told what class of compound the name belongs to. It is up to you to determine the class of compound the name belongs. This is important because steps to writing or determining formula from name varies from one group of compound to another. It is, therefore, important that you know how to identify a name of a compound as molecular, ionic, or containing polyatomic ion..etc.

As the notes in the following sections are given on how to write appropriate formula, you will be told what to look for in names to correctly identify the type of compound based on the name that is given.

⇐ **LOOKING back: Topic 4: Chemical bonding.** You learned how to recognize formulas as ionic or molecular

8. Binary ionic Compounds: Writing formulas for binary ionic compounds

Binary ionic compounds have formulas that are composed of two different elements;
A metal and a nonmetal

Names of binary compounds always ends with –ide

Examples: Calcium brom*ide*, Aluminum sulf*ide*, and Zinc ox*ide*

Once you have established that the name given in a question is a binary ionic compound, follow steps shown in the three examples below to learn how to write its correct formula.

Concept Task: Be able to write correct chemical formulas to binary compounds.

Three binary ionic compound names are given below.
You are shown how to write correct formula to each of these compounds.
Study the steps below to learn how to write correct formulas to other binary ionic compounds.

As you study the steps to writing the correct formulas, KEEP IN MIND that the purpose of going through these steps is to MAKE SURE that your final (correct) formula has the correct element symbols and correct subscripts for name given. If you can write correct formulas without going through these steps, you should do so.

	Example 8 **Calcium brom**ide	*Example 9* **Aluminum Sulf**ide	*Example 10* **Zinc Ox**ide
Step 1: Locate and write down symbols and charges of the elements (USE THE PERIODIC TABLE). The charge of the elements is the oxidation number.	Ca^{2+} Br^{1-}	Al^{3+} S^{2-}	Zn^{2+} O^{2-}
Step 2: Criss-cross the values of the + and - charges so that each becomes the subscript for the other element.	Ca^{2+} Br^{1-} ↘ Ca_1 Br_2	Al^{3+} S^{2-} ↘ Al_2 S_3	Zn^{2+} O^{2-} ↘ Zn_2 O_2
Step 3: Rewrite the formula with Subscripts BUT without the charges	Ca_1Br_2	Al_2S_3	Zn_2O_2
Step 4: Clean up formula to get the *correct formula:* · Reduce formulas to empirical form (if necessary) · Subscript of 1 (one) should not be written.	$CaBr_2$	Al_2S_3	ZnO

These formulas are all correct for the names because each contains:
Correct atom symbols and correct ratio of the atoms (correct subscripts).
Subscripts allowed the sum of (+) and (-) in each formula to equal Zero.

Copyright © 2010 E3 Scholastic Publishing. All Rights Reserved.

Topic 5 – Chemical formulas and equations

9. Polyatomic ion compounds: Recognizing names of compounds containing a polyatomic ion

Polyatomic ions are ions composed of two or more atoms with excess charge.
Most polyatomic ions have negative charges (they contain more electrons than protons).
A polyatomic ion can combine with elements (or other polyatomic ions) of opposite charge to form variety of compounds.

See **Table E** for a list of common polyatomic ions

Formulas of these compounds are different from those of binary compounds in two ways:
. They usually contain three or more elements : **ex. Na**NO_3 (contains Na, N, and O)
. There may be parenthesis around the polyatomic atoms : ex (NH_4)$_2$O   (NH_4 is a polyatomic ion)

To determine if a chemical name given in a question contains a polyatomic ion:
  Look and note if: The second name ends with –*ate* (Sodium Nitr*ate*)   Or –*ite* (Calcium sulf*ite*)
             OR the second name is *hydroxide* (magnesium *hydroxide*)
             OR the first name is *ammonium* (*ammonium* oxide)

Once you have established that name given in a question is a compound containing a polyatomic ion, follow steps in the three examples below to learn to write its correct formula.

10. Polyatomic ion compounds: Writing formulas of compounds containing a polyatomic ion

Concept Task: Be able to write correct formulas to compounds containing a polyatomic ion

Below, three polyatomic ion compounds are given.
You are shown how to write correct formula to each of these compounds.
Study the steps below to learn how to write correct formulas to other polyatomic ion compounds.
As you study these steps, KEEP IN MIND that the purpose of going through these steps is to MAKE SURE that your final (correct) formula has the correct element symbols and correct subscripts for the compound.

	Example 11	*Example 12*	*Example 13*
	Sodium Nitr*ate*	**Calcium Sulf***ite*	*Ammonium* **Oxide**
STEP 1: Locate and **Write down:** Symbols and charges using Period Table and/or Table E. **IMPORTANT: PUT parenthesis around polyatomic atoms. PUT + or – charge of the ion outside the parenthesis.**	Na^{+1} $(NO_3)^{-1}$	Ca^{2+} $(SO_3)^{2-}$	$(NH_4)^{1+}$ O^{2-}
Step 2: Criss – Cross values of charges. (Keep the parenthesis)	$Na^{+1}(NO_3)^{1-}$ $Na_1(NO_3)_1$	$Ca^{2+}(SO_3)^{2-}$ $Ca_2(SO_4)_2$	$(NH_4)^{1+} O^{2-}$ $(NH_4)_2 O_1$
Step 3: Rewrite formula with subscripts BUT without the charges (Keep the parenthesis)	$Na_1(NO_3)_1$	$Ca_2(SO_4)_2$	$(NH_4)_2 O_1$
STEP: 4 : CLEAN UP FORMULA : If necessary: **REDUCE** subscripts to empirical form (DON'T EVER CHANGE THE SUBSCRIPTS OF THE POLYATOMIC ATOMS) **REMOVE parenthesis** if subscript outside parenthesis is a 1 **KEEP parenthesis** if subscript outside parenthesis is 2 or more **ERASE any** subscripts that is a 1	**Na** NO_3		$(NH_4)_2$ **O**

Copyright © 2010 E3 Scholastic Publishing. All Rights Reserved.

Topic 5 – Chemical formulas and equations

11. Multiple oxidation number compounds: Understanding names with Roman numeral

RECALL that most transition metals have multiple positive oxidation numbers.
LOOK on the periodic table for elements such as iron (Fe), chromium (Cr) and lead (Pb).
Note that each has more than one (+) oxidation numbers.
If an element has many positive oxidation numbers, a compound made with one positive ion is different in many ways from a compound made with a another positive ions of the element.

For example: A compound of Fe^{2+} ion with chlorine (Cl) has a different formula ($FeCl_2$) and different properties than a compound of Fe^{3+} ion with chlorine ($FeCl_3$).

The stock system of naming uses Roman numeral in parenthesis to distinguish the names of compounds produced by the different oxidation charges of an atom.

Examples of stock system naming and the meaning of a Roman numeral in parenthesis are given below:

Iron (II) chloride   (II) indicates that Iron with a charge of +2 forms this compound with chlorine.
Iron (III) oxide   (III) indicates that Iron with a charge of +3 forms this compound with oxygen.
Lead (IV) nitrate   (IV) indicates that Lead with a charge of +4 forms this compound with nitrate.

NOTE: The (Roman numeral) indicates the **value** of the **positive charge** for the first element.

12. Multiple oxidation numbers compounds: Writing correct formulas

Concept Task: Be able to write correct formulas to compounds Roman numeral in their names.

Four compounds with Roman Numeral in their names are given below.
You are shown how to write correct formula to each of these compounds.
Study to learn how to write correct formulas to other compounds containing a Roman numeral.
NOTE: The steps have been shortened (The criss-cross method have been eliminated) for clarity.

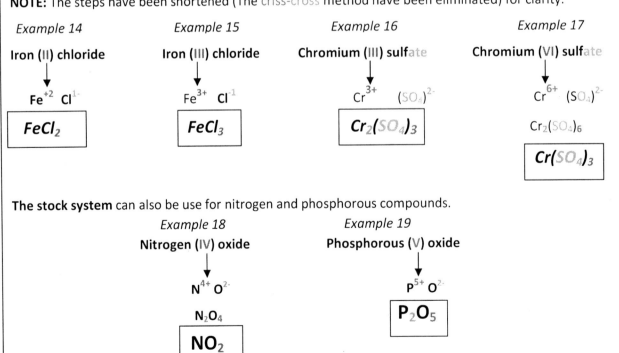

Topic 5 – Chemical formulas and equations

13. Binary molecular (covalent) compounds with prefixes: Understanding prefixes

Molecular (covalent) compounds are composed of nonmetal atoms only.

Binary molecular compounds, which contain two different nonmetals, are commonly named with prefixes.

A prefix in a chemical name indicates how many nonmetal atom is in the compound.

Examples of some common binary molecular compounds named with prefixes:

Carbon _di_oxide	Carbon _mono_xide	_di_nitrogen _mono_xide
CO_2	CO	N_2O

In order to understand these names and be able to write formulas to these compounds, you need to know prefixes and rules given below.

A. Know the common prefixes relating to the number of atoms in a formula.

Number of atom	Prefixes	Number of atom	Prefixes
1	mono-	6	hexa-
2	di-	7	hepta-
3	tri-	8	octo-
4	tetra-	9	non-
5	penta-	10	deca-

B. Know these four simple rules.

1. The only time a prefix is NOT used is when there is ONLY ONE of the first nonmetal atom

   Ex. CO_2: Carbon is the **first nonmetal**, and there is just one Carbon in the formula
   Monocarbon dioxide would be wrong naming for CO_2.
   Carbon dioxide (as you know) is the correct name for CO_2.

2. The prefixes are the subscripts.
3. NO criss – crossing
4. No reducing to empirical formula

14. Binary molecular (covalent) compounds with prefixes. Writing correct formulas

Concept Task: Be able to write formulas to binary molecular compounds.

Three binary molecular formulas are given below.

You are shown how to write correct formula to each of these compounds.
Study to learn how to write correct formulas to other binary molecular compounds.

	Example 20	Example 21	Example 22
Names given:	Phosphorous _tri_chloride	_di_nitrogen _penta_oxide	_di_hydrogen _mono_sulfide
Translations:	1 Phosphorous 3 Chlorine	2 Nitrogen 5 Oxygen	2 Hydrogen 1 Sulfur
Correct formulas:	PCl_3	N_2O_5	H_2S

Topic 5 – Chemical formulas and equations

B. Chemical names:

15. Chemical naming: What to expect on multiple choice questions

On multiple choice questions, you will be given a chemical formula in a question, and be asked to choose the name that is correct for that formula. It is important to note that names that you will get as choices usually look very similar. One name may be different from the others by just one letter in the name ending or by the presence (or absence) of a Roman numeral.
To further explain what this means, look at the table below.

The Table below shows:

In the left column, chemical formulas of three chemical substances are given.

In the middle column, correct name to each formula is given.

In the right columns, three choices representing wrong choices on a multiple choice test are given.

Given formula	Correct name	Wrong names that can be given as choices		
$MgCl_2$	Magnesium chloride	Magnesium chlorite	Magnesium chlorine	Magnesium chlorate
K_2SO_4	Potassium sulfate	Potassium (II) sulfate	Potassium sulfide	Potassium (II) sulfide
MnO	Manganese (II) oxide	Manganese (I) oxide	Manganese (III) oxide	Manganese (IV) oxide

Because all four multiple choices are usually very similar, you MUST take the time to figure out for sure which of the choices is the correct name to a formula that is given in the question.
In this is section of lesson 3, you will learn the steps of determining (or writing) the correct name when a formula of a compound is given.

The use of the Periodic Table and Reference Table E, is highly recommended in formula writing.

When a formula of a substance is given in a question and you asked to determine its correct, you will not be told that the formula is ionic or molecular, or that it contains a metal with many positive charges. It is up to you to know the class of compound the formula belongs. This is important because how compound formulas are named varies quite a bit from one class of compound to another. It is, therefore, important that you know how to identify a formula as molecular, ionic, or containing polyatomic ion..etc.

As the notes in the following sections are given on how to write appropriate name, you will be told what to look for in a formula to correctly identify the group of compounds the formula belongs.

Topic 5 – Chemical formulas and equations

16. Binary ionic compounds: Naming binary ionic compounds

Concept Task: Be able to name binary ionic compound formulas

To determine if a given formula is a binary ionic:
The formula MUST have two different element symbols: A metal and a Nonmetal

Once you have determined that the formula given is a binary ionic compound, follow the steps in examples below to learn how to write the correct name of the binary ionic compounds.

Three formulas of binary ionic compounds are given below:
You are shown how to determine correct names to these compounds.
Study these steps to learn how to determine names to other binary ionic compounds formulas.

As you study these steps, KEEP IN MIND that the purpose of going through the steps is to ensure that the chemical name to the formula given has correct element names and correct name endings.

NOTE: The metal in each formula has only one positive charge. (Confirm this on the Periodic Table) Therefore, no Roman numerals are needed in names.

	Example 23	*Example 24*	*Example 25*
	$ZnCl_2$	CaO	Al_2N_3
STEP 1: Locate and write down names of elements in formula (Use the Periodic Table)	Zinc Chlor*ine*	Calcium Ox*ygen*	Aluminum Nitr*ogen*
Step 2: Write correct name: - Keep metal's name - Change the nonmetal ending to -ide	Zinc Chlor*ide*	Calcium ox*ide*	Aluminum Nitr*ide*

When a nonmetal is listed second in a formula, its name ending MUST BE CHANGED to *-ide*

17. Compounds with polyatomic ion: Naming compounds with polyatomic ions

Concept Task: Be able to name formulas containing polyatomic ions.

To determine if formula given contains polyatomic ion:
. The formula Must have three or more different elements.

Once you have determined that the formula given contains a polyatomic ion:
Follow steps in examples below to learn how to write correct names to compounds with polyatomic ions:

Three formulas of polyatomic ion compounds are given below:
You are shown how to determine correct names to these compounds.
Study these steps to learn how to determine names to other binary ionic compounds formulas.

	Example 26	*Example 27*	*Example 28*
	$Mg_2(PO_4)_3$	NH_4NO_3	NH_4Cl
Step 1: Locate and Write down names of symbols in formula (Use Periodic Table and Table E)	Magnesium Phosphate	Ammonium Nitrate	Ammonium Chlor*ine*
Step 2: Write correct name - Keep name of metal - Keep name of polyatomic NOTE: When NH_4 (a poly ion) is combined with a nonmetal, in a formula, the nonmetal ending is changed to -ide	Magnesium Phosphate	Ammonium Nitrate	Ammonium Chlor*ide*

In naming, NO CHANGE is made to name of a metal atom or polyatomic ion.

Topic 5 – Chemical formulas and equations

18. Compounds of element with multiple oxidation numbers: Writing correct name

RECALL that a compound containing a metal of multiple + oxidation numbers are named using Roman numeral in parenthesis. This is called the stock system of naming.

Concept Task: Be able to name formulas containing metals with multiple oxidation numbers.

IMPORTANT NOTE: To use Roman numeral in naming, be sure that the metal (or the first) element in the formula has more than one positive number.
    LOOK on your periodic table and note how many + numbers are listed for the metal (first) element.

If the metal (or the first) element in the formula has ONLY one + charges listed on the Periodic Table, the formula CANNOT be named with Roman numeral inside a parenthesis:

If the metal (or the first) element in the formula has MORE than one + charges listed on the Periodic Table, the name of the formula **MUST** contain a Roman numeral in parenthesis.

RECALL that the Roman numeral indicates which + charge of an atom is used in the formula.

Once you have established that the formula given should be named using a Roman numeral in parenthesis, you can follow one of the two methods below to get the correct Roman numeral.

Two methods of getting the correct Roman numeral.

1. USE subscript of second symbol as Roman numeral value.
    Easy to do, BUT may give you the wrong Roman numeral some of the times.

    Three formulas containing element (the first element) that has multiple + charges.
    The name of the each formula given is determined using two simple steps.

	Example 29	*Example 30*	*Example 31*
	Sn F$_4$	**N$_2$O**	**Fe$_3$(PO$_4$)$_2$**
STEP 1: Write names of first and last symbols in the formula (use Tables). Put a ( ) parenthesis between the names. **NOTE:** If second symbol is a nonmetal, change ending to *–ide*. If second symbol is a polyatomic ion, leave name as is.	Tin ( ) fluor*ide*	Nitrogen ( ) ox*ide*	Iron ( ) phosphate
STEP 2: Determine the correct Roman numeral: Use the **subscript** of the second symbol as the Roman numeral value to be placed in ( ).	**Tin (IV) fluor*ide***	**Nitrogen (I) ox*ide***	**Iron (II)**
	Subscript of F (second symbol) in SnF$_4$ is 4, so Roman numeral IV (4) is used in parenthesis to name Sn F$_4$	Subscript of O (second symbol) in N$_2$O is 1, so Roman numeral I (1) is used in parenthesis to name N$_2$O	Subscript of PO$_4$ (second symbol) in Fe$_3$(PO$_4$)$_2$ is 2, so Roman numeral II (2) is used in parenthesis to name Fe$_3$(PO$_4$)$_2$

Although the use of subscript of the second symbol as Roman numeral value is easy to do, it may gives a wrong result sometimes. It is important to double check to make sure that the name that you chose or write is appropriate for the formula that is given. **The second method is explained on the next page.**

Topic 5 – Chemical formulas and equations

18. cont.

2. Use math to determine the value of the Roman numeral.

A bit more complicated, BUT if done correctly, will ALWAYS give you the correct Roman numeral.

It is highly recommend that you try method 1 on the previous page to determine the correct Roman numeral.

Two formulas containing a metal that has multiple positive charges are given below.

The Roman numeral to be placed in parenthesis when naming each formula is determined mathematically by using the steps below.

Example 32   *Example 33*

CrN_2 $CuSO_4$

Step 1: Assign negative (–) charge to nonmetal or polyatomic
For nonmetals: Use Periodic Table
For polyatomic ions: Use Table E
Put polyatoms in parenthesis ( )
Put - charge outside parenthesis

$Cr \; N_2^{3-}$ $Cu \; (SO_4)^{2-}$

Step 2: Find the total negative (-) in the formula: (subscript x charge)

$2 \times 3- = -6$ $1 \times 2- = -2$

Step 3: Determine a positive (+) number that when added to the total negative value (in step 2) will have a sum of Zero (0).
JUST THINK!

$+6$ $+2$

Step 4: Name the formulas:
. Write names of symbols in formula (Use Tables)
. Use value of + charge (step 3) as Roman numeral in parenthesis
. Change nonmetal ending to –ide
. Keep polyatomic ion name

Chromium ( ) nitrogen   Copper ( ) sulfate

Chromium (VI) nitride   **Copper (II) sulfate**

NOTE: Trying to figure out names of the above formulas in the same way as the in method 1 would have given you wrong names.

You could use method 1 to figure out the names, but you must always think the formulas through, and double check and make sure that the names you come up with make sense for the formulas.

THE SUM OF CHARGES IN FORMULA MUST ALWAYS BE ZERO (0)

Always remember, there are many ways to solve chemistry problems. Find one of the ways that is appropriate and comfortable for you to solve the problem.

Topic 5 – Chemical formulas and equations

19. Binary molecular compounds: Naming binary molecular compounds

Concept Task: Be able to name formulas of binary molecular compounds

RECALL that molecular (covalent) substances are commonly named using prefixes.

Prefixes indicate the number of each atom in the formula.

Review the list of prefixes and rules of using prefixes to name molecular compounds on page 105.

To determine if a formula is a molecular compound formula:

   The formula must contain two different nonmetals (Ex. P_2Cl_3 H_2O_2 CF_4)

Once you have determine that a formula is a binary molecular

   Use appropriate prefix to name the given formula.

Three formulas of binary molecular compounds are given below.
The name of each formula is determined using two simple steps below.
Study these step to learn how to name other binary molecular formulas.

	Example 34	Example 35	Example 36
Given molecular formula	P_2Cl_3	H_2O_2	CF_4
Step 1: Translate formulas: Write number of each atom	2 P 3 Cl	2 H 2 O	1 C 4 F
Step 2: Name formulas .Change numbers to prefixes .Write name of element after each prefix .Keep name of first element .Change second nonmetal ending to *ide*	**di**phosphorous **tri**chlor*ide*	**di**hydrogen **di**ox*ide*	Carbon **tetra**fluor*ide*

RECALL: no prefix is needed when there is just one of the first nonmetal.

Monocarbon tetrafluoride is a wrong name for CF_4

See rules on page 105.

See page 105 for Table of Prefix and its Rules.

Topic 5 – Chemical formulas and equations

Lesson 4 – Chemical equations

Introduction

Equation shows changes that are taking place in a substance.
There are three major types of changes. Each can be represented with an equation.
Study and note the similarities and differences among the three types of equations listed below.

Type of change	Definition	Example of equation
1. **Chemical change**	A change in chemical composition of one or more substances to other substances	$H_2(g) + O_2(g) \longrightarrow H_2O(l)$
2. **Physical change**	A change of a substance from one form (phase) to a different form without changing its chemical composition.	$H_2O(s) \longrightarrow H_2O(l)$
3. **Nuclear change**	A change in the nucleus contents of one atom to that of another atom	$^{220}Fr \longrightarrow {}^{4}He + {}^{216}At$

In this lesson of Topic 5, only chemical changes and equations will be discussed.

⇐ **LOOKING BACK:** Topic 1 – Matter and energy : Phase changes and equations were discussed.

LOOKING AHEAD ⇨ Topic 12 - Nuclear chemistry: Nuclear changes and equations will be discussed.

20. Chemical equations: Reading and interpreting a chemical equation

A chemical equation uses symbols to show changes in chemical compositions of substances during a chemical change.

A chemical reaction is a mean in which chemical changes occur.

For any chemical equation, the following information can be determined.

Reactants are the starting substances that will go through chemical changes (Shown to the LEFT of arrow in equations)

Products are the substances that are remaining after a change had occurred (Shown to the RIGHT of arrow in equations)

Coefficient is a whole number in front of each substance to show the number of moles (how many units) of each substance is taking part in the reaction.

LOOKING AHEAD ⟹ Topic 6: Moles will be discussed in more details.

Arrow separates Reactants from Products, and can be read as "**yields**" or "**produces**."

Example chemical equation is shown below.

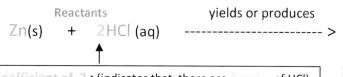

Reactants — yields or produces — Products

$Zn(s) + 2HCl(aq) \longrightarrow ZnCl_2(aq) + H_2(g)$

Coefficient of 2 : (indicates that there are 2 moles of HCl)
Coefficient of Two or more is always written in front of substances in equations.

Coefficient of 1: Indicates that there is 1 mole of $ZnCl_2$.
A coefficient of 1 is never written in front of the substance.

(s), (l), (g), (aq) are sometimes written to show phases of the substances taking part in the reaction.

Topic 5 – Chemical formulas and equations

21. Chemical equation: Determining reactants and products in equation

Concept Task: Be able to identify reactants and /or products from a given equation.

To identify reactants:
 LOOK for a choice of substances to the LEFT of arrow

To identify products:
 LOOK for a choice of substances to the RIGHT of arrow:

Example 37

In the equation

$CH_4 + 2O_2 \longrightarrow CO_2 + 2H_2O$

Which correctly identifies the products?

1) CO_2 and O_2 3) CH_4 and O_2
2) CO_2 and H_2O 4) CH_4 and H_2O

Answer: Choice 2. CO_2 and H_2O are the substances to the RIGHT of the arrow.

22. Chemical equation: Determining coefficient and sums of all coefficient in an equation

Concept Task: Be able to determine number of moles of a substance or the sum of all coefficients in an equation.

To determine coefficient or mole of a substance:
 LOOK at the whole number in front of the substance

To determine sum of all coefficients:
 Identify all coefficients and add them up

NOTE: DO NOT forget to add coefficient of 1, which will not be written in front of a substance in a balanced equation.

Example 38

Given the equation

$2Li + 2H_2O \longrightarrow 2LiOH + H_2$

What is the sum of all coefficients?

1) 10   2) 9   3) 8   4) 7

Before choosing:
 Identify all coefficients and add them up
 $2Li + 2H_2O \longrightarrow 2LiOH + \_H_2$
 $2 + 2 + 2 + 1 = 7$

Answer: Choice 4

23. Type of reactions: Definitions and facts

There are four major types of chemical reactions:

Synthesis reactions always involve two or more substances as reactants. During a synthesis reaction, the reactants combine to form one product.

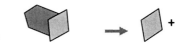

Decomposition reactions always involve one single substance as a reactant. During a decomposition reaction, the reactant breaks down (or decomposes) into two or more products.

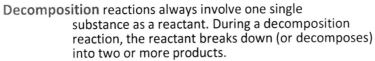

Single replacement reactions likely involve a compound and a free element as reactants. During a single replacement reaction, the free element replaces one of the elements in the compound to form a different compound and a different free element. This reaction occurs only when the free element reactant is more reactive than the similar element in the compound.

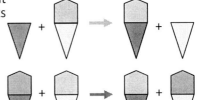

Double replacement reactions usually involve two compounds in aqueous phase. During a double replacement reaction, the ions of compounds switch with each other. The result is a formation of products with two different compound formulas.

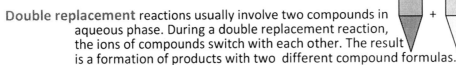

On the next page, you will be given example equation showing each type of reaction defined above.

Topic 5 – Chemical formulas and equations

24. Types of chemical reaction: Example equations and example questions

Below are example equations to represent the different types of reactions defined on the previous page. For each type of reaction, the general equation and example equation are given.

Concept Facts: Be able to relate equation to type of a reaction

Type of reaction	Example chemical reaction equation
Synthesis (Combination)	$2H_2 + O_2 \longrightarrow 2H_2O$
Decomposition (Analysis)	$2H_2O \longrightarrow 2H_2 + O_2$
Single replacement	$Zn + 2HCl \longrightarrow ZnCl_2 + H_2$
Double replacement	$NaCl + AgNO_3 \longrightarrow NaNO_3 + AgCl$

Concept Task: Be able to determine the type of a reaction given an equation.	**Concept Task:** Be able to determine a correct equation given a name of a reaction.
Example 39 *The equation* $$3CaO + P_2O_5 \longrightarrow Ca_3(PO_4)_2$$ *Can be best described as* 1) Synthesis 2) Decomposition 3) Single replacement 4) Double replacement **Answer: Choice 1:** In the equation two compounds, CaO and P_2O_5, are combining to make one single compound, $Ca_3(PO_4)_2$. This is what occurs in synthesis reactions.	**Example 40** *Which of the equation represents a single replacement reaction?* 1) $H^+ + OH^- \longrightarrow H_2O$ 2) $2Cu + O_2 \longrightarrow 2CuO$ 3) $CuCO_3 \longrightarrow CuO + CO_2$ 4) $Ag + 2CuNO_3 \longrightarrow Ag(NO_3)_2 + 2Cu$ **Answer: Choice 4:** The equation is showing a single element (Ag) replacing another element (Cu) in $CuNO_3$ to make $Ag(NO_3)_2$

25. Conservation of atoms in a balanced equation: Definition and fact

Law of conservation states that during a chemical reaction:

. Neither atoms, mass, charge nor energy are created nor destroyed.

This means that during a chemical, atoms, mass, charges, and energy are conserved so that their amounts are the same before and after a reaction.

A Balanced chemical equation is a way of showing **conservation** in chemical reactions.

In the balanced equation below:

$$N_2 + 3H_2 \longrightarrow 2NH_3$$

There are: 2 N   2 N
            6 H   6 H

atoms of reactants (before a reaction) = atoms of products (after a reaction)

A balanced chemical equation contains the correct combinations of smallest whole-number coefficients that allow **number of atoms** on both sides of the equation to be **equal**.

Topic 5 – Chemical formulas and equations

26. Conservation in equation: Determining which equation is balanced.

Concept Task: Be able to determine which equation is balanced (demonstrates conservation).

The only way to determine for sure is to count the number of each atom on both sides of the equation. The equation that is balanced will have an **equal number of each atom on** both sides.

To determine which equation is balanced or demonstrates conservation of atoms:

COUNT the atoms on both sides of each equation

CHOOSE the equation in which atoms are equal on both sides

NOTE: When counting atoms in equations, BE SURE TO COUNT THE NUMBER OF ATOMS CORRECTLY.

Incorrect counting can lead you to choose the wrong choice.

 LOOkING Back: Topic 5- Lesson 1:
You learned how to count atoms in formulas.

Example 41

Which of the following equations is correctly balanced?

1) $CO + O_2 \longrightarrow 2CO_2$
2) $2SO_2 + O_2 \longrightarrow SO_3$
3) $CO + 2O_2 \longrightarrow CO_2$
4) $2SO_2 + O_2 \longrightarrow 2SO_3$

Answer Choice 4. In this equation, there are 2 S atoms and 6 O atoms on each side. This equation demonstrates a conservation of atoms. Conservation of atoms is not demonstrated in choices 1, 2, 3 equations.

27. Balancing equations: How to balance equations.

As mentioned earlier, an equation is balanced when it contains the correct combination of smallest whole number coefficients. The coefficients allow number of each atoms on both sides of an equation to be the same.

On tests, you will be given an equation that is not balanced, and you will be asked to balance the equation. If the question is multiple choice, there will be a follow up question such as " what is the sum of all coefficients?"

To balance an unbalanced equation:

You need to change one or more coefficients in front of the substances in the equation. The right combination of coefficients will make the number of atoms on both sides equal.

Which coefficient should you change and which one shouldn't you change?

What whole number coefficient should you place in front of the substances?

These questions cannot be answered since it all depends on the equation that is given. Some unbalanced equations require a change of just one of the coefficients to make it balanced. Other unbalanced equations may require changing all of the coefficients to make it balanced. It all depends on the equation.

Finding the right combination of coefficients to balance an equation is by trial and error. When a change of one of coefficient does not work, try a different coefficient. The first coefficient you change could be the difference between balancing the equation quickly and correctly, or struggling to balance it.

You will be able to balance some equations quickly because you can see, right away, which coefficients need to be changed, and what the coefficients should be changed to in the equation. In other equations, the changes in coefficients that are needed may not be so obvious. On the next page, a list of helpful suggestions to balancing equations is given. Example equations are balanced using tables to keep tract of atoms.

Topic 5 – Chemical formulas and equations

28. Balancing equations: Helpful suggestions

Helpful suggestions to balancing equations:

- Make a table to keep track of the number of atoms as you change coefficients.
- Always try balancing one atom at a time.
- Every time a coefficient is changed, RECOUNT the number of each atom affected by the change. NOTE the change on the table. (BE SURE TO COUNT ATOMS CORRECTLY)
- Always change coefficients of free elements last. (Free elements are elements that are not bonded to any other atom (Ex. Na and Cl_2 are free elements)
- Be sure that coefficients are in smallest whole-number ratio. That means the coefficients should NOT BE reducible by a common factor.

29. Balancing equations: Balancing equation using the RAP table

Concept Task: Be able to balance equation

When balancing equation, all you need to do is change coefficients. **The use of a table is optional.** However, a table is recommended if you are struggling to balance an equation. By making a table, you can keep track of the number of atoms as the coefficients are being changed.
Below, an unbalanced equation is given. The equation will be balance using a "RAP" table to keep track of the number of atoms. You can always refer to this step-by-step example if you find yourself struggling to balance an equation.

As you study these steps, KEEP IN MIND that the purpose of making a table is to help you keep track of the number of atoms as the coefficients are changed. IF you can balance equation without making a table, you should do so.

Example 42. Balance the equation:
Follow these steps to balance it:

$Li_3N \longrightarrow Li + N_2$

Step 1: Make a RAP Table as shown to the right
. **List Atoms** in the equation (middle column)
. **Count and note** number of each atom on both (Reactants and Products) sides.

R(reactants)	A(atom)	P(products)
3	Li	1
1	N	2

Step 2: Choose one atom to balance.
Decide which atom to balance first.
You need 2 N on the Left

Change coefficient of Li_3N to 2 Li_3N
Recount each atom affected by the change
2Li_3N = 6 Li and 2 N
Write these changes on the Table as shown

$2Li_3N \longrightarrow Li + N_2$

R(reactants)	A(atom)	P(products)
6 3	Li	1
2 1	N	2

Step 3: As you can see, equation is not balance:
Li is not equal on both sides.
You need 6 Li on the right

Change coefficient of Li to 6 Li
Recount each atom affected by the change.
6 Li = 6 Li
Write this change on the table as shown.

$2Li_3N \longrightarrow 6Li + N_2$

R(reactants)	A(atom)	P(products)
6 3	Li	1 6
2 1	N	2

The equation

$2Li_3N \longrightarrow 6Li + N_2$

is balanced. The combination of coefficients 2 : 6 : 1 allows the number of each atom to be equal on both sides (As shown on the RAP table).

Topic 5 – Chemical formulas and equations

30 Balancing equations: Another Table for balancing equation

Concept Task: Be able to balance complicated equations

Below is a more complicated equation to balance than the one on the previous page. This equation contains four different atoms; There are polyatomic ions in the equation. Equations like these may look difficult to balance, however, they can be as easy to balance as those equations with just two atoms. The key, again, is to change one coefficient at a time, and to try balancing one atom a time.

In the equation below, the polyatomic ion PO_4 appears on both sides of the equations. If equation given contains a polyatomic ion that appears on both sides of the equation:

. When listing atoms on a table, Keep the polyatomic ion together as a unit (Do not break up the polyatomic ion into individual elements . (See example and table below)

The equation below is balanced using a different table to keep track of the number of atoms.
As you study the steps, keep in mind that the table is to help you keep track of number of atoms as coefficients are changed. Your goal is to get the right combination of smallest-whole number coefficients to make atoms equal on both sides.

Example 43. Balance the equation $\quad Ca(OH)_2 + H_3PO_4 \text{---------> } Ca_3(PO_4)_2 + H_2O$

Step 1: Make tables as shown

List atoms in the same order on both tables. Keep polyatomic atoms (PO_4) as a unit

Count atoms correctly, and write how many on each tables.

Ca	O	H	PO$_4$
1	2	5	1

Ca	O	H	PO$_4$
3	1	2	2

Step 2: Decide which atom to balance first. If necessary, balance polyatomic (PO_4) ion first.

Change: H_3PO_4 to $2H_3PO_4$
Recount: $2H_3PO_4$: 6H   2PO$_4$
Count H in Ca(OH)$_2$: 2 H
Note total: 8 H   2 PO$_4$

$Ca(OH)_2 + 2H_3PO_4 \text{--------> } Ca_3(PO_4)_2 + H_2O$

Ca	O	H	PO$_4$
1	2	5	1
1	2	8	2

Ca	O	H	PO$_4$
3	1	2	2
3	1	2	2

Step 3: Equation IS NOT balance. You need to change another coefficient.

Try balancing Ca.
Change: Ca(OH)$_2$ to 3Ca(OH)$_2$
Recount: 3Ca(OH)$_2$: 3Ca 6O   6H
Count H in 2H$_3$PO$_4$:   6H
NOTE Total: 3Ca 6O 12H

$3Ca(OH)_2 + 2H_3PO_4 \text{--------> } Ca_3(PO_4)_2 + H_2O$

Ca	O	H	PO$_4$
1	2	5	1
1	2	8	2
3	6	12	2

Ca	O	H	PO$_4$
3	1	2	2
3	1	2	2
3	1	2	2

Step 4: Equation still is not balance.
Try balancing another atom.
Change: H$_2$O to 6H$_2$O
Recount: 6H$_2$O: 12 H   6O
NOTE changes on the right table

$3Ca(OH)_2 + 2H_3PO_4 \text{--------> } Ca_3(PO_4)_2 + 6H_2O$

Ca	O	H	PO$_4$
1	2	5	1
1	2	8	2
3	6	12	2
3	6	12	2

Ca	O	H	PO$_4$
3	2	2	2
3	2	2	2
3	2	2	2
3	6	12	2

With the three changes made to coefficients, the number of atoms on both sides (notice bottom row numbers on the tables) is equal. **Equation above is balanced with coefficients of** 3 : 2 : 1 : 6

Topic 5 – Chemical formulas and equations

31. Balancing equation: Determining coefficient of or the sum of coefficients

When a balancing equation problem is given as a multiple choice question, you are likely to be asked one of the following questions.

1. What is the coefficient in front of one of the substances in the equation?

2. What is the sum of all coefficients?

3. What is the mole ratio of the substances.

To correctly answer any of these questions, you must first balance the given equation correctly. Keep in mind that if you do not balance the equation correctly, you are likely to choose the wrong choice as your answer. If the equation is balanced correctly, any of the above questions is easy to answer correctly.

Two examples multiple questions on balancing equations are given below.

Concept Task: Be able to balance equation and choose the correct coefficient of a substance

Example 44

Given the equation

$$NH_3 + O_2 \longrightarrow HNO_3 + H_2O$$

What is the smallest whole-number coefficient of O_2 when the equation is correctly balanced?

1) 1   2) 2   3) 3   4) 4

Before choosing

Balance the equation correctly: $NH_3 + 2O_2 \longrightarrow HNO_3 + H_2O$

Answer: Choice 2   because O_2 has a coefficient of 2.

Concept Task: Be able to balance equation and choose the correct sum of all coefficients

Example 45

Given the unbalanced equation below:

$$C_3H_4 + O_2 \longrightarrow CO_2 + H_2O$$

What is the sum of all coefficients when the equation is correctly balanced with the smallest whole-number coefficients?

1) 20   2) 9   3) 10   4) 15

Before choosing:

Balance the equation correctly: $C_3H_4 + 4O_2 \longrightarrow 3CO_2 + 2H_2O$

Add up all the coefficients: $1 + 4 + 3 + 2 = 10$

Answer: Choice 3

> **NOTE:** Don't forget to add the coefficient of 1 (C_3H_4 has a coefficient of 1).
> A common mistake made by students, even after they had correctly balance a difficult equation, is forgetting to add a coefficient of 1 to the sum. In the above question, choice 2 (sum of 9) reflects failure to add the coefficient of 1 that is in front of C_3H_4. This would obviously be the wrong answer.
>
> ALWAYS ADD THE COEFFICIENT OF 1 to get the correct sum.

Topic 5 – Chemical formula and equation

Check-A-list

Concept Terms

Below is a list of vocabulary terms from Topic 5. You should know definition and facts related to each term.

Put a check in the box [√] next to each term if you know its definition and other facts related to the term.

[ ] Chemical formula
[ ] Qualitative
[ ] Quantitative
[ ] Subscript
[ ] Molecular formula
[ ] Empirical formula
[ ] Structural formula
[ ] Binary compound
[ ] Polyatomic ion
[ ] Molecular compound

[ ] Chemical equation
[ ] Reactant
[ ] Product
[ ] Coefficient
[ ] Balanced equation
[ ] Law of conservation

If you don't have a check next to a term, look it up or ask your teacher.

Concept Tasks

Below is a list of concept tasks from Topic 5. You should know how to solve problems and answer questions related to each concept task.

Put a check in the box [√] next a concept task if you know how to solve problems and answer questions related to it.

[ ] Determining number of each atom and total number of atoms in simple formulas
[ ] Determining number of an atom and total number of atoms in formulas with parenthesis
[ ] Recognizing empirical formulas
[ ] Determining empirical formula of a given molecular formula
[ ] Writing and recognizing appropriate chemical formulas from binary compound names
[ ] Writing and recognizing appropriate chemical formulas from name containing polyatomic ions
[ ] Writing and recognizing appropriate chemical formulas from names containing Roman numeral
[ ] Writing and recognizing appropriate chemical formula from names containing prefixes
[ ] Naming and recognizing formulas of binary ionic compounds
[ ] Naming and recognizing formulas of compounds containing polyatomic ions
[ ] Naming and recognizing formulas of compounds containing an element with multiple + charges
[ ] Naming and recognizing formulas of compounds containing prefixes
[ ] Determining reactants and products of a chemical equation
[ ] Determining coefficient (number of mole) of a substance in an equation
[ ] Determining sum of all coefficient (total number of moles) in an equation
[ ] Determining mole ratio of substances in an equation
[ ] Determining type of a reaction from equation
[ ] Determining and recognizing equation of a given type of reaction
[ ] Determining which equation is balanced or demonstrates conservation of mass
[ ] Balancing equations

If you do not have a check next to a concept task, look it up or ask your teacher.

Topic 5 – Chemical formula and equation

Concept Fact Review Questions

1. A chemical formula is an expression of
   1) Qualitative composition, only
   2) Quantitative composition, only
   3) Both qualitative and quantitative composition
   4) Neither qualitative nor quantitative composition

2. A type of formula showing the simplest ratio in which atoms are combined is called
   1) A molecular formula
   2) An empirical formula
   3) A structural formula
   4) A condensed formula

3. What is conserve during chemical reactions?
   1) Energy, only
   2) Matter, only
   3) Both matter and energy
   4) Neither matter nor energy

4. Given a balanced chemical equation, it is always possible to determine
   1) Whether a reaction will or will not take place
   2) The conditions necessary for the reaction to take place
   3) The relative number of moles taking place in the reaction
   4) The physical state of the products and reactants

5. Which list is composed only of types of chemical reactions?
   1) Synthesis, decomposition, single replacement
   2) Decomposition, evaporation, and double
   3) Synthesis, decomposition, freezing
   4) Decomposition, melting, combustion

Concept Task Review Questions

6. In the compound, $Ca_3(PO_4)_2$, what is the total number of phosphate ions the formula?
   1) 3   2) 2   3) 8   4) 4

7. The total number of atoms in the hydrate $CuSO_4 \cdot 3H_2O$ is
   1) 9   2) 12   3) 15   4) 24

8. What is the ratio of ammonium ion to sulfate ion in the formula $(NH_4)_2SO_4$?
   1) 2 : 1   2) 1 : 2   3) 8 : 4   4) 4 : 1

9. Which formula is an empirical formula?
   1) H_2CO_3 2) $H_2C_2O_4$ 3) CH_3COOH 4) CH_2OHCH_2OH

10. Which two compounds have the same empirical formula?
    1) C_2H_2 and C_2H_4 2) CH_2 and C_3H_8 3) HO and H_2O 4) NO_2 and N_2O_4

11. Which is the correct formula for iron (II) sulfide?
    1) FeS   2) Fe_5O_3 3) Fe_2S_3 4) $Fe_2(SO_4)_2$

12. The correct name for $NaClO_4$ is sodium
    1) Chloride
    2) Chlorate
    3) Perchlorate
    4) chlorite

13. Which formula is a binary compound?
    1) KOH   2) $NaClO_3$ 3) Al_2S_3 4) $Bi(NO_3)_3$

Topic 5 – Chemical formula and equation

14. What is the simplest ratio of nitrogen to oxygen atom in the compound nitrogen (IV) oxide?
    1) 1 : 2   2) 2 : 1   3) 2 : 4   4) 4 : 2

15. A single replacement reaction is shown in which equation?
    1) $Ca(OH)_2$ + HCl ------------> $CaCl_2$ + H_2O
    2) Ca + $2H_2O$ ----------> H_2 + $Ca(OH)_2$
    3) $2H_2O_2$ --------------------> $2H_2O$ + O_2
    4) $2H_2$ + O_2 --------------> $2H_2O$

16. Which of these equations shows conservation of atoms?
    1) KBr -------> K + Br_2
    2) $2KClO_3$ ------> $2KCl$ + $2O_2$
    3) $CuCO_3$ ---------> CuO + CO_2
    4) $CaCO_3$ -------> CO_2 + $2CaO$

17. Given the incomplete equation:
    $$2N_2O_5 \longrightarrow$$
    Which set of products completes and balances the incomplete equation?
    1) $2N_2 + 3O_2$ 2) $2N_2 + 2O_2$ 3) $4NO_2 + O_2$ 4) $2NO + 2O_2$

18. Given the unbalanced equation:
    ___$Ca(OH)_2$ + ___$(NH_4)_2SO_4$ -----> ___$CaSO_4$ + ___NH_3 + ___H_2O

    What is the sum of all coefficients when the equation is correctly balanced using the smallest whole-number coefficients?
    1) 5   2) 7   3) 9   4) 11

Constructed Response Questions

Answer questions 19 and 20 based on the equation and information below.

19. What is the correct formula for ammonium dichromate?   19.

20. What is the correct IUPAC name for the formula BeO ?   20.

Base your answers to questions 21 through 23 on the equation below.

___ C_2H_6 + ___ O_2 ---------> ___ CO_2 + ___ H_2O

21. Balance the equation above, using the smallest whole number coefficients.

22. What is the sum of all coefficients when the equation is balanced.   22.

23. What type of a chemical reaction is represented by the equation?   23.

Topic 6 – Mole interpretation : Mathematics of Formulas and Equations

Topic outline

In this topic, you will learn about the following concepts:

. Mole interpretation

. Math of formulas
. Gram formula mass calculation
. Mole - mass calculation
. Percent composition
. Molecular formula

. Math of equations
. Mole ratio in balanced equations
. Mole – mole problems
. Volume – volume problems

Lesson 1 – Mole interpretation in Formulas

Introduction

A mole is a unit that describes a quantity of 6.02×10^{23}.

A mole is, therefore, a unit of quantity in the same sense that a dozen refers to a quantity of 12.

Consider the following units of quantities:

1 dozen eggs = 12 eggs

1 gross of apples = 144 apples.

1 mole of atoms = 602000000000000000000000 atoms.

A mole is a very large unit of quantity that is only used to describe quantity of particles (atoms, molecules, ions, or electrons..etc) in chemical substances.

The number, 602000000000000000000000, is called the Avogadro's number.
It is always written in its scientific notation form: 6.02×10^{23}

$$1 \text{ mole} = 6.02 \times 10^{23}$$

1. Mole interpretations in chemistry questions

The term "mole" shows up often in chemistry questions that involve formulas and equations. How you interpret the term "mole" in a question depends on the context in which it is being used in that question.

Below are example questions in which the term "mole" is used.

Question 1: How many moles of hydrogen are in 1 mole of the formula H_3PO_4?

Question 2: What is the mass of one mole of H_3PO_4?

Question 3: What is the mole ratio of H_2 to O_2 in the equation: $2H_2 + O_2 \longrightarrow 2H_2O$

The mole terminology is used in a slightly different sense in each question.
Your ability to answer the above questions correctly depends on your understanding of mole concepts and its many interpretations.

In this lesson, you will learn about mole concepts and its interpretations in chemical formulas.

Topic 6 – Mole interpretation : Mathematics of formulas and Equations

2. Mole of atoms in formulas : Determining the number of moles of atoms in formulas

The number of moles of atoms in a given formula can be determined by counting how many atoms there are in the formula.

⬅ L👀king Back: **Topic 5: Chemical formulas.** You learned how to count atoms in formulas.

However, when there are more (or less) than one mole of a formula, determining the number of moles of atoms becomes a little bit more involved than just counting atoms.

Concept Task: Be able to determine the number of moles of each atom in a given mole of formula

  To determine number of moles of any atom in a formula:

  Count how many of the atom is in the formula.
  Multiply the number of that atom by the given number of moles of the formula.

  Number of mole of each atom = Given moles   x   Number of the atom in the formula

Concept Task: Be able to determine the total number of moles of atoms in a given formula

  To determine total number of moles atoms:

  Determine how many moles of each atom
  Add up all the moles of atoms

  Total number of moles of atoms = Sum of all the moles of atoms

NOTE: YOU MUST COUNT ATOMS CORRECTLY IN THE GIVEN FORMULA:

In examples below, different numbers of moles of two formulas are given below.
You are shown how to determine the number of moles of each **atom and the** total number of moles of atoms in each formula.
Study these examples to learn how to do the same for any given formula.

Example 1
1 mole of $Al_2(SO_4)_3$ consists of
  1   x   2 Al   =   2 moles of Al atoms
  1   x   3 S   =   3 moles of S atoms
  1   x   12 O =   12 moles of O atoms

  Total moles of atoms = 17 moles of atoms
                  in 1 mole of $Al_2(SO_4)_3$

Example 2
2 moles of $Al_2(SO_4)_3$ consist of:
  2   x   2 Al   =   4 moles of Al atoms
  2   x   3 S   =   6 moles of S atoms
  2   x   12 O =   24 moles of

  Total moles of atoms = 34 moles of atoms
                  in 2 moles $Al_2(SO_4)_3$

Example 3
1 mole of $CaCO_3 \cdot 2H_2O$ consists of:
  1   x   1 Ca   =   1 mole of Ca atoms
  1   x   1 C   =   1 mole of C atoms
  1   x   5 O   =   5 moles of O atoms
  1   x   4 H   =   4 moles of H atoms

  Total moles of atoms = 11 moles of atoms
                  in 1 mole $CaCO_3 \cdot 2H_2O$

Example 4
0.5 mole of $CaCO_3 \cdot 2H_2O$ consists of
  0.5   x   1 Ca   =   0.5 mole of Ca atoms
  0.5   x   1 C   =   0.5 mole of C atoms
  0.5   x   5 O   =   2.5 moles of O atoms
  0.5   x   4 H   =   2.0 moles of H atoms

  Total moles of atoms = 5.5 moles of atoms
                  in 0.5 mole $CaCO_3 \cdot 2H_2O$

Topic 6 – Mole interpretation : Mathematics of formulas and Equations

3. Molar Mass – The mass of 1 mole of a substance: Definition and facts:

Molar mass of a substance is the mass, in grams, of 1 mole of that substance
What does this means?
RECALL that one mole of a substance contains 6.02×10^{23} of particles (atom, molecule, or ion) found in that substance.

For example: Water is composed of water molecules.
. One mole of water contains 6.02×10^{23} (602000000000000000000000) molecules of water.
(That's a lot of molecules).
. **Molar mass of water** is known to be 18 grams. That is to say:
If you put 6.02×10^{23} molecules of water on a scale and weigh it, it will weigh exactly 18 grams.

Below are different variations of molar mass. You will learn how to determine each in the next few sets.

Atomic mass specifically refers to the mass of 1 mole of an element.
Formula mass is commonly used when referring to the mass of 1 mole of an ionic substance.
Molecular mass is commonly used when referring to the mass of 1 mole of a molecular substance.

Regardless of the formula, the mass of one mole of a substance is easy to determine.
You are shown how to do so in the following two sets.

4. Atomic mass: Determining gram atomic mass of elements

Concept Task: Be able to determine the gram atomic mass of an element.

Note and Use the following to determine gram atomic mass of an element

Atomic mass = mass of 1 mole of atoms = Atomic mass of the element on the Periodic Table

To determine the gram-atomic mass of an element
LOOK on the Periodic Table for its atomic mass.

In the notes below, you are shown how to determine the gram atomic masses of two elements.
Study this example to learn how to determine gram atomic mass of any element.

Element	Atomic mass (Atomic mass on the Periodic Table
Mg (Magnesium) =	24.305 g
Kr (Krypton) =	83.80 g

Atomic mass → 83.80
Kr
36

Example 5
Which of these elements has the greatest gram-atomic mass?
1) Br   2) Ge   3) Fe   4) Ca

Before Choosing:
LOOK up mass of the each element on the Periodic Table.
Br	Ge	Fe	Ca
79.9g	72.6g	55.8g	40.1g

Answer: Choice 1

Topic 6 – Mole interpretation : Mathematics of formulas and Equations

5. Formula (or molecular) mass: Determining mass of 1 mole of a formula

Concept Task: Be able to determine the formula or molecular mass of a given compound

NOTE and USE the following relationship to determine gram-formula mass.

> Formula mass = Mass of 1 mole of a formula = The sum of all atomic mass in a formula

To determine formula or molecular mass of a substance

Determine the number of each element in the formula
Multiply number of each element by their atomic mass (from Periodic Table)
Add up the total mass of all the elements in the formula to get the formula mass.

What is the Formula mass of H_2O $Al(OH)_3$ $NaNO_3 \cdot 4H_2O$?
Below, gram-formula mass of these four formulas are calculated.
Study the step-by step set up to learn how to calculate gram-formula mass of any formula.

		step 1 Determine number of each atom	step 2 multiply by (atomic mass) =	Total mass of each atom =	step 3 Find Formula mass (Add up all masses)
Example 6	H_2O	2 H 1 O	2 (1) 1 (16)	2 g 16 g	+ → **18 g** Formula mass of water
Example 7	$Al(OH)_3$	1 Al 3 O 3 H	1 (27) 3 (16) 3 (1)	27 g 48 g 3 g	+ → **78 g** Formula mass of $Al(OH)_3$
Example 8	$NaNO_3 \cdot 4H_2O$	1 Na 1 N 7 O 8 H	1 (23) 1 (14) 7 (16) 8 (1)	23 g 14 g 112 g 8 g	+ → **157 g** Formula mass of $NaNO_3 \cdot 4H_2O$

You can make a table like the one below to set up and calculate formula mass of a substance.

Example 9 What is the formula mass of $(NH_4)_2SO_4$

Atoms	Atomic mass (from periodic Table)	X	How many (count atoms)	=	Mass (of each atom)
N	14		2		28
H	1		8		8
S	32		1		32
O	16		4		64

132 g = formula mass of $(NH_4)_2SO_4$

NOTE: To Calculate formula mass of a substance correctly: You must:
. Count number of each atom correctly
. Multiply by the correct (rounded) atomic mass
. Add up all the masses correctly

Error in any of these steps will lead to incorrect formula mass.

Topic 6 – Mole interpretation : Mathematics of formulas and Equations

6. Mass – mole relationship: Understanding the relationship between mass and moles

Remember that the mass of one mole of a substance is the formula mass of that substance. In another word, 6.02×10^{23} particles (one mole) of a given substance will always weigh a mass equal to its formula mass. What if there is more than one mole of that substance? In another word, what if there are more than 6.02×10^{23} particles of that substance in a given sample. It makes sense to think that a sample containing more than one mole of the substance (more than 6.02×10^{23} particles) will have a mass that is greater than its formula mass. A sample containing less than one mole of the substance (less than 6.02×10^{23} particles) will have a mass that is less than its formula mass.

7. Mass from moles calculation: Calculating mass of a given moles of a substance

Concept Task: Be able to calculate the mass of a given number of moles of a substance

Reference Table T equation:

$$\text{Moles given} = \frac{\text{Mass}}{\text{Formula mass}} \quad \text{OR} \quad \text{Mass} = \text{moles given} \times \text{formula mass}$$

To calculate the mass of any given number of mole of a substance:

Determine the formula mass of the substance (As shown on last page).
Multiply the number of moles in question by formula mass you determined.

Below, different numbers of moles of substances are given in the example problems.
Each problem is setup and the mass is calculated.
Study the steps in these examples to learn how to calculate mass for any given mole of a substance.

Step 1: Determine formula mass

Example 10

What is the mass of 0.25 mole of HNO_3?

Mass = mole × Formula mass of HNO_3
Mass = 0.25 × 63 = 15.75
Mass of 0.25 mole of HNO_3 = 15.75 g

Formula mass of HNO_3:			
1 H	1(1)	=	1
1 N	1(14)	=	14
3 O	3(16)	=	48
Mass of 1 mole (formula mass)		**=**	**63g**

Example 11

What is the mass of 2 moles of $Mg(C_2H_3O_2)_2$?

Mass = mole × Formula-mass of $Mg(C_2H_3O_2)_2$
Mass = 2 × 118 = 236
Mass of 2 moles of $Mg(C_2H_3O_2)_2$ = 236 g

Formula mass of $Mg(C_2H_3O_2)_2$			
1 Mg	1(24)	=	24
2 C	2(12)	=	24
6 H	6(1)	=	6
4 O	4(16)	=	64
Mass of 1 mole (formula mass)		**=**	**118 g**

Example 12

What is the mass of 1 mole of $H_2SO_4 \cdot 3H_2O$
Mass = mole × Formula-mass
Mass = 1 × 126 = 126
Mass of 1 mole of $H_2SO_4 \cdot 3H_2O$ = 126 g

Formula mass of $H_2SO_4 \cdot H_2O$			
4 H	4(1)	=	4
1 S	1(32)	=	32
5 O	5(16)	=	90
Mass of 1 mole (formula mass)		**=**	**126 g**

Step 2: Substitute formula mass into equation (as shown to the see left)

NOTE: You MUST calculate the formula mass correctly or your calculated mass (answer) will be wrong.

Copyright © 2010 E3 Scholastic Publishing. All Rights Reserved.

Topic 6 – Mole interpretation : Mathematics of formulas and Equations

8. Mole – mass calculation: Understanding the relationship between moles and mass

As mentioned earlier, a formula mass of a substance is the mass of one mole (or 6.02×10^{23} particles) of a substance. It makes sense to think that if a sample of a substance weighs less than its formula mass, there is less than one mole (less than 6.02×10^{23} particles) of that substance in the sample. If a sample of a substance weighs more than its formula mass, there are more than one mole (or more than 6.02×10^{23} particles) of that substance in the sample.

9. Moles calculation from mass: Calculating moles from a given mass of a substance.

Concept Task: Be able to calculate number of the moles of a substance from a given mass of the substance.

Note and Use Reference Table T equation below

$$\text{Number of moles} = \frac{\text{Given mass}}{\text{Formula mass}}$$

Reference Table T equation

To determine number of moles from mass of a substance:

Determine the formula mass of the substance
Divide the mass given in the question by the formula or the atomic mass you determined

Below, mass of substances is given in each example problem.
Each problem is setup and the number of moles is calculated.
Study the steps, the setup and calculation for each problem to learn to do the same for similar problems.

Example 13:
What is the number of moles in a 32.7-gram sample of zinc?

$$\text{Moles} = \frac{\text{Given mass of Zinc}}{\text{Atomic mass of zinc}}$$

$$\text{Moles} = \frac{32.7}{65.4} = 0.5 \text{ mole}$$

Step 1: Determine formula mass

Atomic mass of Zn = **65.4 g**
(Found on the Periodic Table)

Example 14
What is the number of moles of O_2 in 96 grams of the substance?

$$\text{Moles} = \frac{\text{Given mass of } O_2}{\text{Formula mass of } O_2}$$

$$\text{Moles} = \frac{96}{32} = 3.0 \text{ moles}$$

Molecular mass of O_2

2 O   2 (16) = **32 g**

Example 15
What are the number of moles in 77.5 grams of $Ca_3(PO_4)_2$?

$$\text{Moles} = \frac{\text{Given mass of the } Ca_3(PO_4)_2}{\text{Formula mass of } Ca_3(PO_4)_2}$$

$$\text{Moles} = \frac{77.5}{310} = 0.25 \text{ mole}$$

Formula mass of $Ca_3(PO_4)_2$

3 Ca   3 (40) = 120 g
2 P   2 (31) = 62 g
8 O   8 (16) = 128 g

Gram formula mass of $Ca_3(PO_4)_2$ = 310 g

Step 2: Substitute formula-mass into equation and solve (SEE LEFT for work)

Topic 6 – Mole interpretation : Mathematics of formulas and Equations

10. Percent composition: Determining the percent by mass of each element in formulas

Percent composition **by mass** indicates what portion of a mass of a substance is due to the mass of an individual element in its formula.

Concept Task: Be able to calculate percent composition of elements in a formula

Note and Use the Reference Table T equation below to calculate percent composition

Reference Table T equation

$$\text{Percent composition} = \frac{\text{Total mass of the element in a formula}}{\text{Formula mass of the given formula}} \times 100$$

To determine percent composition of any element in a formula:
  Determine the total mass of each element in the formula
  Add up all masses to get the formula mass
  Divide the mass of the element in the question **by** the formula mass, then multiply by 100

Below, two formulas are given. Percent by mass of each element in the formulas is calculated in three steps.
Study the steps, setups, and calculations of the examples to learn how to calculate percent composition.

Example 16

What is the percent composition of each element in the $MgCl_2$?

$\% \text{ Mg} = \dfrac{\text{Total mass of Mg}}{\text{Formula mass of MgCl}_2} \times 100$

$\% \text{ Mg} = \dfrac{24}{94} \times 100 = 25.5\%$

$\% \text{ Cl} = \dfrac{\text{Total mass of Cl}}{\text{Formula mass of MgCl}_2} \times 100$

$\% \text{ Cl} = \dfrac{70}{94} \times 100 = 74.5\%$

Step 1: Determine the total mass of each element in $MgCl_2$
  $1 \text{ Mg} = 1(24) = 24 \text{ g}$
  $2 \text{ Cl} = 2(35) = 70 \text{ g}$

Step 2: Determine formula mass of $MgCl_2$ = **94 g**

Step 3: Calculate % of each element
  . Put mass of each element and formula-mass into equation
  (as shown to the left)

Example 17

What is the percent by mass of each element in $Ba(NO_3)_2$?

$\% \text{ Ba} = \dfrac{\text{Total mass of Ba}}{\text{Formula mass of Ba(NO}_3)_2} \times 100$

$\% \text{ Ba} = \dfrac{137}{261} \times 100 = 52.5\%$

$\% \text{ N} = \dfrac{\text{Total mass of N}}{\text{Formula mass of Ba(NO}_3)_2} \times 100$

$\% \text{ N} = \dfrac{28}{261} \times 100 = 10.7\%$

$\% \text{ O} = \dfrac{\text{Total mass of O}}{\text{Formula mass of Ba(NO}_3)_2} \times 100$

$\% \text{ O} = \dfrac{96}{261} \times 100 = 36.8\%$

Step 1: Determine the total mass of each element in the formula $Ba(NO_3)_2$
  $1 \text{ Ba} = 1(137) = 137 \text{ g}$
  $2 \text{ N} = 2(14) = 28 \text{ g}$
  $6 \text{ O} = 6(16) = 96 \text{ g}$

Step 2: Determine formula mass of $Ba(NO_3)_2$ = **261 g**
  (add up masses in step 1)

Step 3: Calculate % of each element
  .Substitute mass of each element and formula-mass into equation (as shown to the left)

Topic 6 – Mole interpretation : Mathematics of formulas and Equations

11. Percent composition of hydrates: Calculating the percent of water in a hydrate

Hydrates are groups of ionic compounds that contain water within their crystalline structures.

Example formulas and names of some common hydrates are given below:

$CaCl_2 \cdot 2H_2O$ Calcium chloride dihydrate   (dihydrate means $2H_2O$)

$MgSO_4 \cdot 7H_2O$ Magnesium sulfate heptahydrate   (heptahydrate means $7H_2O$)

$CuSO_4 \cdot 5H_2O$ Copper sulfate pentahydrate   (pentahydrate means $5H_2O$)

A particle of $CuSO_4 \cdot 5H_2O$

Formula mass (mass of 1 mole) of a hydrate is due in parts to the mass of the water.

Concept Task: Be able to calculate percent by mass of water in a hydrate

Percent composition of the water in a hydrate can be calculated using the equation below.

$$\text{Percent } H_2O \text{ in a hydrate} = \frac{\text{Total mass of } H_2O}{\text{Formula mass of the hydrate}} \times 100$$

To determine percent of water in a hydrate:
- **Determine** Total mass of water
- **Determine** the formula mass of the hydrate.
- **Divide** the mass of water by the formula mass of the hydrate, then multiply by 100

Below, percentages of water in two hydrates are calculated. **Study** the steps, set up, and the calculation of percent of water in these two examples to learn how to do the same for other hydrates

Example 18
What is the percent of water in the hydrate $CaCl_2 \cdot 2H_2O$

$\% \ H_2O = \dfrac{\text{Total mass of } H_2O}{\text{Formula mass of } CaCl_2 \cdot H_2O} \times 100$

$\% \ H_2O = \dfrac{36}{146} \times 100 = \mathbf{27\%}$

Step 1: Determine mass of water in $CaCl_2 \cdot 2H_2O$
$2H_2O = 4H = 4(1) = 4 \text{ g}$
$ 2O = 2(16) = 32 \text{ g}$
Total mass of $2H_2O = 36 \text{ g}$

Step 2: Determine formula mass of $CaCl_2 \cdot 2H_2O$
$1 Ca = 1(40) = 40 \text{ g}$
$2 Cl = 2(35) = 70 \text{ g}$
$4 H = 4(1) = 4 \text{ g}$
$2 O = 2(16) = 32 \text{ g}$
Formula mass $= 146 \text{ g}$

Step 3: Substitute mass into equation to find % of H_2O (see work on left)

Example 19
What is the percent by mass of H_2O in the hydrate $MgSO_4 \cdot 7H_2O$

$\% \ H_2O = \dfrac{\text{Total mass of } H_2O}{\text{Formula mass of } MgSO_4 \cdot 7H_2O} \times 100$

$\% \ H_2O = \dfrac{126}{246} \times 100 = \mathbf{51\%}$

Mass of $7H_2O = 7 \text{ (mass of 1 } H_2O)$
$7(18 \text{ g}) = 126 \text{ g}$
Total mass of $H_2O = 126 \text{ g}$

Formula mass of $MgSO_4 \cdot 7H_2O$
$1 Mg = 1(24) = 24 \text{ g}$
$1 S = 1(32) = 32 \text{ g}$
$4 O = 4(16) = 64 \text{ g}$
$7 H_2O = 7(18) = 126 \text{ g}$
Formula mass $= 246 \text{ g}$

Topic 6 – Mole interpretation : Mathematics of formulas and Equations

12. Percent composition of hydrates. Calculating percent of water using experimental data

A **hydrate** can be heated to remove its water (by evaporation) in a laboratory experiment.
Anhydrous is a hydrate with its water removed. If the mass of a hydrate and of the anhydrous are known, the mass of water that was in the hydrate can be determined. From this mass, percent of water in the hydrate can be calculated.

NOTE the following equation for calculating percent of water in hydrates:

$$\% \text{ water} = \frac{\text{Mass of water}}{\text{Mass of hydrate}} \times 100$$

Concept Task: Be able to calculate percent composition of water in a hydrate from lab information

Two example problems of calculating percent of water from lab data are given below.
Study the steps the set up, and the calculation for each example to learn how to do the same.

Example 20
A 2.8 grams sample of a hydrated substance is heated until all the water of hydration is driven off. The substance remaining in the evaporation dish has a mass of 2.1 grams. What is the percent of water in the hydrate?

$\% \text{ water} = \dfrac{\text{Mass of water}}{\text{Mass of hydrate}} \times 100$

$\% \text{ water} = \dfrac{0.7}{2.8} \times 100 = 25\%$

Step 1: Determine the mass of water:
Mass of water = mass of hydrate – Mass anhydrous
Mass of water = 2.8 – 2.1 = 0.7 g

Step 2: Calculate percent of water:
Substitute masses into equation as shown to the left

Example 21
During a laboratory experiment to determine percent of water in a hydrate, a student collected the following data.

Mass of evaporated dish	32.5 g
Mass of hydrate + dish	37.5 g
Mass of anhydrous + dish	35.8 g

What is the percent of water in the hydrate?

$\% \text{ of water} = \dfrac{\text{Mass of water}}{\text{Mass of hydrate}} \times 100$

$\% \text{ of water} = \dfrac{1.7}{5.0} \times 100 = 52 \%$

Step 1: Use data to determine mass of hydrate and mass of water.

Mass of hydrate = 37.5 – 32.5 = 5.0 g
Mass of anhydrous = 35.8 – 32.5 = 3.3 g

Mass of water = Hydrate – anhydrous
Mass of water = 5.0 – 3.3 = 1.7 g

Step 2: Substitute masses in the equation to calculate percent of water in the hydrate (SEE LEFT for work)

Topic 6 – Mole interpretation : Mathematics of formulas and Equations

13. Molecular formula: Determining molecular formula from molecular mass and empirical formula

Molecular formula of a substance shows the true composition of a substance.
For example, water has a molecular formula of H_2O. This formula shows the true composition of water.
Molecular mass (mass of 1 mole) of water (18 grams) is the mass calculated from this formula.
Empirical formula of a substance shows atoms in a formula in their lowest ratio.

Concept Task: Be able to determine a molecular formula of a substance from a molecular mass and an empirical formula

Two example questions on determining molecular formula from mass and empirical formula.
Molecular formula in each problem is determined using a few steps.
Study the steps, the set up, and the calculations for both examples to learn how to do the same.

Example 22. NOTE: This is not a multiple choice question
A substance has a molecular mass of 116 and empirical formula of C_2H_5. What is the molecular formula of this substance?

As you study the three steps below, **KEEP IN MINE** the purpose of going through these steps:
You are looking to determine JUST ONE molecular formula that has a mass of exactly 116 g, and can be reduced to the given empirical formula C_2H_5.

Step 1: Determine the mass of the empirical formula: C_2H_5 2C   2(12) = 24
                                                                5 H   5(1) = 5   } 29 g

Step 2: Determine how many empirical formula
there are in the given molecular mass $= \dfrac{\text{Molecular mass}}{\text{Empirical formula mass (step 1)}} = \dfrac{116}{29} = 4$

Step 3: Determined molecular formula by:
Multiplying each subscript of empirical formula by step 2 answer (4) :   4(C_2H_5)

$$\text{Molecular formula} = C_8H_{20}$$

Example 23. NOTE : This is a multiple choice type question.
What is the molecular formula of a substance with a molecular mass 54 g and an empirical formula of C_2H_3?

1) C_2H_3 2) C_6H_9 3) C_4H_6 4) C_3H_2

SUGGESTIONS:
On multiple choice questions, you can:
  A. Use the three steps in example 1 to figure out the correct molecular formula.
     OR
  B. Go through each choice and **eliminate** any choice that neither has the molecular mass given nor the empirical formula given.

Eliminate the following wrong choices:
Choice 1. Wrong because C_2H_3 has the empirical formula of C_2H_3, **BUT**, its mass is NOT 54 g
Choice 2. Wrong because C_6H_9 has the empirical formula of C_2H_3, **BUT**, its mass is NOT 54 g
Choice 4. Wrong because C_3H_2 neither has the empirical formula of C_2H_3 **NOR** a mass of 54 g

Answer: Choice 3. Correct because C_4H_6 has empirical formula of C_2H_3 AND a mass of 54

Topic 6 – Mole interpretation : Mathematics of formulas and Equations

Lesson 2 – Mole interpretation in Equations

Introduction:

> ⬅️ **LOOKING BACK: Topic 5 : Chemical equation.** You learned about equations.
>
> **Recall** that a chemical equation shows changes that are taking place in a chemical reaction.
>
> **A balanced chemical equation** is a recipe for changing one or more chemical substances to different substances.
>
> **Consider the equation:** $N_2 + 3H_2 \longrightarrow 2NH_3$
>
> This balanced equation reads as a recipe in the following way:
>
> To make 2 moles of ammonia ($2NH_3$), 1 mole of nitrogen (N_2) is needed to combine (or react) with 3 moles of hydrogen ($3H_2$).
>
> A balanced chemical equation shows substances that are reacting and are being produced, and also the mole proportions (or mole ratios) of the substances in the reaction. Knowing the mole ratio of reacting substances in a balanced equation, you can make any number of moles of the products by combining **more** or **less** of reactants in the same proportion.
>
> In this lesson, you will learn how to solve problems that involved mole proportions in chemical equations.

14. Mole ratio: Determining the mole ratio of substances in a balanced equation

RECALL that the coefficients in front of substances in a balanced equation indicate number of moles of the substances.

Concept Task: Be able to determine mole ratio of substances in a balanced equation.

To determine mole ratio **of substances in a reaction:**
  Indicate the coefficients of the substances in the question.

  NOTE: If the coefficients you indicated are reducible, be sure to reduce them with a common greatest factor (CGF).

Below, an example equation is given.

$4NH_3 + 5O_2 \longrightarrow 4NO + 6H_2O$

Mole ratios (proportions) of substances in the equation are listed below.

Study the mole ratios for this equation to learn to do the same for any given equation.

  Mole ratio of NH_3 to O_2 is 4 : 5
  Mole ratio of NH_3 to NO is 1 : 1
    (reduced from 4 : 4)
  Mole ratio of NO to H_2O is 2 : 3
    (reduced from 4 : 6)

Example 24

In the balanced equation below:

$2KClO_3 \longrightarrow 2KCl + 3O_2$

What is the mole ratio of $KClO_3$ decomposed to O_2 produced?

1) 2 : 2   2) 1 : 3   3) 2 : 3   4) 2 : 5

Answer: Choice 3 : $2KClO_3$ and $3O_2$
    Mole ratio   2   :   3

Example 25

Given the balanced equation

$2C_2H_6 + 7O_2 \longrightarrow 4CO_2 + 6H_2O$

What is the mole ratio of C_2H_6 combusted to that of H_2O produced in the reaction?

1) 4 : 6   2) 1 : 3   3) 3 : 1   4) 1 : 1

Answer: Choice 2 : $2C_2H_6$ to $6H_2O$
Mole (coefficient) ratio: 2   to   6
Reduce ratio by CGF of 2:   1   to   3

Copyright © 2010 E3 Scholastic Publishing. All Rights Reserved.

Topic 6 – Mole interpretation : Mathematics of formulas and Equations

15. Balance chemical equations: Understanding and relating equations to recipe

As noted in the introduction, a balanced chemical equation is a recipe for making chemical substances. The coefficients give you the mole proportion of substances reacting and being produced.

Consider this recipe that shows proportion of cake mix to eggs needed for making 24 cupcakes.

   1 box cake mix   +   3 eggs   -------> 24 cup cakes

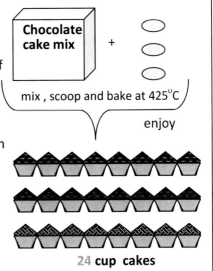

It is understandable that if 48 cup cakes are to be made, the amount of cake mix and eggs must be changed.

Many of you can determine how many boxes of cake mix and the number of eggs that are needed to make 48 cup cakes.
Since 48 cup cakes is twice (or doubled) the number of cupcakes (24) in the recipe, every ingredient in the recipe must be doubled. 48 cup cakes, therefore, requires 2 boxes of cake mix and 6 eggs. The math involved in figuring these out is simple algebra.

When there is no clear relationship between the number of cupcakes you need to make and the number of cupcakes in the recipe, then it is necessary to set up the problem using proportion to solve it.
For example, to make 32 cup cakes, it will be necessary to set up proportion to solve for the number of eggs and cake mix you will need.
The set up to figuring out the how much ingredient to make 32 cup cakes are as follows.

To determine how many eggs to make 32 cupcakes?:

3 eggs	=	24 cupcakes	
X eggs	=	32 cupcakes	
24 X	=	96	(cross multiply)
$\dfrac{24 X}{24}$	=	$\dfrac{96}{24}$	(divide both sides by 24)
X	=	4 eggs	needed to make 32 cupcakes

To determine how many boxes of cake mix to make 32 cupcakes:

1 box	=	24 cupcakes	
X	=	32 cupcakes	
24 X	=	32	(cross multiply)
$\dfrac{24 X}{24}$	=	$\dfrac{32}{24}$	(divide both sides by 24)
X	=	1.33	($1\,{}^{1}/_{3rd}$) **boxes** of cake mix are needed to make 32 cupcakes.

In the next few sections, you will apply the same method to solving mole problems in balanced chemical equations.

Topic 6 – Mole interpretation : Mathematics of formulas and Equations

16. Mole – mole problems: Calculating the number of moles of substance in equation

In mole to mole problems, you will be given:
- A balanced chemical equation (A recipe for making chemical substances)
- A follow up question that gives a different number of moles of one the substances in the equation.
- You'll be asked to determine a number of moles of another substance in the equation.

To determine, You can:
- **Think the problem through** based on proportion (See example 1 below)
- **Set up proportion** and solve (See example 2 below)

Concept Task: Be able to solve mole to mole problem in a balanced chemical equation

Below, a typical mole – mole multiple choice question is given
The problem is solved by just thinking the question through.
Study and learn how this is done so you'll be able solve similar problems.

Example 26:

Given the balanced equation below:

$$2 C + 3 H_2 \longrightarrow C_2H_6$$

How many moles of C is needed to react with 12 moles of H_2?

1) 2 moles   2) 6 moles   3) 24 moles   4) 8 moles

JUST THINK: What is the relationship between the 12 moles of H_2 (in the follow up question) to the 3 moles of H_2 (in the equation)?
The 12 moles of H_2 in question is **4** times the 3 moles of H_2 in the balanced equation.
Therefore,
The number of moles of C that is needed MUST also be **4** times the number of moles of C (2 moles) in the balanced equation.
8 moles of C (**4** times the 2 moles in equation) are needed.

Answer: Choice 4

Below, a typical mole-mole short answer type question is given .
Study how the number of moles is determined using proportion set up.

Example 27. You can solve by setting up a proportion.

Given the balanced equation below:

$$2 KClO_3 \longrightarrow 2 KCl + 3 O_2$$

What is the total number of moles of O_2 produced when 5.5 moles of $KClO_3$ is decomposed?
Show set up and solve.

Step 1: Rewrite the equation	$2 KClO_3 \longrightarrow 2 KCl$	$+ 3 O_2$
Step 2: Write X and the given number of moles (5.5) underneath the substances (O_2 and $KClO_3$) mentioned in the follow up question.	5.5	X
Step 3: Write out the proportion and solve	$\dfrac{2}{5.5}$ =	$\dfrac{3}{X}$
(cross multiply to get)	2X =	16.5
(divide both sides by 2)	$\dfrac{2X}{2}$	$\dfrac{16.5}{2}$
	X =	8.25 moles of O_2 produced

Topic 6 – Mole interpretation: Mathematics of formulas and Equations

17. Volume – Volume problems: Calculating the volume of substance in equation

In volume to volume problems, you'll be given:
. A balanced chemical equation (A recipe for making chemical substances)
. A follow up question that gives a volume of a substance in the equation.
. You'll be asked to determine the volume of another substance in the equation.

To determine, You can:
Think the problem through based on proportion (See example 1 below)
Set up proportion and solve (See example 2 below)

Concept Task: Be able to solve volume to volume problem in a balanced chemical equation

A typical volume to volume multiple choice question is given below.
The problem is solved by just thinking the question through.
Study and learn how this is done so you'll be able solve similar problems the same way.

Example 28:

Given the balanced equation below:
$$C_3H_8 + 5O_2 \longrightarrow 3CO_2 + 4H_2O$$

How much volume of propane, C_3H_8, will react to produce 9 liters of CO_2?

1) 12 liters   2) 9 liters   3) 45 liters   4) 3 liters

JUST THINK: What is the relationship between the 9 liters of CO_2 (in the follow up question) to the 3 moles of CO_2 (in the equation)?
The 9 liters of CO_2 in question is **3** times the 3 moles of CO_2 in the balanced equation.
Therefore,
The Volume of C_3H_8 that will react MUST also be **3** times the number of moles of C_3H_8 (1 moles) in the balanced equation.
3 moles of C_3H_8 (**3** times the 1 mole in equation) must react

Answer: Choice 2

A typical volume – volume short answer question is given below.
The problem is solved by setting a proportion.
Study and learn how this is done so you'll be able solve similar problems the same way.

Example 29. You can solve by setting up a proportion.

Given the balanced equation below:
$$C_3H_8 + 5O_2 \longrightarrow 3CO_2 + 4H_2O$$

How much volume of oxygen, O_2, will react to produce 13 liters of CO_2?
Show set up and solve.

Step 1: Rewrite equation $C_3H_8 + 5O_2 \longrightarrow 3CO_2 + 4H_2O$
Step 2: Write X and the given volume (13)
underneath the substances (O_2 and CO_2)   X   13
mentioned in the follow up question
Step 3: Write out the proportion and solve $\dfrac{5}{X} = \dfrac{3}{13}$

NOTICE in step 2 how the proportion is very much set when X and the given volume (13) are written *directly underneath* the correct two substances (O_2 and CO_2) mentioned in the question.

(cross multiply to get) $3X = 65$

(divide both sides by 2) $\dfrac{3X}{3} = \dfrac{65}{3}$

          $X = 21.7$ liters
          of O_2 will react

Topic 6 – Mole interpretation: Mathematics of formulas and Equations

18. Mass – Mass problems: Calculating the mass of a substance in equation

In mass to mass problems, you'll be given:
- A balanced chemical equation (A recipe for making chemical substances)
- A follow up question that gives a mass of a substance in the equation.
- You'll be asked to determine the mass of another substance in the equation.

To determine, you must :
Set up mass proportion and solve

Unlike the previous two types of problems (mole – mole and volume – volume), mass – mass problems should solved by using mass proportion. Mass proportion is set up differently from the two previous proportions.

Concept Task: Be able to solve mass to mass problem in a balanced chemical equation.

A typical mass – mass problem is given below is given below.
The problem is solved by setting up mass proportion.
Study and learn how this is done so you'll be able solve similar problems the same way.

Example 30

Given the balanced equation below:

$$2 KClO_3 \longrightarrow 2 KCl + 3 O_2$$

How many grams (mass) of KCl is produced by decomposing 100 g of $KClO_3$
Show set up and solve.

Step 1: Re-write equation

$$2 KClO_3 \longrightarrow 2 KCl + 3 O_2$$

Step 2: Write X and the given mass (100 g) underneath the two substances (KCl and $KClO_3$) mentioned in the question.

100   X

Step 3: Set up mass proportion equation

$$\frac{\text{Mass of } 2KClO_3}{100} = \frac{\text{Mass of } 2KCl}{X}$$

Step 4: Calculate the masses (See work below). Substitute the masses into equation.

$$\frac{244}{100} = \frac{148}{X}$$

Step 5: Solve your set up by:

Cross multiplying.   244 X = 14800

Divide both sides by 244 $\frac{244 X}{244} = \frac{14800}{244}$

$$X = 60.65 \text{ g}$$

of KCl is produced from 100 g of $KClO_3$

Mass of 2 $KClO_3$	Mass of 2 KCl
2 K 2(39) = 78 g	2 KCl 2 (39) = 78
2 Cl 2 (35) = 70 g	2 Cl 2 (35) = 70
6 O 6 (16) = 96 g	148 g
244g	

Topic 6 – Mole interpretation: Mathematics of formulas and Equations

Check-A-list

Concept Terms

Below is a list of vocabulary terms from Topic 6. You should know definition and facts related to each term.

Put a check in the box [V] next to each term if you know its definition and other facts related to the term.

[ ] Mole
[ ] Avogadro's number
[ ] Molar mass
[ ] Gram-atomic mass
[ ] Gram-formula mass
[ ] Gram-molecular mass
[ ] Percent composition
[ ] Hydrate
[ ] Anhydrous
[ ] Percent composition of hydrate

If you don't have a check next to a term, look it up or ask your teacher.

Concept Tasks

Below is a list of concept tasks from Topic 6. You should know how to solve problems and answer questions related to each concept task.

Put a check in the box [V] next a concept task if you know how to solve problems and answer questions related to it.

[ ] Determining the number of moles of each atom in a given mole of formula
[ ] Determining the total number of moles of atoms in a given formula
[ ] Determining the gram-atomic mass (molar mass) of an element.
[ ] Calculating the gram-formula mass (gram-molecular mass, molar mass) of a compound
[ ] Calculating the mass of any given mole of a substance
[ ] Calculating number of moles of any given mass of a substance
[ ] Calculating percent composition by mass of an element in a formula
[ ] Calculating percent of composition of water in a hydrate
[ ] Calculating percent composition of water in a hydrate from lab information
[ ] Determining molecular formula from molecular mass and empirical formula
[ ] Determining mole ratio of substance in a balanced equation
[ ] Setting up and solving mole to mole problem in a balanced chemical equation
[ ] Setting up and solving volume to volume problem in a balanced chemical equation
[ ] Setting up and solving mass to mass problem in a balanced chemical equation

If you do not have a check next to a concept task, look it up or ask your teacher.

Topic 6 – Mole interpretation: Mathematics of formulas and Equations

Concept Task Review Questions

1. What is the total number of moles of hydrogen atoms in 4 mole of $(NH_4)_2SO_4$?
   1) 8
   2) 10
   3) 16
   4) 32

2. How many different types of atoms are in the formula $Ba(OH)_2 \cdot 8H_2O$?
   1) 3
   2) 2
   3) 3
   4) 8

3. The formula mass of $C_3H_5(OH)_3$ is
   1) 48 g/mole
   2) 58 g/mole
   3) 74 g/mole
   4) 92 g/mole

4. What is the mass in grams of 0.5 mole of Co?
   1) 27
   2) 28
   3) 12
   4) 59

5. The number of moles of H_2SO_4 that weighs 245 grams is equal to
   1) 0.4 mole
   2) 1 moles
   3) 2.5 moles
   4) 3 moles

6. The number of moles of the element lead that will have a mass of 311 grams is equal to
   1) 2 mole
   2) 1.5 mole
   3) 0.67 mole
   4) 1.0 mole

7. What is the total mass in grams of 3 moles of $Al_2(CrO_4)_3$?
   1) 134
   2) 402
   3) 1206
   4) 1530

8. The mass in grams of two moles of $(NH_4)_2CO_3$ is equal to
   1) 96 x 2
   2) 108 x 2
   3) $\frac{96}{2}$
   4) $\frac{2}{96}$

9. What is the percent composition of nitrogen in the compound NH_4NO_3?
   1) 35 %
   2) 29 %
   3) 18 %
   4) 5.7 %

10. What is the approximate percent composition of $CaCO_3$?
    1) 48 % Ca, 12 % C and 40 % O
    2) 12 % Ca, 48 % C, and 40 % O
    3) 40 % Ca, 12 % C and 48 % O
    4) 40 % Ca, 48 % C, and 12 % O

11. During an experiment to determine the percent by mass of water in a hydrated crystal, a student found the mass of a hydrated compound to be 4.10 grams. After heating to constant mass, the mass was 3.70 g. What is the percent by mass of water in this crystal?
    1) 9.8 %
    2) 90 %
    3) 11%
    4) 0.40 %

12. A compound has a molecular mass of 284 g and an empirical formula of P_2O_5. What is the molecular formula of this compound?
    1) P_4O_{10}
    2) P_5O_2
    3) P_2O_5
    4) $P_{10}O_4$

13. Acetic acid has a formula of $HC_2H_3O_2$. What is the ratio by mass of hydrogen to carbon to oxygen in this formula?
    1) 1 : 2 : 2
    2) 2 : 3 : 3
    3) 1 : 6 : 8
    4) 1 : 2 : 4

T6Q

Topic 6 – Mole interpretation: Mathematics of formulas and Equations

14. Given the reaction:

$$2C_2H_6 + 7O_2 \longrightarrow 4CO_2 + 6H_2O$$

What is the moles ratio of CO_2 produced to moles of C_2H_6 consumed?

1) 1 to 1   2) 2 to 1   3) 3 to 2   4) 7 to 2

15. Given a balanced chemical equation below:

$$3Cu(s) + 2H_3PO_4 \longrightarrow Cu_3(PO_4)_2 + 3H_2$$

How many moles of copper are needed to react with 5 moles of phosphoric acid?

1) 10.0 moles   2) 5.00 moles   3) 15.0 moles   4) 7.50 moles

16. According to the reaction below:

$$2SO_2(g) + O_2(g) \longrightarrow 2SO_3(g)$$

What is the total number of liters of $O_2(g)$ that will react completely with 89.6 liters of SO_2 at STP?

1) 1.0 L   2) 0.500 L   3) 22.4 L   4) 44.8 L

17. Given the reaction:

$$4Al(s) + 3O_2(g) \longrightarrow 2Al_2O_3(s)$$

What is the minimum number of grams of O_2 gas required to produce 102 grams of Al_2O_3?

1) 32.0 g   2) 192 g   3) 96.0 g   4) 48.0 g

Constructed Response Questions

Base your answers to questions 18 through 19 on the information below.

Gypsum is a mineral that is used in the construction industry to make drywall (sheetrock). The chemical formula for this hydrated compound is $CaSO_4 \cdot 2H_2O$. A hydrated compound contains water molecules within the crystalline structures. Gypsum contains 2 moles of water for each 1 mole of calcium sulfate.

18. What is the gram-formula mass of $CaSO_4 \cdot 2H_2O$.   18.

19. Show a correct numerical setup for calculating the percent composition by mass of water in this compound and record your result.   19.

Base your answers to questions 20 through 21 on the balanced chemical equation below.

$$2H_2O \longrightarrow 2H_2 + O_2$$

Show work and write your answers here.

20. What is the total number of moles of O_2 produced when 8 moles of H_2O is completely consumed?   20.

21. How does the balanced chemical equation show the Law of Conservation of Mass?   21.

T6Q

Topic 7 - Solutions

Topic outline

In this topic, you will learn the following concepts:
. Properties of aqueous solutions
. Description of solutions   . Expression (calculation) of concentration of solutions
. Solubility factors   . Molarity and parts per million
. Soluble and insoluble substances   . Vapor pressure
. Types of solutions   . Effects of solute on physical properties of water

Lesson 1 - Properties of aqueous solutions

Introduction

RECALL that a solution is a homogeneous mixture. Homogenous mixture is a type of mixture in which all of the components are evenly and uniformly mixed throughout the mixture.

One of the best examples of a solution is when salt is mixed in water to produce a salt solution. Milk is also a homogeneous mixture (or solution).

Although there are many different kinds of solutions, the discussion of solution in this topic will focus on aqueous solutions only.

Aqueous solutions are solutions in which a substance (solute) is dissolved in water (solvent).

In this lesson, you will learn about the properties of aqueous solutions.

1. Components of aqueous solutions: Definitions and facts

All aqueous solutions consist of two main components:
Below are definitions and facts about the two components of all aqueous solutions.

Concept Facts: Study to remember the following solution related information

Solute:
Solute is the substance being dissolved.
Solute is always present in a smaller amount than the solvent.
Solute is usually a solid, but can also be a liquid or a gas.

Solvent (Water)
Solvent is the substance in which the solute is dispersed.
Solvent is the substance that dissolves (disperses) the solute.
Solvent is always present in a greater amount than the solute.
In aqueous solutions, the solvent is always water.
In all solutions, the solvent is usually a liquid.

Aqueous solution
Aqueous solution is a mixture of solvent (water) and the solute

The equation below shows the dissolving of a salt (solute) in water.
NOTE how the different components of the mixture are represented.

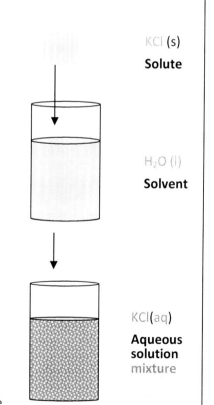

$KCl_{(s)}$ + $H_2O_{(l)}$ ------------------> $KCl_{(aq)}$
Solute   solvent   mixture

(s) means solid   **(l)** means liquid   **(aq)** means aqueous mixture

Topic 7 - Solutions

2. Solute and solvent of a solutions: Interpreting symbol of solutions

RECALL: A chemical formula can only be used to represent pure substances such as elements and compounds. Aqueous solutions can be represented by symbols, not by chemical formulas. A symbol of an aqueous solution is not a chemical formula of that solution.

Concept Task: Be able to interpret symbol of a solution

Below are examples of four aqueous solutions:

NOTE that the solution name, symbol of the solution, the solute and the solvent are given.

Study the information below to learn how to interpret solutions, and determine its solute and solvent.

Solution name	Solution (mixture) symbol	Solute formula	Solvent formula
Sodium chloride solution	$NaCl\,(aq)$	$NaCl\,(s)$	$H_2O\,(l)$
Potassium nitrate solution	$KNO_3\,(aq)$	$KNO_3\,(s)$	$H_2O\,(l)$
Sugar solution	$C_6H_{12}O_6\,(aq)$	$C_6H_{12}O_6\,(s)$	$H_2O\,(l)$
Carbon dioxide solution	$CO_2\,(aq)$	$CO_2\,(g)$	$H_2O\,(l)$
Ethanol (alcohol) solution	$C_2H_5OH\,(aq)$	$C_2H_5(OH)\,(l)$	$H_2O\,(l)$

NOTE: The aqueous symbol (aq) next to a formula of a substance always means that the substance is dissolved in water, $H_2O\,(l)$

3. Solutes and solvent: Determining solute and solvent of solutions

Concept Task: Be able to determine solute and solvent of a solution.

To determine solvent of a solution
  CHOOSE Water (H_2O) as solvent if the solution is aqueous
  CHOOSE the liquid of the solution for all other solutions.

To determine solute of a solution
  CHOOSE the formula or name of the substance

RECALL: Ionic substances are composed of + and – ions.

  Ex: LiCl (an ionic compound) is really Li^+Cl^-.

  In a LiCl solution, both Li+ and Cl- (or LiCl) are the solutes, not just Li+ ion and not just Cl- ion.

Example 1

In the aqueous solution of NH_3, the solute is

1) $H_2O(l)$ 3) $NH_3(aq)$
2) $H_2O(s)$ 4) $NH_3(g)$

Answer: Choice 4

Example 2

In LiCl (aq), the solute is

1) Li+   3) Cl-
2) LiCl   4) H_2O

Answer: Choice 2, LiCl is the substance that dissolved in water to make LiCl (aq)

Dissolving LiCl salt.

Molecule-ion attraction

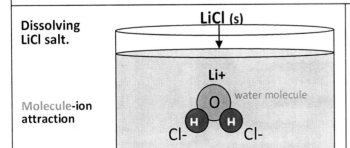

When a salt (**LiCl**) is place in water, it interact with water molecules, H_2O, to dissolve.

In LiCl solution : LiCl $_{(aq)}$

Li+ (the positive ion of the salt) attracts
  O (negative end of a water molecule)

Cl- (negative ion of the salt) attracts
  H (positive ends of water of a water molecule)

(Recall: Opposites attract)

Topic 7 - Solutions

4. Properties of solution: Facts

A properly made solution will have the following characteristics.

Concept Facts: Study to remember these characteristics of solutions

- Solutions are homogenous mixtures
- Solution are generally clear
- Solution are transparent and do not disperse light
- Solutions can be colorful (*compounds likely contains a transition element*)
- Particles in the solution will not settle to the bottom of the container
- Solute and solvent can be separated by boiling, evaporation and distillation processes

A $KMnO_4$ (potassium permanganate) solution has a purple color

Crystallization is a process of recovering a salt (solute) from a mixture by evaporation (or boiling).
- Particles of water is evaporated out of a mixture, leaving particles of the solute behind

Filtration CANNOT be used to separate solute from solvent of a mixture.
- Particles of solvent and solute will both pass through a filter paper

Lesson 2 – Solubility factors

Introduction:

Not every substance that is put in water will dissolve. Some substances dissolve very well, others very little, while some not at all. In addition, how well a given substance dissolves in water is affected by conditions such as temperature and / or pressure.

In this lesson, you'll learn about factors that affects how well substances dissolve in water. You will also learn how to determine which substance will dissolve or will not dissolve in water.

5. Solubility: Definitions and facts

Solubility describes the extent to which a substance will dissolve in water at certain conditions.

Miscibility describes the extent to which two liquids will mix

Below are terms that are used to describe the extent to which a substance will dissolve in a given solvent.

Concept Facts: Study to remember them.

Soluble means that a substance has HIGH solubility.
  Soluble salts dissolve very well in water.
   Ex. NaCl (sodium chloride salt) is soluble in water.

Insoluble means that a substance has LOW solubility.
  Insoluble salts do not dissolve well in water.
   Ex. AgCl (silver chloride salt) is insoluble in water.

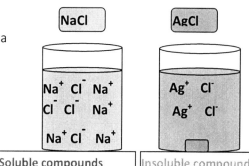

Soluble compounds completely dissolve to produce high ion concentration.

Insoluble compounds dissolve very little to produce low ion concentration.

Miscible refers to two liquids with HIGH miscibility.
  Two miscible liquids will mix evenly, and will not form layers.
   Ex. Alcohols and water are miscible liquids. They will mix evenly and uniformly.

Immiscible refers to two liquids with LOW miscibility.
  Two immiscible liquids will not mix evenly, and will form (or separate) into layers.
   Ex. Oil and water are immiscible liquids and will separate into layers.

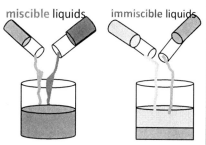

miscible liquids   immiscible liquids

Topic 7 - Solutions

6. Solubility factors: Facts

The extent to which a solute dissolves in water depends largely on the following three factors:
Temperature, pressure, and the nature of the solute.

In the notes below, you will learn how these three factors affect how well a solute dissolves in water.
solutes.
Concept Facts: Study to remember these on factors that affect solubility

Temperature:

For any given solute, its solubility (how well it dissolves) changes with change in temperature of water.
The effect of temperature on solubility of solutes varies depending on if the solute is a solid or a gas.

Solid solutes: Ex, $NaNO_3(s)$ salt, $KCl(s)$ salt, Sugar
Solubility of solids increases when the temperature of water increases.
The amount of solid that can be dissolved in water increases as
the temperature of the water increases
   $NaNO_3(s)$, $KCl(s)$ and sugar dissolve better in hot water than in
   cold water.

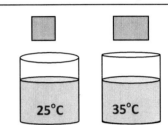
At a higher water temp of $35°C$, a greater amount of the solid can be dissolved in water.

Gaseous Solutes: Ex. $O_2(g)$, $CO_2(g)$, nitrogen gas
Solubility of gases increases when the water temperature decreases.
The amount of gas that can be dissolved in water increases as
the water temperature decreases.
   $O_2(g)$, $CO_2(g)$, and nitrogen dissolve better in cold water than in
   hot water.

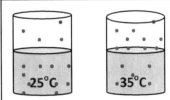
At a lower temperature of $25°C$, the water contains more dissolved gas particles.

Pressure

For a given gaseous solute, the solubility of the solute changes
with a change in pressure.

Gaseous solutes
Solubility of gases increases when the pressure on a gas increases.
As pressure increases, solubility of a gas in water increases.
   $O_2(g)$ and $CO_2(g)$ will dissolve better in a high pressure system
   than in a low pressure system.

Solid solutes
Pressure has no effect on the solubility of a solid in water
   The amount of $NaNO_3(s)$ and $KCl(s)$ that dissolve in water will
   not be affected by a change in pressure.

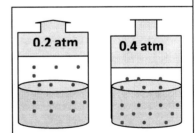
At a higher pressure of 0.4 atm, more gas particles are pushed into the water, and the water will contain more dissolved gas particles.

Nature of solutes
"Like dissolves like" is a saying that emphasizes the fact that polar solutes and ionic solutes
dissolves better in polar solvents.
   Ionic solutes (such as NaCl) dissolve well in water because they are alike in terms of polarity.
   .Water is a polar substance with + and – ends. Ionic substances are composed of + and – ions
   Nonpolar solutes, which have no + and no – ends, do not dissolve well in water.

Topic 7 - Solutions

7. Solubility factors: Determining substances that change solubility when pressure or temperature is changed.

Concept Task: Be able to determine a substance whose solubility will be affected by an increase or decrease in temperature (or pressure).

To determine the type of substance correctly, you must consider the following about the question.

If the question asks for a substance that:
  Increases its solubility as water temperature increases
  Decreases its solubility as water temperature decreases
  Shows no change in solubility as pressure changes
  LOOK for a solid (or ionic) solute

If a question asks for a substance that:
  Increases its solubility as water temperature decreases
  Decreases its solubility as water temperature increases
  Changes its solubility as pressure changes
  LOOK for a gaseous solute

Example 3
The solubility of which substance will not be affected by an increase in pressure?
1) N_2 3) CO_2
2) SO_3 4) LiCl

Before choosing:
  RECALL: solid solutes are not affected by change in pressure
  LOOK for: a solid solute:
Answer: Choice 4: LiCl is a solid (ionic) salt. The rest of the choices are gases.

Example 4
As temperature of water increases, which substance will show a decrease in solubility?
1) $CaBr_2$ 3) KNO_3
2) CO   4) KBr

Answer: Choice 2: Because CO is a gas, and gaseous solutes have a decrease in solubility as water temperature increases

8. Solubility factors: Determining the condition of temperature and / or pressure that a given solute is most or least soluble

Concept Task: Be able to determine the temperature and pressure that a solute is most or least soluble.

To determine correctly the conditions, you must consider if the substance (given in the question) is a solid or a gas.

First Determine: If solute formula in given in the question is a gas OR a solid

Then consider:
  If Solid, and the question asks for condition of:
    Most soluble: LOOK for the highest temperature
    Least soluble: LOOK for the lowest temperature

  If Gaseous, and the question asks for condition of:
    Most soluble: LOOK for the lowest temperature and the highest pressure
    Least soluble: LOOK for highest temperature and the lowest pressure

Example 5
Under which condition of temperature would Li_2SO_4 be least soluble?
1) 20°C   3) 30°C
2) 40°C   4) 50°C

Correct: Choice 1. Since Li_2SO_4 is a solid salt, it will be **least soluble** at the lowest temperature.

Example 6
At which temperature and pressure would Chlorine be most soluble in water?
1) 300 K and 0.5 atm
2) 300 K and 1.0 atm
3) 250 K and 0.5 atm
4) 250 K and 1.0 atm

Correct: Choice 4. Since Chlorine is a gas, it will be **most soluble** at lowest temperature and highest pressure.

Topic 7 - Solutions

9. Soluble and insoluble salts: Reading and understanding the Solubility Guideline Table F.

As mentioned earlier, not every substance will dissolve in water. Soluble substances dissolve well in water, while insoluble substances dissolve slightly or not at all.

Solubility of an ionic solute depends on the nature of the ions it contains.

Solubility Guideline Table F shown below lists ions that form soluble and insoluble compounds.

The Table can be used for determining which substance is soluble or insoluble.

NOTE that this table is composed of two different tables

Table F
Solubility Guidelines

Soluble ions Table | Insoluble ions Table

Ions That Form Soluble Compounds	Exceptions
Group 1 ions (Li^+, Na^+, etc.)	
ammonium (NH_4^+)	
nitrate (NO_3^-)	
acetate ($C_2H_3O_2^-$ or CH_3COO^-)	
hydrogen carbonate (HCO_3^-)	
chlorate (ClO_3^-)	
perchlorate (ClO_4^-)	
halides (Cl^-, Br^-, I^-)	when combined with Ag^+, Pb^{2+}, and Hg_2^{2+}
sulfates (SO_4^{2-})	when combined with Ag^+, Ca^{2+}, Sr^{2+}, Ba^{2+}, and Pb^{2+}

Ions That Form Insoluble Compounds	Exceptions
carbonate (CO_3^{2-})	when combined with Group 1 ions or ammonium (NH_4^+)
chromate (CrO_4^{2-})	when combined with Group 1 ions or ammonium (NH_4^+)
phosphate (PO_4^{3-})	when combined with Group 1 ions or ammonium (NH_4^+)
sulfide (S^{2-})	when combined with Group 1 ions or ammonium (NH_4^+)
hydroxide (OH^-)	when combined with Group 1 ions, Ca^{2+}, Ba^{2+}, or Sr^{2+}

Left Table lists ions that form soluble compounds   **Right** Table lists ions that form insoluble compounds

Both Tables have an exception column.

Concept Task: Be able to determine which substance is soluble or insoluble

To determine if a given compound is soluble or insoluble. Consider the following notes:

Soluble compounds

A formula or a name contains an ion found on the soluble (LEFT) table, BUT is not combined with an exception.

A formula or name contains an ion in the insoluble Table, BUT is combined with an ion in the exception column.

Insoluble compounds

A formula or a name contains an ion found on the insoluble (RIGHT) table, BUT is not combines with an exception

A formula or name contains an ion that is found in the Soluble Table, BUT is combined with an ion in the exception.

Topic 7 - Solutions

10. Soluble and insoluble solutes: Examples of soluble and insoluble salts

The following notes give you four solutes.
The second column indicates whether the compound is soluble or insoluble. Explanation as to why the compound is soluble or insoluble based on information from **Solubility Table F** is also given.
As you study these examples, refer to **Solubility Table F** to see the side the ions of the formulas are located.

Formula or name of solutes

LiCl   Soluble
Li+ ion (and all Group 1 ions) is listed on the soluble table.
Cl- ion, a halide, is also listed on the soluble table.
Neither ion is listed as an exception for the other.
Therefore, Li+ ion combines with Cl- ion to form a compound (LiCl) that is soluble

$AgSO_4$ Insoluble
SO_4^{2-} ion (sulfate ion) is listed on the soluble table with some exceptions
Ag^{2+} (silver) ion is listed as one of the exceptions for sulfate.
Therefore, SO_4^{2-} ion combines with Ag^{2+} ion to form a compound ($AgSO_4$) that insoluble

Barium hydroxide   Soluble
Hydroxide ion (OH-) is listed on the insoluble table with some exceptions.
Barium (Ba^{2+}) is listed as one of the exceptions for (OH-) ion.
Therefore, hydroxide ion combines with barium to form a compound (barium hydroxide) that is soluble.

Magnesium sulfide   Insoluble
Sulfide (S^{2-}) ion is listed on the insoluble side with some exceptions.
Magnesium (Mg^{2+}) ion is not listed as an exception for S^{2-} ion.
Therefore, sulfide combines with magnesium to form a compound (magnesium sulfide) that is insoluble

11. Soluble and insoluble salt: Determining which solute is soluble and which is insoluble

Concept Task: Be able to determine which substance is soluble or insoluble in multiple choice questions.

Example 7
Which of the following compounds is insoluble in water?
1) $Ca(NO_3)_2$ 2) Na_2CO_3 3) K_2S 4) $Ca_3(PO_4)_2$

Before choosing:
Go through each formula one at a time using the **Solubility Table F** to determine
$Ca(NO_3)_2$: Contains soluble NO_3^- ion, Ca ion not in exception (SOLUBLE)
Na_2CO_3 : Contains soluble Na^+ ion , CO_3 is not in exception column (SOLUBLE)
K_2S : Contains soluble K^+ ion, S ion not in exception column (SOLUBLE)
$Ca_3(PO_4)_2$: Contains insoluble PO_4^{3-} ion, Ca ion not in the exception column (INSOLUBLE)

Answer: choice 4

Example 8
Which compound is the most soluble?
1) Lead iodide   3) Barium carbonate
2) Lead sulfate   4) Calcium hydroxide

Answer: Choice 4. Hydroxide ion generally forms insoluble compounds. However, when it combines with **calcium**, it forms a compound (calcium hydroxide) that is soluble. All others choices are contain insoluble compounds.

Topic 7 - Solutions

Lesson 3 - Descriptions of solution and the solubility curves.

Introduction

A solution can be described as saturated, unsaturated, supersaturated, dilute, or concentrated depending on four factors of the solutions: These factors are:

Type of solute, amount of the solute, amount of water, and temperature of water.

It is hard to classify a solution just by looking at it. For example, if there are three beakers on a table, each containing a clear solution, you will not be able to classify the types of solution in all three beakers just by looking at the solutions. To accurately classify the type of solution in each beaker, you'll need to know the type and the amount of solute, amount of water, and the temperature of each solution. You will then use the **Solubility Curve Table G** to help you classify the solutions.

In this lesson, you will learn terms that are used to describe solutions. You will also learn how to use the **Solubility Curve Table G** to describe different solutions.

12. Description of solutions: Definitions and facts

Below are a list of terms that are used to describe solutions.

Concept Facts: Study to remember these solution description terms.

Saturated solution
> A solution containing the maximum amount of solute that can be dissolved at a given water temperature.
> In a saturated solution, equilibrium exists between dissolved and undissolved particles.

Unsaturated solution
> A solution containing less than the maximum amount of solute that could dissolved at a given water temperature.
> An unsaturated solution will dissolve more solute.

Supersaturated solution
> A solution containing more than the maximum amount of solute that can dissolve at a given water temperature.
> In a supersaturated solution, the undissolved solute will settle to the bottom of the container.

Dilute solution
> A solution containing a small amount of solute in a large amount of water (solvent)
>> Ex.   10 grams of salt in 100 grams of water makes a dilute solution

Concentrated solution
> A solution containing a large amount of solute in a small amount of water
>> Ex.   Ten spoonful of salt in one glass of water makes a concentrated solution

IN THE NEXT FEW PAGES, you'll learn how to use the Solubility Curve Table G to classify solutions.

Topic 7 - Solutions

13. The solubility Curve Table G: Reading and understanding the Solubility Curves

Below, the Solubility Curves Reference Table G is given.

Below the Table, you will find important information, as well as questions relating to solutions that you can answer by using this Table.

Table G   Solubility Curves

[Graph showing solubility curves for KI, NaNO₃, KNO₃, HCl, NH₄Cl, KCl, NaCl, KClO₃, NH₃, SO₂ with Solute per 100 g of H₂O (g) on y-axis (0-140) and Temperature (°C) on x-axis (0-100)]

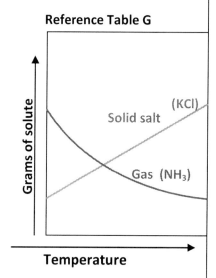

Reference Table G

NOTE the followings important facts about the table:

. The x axis is labeled with water (solvent) temperatures

. The y axis is labeled with grams of solute per 100 grams of H_2O

. Each curve is labeled with the formula of the solute.

. Solid solutes have curves with positive slopes

  Solubility of solids increase as the water temperature increases

. Gaseous solutes have curve with negative slopes

  Solubility of gases decrease as the water temperature increases

The solubility curve table can help you answer the following questions about a solution:

. How many grams of a solute is needed to form a saturated solution?

. Is a solution saturated, unsaturated, or supersaturated?

. Which solute is most or least soluble, most or least dilute, and most or least concentrated?

In the next few sections, you will learn how to answer these questions using the

Solubility Curve Table G:

Topic 7 - Solutions

14. Saturated solution: Determining the amount of solute needed to form a saturated solution

RECALL that a *saturated* solution contains the maximum amount of solute that can be dissolved in a given amount of water at a specified temperature.

Concept Task: Be able to determine the grams of solute to form a saturated solution using Solubility Curve Table G.

Below, steps on how to use Solubility Curve Table G to determine the saturated amount of any solute. **Study** the steps and the information about adjusting grams of solute.

Step 1: Locate the given temperature on the x axis
Step 2: Go up from the temperature point to intersect the curve for the given substance
Step 3: Go left (from where you intersect) to the y axis and read the grams of solute

NOTE: Amount of solute you determined on the y axis is for 100 grams of water only.

You can adjust the grams of solute to saturate if the amount of water is different from 100 g.

If amount of water is 100 grams: The amount you determined in step 3 is your answer

If amount of water is 200 grams: Double the amount you determined in step 3

If amount of water is 50 grams : Half the amount you determined in step 3

Below are example questions on determining amount of solute to form a saturated solution.
Study how each problem is solved using the three steps listed above. Be able to solve similar problems.

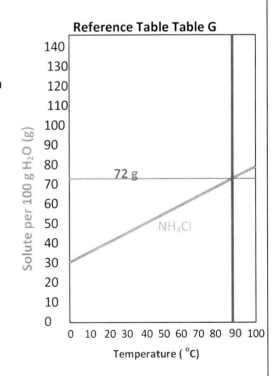
Reference Table Table G

Example 9
What is the maximum amount of grams of NH_4Cl that is needed to saturate 100 g of water at 90°C?

1) 100 g   2) 90   3) 144 g   4) 72 g

Answer: Choice 4. See graph to the right for explanation

Example 10
What is the maximum amount of grams of NH_4Cl that is needed to saturate 50 grams of water at 90°C?

1) 36 g   2) 90   3) 144 g   4) 72 g

Answer: Choice 1. According to example 1 answer:
In 100 g H_2O: 72 grams of NH_4Cl is saturated.
Therefore, In 50 g H_2O: 72 ÷ 2 = 36 g NH_4Cl is saturated

Example 11
What is the maximum amount of grams of NH_4Cl that is needed to saturate 300 grams of water at 90°C?

1) 72 g   2) 144 g   3) 300 g   4) 216 g

Answer: Choice 4. According to example 1 answer:
In 100 g H_2O: 72 grams of NH_4Cl is saturated.
Therefore, In 300 g H_2O: 72 x 3 = 216 g NH_4Cl is saturated.

Topic 7 - Solutions

15. Saturated amount: Determining how much more solute is needed to bring a solution to saturation

RECALL that an unsaturated solution contains less solute than can be dissolved. A solution that is unsaturated can be made saturated by adding more of the solute. How much more solute should be added can be determined by taking the difference between the gram of solute to saturate at the given temperature, and the amount of solute that is in the unsaturated solution.
Again, you will need you Solubility Curve Table G.

Concept Task: Be able to determine amount of solute that must be added to a solution to bring the solution to saturation.

Below, three steps are given for this concept task.
Study these steps and the example question to the right to learn how to solve similar problems.

Step 1: Determine amount of solute to make a saturated solution using the Solubility Curve Table G
(See previous page on determining saturation amount)

Step 2: Note the amount of solute in solution

Step 3: Determine amount of solute needed to bring the solution to saturation:

Saturated amount - grams of solute in the question
(step 1)   -   (step 2)

Example 12

How many more grams of NH_4Cl solute must be added to solution containing 37 grams of the solute in 100 grams of water at $40°C$?

1) 30 g   2) 10 g   3) 63 g   4) 3 g

Before choosing, go through the steps.

Step 1: Saturation amount of NH_4Cl at $40°C$ (Use Table G) = 47 g
Step 2: Grams of NH_4Cl in solution = 37 g
Step 3: Grams NH_4Cl needed = 47 – 37 = **10 g**
Answer: Choice 2

16. Saturated solution: Determining the amount of solute that will re-crystallized when a saturated solution is cooled to a lower temperature

Recall that a supersaturated solution contains more solute than can be dissolved at a given temperature. When a salt solution that is saturated at one temperature is cooled to a lower temperature, fewer amount of the solute will be soluble. As a result, the ions of the solute in the solution will re-crystallize and precipitate (settle out) from solution. The solution at the lower temperature is a supersaturated solution because it contains more solute than can be dissolved.
Precipitate is a solid that forms out of a solution.
The amount of solute that precipitated (settle out) at the lower temperature can be determined by taking the difference between the saturated amounts of the solute at the two temperatures given.

A saturated solution of $KClO_3$ at $80°C$

cooled to $60°C$

Undissolved $KClO_3$ settled out at a lower temperature of $60°C$.

Concept Task: Be able to determine the amount of solute that will precipitate out at a lower temp.

Use the Solubility Curve Table G
Step 1: Determine saturated amount at the higher temperature
Step 2: Determine saturated amount at the lower temperature
Step 3: Determine amount of solute that will precipitate:
saturation at higher temp – saturation at lower temp
(step 1)   –   (step 2)

Example 13

How many grams of a $KClO_3$ solution will precipitate when a saturated solution made with 100 grams of water at $80°C$ is cooled to $60°C$?

1) 140 g   2) 56 g   3) 18 g   4) 20 g

Before choosing, go through the steps.
Use Table G to determine saturation of $KClO_3$:

Step 1: Saturation at $80°C$ = 46 g
Step 2: Saturation at $60°C$ = 28 g
Step 3: Amount that precipitate or will settle out = 46 - 28 = 18 g
Answer: Choice 3

Topic 7 - Solutions

17. Type of solution: Using the solubility curve to determine types of solutions.

A solution is described as saturated, unsaturated, or supersaturated based on how much of the solute is in the solution, the amount of water, and the temperature of the water.
Using the **Solubility Curve Table G**, you can determine the type of solution when all the above information are known in a question.

Concept Task: Be able to determine if a solution is saturated, unsaturated, or supersaturated

Below, steps to determining the type of solution using the Solubility Curve Table G are given.
Study the steps and the graph to the right to learn how to determine the type of solution.

Step 1: Locate the temperature given in question

Step 2: Go up the temperature line and **stop** when you had gone up as high up as the amount of solute in the question

Step 3: Determine solution as:
  Saturated: If where you stopped is ON THE CURVE
  (solution contains SAME amount of solute as can be dissolved)

  Supersaturated: If where you stopped is ABOVE THE CURVE
  (Solution contains MORE solute than is capable of being dissolved)

  Unsaturated: If where you stopped is BELOW THE CURVE
  (Solution contains LESS solute than is capable of being dissolved)

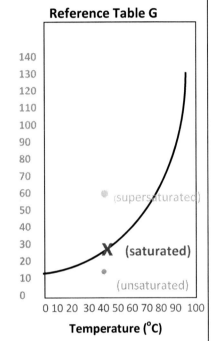

Reference Table G

18. Type of solution: Determining if solution is saturated, unsaturated or supersaturated

Concept Task: Be able to determine if a solution is saturated, unsaturated, or supersaturated

Study the example questions and the steps to learn to answer similar questions.

Example 14

A solution of NH_4Cl containing 70 g of the solute in 100 g of H_2O at $45°C$ is best described as

1) Saturated   2) Unsaturated   3) Supersaturated

Before choosing: Use the solubility Table G to:

Step 1: **Locate** temperature of $45°C$ on x axis

Step 2: **Go up** $45°C$ and Stop at 70 g

Step 3: **Determine** type of solution:
Where you stopped at 70 g is ABOVE the NH_4Cl CURVE. Solution in question is supersaturated solution

Answer: Choice 3

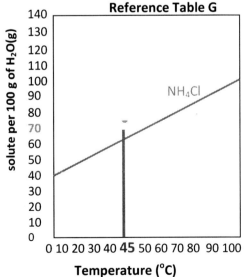

Reference Table G

Topic 7 - Solutions

18. Cont.

IMPORTANT NOTE: When amount of water in a question is MORE or LESS than 100 grams, You will need to adjust the grams of solute in the question before you can accurately determine the type of solution using the three steps described on the previous page.

Concept Task: Be able to determine type of solution when amount of water is less or more than 100 g

If amount of water in question is 50 grams,
Double the solute amount in question before using the solubility curve table.

If amount of water in question is 200 grams
Cut the solute amount in question in half before using the solubility curve.

Example 15

A solution containing 140 grams of $NH_3(g)$ in 200 grams of water at $10^\circ C$ is best described as

1) Saturated
2) Unsaturated
3) Supersaturated

Before choosing a choice:

Cut in half the amount of solute in question (b/c H₂O amount is 200 g)

Solute amount in question = 140 g

Cut solute amount in half = 140/2 = 70 g

Go up $10^\circ C$, **stop at** 70 g on the solubility curve.

Answer: **Choice 1:** Where you stopped (at 70 g) is ON the NH_3 curve.
Solution in question is saturated

(see blue line on the graph)

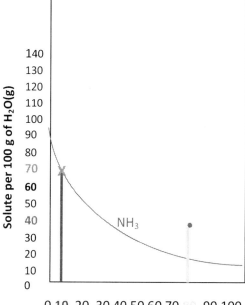

Example 16.
What type of solution is formed when 20 grams of $NH_3(g)$ is dissolved in 50 grams of water at $80^\circ C$?

1) Saturated
2) Unsaturated
3) Supersaturated

Before choosing a choice

Double the solute amount in question (b/c amount of H₂O is 50 g)
Solute amount in question = 20 g

Double solute amount = 20 x 2 = 40 g

Go up $80^\circ C$, **Stop at** 40 g on the solubility Table.

Answer: **Choice 3:** Where you stopped (at 40 g) is
ABOVE the NH_3 curve.
Solution in question is a supersaturated

(see green line on the graph)

Topic 7 - Solutions

19. Type of solution: Determining if solution is concentrated or dilute

Concentrated and dilute are other terms that are used to describe solutions.

Concept Facts: Study to remember facts related to these two terms.

A **concentrated solution** contains a large amount of solute relative to the amount of water.

A **dilute solution** contains a small amount of solute relative to the amount of water.

It is important to note that a solution that is dilute **is not** necessarily unsaturated. In the same sense, a solution that is concentrated **is not** necessarily supersaturated. A given amount of a solute can form a solution that is both dilute and unsaturated at one temperature. However, at a different temperature, that same amount of solute can form a solution that is dilute and supersaturated.

Solutions can, therefore, be described by the combination of two terms.

   Dilute and saturated   Concentrated and saturate
   Dilute and unsaturated   Concentrated and unsaturated
   Dilute and supersaturated   Concentrated and supersaturated

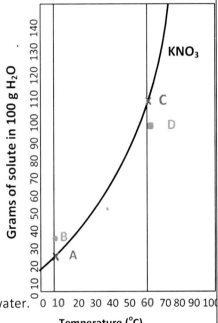

The Solubility curve to the right shows four different solutions of KNO_3 at $10°C$ and $60°C$ in $100 g$ of H_2O
These four solutions can be described as follows.
Study these descriptions to learn how to do the same.

   A: Saturated and Dilute
   B: Supersaturated and Dilute
   C: Saturated and Concentrated
   D: Unsaturated and Concentrated

Solution A and B are dilute because each contains small amount (23 g and 38 g) of KNO_3 in a large amount (100 g) of water.

Solution C and D are concentrated because each contains large amount (105 g and 98 g) of KNO_3 relative to the amount (100 g) of water.

20. Type of solution: Determining if solution is dilute or concentrated

Concept Task: Be able to describe solutions as dilute or concentrated.

Example 17
A solution containing 10 grams of $KClO_3$ in 100 grams of water at $40°C$ is best describe as
1) Dilute and saturated
2) Concentrated and supersaturated
3) Dilute and unsaturated
4) Concentrated and unsaturated

   Before choosing, go through the steps. Be sure to use the Solubility Curve Table.
   Step 1: Determine if solution is dilute or concentrated.
      Dilute: Because 10 g of $KClO_3$ is a **small amount** of solute compares to 100 g of water

   Step 2: Determine if saturated, unsaturated, or supersaturate (LOOK at a solubility curve table)
      Unsaturated: Because 10 g of $KClO_3$ is LESS than the saturated amount (15 g) at $40°C$.

   Answer: Choice 3 : Dilute and unsaturated

Topic 7 - Solutions

21. The solubility Curve Table: Determining Most and Least of solutions

Using the Solubility Curve Table G, you can determine which solute is most or least soluble at any given temperature

Concept Task: Be able to determine which saturated solution is the most or least soluble, the most or least dilute, or the most or least concentrated at a given temperature.

To determine which solution is the most or least soluble at any given temperature:

Step 1: Locate and note the saturated point of each substance at the given temperature

Step 2: Choose most or least based on the following information:

At any given temperature:

To determine which saturated solution is :

Most soluble
Most concentrated   } **LOOK** for the saturated point **Closest to the TOP**
Least dilute

To determine which saturated solution is:

Least soluble
Least concentrated   } **LOOK** for the saturated point **Closest to the BOTTOM**
Most dilute

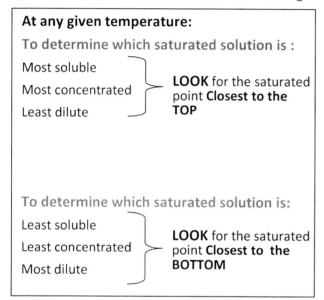

Below is an example problem :

Example 18

*A saturated solution of which substance is the **most dilute** at 60°C?*

1) NH_4Cl 2) KCl   3) KNO_3 4) $NaNO_3$

Before choosing, take the time to:

Locate and note the saturated point (intersects of 60°C temperature and the curve) for each substance. (SEE curves to the right.)

Most dilute will be the saturated solution closest to the bottom.

Answer: Choice 2 : KCl is the closest to the bottom of the four choices.

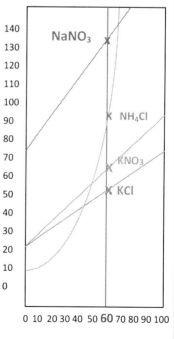

Copyright © 2010 E3 Scholastic Publishing. All Rights Reserved.   153

Topic 7 - Solutions

Lesson 4 – Expression of concentration of solutions

Introduction

Concentration of a solution indicates how much of dissolved solute is in a given amount of the solution (or the solvent).
The concentration of a solution can be expressed in few different ways.

In this lesson, you will learn of two concentration expressions: Molarity and parts per million.

Most questions dealing with concentration involve calculations using information given in a question about a solution. Equations for concentration calculations can be found in your **Reference Table**.

Be sure to have your Reference Table and a calculator as you study this lesson.

22. Molarity: Definition and interpretation of Molarity concentrations

Molarity expresses concentration of a solution in number of moles of solutes per liter of solution.
Molarity of a solution can be calculated using the equation:

$$\text{Molarity} = \frac{\text{moles of solutes}}{\text{Liter (volume) of solution}}$$

Reference Table T equation

When Molarity concentration of a solution is calculated, the unit is in moles/liter.

Moles per liter can also be written as "M" or "molar".

Interpreting Molarity concentration numbers.

Below, examples Molarity concentrations are given on the left column.
The right column shows the interpretation of these concentrations.

Molarity concentration	Interpretation
0.5 M Solution	There are 0.5 mole of the solute in 1 liter of the solution
1.0 M NaCl solution	This solution contains 1.0 mole of NaCl solute in every 1 Liter
1.6 molar KNO_3 solution	1 Liter of this solution contains 1.6 moles of KNO_3 solute

Concept Task: Be able to interpret Molarity concentration value (M) of a solution.

Below, example question on interpreting Molarity concentration of a solution
Study the notes above and the example question below to learn how to do the same on similar questions

Example 19
Which statement is true of a 3 M aqueous solution of HCl?
1) 3 Liter of the solution contains 1 mole of HCl solute
2) 3 Liter of the solution contains 3 moles of HCl solute
3) 1 Liter of the solution contains 1 mole of HCl solute
4) 1 Liter of the solution contains 3 moles of HCl solute.

Answer: Choice 4. The moles of the solute is always the same as the Molarity (M): $3 M = \frac{3 \text{ moles}}{1 \text{ liter}}$
The volume of the solution is always 1 Liter :

Topic 7 - Solutions

23. Molarity calculations: Calculating concentration using Molarity equation

Molarity concentration of a solution can be calculated using the following Reference Table T equation

$$\text{Molarity (M)} = \frac{\text{moles of solute}}{\text{Volume (L) of solution}}$$

You can also use this equation to calculate volume of a solution or the number of moles of solute in a solution.

Below, concept tasks related to the use of Molarity equation are given.

Equation and example question for each concept task are given.
Study example question and set up of each problem to learn how to do the same on similar questions.

Concept Task: Be able to set up and calculate Molarity from moles of solute and volume (L) of solution

$$\text{Molarity} = \frac{\text{moles of solute}}{\text{Volume (L) of solution}}$$

Example 20
What is the concentration of a solution that contains 1.4 moles of solute in 2 L of the solution?

$$\text{Molarity} = \frac{1.4}{2} = 0.7 \, M$$

Concept Task: Be able to set up and calculate Molarity from mass of solute and volume (L) of solution

$$\text{Molarity} = \frac{\text{Mass of solute}}{(\text{Formula mass of solute}) \times (\text{Volume})}$$

Example 21
NaOH solution contains 20 grams of NaOH in 0.5 L of solution. What is the concentration of this solution
(formula mass of NaOH = 40 g)

$$\text{Molarity} = \frac{20}{(40) \times (0.5)} = 1 \, M \text{ or } 1 \text{ mole/L}$$

Concept Task: Be able to set up and calculate moles from Molarity and volume (L) of solution

moles = Molarity x liter of solution

Example 22
What is the number of moles of a solute in a 400 ml of a 0.1 molar solution?
NOTE: Change 400 ml to 0.4 L

moles = (0.1) x (0.4) = **0.04 moles of solute**

Concept Task: Be able to set up and calculate Mass of solute from Molarity and volume (L) of solution

Mass = Molarity x liter x formula mass

Example 23
What is the mass of NaCl that is dissolved in a 1 L of 0.5 M NaCl solution?
(Formula mass of NaCl = 58 g)

Mass = 0.5 x 1 x 58 = **29 g of NaCl**

Concept Task: Be able to calculate volume of a solution from Molarity and moles of solute.

$$\text{Volume} = \frac{\text{moles of solutes}}{\text{Molarity (M)}}$$

Example 24
How much volume of 3 M H_2SO_4 solute will contain 2 moles of the solute?

$$\text{Volume} = \frac{2}{3} = 0.67 \, L$$

Topic 7 - Solutions

24. Parts per million: Definition and interpretation

Parts per million expresses the concentration of a solution in number of grams of solute that is in every one million parts of the solution.

Parts per million (ppm) concentrations can be calculated using the equation below:

$$\text{Parts per million} = \frac{\text{Grams of solute}}{\text{Grams of Solution}} \times 1\,000\,000$$

Reference Table T equation

ppm is the unit for parts per million concentration of a solution.

Interpreting parts per million concentrations

Below, parts per million (ppm) concentrations of two solutions are given on the left column.
The right column shows the interpretation of these concentrations.

ppm concentration	Interpretation
0.3 ppm Solution	Every 1 million parts of this solution contains 0.3 grams of the solute.
0.001 ppm O_2 solution	There are 0.001 gram of O_2 in every 1 million part of this O_2 solution

25. Part per million calculation: Calculating concentration using ppm equation

Below, concept tasks related to parts per million calculations are given.
Study the example question and set up of each example problem to learn how to do the same on similar questions.

Concept Task: Be able to calculate ppm from grams of solute and grams of solution

$$\text{ppm} = \frac{\text{Grams of solute}}{\text{Grams of solution}} \times 1\,000\,000$$

Example 25
A solution of carbon dioxide contains 0.5 grams of the solute in 500 grams of the solution. What is the concentration in part per million?

$$\text{ppm} = \frac{0.5}{500} \times 1000000 = .001 \text{ ppm}$$

Concept Task: Be able to calculate ppm from grams of solute and grams of water

$$\text{ppm} = \frac{\text{Grams of solute given}}{(\text{Grams of solute} + \text{Grams of water})} \times 1\,000\,000$$

Grams of solute + Grams of water = Grams of solution

Example 26
A solution of sodium nitrate contains 50 grams of the solute in 1000 grams of water. What is the concentration of the solution in parts per million?

$$\text{ppm} = \frac{50}{(50 + 1000)} \times 1000000$$

$$\text{ppm} = \frac{50}{1050} \times 1000000 = 4.8 \times 10^4 \text{ ppm}$$

Concept Task: Be able to calculate grams of solute from ppm and grams of solution

$$\text{Grams of solute} = \frac{\text{ppm} \times \text{Grams of solute}}{1\,000\,000}$$

Example 27
How many grams of NH_4Cl is dissolved in 2000 grams solution to produce a concentration of 1.5 ppm?

$$\text{Grams of solute} = \frac{1.5 \times 2000}{1000000} = .003 \text{ g}$$

DO NOT forget to multiply or divide by 1000000 in parts per million problems.

Topic 7 - Solutions

Lesson 5 : Boiling and Vapor pressure

26. Boiling and vapor pressure: Definitions and facts

Vapor pressure is a pressure exerted by evaporated particles (vapor, gas) of a liquid on the surface of the liquid.

Vapor is a gas form of a substance that is normally a liquid.

For example: Water is normally a liquid. **Water vapor** is evaporated molecules of water in the gas phase.

Concept Facts: Study to remember the facts below about vapor pressure.
. Vapor pressure varies depending on the temperature of a liquid
. The higher the temperature of a liquid, the higher its vapor pressure
. Different substances have different vapor pressure at given temperatures
. Substances with low vapor pressure have strong intermolecular forces
. Substances with high vapor pressure have weaker intermolecular forces

RECALL that intermolecular forces are forces holding molecules of a substance together.
A molecule of a substance enters into the vapor (gas) phase when the intermolecular forces holding it to other molecules are broken.

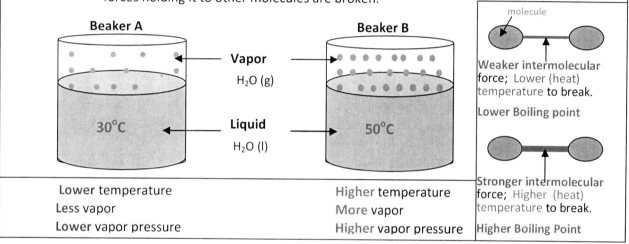

Beaker A	Beaker B	
Lower temperature	Higher temperature	Weaker intermolecular force; Lower (heat) temperature to break. Lower Boiling point
Less vapor	More vapor	
Lower vapor pressure	Higher vapor pressure	Stronger intermolecular force; Higher (heat) temperature to break. Higher Boiling Point

27. Boiling and Pressure: Definitions and facts

Boiling is a rapid phase change of a liquid to the vapor phase.
Boiling occurs when the vapor pressure of a liquid is equal to the atmospheric pressure

Concept Facts: Study to learn the relationship between boiling of a liquid and vapor pressure

Atmospheric pressure is the pressure exerted by the weight of air on the surface of objects here on earth.

Normal atmospheric pressure = Standard Pressure = 101.3 KPa or 1 atm   (SEE TABLE A)

Boiling point is the temperature at which vapor pressure of a liquid equals the atmospheric pressure.

Water boils at 100°C at normal atmospheric pressure (101.3 KPa or 1 atm) because 100°C is
the temperature of water that will produce a vapor pressure of 101.3 KPa (or 1 atm). **(SEE Table H)**
. At a different atmospheric pressure (higher or lower elevation), water boils at a different temperature

Different substances have different boiling points because strength of intermolecular forces varies from one substance to another.
. Substances with strong intermolecular forces have higher boiling points than those with weak intermolecular forces **(See Diagram above)**

Reference Table H on the next page shows the relationship between temperature and vapor pressure of four liquids.

Topic 7 - Solutions

28. Reference Table H: Temperature vs. Vapor pressure table

Table H below shows the relationship between temperature and vapor pressure of four liquids: propanone, ethanol, water, and ethanoic acids

Use this Table to also determine boiling points of the liquids at any atmospheric pressure.

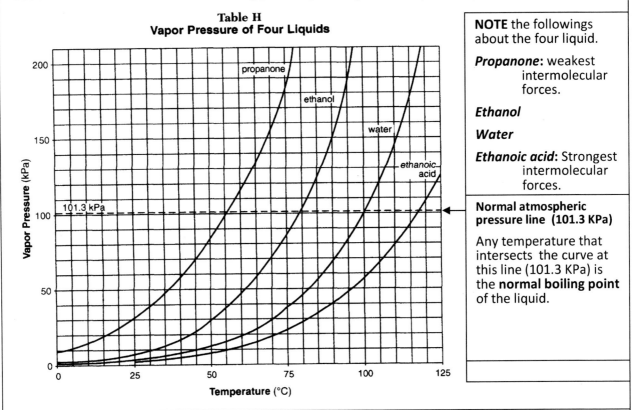

NOTE the followings about the four liquid.

Propanone: weakest intermolecular forces.

Ethanol

Water

Ethanoic acid: Strongest intermolecular forces.

Normal atmospheric pressure line (101.3 KPa)

Any temperature that intersects the curve at this line (101.3 KPa) is the **normal boiling point** of the liquid.

Below, Concept Tasks and example questions related to vapor pressure and the use of Table H are given. **Study** each question and be sure to confirm the answer given by looking at Table H.

Concept Task: Be able to determine the vapor pressure of a liquid at any given temperature.

Example 28
What is the vapor pressure of propanone at 45°C?
1) 60 KPa   2) 101.3 KPa   3) 120 KPa   4) 145 KPa

Answer: Choice 1

Concept Task: Be able to determine the normal boiling point of the liquids:

Example 29
Which liquid has the highest normal boiling point?
1) Propanone   2) Ethanol   3) Water   4) Ethanoic acid

Answer: Choice 4

Concept Task: Be able to determine boiling point of the liquids at any given atmospheric pressure.

Example 30
What is the boiling point of propanone at normal atmospheric pressure?
1) 100°C   2) 50°C   3) 101.3 °C   4) 28°C

Answer: Choice 2

Topic 7 - Solutions

Lesson 6 : Effect of solute on the physical properties of a water.

Introduction:

When a solute is dissolved in water to make a solution, physical properties of the solution will be different than those of water.

In this lesson, you will learn about changes in physical properties of water when a solute is added to water to make a solution. You will also learn how to determine which solute and which concentration of a solution will have the greatest or least effect on the properties of water.

29. Effect of solute: Comparing physical properties of solution to that of pure of water

Pure water has a certain set of physical properties. Some of these properties are listed below.

Concept Facts: Study to remember these properties of pure water.

   Boiling point at $100°C$
   Freezing point at $0°C$
   Vapor pressure of 101.3 KPa (at $100°C$)
   No electrical conductivity

When a solute is dissolved in water to make a solution, these physical properties of water will change.
   These changes are listed below.

Concept Task: Study to remember these changes to properties of water.

   Number of dissolved particles in the water increases ↑
       As a result:
   Boiling point is increased or elevated   ↑
       This means a solution will boil at a temperature that is higher than $100°C$.
   Freezing point is decreased or depressed ↓
       This means a solution will freeze at a temperature that is lower than $0°C$.
   Vapor pressure is decreased or lowered ↓
       This means a solution will have a vapor pressure that is less than 101.3 KPa at $100°C$.
   Electrical Conductivity is increased   ↑
       This means a solution will conduct electrical current better than pure water

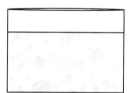

Pure water: No dissolved particles

   Higher freezing point
   Lower boiling point

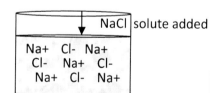

NaCl solution: More dissolved particles

   Lower Freezing point
   Higher boiling point

How much higher or lower are the boiling and freezing points of a solution when compared to those of pure water depends on the following factors.
   . Number of dissolved particles the solute produced (ionized to) in the water.
   . Concentration of particles in the solution

On the next page, you will learn how to determine:
   .Which concentration and which solute will cause the greatest or the least change on boiling and freezing points.

Topic 7 - Solutions

30. Effect of concentration on physical properties: Concept Facts and examples

Consider the following diagrams comparing freezing and boiling points of three KCl solutions.

NOTE the followings: The three solutions contain the same solute (KCl)

Their Molarity concentrations are different.

Lowest concentration   Highest concentration

Lowest Boiling point   Highest boiling point

Highest Freezing point   Lowest Freezing point

FACT: A solution of a higher concentration will produce a lower freezing point and a higher boiling point than a solution of a lower concentration.

31. Effect of concentration: Determining concentration effect on physical properties

Concept Task: Be able to determine which concentration will produce a solution with the lowest or highest freezing (or boiling) point.

Below, are notes on how to figure this out. **Study** information below and the example questions to the right to learn to do the same.

To determine the concentration that produces:

Lowest Freezing point

OR

Highest Boiling point

LOOK for Highest Molarity (M) concentration

To determine the concentration that produces:

Highest Freezing Point

OR

Lowest Boiling Point

LOOK for Lowest Molarity (M) concentration

Example 31

A concentration of which $CaCl_2$ solution will have the lowest freezing point?

1) 1 M   2) 2 M   3) 3M   4) 4 M

Answer: Choice 4 : The higher the concentration the lower the freezing point of the solution.

Example 32

Compare to a solution of 0.5M LiBr solution, a solution of 0.1M LiBr will have a

1) Lower freezing and lower boiling points
2) Lower freezing and higher boiling points
3) Higher freezing and lower boiling points
4) Higher freezing and higher boiling points

Before choosing: Consider the comparison:

You are comparing:

Lower Molarity	TO	Higher Molarity
0.1 M	TO	0.5 M
Lower FP / Higher BP		Higher FP / Lower BP

Answer: Choice 3. Lower Molarity concentration solution will always have a higher freezing point (FP) and a lower boiling point (BP) when compared to solutions with higher Molarity concentrations.

Topic 7 - Solutions

32. Effect of solutes on physical properties: Facts and diagrams

Consider the following diagrams comparing the freezing and boiling points of three solutions.

NOTE the followings: Each solution contains different solute (different number of dissolved particles)

Their Molarity concentrations are the same (1 M)

 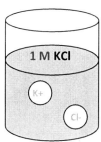 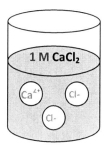

Molecular solute (CH_3OH)　　Ionic solute (KCl)　　Ionic solute ($CaCl_2$)

(1 dissolved particle)　　2 dissolved (K+ , Cl-) particles　　3 dissolved (Ca^{2+}, Cl- , Cl-) particles

Lowest Boiling point　　　　　　　　　　　　　　　Highest boiling point

Highest Freezing point　　　　　　　　　　　　　Lowest Freezing point

IMPORTANT NOTES:

Molecular substances (such as CH_3OH) DO NOT dissolve into ions or break up into element individual element when placed in water to dissolve.
In solutions, they stay as one molecule (CH_3OH) or one dissolved particle.

Ionic substances (such as KCl and $CaCl_2$) dissolve or break up into ions when placed in water.

The number of dissolved particles in an ionic solution depends on the total number of + and – ions that makes up the ionic formula.

 LOOKING BACK: Topic 5- Chemical formulas, You learned how to count ions in formulas.

 LOOKING BACK: Topic 4: Chemical Bonding: You learned how to determine chemical formulas of molecular and ionic compounds.

Concept Fact: The effect of solute on boiling and freezing points depends on the number of dissolved particles a solute produced when in solutions.

According to the above diagrams:

. Ionic solutes will always produce more dissolved particles than molecular (covalent) solutes.
Therefore, a solution of ionic solute (KCl and $CaCl_2$) will always have a lower freezing point and a higher boiling point than a solution of a molecular compound (CH_3OH) of the same concentration.

. Ionic solutes that produced three particles will have a lower freezing point and a higher boiling point than ionic solutes that produced two particles in solution.
Therefore, a solution of $CaCl_2$ (three dissolved ions) will always have a lower freezing point and a higher boiling point than a solution of KCl (two dissolved ion) of the same concentration.

See next page for example questions.

Copyright © 2010 E3 Scholastic Publishing. All Rights Reserved.　　161

Topic 7 - Solutions

33. Effect of solutes: Determining which solute will produce a solution with the highest (or lowest) freezing and boiling points

Concept Task: Be able to determine which solute will produce a solution with the highest or lowest freezing (or boiling) point.

To determine which solute will produce solution with

Highest Freezing point OR LOWEST Boiling point

LOOK for a molecular (only nonmetal) formula.
If there is no Molecular formula,
CHOOSE ionic formula with JUST two total ions

To determine which solute will produce solution with:

Lowest Freezing point OR Highest Boiling point

LOOK for ionic (metal-nonmetal) formula
If more than one ionic
CHOOSE the ionic formula with the most ions

Example 33

A 2 M solution of which solute would have the *highest freezing point*?

1) $CaCl_2$ 3) KCl
2) $C_6H_{12}O_6$ 4) KNO_3

Before choosing, Consider what to look for:

For Highest Freezing point

LOOK for molecular (only nonmetal) formula

Answer: Choice 2. $C_6H_{12}O_6$ is molecular (contains of only nonmetal atoms)

The rest of the choices are ionic (each contains a metal)

Example 34

Which 0.1 M solution will have the highest boiling point?

1) $NaNO_3$ 3) CH_3OH
2) $Mg(NO_3)_2$ 4) C_2H_5OH

Before choosing: consider what to look for:

For Highest Boiling Point

LOOK for ionic (metal-nonmetal) formula

Choice 1: $NaNO_3$ is ionic (2 total ions)

Choice 2: $Mg(NO_3)_2$ is also ionic (3 total ions)

Answer : Choice 2. $Mg(NO_3)_2$ contains more ions

Example 35

Which solution will have the *lowest freezing point*?

1) 1 M CH_3OH 3) 2 M CH_3OH
2) 1 M LiBr   4) 2 M LiBr

Answer: Choice 4. it contains higher concentration (2 M) of ionic solute (LiBr)

Topic 7 – Solutions

Check-A-list

Concept Terms

Below is a list of vocabulary terms from Topic 7. You should know the definition and facts related to each term.

Put a check in the box [V] next to each term if you know its definition and other facts related to the term.

[ ] Aqueous solution
[ ] Homogeneous mixture
[ ] Solution
[ ] Properties of solutions
[ ] Solute
[ ] Solvent
[ ] Solubility
[ ] Soluble
[ ] Miscibility
[ ] Miscible
[ ] Immiscible
[ ] Solubility factors

[ ] Saturated
[ ] Unsaturated
[ ] Supersaturated
[ ] Dilute
[ ] Concentrated
[ ] Molarity
[ ] Part per million
[ ] Vapor
[ ] Vapor pressure
[ ] Boiling Point

If you do not have a check next to a term, look it up or ask your teacher.

Concept Tasks

Below is a list of concept tasks from Topic 7. You should know how to solve problems and answer questions related to each concept task.

Put a check in the box [V] next a concept task if you know how to solve problems and answer questions related to it.

[ ] Interpreting symbol of a solution
[ ] Determining solute and solvent of a solution.
[ ] Determining a substance whose solubility changes with increase or decrease in temperature (or pressure).
[ ] Determining temperature and pressure that a solute is most or least soluble.
[ ] Determining and recognizing which substance is soluble or insoluble Using Table F
[ ] Determining grams of solute to form a saturated solution using Solubility Curve Table G.
[ ] Determining grams of solute needed to add to a solution to make it saturated
[ ] Determining if solution is saturated, supersaturated or unsaturated in 100 g of water
[ ] Determining if solution is saturated, supersaturated or unsaturated in MORE or LESS than 100 g of water.
[ ] Determining if a solution is concentrated or dilute using Table G
[ ] Determining which saturated solution is most or least soluble, dilute, or concentrated from Table G
[ ] Interpreting Molarity concentration value (M) of a solution.
[ ] Calculating Molarity (M) concentration from moles of solute and volume (L) of a solution
[ ] Calculating Molarity (M) concentration from mass (g) of solute and volume (L) of a solution
[ ] Calculating moles of solute from Molarity (M) and volume (L) of a solution
[ ] Calculating of mass of solute from Molarity and volume (L) of a solution
[ ] Calculating volume (L) of a solution from Molarity (M) and moles of solute
[ ] Interpreting part per million (ppm) concentration of a solution
[ ] Calculating ppm concentration from Grams of solute and Grams of solution
[ ] Calculating ppm concentration from Grams of solute and Grams of water
[ ] Calculating Grams of solute from ppm concentration and Grams of solution
[ ] Determining vapor pressure of any liquid at a given temperature using Reference Table H
[ ] Determining normal boiling point of the four liquids using Table H
[ ] Determining boiling point of any of the liquids at a given atmospheric pressure

If you do not have a check next to a concept task, look it up or ask your teacher.

Topic 7 – Solutions

Concept Fact Review Questions

1. The process of recovering a salt from a solution by evaporating the solvent is known as
   1) Decomposition   2) Crystallization   3) Reduction   4) Filtration

2. In a true solution, the dissolved particles
   1) Are visible to the eyes
   2) Will settle out on standing
   3) Are always solids
   4) Cannot be removed by filtration

3. Which change will increase the solubility of a gas in water?
   1) Increase in pressure and increase in temperature
   2) Increase in pressure and decrease in temperature
   3) Decrease in pressure and increase in temperature
   4) Decrease in pressure and decrease in temperature

4. The solubility of a salt in a given volume of water depends largely on the
   1) Surface area of the salt crystals
   2) Pressure on the surface of the water
   3) Rate at which the salt and water are stirred
   4) Temperature of the water

5. A solution in which equilibrium exists between dissolved and undissolved particles is also a
   1) Saturated solution
   2) Concentrated solution
   3) Supersaturated solution
   4) Dilute solution

6. Molarity (M) of a solution is equal to the
   1) $\dfrac{\text{Number of grams of solute}}{\text{Liter of solution}}$
   2) $\dfrac{\text{Number of moles of solute}}{\text{Liter of solvent}}$
   3) $\dfrac{\text{Number of grams of solute}}{\text{Liter of solvent}}$
   4) $\dfrac{\text{Number of moles of solute}}{\text{Liter of solution}}$

7. When the vapor pressure of a liquid is equal to the atmospheric pressure, the liquid will
   1) Freeze   2) Melt   3) Boil   4) Condense

8. As a solute is added to a solvent, what happens to the freezing point and the boiling point of the solution?
   1) The freezing point decreases and the boiling point decreases
   2) The freezing point decreases and the boiling point increases
   3) The freezing point increases and the boiling point decreases
   4) The freezing point increases and the boiling point increases

9. As water is added to a solution, the number of dissolved ions in the solution
   1) Increases, and the concentration of the solution remains the same
   2) Decreases, and the concentration of the solution increases
   3) Remains the same, and the concentration of the solution decreases
   4) Remains the same, and the concentration of the solution remains the same

10. The depression of the freezing point is dependent on
    1) The nature of the solute
    2) The concentration of dissolved particles
    3) Hydrogen bonding
    4) The formula of the solute

Topic 7 – Solutions

Concept Task Review Questions

11. What happens when $Ca(NO_3)_2(s)$ is dissolved in water?
    1) NO_3^- ions are attracted to the oxygen atoms of water
    2) Ca^{2+} ions are attracted to the oxygen atoms of water
    3) Ca^{2+} ions are attracted to the hydrogen atoms of water
    4) No attractions are involved, the crystal just falls apart

12. A decrease in water temperature will increase the solubility of
    1) $C_6H_{12}O_6(s)$ 2) $NH_3(g)$ 3) $KCl(s)$ 4) $Br_2(l)$

13. Under which two conditions would water contain the least number of dissolved $NH_3(g)$ molecules?
    1) 101.3 KPa and 273 K
    2) 101.3 kPa and 546 K
    3) 60 KPa and 273 K
    4) 60 KPa and 546 K

14. According to Reference Table F, which of these compounds is soluble in water at STP?
    1) $ZnSO_4$ 2) $BaSO_4$ 3) $ZnCO_3$ 4) $NaCO_3$

15. According to Table F, which chromate salt is least soluble?
    1) Potassium chromate
    2) Calcium chromate
    3) Ammonium chromate
    4) Lithium chromate

16. How many grams of KCl must be dissolved in 100 g of H_2O at 60°C to make a saturated ?
    1) 30 g   2) 45 g   3) 56 g   4) 90 g

17. Which is a saturated solution?
    1) 40 g NH_4Cl in 100 g of water at 50°C
    2) 2g SO_2 in 100 g water at 10°C
    3) 52 g KCl in 100 g of water at 80°C
    4) 120 g KI in 100 g water at 20°C

18. What amount of potassium chloride must be added to a solution made by dissolving 80 g of the solute in 200 grams of H_2O at 60°C to produce a saturated solution?
    1) 45 g   2) 160 g   3) 100 g   4) 120 g

19. One hundred grams of water is saturated with NH_4Cl at 50°C. If the temperature of the solution is decreased to 10°C, what amount of the solute will precipitate?
    1) 5 g   2) 17 g   3) 30 g   4) 50 g

20. Based on Reference Table G, a solution of $NaNO_3$ that contains 120 g of solute dissolved in 100 gram of H_2O at 50 °C is best described as
    1) Saturated   2) Unsaturated   3) Supersaturated

21. A solution containing 140 grams of potassium iodide in 100 grams of water at 20°C is best classified as
    1) Unsaturated and dilute
    2) Unsaturated and concentrated
    3) Saturated and dilute
    4) Supersaturated and concentrated

22. A saturated solution of which compound will be the least concentrated solution in 100 g of water at 40°C?
    1) SO_2 2) NaCl   3) $KClO_3$ 4) NH_4Cl

Topic 7 – Solutions

23. According to Reference Table G, how does a decrease in temperature from 40°C to 20°C affect the solubility of $NH_3(g)$ and that of NH_4Cl?
    1) The solubility of NH_3 increases, and the solubility of NH_4Cl increases
    2) The solubility of NH_3 decreases, and the solubility of NH_4Cl increases
    3) The solubility of NH_3 increases, and the solubility of NH_4Cl decreases
    4) The solubility of NH_3 decreases, and the solubility of NH_4Cl decreases

24. A solution of NaCl contains 1.8 moles of the solute in 600 ml of solution. What is the concentration of the solution?
    1) 333 M   2) 0.003 M   3) 3 M   4) 0.05 M

25. A student dissolved 48 grams of $(NH_4)_2CO_3$ in 2000 ml of water. What will be the molarity of this solution?
    1) 1 M   2) 2 M   3) 0.25   4) 0.5 M

26. How many moles of KNO_3 are required to make .50 liter of a 2 molar solution of KNO_3?
    1) 1.0   2) 2.0   3) 0.50   4) 4.0

27. How many liters of 1.5 M $Ca(NO_3)_2$ solution would contain .45 mole of the $Ca(NO_3)_2$ solute?
    1) 0.3 L   2) 0.67 L   3) 1.95 L   4) 243 L

28. A 500 gram of oxygen solution contains .05 grams of dissolved oxygen. The concentration of this solution expressed in parts per million is closest to
    1) 1.0×10^4 ppm   3) 1.0×10^{-4} ppm
    2) 1.0×10^2 ppm   4) 2.5×10^7 ppm

29. The vapor pressure of a liquid is 0.92 atm at 60°C. The normal boiling point of the liquid could be
    1) 35°C   2) 45°C   3) 55°C   4) 65°C

30. Which preparation will produce the greatest increase in the boiling point of water?
    1) 0.3 moles of $CaCl_2$ in 100 g of water
    2) 0.3 moles of $CaCl_2$ in 1000 g of water
    3) 0.3 moles of KCl in 100 g of water
    4) 0.3 moles of KCl in 1000 g of water?

31. Which of the preparation of solutions will have the lowest freezing point?
    1) 0.2 M KOH   3) 0.2 M $Mg(OH)_2$
    2) 0.2 M NaOH   4) 0.2 M $CH_2(OH)_2$

Topic 7 – Solutions

Constructed Response Questions

Base your answers to questions 32 and 33 on the information below.

A student is instructed to make 0.250 liter of a 0.200 M aqueous solution of $Ca(NO_3)_2$.

32. In order to prepare the described solution in the laboratory, two quantities must be measured accurately. One of these quantities is the volume of the solution. What other quantity must be measured to prepare this solution?

33. Show a correct numerical setup for calculating the total number of moles of $Ca(NO_3)_2$ needed to make 0.250 liter of the 0.200 M calcium nitrate solution.

34. Show a correct numerical setup for determining how many liters of a 1.2 M solution can be prepared with 0.50 mole of $C_6H_{12}O_6$.

35. What is the concentration of a solution that contains 2 moles of solute in 1.2 L of solution.

Given the balanced equation for the dissolving $NH_4Cl(s)$ in water:

$$NH_4Cl(s) \xrightarrow{H_2O} NH_4^+(aq) + Cl^-(aq)$$

36. A student is holding a test tube containing 5.0 milliliters of water. When a sample of $NH_4Cl(s)$ is placed in the test tube, the test tube feels colder to the student's hand. Describe the direction of heat flow between the test tube and the hand.

37. Using the key to the right, draw at least two water molecules in the box showing the correct orientation of each water when it is near the Cl^- ion in the aqueous solution

Key
● = Hydrogen atom
○ = Oxygen atom
●○● = Water molecule

Topic 8 – Acids, Bases and Salt

Topic outline:

In this topic, you will learn about the following concepts:
- General properties of acids and bases
- Definitions of acids and bases by:
  - Arrhenius theory
  - Alternate theory
- Relative ion concentration
- pH values
- Changes on indicators
- Relating H+ to pH
- Reactions of acids and bases
- Titration
- Salts

1. Properties of Acids and Bases: Summary of general characteristics

Acids and bases have a certain set of properties that are used to identify them. Below is a summary of these properties. In the next few sets, you will learn more about these characteristics of acids and bases.

Concept Facts: Study to remember the following properties of acids and bases. Note similarities and differences between them.

Acids

1) Are electrolytes
2) Change color of indicators
3) React with bases (Neutralization reaction) to produce Water and Salt
4) Produce H+ as only positive ion in solutions
5) Contain MORE H^+ than OH^- in solutions
6) When added to water, increase H+ concentration of the water
7) When added to water, decrease OH- concentration of the water
8) When added to water, decrease pH
9) Have pH LESS than 7
10) Turn litmus red
11) Turn blue litmus red
12) Have no effect on phenolphthalein (stays colorless)
13) Taste sour
14) React with certain metals to produce salt and hydrogen gas

Bases

1) Are electrolytes
2) Change color of indicators
3) React with acids (Neutralization reaction) to produce water and salt
4) Produce OH- as the only negative ion in solutions
5) Contain More OH- than H+ in solutions
6) When added to water, decrease H+ ion concentration of the water
7) When added to water, increase OH- ion concentration of the water
8) When added to water, increase pH
9) Have pH GREATER than 7
10) Turn litmus blue
11) Turn red litmus blue
12) Turn colorless phenolphthalein to pink
13) Taste bitter and feels slippery

Neutral substances

1) pH of 7
2) Have equal amount of H+ to OH- ions

Topic 8 – Acids, Bases and Salt

Lesson 1: Defining acids and bases

Introductions

What is an acid? What is a base? These questions cannot be answered with just one simple definition. Acids and bases can be defined by many different characteristics.

In this topic, you will learn how acids and bases are defined by theories and other characteristics. As you study this lesson, pay attention to the similarities and differences between acids and bases.

2. Arrhenius theory of acids and bases: Definitions, facts and examples

Arrhenius theory defines acids and bases by the ion each can produce in solutions.

Below, acids and bases are defined through Arrhenius theory.
Concept Facts: Study to remember the followings

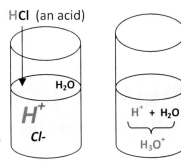

Arrhenius acids: Definitions and facts
Arrhenius acids are substances that can produce
- H^+ (hydrogen ion, proton) in solutions
- H^+ produced by acids is the only positive ion in acidic solutions
- Properties of acids (listed in the summary) are related to properties of H^+ ions they produce
- H^+ ions produced by acids usually combine with H_2O to become H_3O^+ (H^+ and H_3O^+ are synonymous with each other)

$$H^+ + H_2O \longrightarrow H_3O^+$$
hydrogen ion   hydronium ion

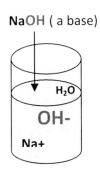

Arrhenius Bases: Definitions and facts:
Arrhenius Bases are substances that can produce OH^- (hydroxide ion) in solutions.
- OH^- produced by bases is the only negative ion in basic solutions
- Properties of bases (listed in the summary) are related to properties of OH^- ions they produce
- Most bases are ionic compounds

3. Alternate theory of acids and bases: Definition and facts

Alternate (a different) theory defines acids and bases by their ability to donate or accept a proton (H^+ or hydrogen ion) during certain chemical reactions.

Concept Facts: Study to remember the following.

Alternate theory of acids:
- An acid is a substance that can *donate a proton* (H^+ or hydrogen ion) during a reaction

Alternate theory of bases:
- A base is a substance that can *accept a proton* (H^+ or hydrogen ion) during a reaction

Topic 8 – Acids, Bases and Salt

4. Arrhenius acids: Determining formulas and names of Arrhenius acids

Concept Task: Be able to determine formulas of Arrhenius acids.
Be able to determine formulas of substances that will produce H+ (hydrogen ion) or H_3O+ (hydronium) ion in solutions.

To determine these substances

LOOK for one of the common acids on Table K (below)
or
LOOK for a formula containing H and another nonmetal

Reference Table K : Common acids

Formula of acid	Name of acid
HCl	Hydrochloric acid
HNO_3	Nitric acid
H_2SO_4	Sulfuric acid
H_3PO_4	Phosphoric acid
H_2CO_3 or CO_2	Carbonic acid
CH_3COOH or HC_2H_3OH	Ethanoic acid (acetic acid)

Example 1

Which of these substances is considered an Arrhenius acid?

1) KOH 2) CH_3OH 3) HNO_3 4) NH_3

Answer: Choice 3. HNO_3 is listed on the **Table K**

Example 2

Which substance will dissolve in water to produce H_3O+ (hydronium ion) as the only positive ion in solutions?

1) HF 2) NaOH 3) NH_4OH 4) KCl

Before choosing: consider what to LOOK for:

THINK: H_3O^+ are produced by acids

LOOK for: formula of an acid:

Answer: Choice 1. HF is a formula of an acid. It contains H and another nonmetal (F)

5. Arrhenius bases: Determining and recognizing formula of bases

Concept Task: Be able to determine or recognize formulas of Arrhenius bases.

To determine if a substance is Arrhenius base, OR
To determine which substance will produce OH^- :

LOOK for one of the common bases on Table L (below)
OR
LOOK for a formula containing a metal and OH

Reference Table L : Common bases

Formula of bases	Name of bases
LiOH	Lithium hydroxide
NaOH	Sodium hydroxide
KOH	Potassium hydroxide
$Ca(OH)_2$	Calcium hydroxide
NH_4OH	Ammonium hydroxide
$NH_3(aq)$	Aqueous ammonia

Example 3

Which formula is an Arrhenius base?

1) HCl 2) Her 3) CH_3OH 4) KOH

Answer: Choice 4. KOH is listed on Table L

Example 4

Aqueous solution of which of these substances contains hydroxide ions as the only negative ion?

1) C_2H_5OH 3) $Mg(OH)_2$
2) NaCl 4) H_2SO_4

Before choosing: consider what to LOOK for:

THINK: Hydroxide ions are produced by bases.

LOOK for: Formula of a base

Answer: Choice 3. $Mg(OH)_2$ is a formula of a base. It contains a metal (Mg) and OH

Copyright © 2010 E3 Scholastic Publishing. All Rights Reserved.

Topic 8 – Acids, Bases and Salt

6. Relative ions concentration of acids and bases: Definitions and facts

NOTE: All solutions made with water contain both H^+ and OH^- ions.
A solution can be defined as acidic or basic depending on how much H^+ and OH^- are in the solution.
In the notes below, acids and bases are defined based on their relative ions concentration.

Concept Facts: Study to remember the following definitions.

Defining acids and bases by relative ions concentration:

Acidic solutions contain *more* (higher concentration of) H^+ ions than OH^- ions.
Acidity describes how acidic is a solution.
    Example of acidic solution that will contain more H^+ ions than OH^- ion
        HCl(aq)   and HNO_3(aq)

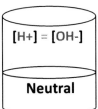

Neutral solutions and pure water contain *equal* amount of H^+ and OH^-

    Example of neutral solutions that contain equal amount of H^+ to OH^-
        Pure H_2O (l)   and   NaCl (aq)

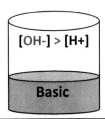

Basic solutions contain *more* (higher concentration of) OH^- ions than H^+ ions
Alkalinity describes how basic is a solution.
    Example of basic solutions that will contain more OH^- ions than H^+ ions
        NaOH(aq)   and NH_3(aq)

7. Relative ions concentration: Determining substances with more or less of the ions

Concept Task: Be able to determine formulas or names of substances based on ion concentrations.

Below, information on this concept task and example questions are given.
Study to learn how to answer similar questions.

To determining which substance will produce more H^+ (H_3O^+) **ions than** OH^- **ions:**	**Example 5** *Which of these solutions contains higher concentrations of H_3O^+ ion than OH^- ions?* 1) NH_3(aq) 3) $C_6H_{12}O_6$(aq) 2) HNO_3(aq) 4) $Ca(OH)_2$ (aq)
LOOK for a formula or name of an acid (Use Table K to confirm acid formula)	**Answer: Choice 2.** Acids have more H_3O^+ than OH^-. HNO_3 is an acid
To determining which formula will produce more OH^- **ions than** H^+ (H_3O^+) **ions:**	**Example 6** *Which substance will produce a solution with more hydroxide ions than hydrogen ions?* 1) LiOH 2) KCl 3) HCl 4) CH_3COOH
LOOK for a formula or name of a base (Use Table L to confirm base formula)	**Answer: Choice 1.** Bases produce solutions with more hydroxide ion (OH^-) than hydrogen ion (H^+). KOH is a base

Topic 8 – Acids, Bases and Salt

8. pH values of acids and bases: Definitions and facts

pH is a measure of the hydrogen (H^+) ion or the hydronium (H_3O^+) ion concentration of a solution. A pH scale ranges in value from 1 – 14. Acids and bases can be defined by their pH values.

Defining acids and bases by pH values.

Concept Facts: Study to remember the followings.

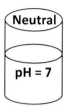
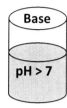

Acids are substances with pH values LESS than 7

Neutral substances have pH = 7

Bases are substances with pH values GREATER than 7

The strength of an acid or a base can be determined by its pH value:
Strong acids have very low pH values. Strong bases have very high pH values

A typical pH scale is shown below.
Some common substances are indicated below the scale to show where their pH values would be.

	Acid		Neutral		Base	
Strong		Weak		Weak		Strong
1---7---14
HCl		Acetic acid	H_2O	NH_3		NaOH
H_2SO_4						KOH

9. pH: Determining which substance has a given pH value

Concept Task: Be able to determine pH of a given substance
Be able to determine a name or formula of a substance based on a given pH

To determine substance if pH given is less than 7
LOOK for a formula or name of an acid

To determine substance if pH given is more than 7
LOOK for a formula or name of a base

To determine substance with pH equal to 7
LOOK for a formula or name of a neutral substance

Example 7

Substance X is dissolved in water to produce a solution with a pH of 2. Substance X is most likely

1) Lithium hydroxide 3) Methanol
2) Ammonia 4) Nitric acid

Before choosing: consider what to look for.

THINK: pH of 2 is less than 7. The substance must be an acid.

Answer: Choice 4.

Topic 8 – Acids, Bases and Salt

10. Acid-base indicators: Defining acids and bases by changes on indicators

Acid – Base **indicators** are substances that can change color in the presence of an acid or a base.

Acid and bases can be defined by the changes caused on these indicators.

The two most common acid-base indicators are phenolphthalein and litmus paper.

Concept Facts: Study to remember the following changes.

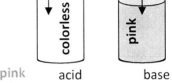

Phenolphthalein is a colorless (acid-base indicator) solution:

Acids are substances that have no effect on phenolphthalein. Phenolphthalein stays colorless in the presence of an acid.

Bases are substances that change colorless phenolphthalein to pink. Phenolphthalein is a good indicator to test for presence of a base

Litmus papers come in variety of colors.
When wet with an acidic or a basic solution, they will change color.

Acids are substances that will change Litmus paper to Red

Bases are substances that will change Litmus paper to Blue

Other common indicators are listed on Table M of the Reference Table

Reference Table M: Common acid-base indicators

Indicator	Approximate pH Range for Color Change	Color Change
methyl orange	3.2–4.4	red to yellow
bromthymol blue	6.0–7.6	yellow to blue
phenolphthalein	8.2–10	colorless to pink
litmus	5.5–8.2	red to blue
bromcresol green	3.8–5.4	yellow to blue
thymol blue	8.0–9.6	yellow to blue

Concept Task: Be able to determine the name or formula of a substance based on change on indicator.

Example 8
Which substance would change colorless phenolphthalein to pink?
1) H_2O 2) KOH 3) CH_3COOH 4) HCl

Before choosing: Use info from Table M

THINK: Phenolphthalein changes from colorless to pink in a solution of pH 8.2 – 10

RELATE: A solution of pH 8.2 - 10 is bases

LOOK for: A formula of a basic substance

Answer: Choice 2: KOH is a base (See Table L)

Example 9
Which substance would likely change bromcresol green from yellow to blue?
1) CH_3COOH 3) NaOH
2) CH_3OH 4) NaCl

Before choosing: LOOK at Table M

THINK: Bromcresol green changes from yellow to blue in a solution of pH 3.8 – 5.4

RELATE: pH 3.8 – 5.4 is a range for acids

LOOK for: Formula of an acid

Answer: Choice 1. CH_3COOH is an acid
(See Table K)

Topic 8 – Acids, Bases and Salt

11. Relating one property of an acid to another:

Concept Task: Be able to determine one property of a substance based on other given properties

For example, a solution that contains a higher concentration of H^+ ion than OH^- ions will also have a pH below 7. Both are properties of acids.

Below, example questions of relating one property of an acid or a base to other properties are given.

For the most part, information on the summary table at the beginning of this topic is needed to correctly answer these questions.

Study the two example questions below, and note how the correct answer to each question is chosen.

NOTE: The question below is testing your ability to relate pH of a solution (given in the choices) to change on litmus paper (given in question).

Example 10

A solution turns litmus red to blue. The pH of this solution could be

1) 1   2) 4   3) 7   4) 9

Before choosing: Use summary table to:
DETERMINE type of solution: Litmus red changes to blue in presence of a base
LOOK for: pH of a base

Answer: Choice 4. Bases have pH greater than 7.

NOTE: The question below is testing your ability to relate pH value and change of phenolphthalein (given in choices) to relative ions concentration of a solution (given in question).

Example 11

A solution contains more hydronium (H_3O^+) ions than hydroxide (OH^-) ions. Which statement is also true of this solution?

1) Its pH is 4, and phenolphthalein will be colorless
2) Its pH is 4, and phenolphthalein will be pink
3) Its pH is 10, and phenolphthalein will be colorless
4) Its pH is 10, and phenolphthalein will be pink

Before choosing:
DETERMINE type of solution: More H_3O^+ than OH^- is a property of acidic solutions.

LOOK for: pH of an acid, and correct effect on phenolphthalein

Answer: Choice 1. pH of 4 is of an acid (pH less than 7).
Phenolphthalein is colorless in acidic solution

Topic 8 – Acids, Bases and Salt

Lesson 2: Reactions of acids and bases

Introduction:
Acids and bases undergo chemical reactions with other substances and with each other.

In this lesson, you will learn about reactions of acids with reactive metals, and reactions of acids and bases with each other.

12. Reaction of acid with a metal: Definitions and facts

Acids react with certain metals to produce hydrogen gas and salt.

The reaction between an acid and a metal is a single replacement reaction.

Below, the general equation and two example equations showing this reaction are given:

NOTE: The reactants and the products.

General equation:	Metal	+	Acid	Salt	+	Hydrogen gas
Example equation 1:	Zn	+	2HCl ---------------→	$ZnCl_2$	+	H_2
Example equation 2:	Mg	+	HNO_3 ---------------→	$Mg(NO_3)_2$	+	H_2

13. Reference Table J – Activity Series: Understanding and using Table J

Which metal will react with acids?

Not every metal will react with acids to produce hydrogen gas and salt.

Reference Table J (SEE RIGHT) shows the activity series of metal (left column of table)

You can use this table to determine which metal will react with acids to produce hydrogen gas and a salt.

NOTE the following about the table.
. The most active metals are located on the top
. The least active metals are found on the bottom.
. H_2 separates metals that will react with acids from those that will not react with acid

Metals above H_2 (Li to Pb) **will react** with acids to produce H_2

Metals below H_2 (Cu to Ag) **will NOT** react with any acid

Reference Table J
Activity Series

Metals	Nonmetals
Li	F_2
Rb	Cl_2
K	Br_2
Cs	I_2
Ba	
Sr	
Ca	
Na	
Mg	
Al	
Ti	
Mn	
Zn	
Cr	
Fe	
Co	
Ni	
Sn	
Pb	
**H_2	
Cu	
Ag	
Au	

Most ↓ Least (both columns)

** Activity series based on Hydrogen standard

Topic 8 – Acids, Bases and Salt

14. Reaction of metal with acids: Determining which metal will react with an acid

Concept Task: Be able to determine a metal that will react with an acid to produce H_2 gas and salt.

You will need to use the **Reference Table J**

To determine which metal will react with an acid
  LOOK for a metal that is above H_2 on the Table J

If equations are given as choices:
  LOOK for equation containing a metal that is above H_2

Example 12
Which of the following metals is likely to react with nitric acid to produce hydrogen gas?

1) Silver   3) Sodium
2) Gold   4) Copper

Answer: Choice 3. Sodium (Na), is above H_2 on Table J

To determine which metal will not react with an acid
  LOOK for a metal that is below H_2 on the table

If equations are given as choices:
  LOOK for equation containing a metal that is below H_2

Example 13
Which reaction will not occur?

1) $Ag + H_2SO_4 \longrightarrow Ag_2SO_4 + H_2$
2) $Pb + H_2SO_4 \longrightarrow PbSO_4 + H_2$
3) $Zn + HCl \longrightarrow ZnCl_2 + H_2$
4) $Li + HCl \longrightarrow LiCl + H_2$

Answer: Choice 1. The metal, Ag, in this equation is **below** H_2 on the activity Table

15. Reactions of a metal with acid: How to determine formula of salt formed from metal – acid reactions

As mentioned, when an acid reacts with a metal, salt and hydrogen gas are produced.

Since the reaction is a single replacement, the salt is formed as the metal replaces hydrogen of the acid.

In the equation:

$$2Li + 2HBr \longrightarrow 2LiBr + H_2$$
(metal)   (acid)   (salt)   (hydrogen gas)

Li (metal) replaces H of HBr (acid) to form the LiBr (salt). The displaced H atoms from acid form H_2 gas.

On tests, you may be given an incomplete metal – acid reaction similar to the one below.

$$Ca + 2HCl \longrightarrow \underline{\qquad} + H_2$$

On the next page, step-by-step instructions on how to determine the correct salt formula to the above equation will be given.

Topic 8 – Acids, Bases and Salt

16. Reaction of acid with metal: Determining correct salt formula

Concept Task: Be able to determine the correct salt formulas from metal - acid reactions.

Below, two incomplete reactions involving an acid and a metal are given below.
The missing salt products are determined using two different methods.

As you study steps in each method, KEEP in mind that these steps will ensure that your salt formula is correct for the reaction given.

Study both examples and **NOTE** which method is the easiest for you in determining the missing salt formula.

Example 14: Determine correct formula of salt by equalizing the charge:

Given the incomplete reaction below:

$$2Na + H_2CO_3 \longrightarrow \underline{\quad} + H_2$$

What is the formula of the salt formed from this reaction?

To determine salt formula:

Replace H of acid H_2CO_3 **with metal** Na:

You'll get: Na_2CO_3

Check if charges are equalized in Na_2CO_3:

Na is a +1 ion (see Periodic Table): $2\,Na^{+1} = +2$

CO_3 is a -2 ion (see Table E): $1\,CO_3^{2-} = -2$

Are charges equalized in formula? Yes, because charges of +2 and -2 in the formula adds up to ZERO (equalized)

The formula: Na_2CO_3 is the correct salt formula

Example 15: Determining correct salt formula by counting atoms

In the reaction?

$$Ca + 2HCl \longrightarrow \underline{\quad} + H_2$$

Which formula represents the missing products?

1) CaH   3) CaCl
2) CaH_2 4) $CaCl_2$

Before choosing:
  Write down equation for the reaction:
  Count atoms on both sides of equation:
  Determine atoms that are missing

$$Ca + 2HCl \longrightarrow H_2 + \underline{\quad}$$
                                                missing
  1 Ca   1 Ca
  2 H   2 H
  2Cl   2 Cl

Correct missing formula of salt : $CaCl_2$

Answer: Choice 4

Topic 8 – Acids, Bases and Salt

17. Neutralization reaction: Definition and facts of acid – base neutralization reaction

Neutralization is a reaction between an acid and a base to produce *water* and *salt*.
Neutralization reaction is a double replacement reaction.

During neutralization reactions:

. Equal moles of H^+ (of an acid) and OH^- (of a base) combine to neutralize each other
. Water and salt are the products of all neutralization reactions
. The salt formula formed depends on the formula of the acid and the base

Below, general equation, example equation, and net ionic equation showing neutralization reaction are given:
NOTE: The reactants and the products.

General equation: Acid   +   Base   ---------->   Water   +   Salt

Example reaction equation: HCl   +   NaOH   --------> H_2O +   NaCl
(hydrochloric acid)   (Sodium hydroxide)   (water)   sodium chloride

Net ionic equation: H+   +   OH-   --------> H_2O

A **net ionic** equation for neutralization reactions shows how water (H_2O) is formed from the H^+ ion of the acid and the OH^- ion of the base

18. Neutralization reactions: Determining which equation represents a neutralization reaction

Concept Task: Be able to determine an equation that represents a neutralization reaction

To determine which equation represents neutralization:

LOOK for an equation showing:

Acid and base as **reactants** (on the LEFT)

OR

Salt and water as **products** (on the RIGHT)

USE Tables K and L to confirm formulas of acids and bases

Example 16
Which reaction represents a neutralization reaction?

1) Pb   + $AgNO_3$ -------->   Ag + $PbNO_3$
2) LiOH   + $HC_2H_3O_2$ --------> H_2O + $LiC_2H_3O_2$
3) NH_4Cl + $AgNO_3$ --------> NH_4NO_3 + AgCl
4) CH_4 + $2O_2$ --------> CO_2 + $2H_2O$

Analyze choices: Reactants must be an acid and a base
Products must be a salt and water
Use Table of acids (Table K) and bases (Table L) to confirm formulas.

Choose: Choice 2 because :
Reactants are LiOH (a base) and $HC_2H_3O_2$ is (an acid)

Topic 8 – Acids, Bases and Salt

19. Neutralization reactions: How to determine correct salt formula in neutralization reactions

RECALL that a neutralization reaction is a double replacement type reaction.
During a double replacement reaction, partners of the two reactants switch.

The **salt formula** can be determined by replacing the H of the acid with the metal (or NH_4) of the base.

Example neutralization equation is shown below.

$$HCl \quad + \quad NaOH \quad \longrightarrow \quad NaCl \quad + \quad HOH$$
(acid)   (base)   (salt)   (water)

In the above equation
The Salt, NaCl, is formed by Na of the base (NaOH) replacing H of the acid (HCl).

The water, HOH (H_2O), is formed by the H (of HCl) and OH (of NaOH).

On tests, you may be given an incomplete neutralization equation as shown below:
$$H_2SO_4 \quad + \quad KOH \quad \longrightarrow \quad \underline{} \quad + \quad H_2O$$

On the next page, you are shown how to determine the correct salt formula to this reaction.

NOTE: As with reactions of an acid with a metal, Just replacing the H of the acid with the metal does not guarantee a correct salt formula. The correct salt formula must contain appropriate combination of **subscripts** to equalize the charges. (**Review Topic 5 – formula writing.**)
In the section below, example questions related to this concept are given. Two ways of determining the correct salt formula will also be shown

20. Neutralization reaction: Determining formula of salt formed

Concept Task: Be able to determine (or write) the correct salt formulas in neutralization reactions.

Below, two incomplete neutralization reactions are given.
Missing salt products are determined using two different methods.
Study both examples and **NOTE** which method is the easiest for you in determining the missing salt formula.

Example 17: Determine the correct formula of salt by equalizing the charges:

$$H_2SO_4 \quad + \quad 2KOH \quad \longrightarrow \quad \underline{} \quad + \quad 2H_2O$$

To determine missing salt product:

Replace H of acid H_2SO_4 with K of base KOH:
You'll get: K_2SO_4

Check if formula K_2SO_4 is correct as written:
    K is +1 ion (See Periodic table): $2K^{+1} = +2$
    SO_4 is a -2 ion (See Table E): $1 SO_4^{2-} = -2$
    Charges in K_2SO_4 are equalized because sum of + and − ions equal Zero (+2 + -2 = 0)

K_2SO_4 is the correct salt formula

Example 18: Determining correct salt formula by counting atoms

Given the incomplete equation
$$2HCl \quad + \quad Mg(OH)_2 \quad \longrightarrow \quad \underline{} \quad + \quad 2H_2O$$
What is the formula of the missing salt product?

1) MgCl   2) H_2 3) Mg_2Cl 4) $MgCl_2$

Before choosing: Determine the missing atoms by counting the atoms on each side.

$2HCl \quad + \quad Mg(OH)_2 \quad \longrightarrow \quad 2H_2O \quad + \quad \underline{}$
    4H   4   missing
    2Cl   2 Cl
    2O   2 O
    1 Mg   1 Mg

Missing atoms: 1 Mg   and   2 Cl
Missing salt formula: $MgCl_2$ (**Answer: CHOICE 4**)

Topic 8 – Acids, Bases and Salt

21. Titration: Definitions and facts

Titration is a lab process used for determining the concentration of an unknown solution by reacting it with a solution of a known concentration.

Titration process usually involves an acid and a base (acid – base titration).
During acid – base titration lab, a base is slowly added to an acid in a beaker. When the number of moles of acid and base in the beaker are equal, neutralization has occurred.
Phenolphthalein (a base indicator) is always added to the acid beaker to indicate the point when the beaker contains only a base. Titration is stopped when the solution in the beaker has a faint pink color. This indicates that all the acid in the beaker has been neutralized, and the solution in the beaker is slightly basic.

If the following information about a titration process are known:
  . Volume of the acid (V_a) that was initially in the beaker.
  . Volume a the base (V_b) used to neutralize the acid
  . Concentration of the acid (M_a) or the base (M_b)

You can calculate for the unknown in the titration process using the titration equation below:

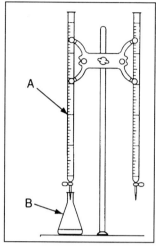

Acid – base titration set up

$M_a \times V_a = M_b \times V_b$

Reference Table T equation

M is the Molarity concentration of acid (M_a) and of base (M_b)
V is the volume of the acid (V_a) and of base (V_b)

22. Titration: Calculating for unknown in a titration problem

Concept Task: Be able to solve for an unknown in a neutralization problem using the titration equation.

Below is an example titration problem. **Study** the steps, set up and calculation of the unknown.

Example 19

A 30 ml of 0.6 M HCl solution is neutralized with 90 ml NaOH solution. What is the concentration of the base?

The steps below show how to solve the above problem using titration equation:

Step 1: Determine the known and unknown: $M_a = 0.6$ M $M_b = X$ (unknown)
                                                $V_a = 30$ ml $V_b = 90$ ml

Step 2: Set up problem using equation: $M_a V_a$ = $M_b V_b$
                                                .6 (30)   = X (90)
Step 3: Solve by : Multiply out: 18   = 90X
                        Divide both sides by 90 $\frac{18}{90}$ = $\frac{90X}{90}$

          Answer: 0.2 M = X = M_b

Molarity concentration of the base that was used to neutralized the 30 ml of 0.6 M of HCl acid solution

Be sure to always keep Molarity and volume of acid together on one side, and Molarity and volume of the base together on the other side of the equation.
When solving math problem in chemistry, be sure your set up is correct. If your set up is wrong, your answer will be calculated value will be wrong for that problem.

Topic 8 – Acids, Bases and Salt

23. Relating pH to H_3O^+ or H^+ ion concentration: Definition and facts.

Mathematically speaking, **pH is defined** as the –log of H^+ ion concentration of solutions.

$$pH = -\log [H^+]$$

pH is, therefore, a measure of how much (concentration of) H^+ or H_3O^+ is in a solution.

In most high school chemistry curriculums, you are not required to use above equation to determine the pH from H^+ Molarity concentration ion in a solution. Most H^+ concentration in high school text books are given in the form of 1×10^{-x} M. The x being a value (between 1 to 14) of a negative exponent.

When the $[H^+]$ or $[H_3O^+]$ of a solution is given in the form of: 1×10^{-x} M

pH value of the solution = x

Example: If [H+] of a solution = 1.0×10^{-4} M.

The pH of the solution = 4

Below, you are given two solutions with different H^+ or H_3O^+ concentration.
Note the relationships between the H+ concentrations to pH values and types of solution.
Study these examples to learn how to determine pH values from $[H_3O^+]$.

H_3O^+ concentration	pH value	Type of solution
1.0×10^{-2} M	2	Acidic
1.0×10^{-8} M	8	Basic

[ ] means concentration of..

24. Relating pH to H^+ concentration: Determining pH from [H3O+] and [H+]

Concept Task: Be able to determine pH of a solution from H^+ (or H_3O^+) concentration.

To determine pH value from given H3O+ (or H^+) concentration
LOOK for pH value equal to the value of negative exponent

Concept Task: Be able to determine H+ (H_3O^+) concentration from pH value

To determine H_3O^+ or H^+ concentration given pH
LOOK for H3O+ or H+ concentration that is equal to: $1 \times 10^{-(\text{value of pH}) \text{ given}}$

Example 20
What is the pH of a solution with H3O+ concentration of 1.0×10^{-6} M?
1) 1   2) 10   3) 6   4) 8

Answer: Choice 3 because pH of 6 is the value of the negative exponent : 1.0×10^{-6}

Example 21
A solution of which H^+ concentration would have a pH of 2?
1) 1×10^{-12} M   3) 1×10^{-2} M
2) 1×10^{-10} M   4) 1×10^{-14} M

Answer: Choice 3. The value of negative exponent must be equal to the pH that is given.

Topic 8 – Acids, Bases and Salt

25. Relating pH to [H+] concentration: Determining change in pH as H+ ion changes

As you know by now, a solution with a pH of 3 is more acidic than a solution with pH of 4.
The difference in level of acidity of one solution to another is due to the difference in H+ concentration of the solutions.
Since the concentration of H+ ions in solutions determines pH, a solution with a pH of 3 has more H+ ions than a solution with a pH of 4.
    . As H+ ion concentration of a solution increases, pH of the solution decreases
    . The lower the pH, the more H+ ions is in a solution

Below, a diagram showing a change in pH of a solution as H+ ion concentration is changed.

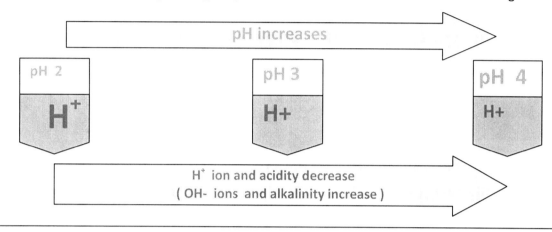

26. Relating pH to [H+] : Difference in [H+] of solutions with two different pH values

How many more (or less) H+ is in one solution in comparison to another solution can be determined if the pH values of the two solutions are known.

Because of the mathematical relation of H+ concentration to pH:

   1 value difference in pH = **10 times (fold) difference in H+ concentration**

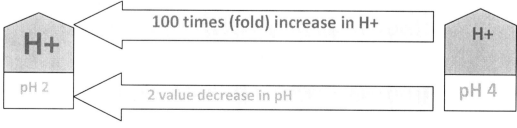

Topic 8 – Acids, Bases and Salt

27. Relative pH to [H+] : Determining difference in H+ of solutions with two different pH values

Concept Task: Be able to compare the level of H+ (or acidity) of two solutions with different pH values.

To determine how many more H+ ions is in a solution of one pH compared to another.

Use the following equation if necessary

$$\text{Difference in H}^+ = 10^{(\text{difference in pH})}$$
$$= 10^{(\text{high pH} - \text{low pH})}$$

Determining if a difference in H+ is more or less:

If a **higher pH** is being **compared** to a **Lower pH**
  The difference in H+ is LESS

If a **Lower pH** is being **compared** to a **Higher pH**:
  The difference in H+ is MORE

Example 22

Compared to a solution with pH of 8, a solution with a pH of 10 has
1) 2 times more H$^+$ ion
2) 2 times less H$^+$ ion
3) 100 times more H$^+$ ions
4) 100 times less H$^+$ ions

Before choosing:
Determine difference in H$^+$ ions $= 10^{(10-8)}$
$= 10^{(2)} = 100$

Consider choosing choice 3 or 4

Determine if there are MORE or LESS H+:
  THINK: The questions is comparing a solution of
      pH 10 **TO** pH 8.
  RECALL: A Higher pH (pH 10) solution
            has less H+ than
            A Lower pH (pH 8) solution

Combine the two determinations:
  pH 10 solution contains 100 times less H+ **than** pH of 8 **solution.**

Answer: Choice 4

Topic 8 – Acids, Bases and Salt
Lesson 3 - Salts

Introduction

Salts are ionic compounds composed of a positive ion (other than H+) and a negative ion (other than OH-).

⬅ **LOOKING Back: Topic 5- Formulas**: You learned how to recognize and write formulas of ionic compounds.

⬅ **LOOKING Back: Topic 7 – Solutions**: You learned how to recognize and determine formulas of soluble salts.

In this lesson of Topic 8, you will learn how to recognize and determine chemical formulas of salts.

28. Salts : Facts and examples

The following are facts related to salts.

Concept Facts: Study to remember the following

. Salts are ionic compounds

. Salts are one of the products formed during acid-base neutralization reactions

. Salts are electrolytes (conducts electricity when dissolved in water)

Example of salt formulas and names are given below.
NOTE the composition of each salt.

NaBr	CaSO$_4$	NH$_4$Cl	NH$_4$NO$_3$
sodium bromide	calcium sulfate	ammonium chloride	ammonium nitrate
Metal - nonmetal atom	Metal - polyatomic ion	NH$_4$ - nonmetal	NH$_4$ - polyatomic ion

29. Salts: Determining formulas and names of salt

Concept Task: Be able to determine formula or name is of a salt.

Study the composition of salts in the above notes to learn how to determine chemical formulas of salts. Study example questions below, and be able to answer similar questions.

Example 23

Which compound is a salt?

1) Ba(OH)$_2$ 2) BaCl$_2$ 3) H$_2$SO$_4$ 4) CH$_3$OH

Answer: Choice 2 . BaCl$_2$ contains a metal (Ba) and a nonmetal (Cl)

Example 24

Which chemical formula represents a salt?

1) HC$_2$H$_3$O$_2$ 2) KOH   3) HF   4) Mg(C$_2$H$_3$O$_2$)$_2$

Answer: Choice 4. Mg(C$_2$H$_3$O$_2$)$_2$ consist of a metal (Mg) and a polyatomic ion (C$_2$H$_3$O$_2$)

Topic 8 – Acids, Bases and Salt

Lesson 4: Electrolytes

One property that acids, bases and salts share is their ability to conduct electricity in aqueous solutions. Acids, bases and salts are considered electrolytes.

In this lesson, you will learn about substances that are electrolytes, and how electrolytes conduct electricity.

30. Electrolytes: Definitions and facts

Electrolytes are substances that conduct electricity when dissolved in water.

The followings are facts related to electrolytes.

Concept Facts: Study to remember them.

. Electrolytes dissolved in water to produce a solution with positive (+) and negative (-) ions

. Electrolytes conduct electricity because of these mobile ions in the solutions

. Acids, bases and salts are electrolytes

31. Electrolytes: Determining which substance is an electrolyte

Concept Task: Be able to determine formulas of electrolytes and nonelectrolytes.

To determine if a substance is an electrolyte:

LOOK for formula of:
  Acid (use Table K of acids to confirm formula)
  Base (use Table L of bases to confirm formula)
  Salt (metal – nonmetal or polyatomic ion)

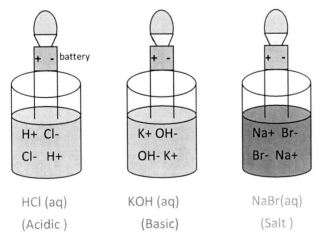

lighted light bulbs

HCl (aq)   KOH (aq)   NaBr(aq)
(Acidic)   (Basic)   (Salt)

The positive and negative ions in acidic, basic and salt solutions allow for a complete circuit, and electrical conductivity.

Example 25

Which two substances are electrolytes?

1) KCl and CH_3OH

2) CH_3COH and $C_6H_{12}O_6$

3) $CaCl_2$ and LiOH

4) HCl and CH_3OH

Answer: choice 3. $CaCl_2$ is a salt

LiOH is a base

Example 26

Which substance is a nonelectrolyte?

1) C_2H_4 3) HCl

2) KOH   4) NaBr

Before choosing:

LOOK for a formula that is neither an acid, nor a base, nor a salt.

Answer: Choice 1. C_2H_4 is neither a salt, nor an acid, nor a base

Topic 8 – Acids, Bases and Salt

Lesson 5 – Formulas and names of acids and bases

Introduction

Acids and bases have distinctive formulas and names that make it easy to identify them.

In this lesson, you will learn how to recognize formulas of acids and bases. You will also learn how to write formulas from given names and names from given formulas.

32. Formulas of acids: Recognizing formula of acids

Formula of acids vary depending on the type of acid. An acid can be classified as organic or inorganic. Inorganic acids can further be classified as binary or ternary acids.

Below, different types of acids and how their formulas are represented are given.
Study the notes below to learn how to recognize formulas of acids

Inorganic acids

Chemical formulas of inorganic acids usually start with H, followed by a nonmetal or a negative polyatomic ion.

Two main categories of inorganic acids are binary and ternary acids.

Binary acid formulas are composed of just two nonmetal atoms:
hydrogen atom and another nonmetal atom

Examples of binary acids: HCl hydrochloric acid H_2S hydrosulfuric acid

Ternary acid formulas are composed of three atoms:
hydrogen atom and a polyatomic ion

Example of a ternary acid: HNO_3 Nitric acid H_2SO_3 sulfurous acid

RECALL that polyatomic ions are listed on your Reference Table E.

Organic acids

Chemical formulas of organic acids usually end with –COOH.

Examples of organic acid formula: CH_3COOH ethanoic (acetic) acid

$HCOOH$ methanoic acid

LOOKING Ahead ⟹ **Topic 10 - Organic Chemistry**: You will learn more about organic acids.

Topic 8 – Acids, Bases and Salt

33. Name of acids: Recognizing and naming acids

Chemical names of acids in these three categories (binary, ternary, and organic acid) vary slightly.

Naming Binary acids

Concept Task: Be able to write the names of binary acids from formulas

RECALL that binary acids are composed of hydrogen and another nonmetal element.
   Binary acids have names that begin with hydro- and ends with –ic.
   Names of binary acids are formed by dropping the –gen of hydrogen
            and modifying the nonmetal ending to –ic.

Below, are steps showing how names of two binary acids are formed from the elements in the formulas. Study the steps in these examples to learn how to name binary acids.

Given the formulas of binary acids:	HCl	and	H$_2$S
The steps below shows how the names of these acids are formed:			
Step 1: Write names of elements in formula:	hydro*gen* chlor*ine*		hydro*gen* sulfur
Step 2: Drop –gen of hydrogen: Modify the nonmetal ending to *ic*:	hydro chlor*ic*		hydro sulfur*ic*
Step 3: Combine to name the acid:	**hydrochloric acid**		**hydrosulfuric acid**

Naming Ternary acids

Concept Task: Be able to write names of ternary acids from formulas

  RECALL that Ternary acids are composed of hydrogen and a polyatomic ion.
   A Ternary acid has a name that reflects only the name of the polyatomic ion in the formula.
    The name of the polyatomic ion in a ternary acid formula is modified to end with –ic or –ous.

The name ending of the polyatomic ion determines if a ternary acid name ends with –ic or –ous.
If an acid formula contains a polyatomic ion ending with –ate, the name ending of the acid is –ic.
If an acid formula contains a polyatomic ion ending with –ite, the name ending of the acid is –ous.

Below, are steps showing how names of two ternary acids are formed from the polyatomic ion in their formulas.
Study these steps to learn how to name and recognize ternary acids.

Given ternary acid formulas:	H$_2$SO$_4$	HNO$_2$
The steps below show how to form names for these ternary acids:		
Step 1: Identify the polyatomic ion in formula	SO$_4$ ion	NO$_2$ ion
Step 2: Name the polyatomic ion (Table E)	Sulf*ate*	Nitr*ite*
Step 3: Name acid by modifying name ending:		
-ate ending changes to –ic	**Sulfuric acid**	
-ite ending changes to –ous		**Nitrous acid**

Topic 8 – Acids, Bases and Salt

34. Formulas of bases: Recognizing and writing formulas of bases.

Recognizing formulas of bases

Chemical formulas of bases usually contain a metal element and OH (hydroxide). These two bases, NH_4OH and $NH_3(aq)$ are the exceptions.

Example of bases formula:	NaOH	Al(OH)$_3$	NH$_4$OH
	a metal element hydroxide	a metal element hydroxide	ammonium hydroxide

NOTE: NOT every formula containing OH is a base.
For an example: **CH$_3$OH** is an alcohol, **not a base**.

Recognizing and determining names of bases:

Chemical names of bases are easy to recognize and to write. Bases are named by the combination of the name of the metal and hydroxide. No modifications or changes are made to these names.

Examples of bases formulas:	Na OH	Al(OH)$_3$	NH$_4$OH
Name of bases from formula:	Sodium hydroxide	Aluminum hydroxide	Ammonium hydroxide

NOTE: Aqueous ammonia, $NH_3(aq)$, is also a base

Topic 8 – Acids, Bases, and Salts

Check-A-list

Concept Terms

Below is a list of vocabulary terms from Topic 8. You should know the definition and facts related to each term.

Put a check in the box [V] next to a term if you know its definition and other facts related to the term.

[ ] Arrhenius acid
[ ] Arrhenius base
[ ] Solution
[ ] Alternate acid theory
[ ] Alternate base theory
[ ] Hydrogen ion
[ ] Hydronium ion
[ ] Hydroxide ion
[ ] Acidity
[ ] Alkalinity

[ ] pH
[ ] Indicator [ ] Neutralization
[ ] Salt
[ ] Titration
[ ] Electrolyte
[ ] Properties of acids
[ ] Properties of bases
[ ] Properties of neutral substances

If you do not have a check next to a term, look it up or ask your teacher.

Concept Tasks

Below is a list of concept tasks from Topic 8. You should know how to solve problems and answer questions related to each concept task.

Put a check in the box [V] next a concept task if you know how to solve problems and answer questions related to it.

[ ] Determining and recognizing formulas of Arrhenius acids
[ ] Determining and recognizing formulas of Arrhenius bases
[ ] Determining and recognizing formulas of a substance based on relative ion concentration
[ ] Determining pH of a based on formula or name of the substance
[ ] Determining and recognizing name of a substance based on pH value
[ ] Determining and choosing a property of a substance based on other given properties
[ ] Determining a metal that will react with an acid to produce H_2 gas and salt.
[ ] Determining correct salt formulas from metal - acid reactions.
[ ] Determining and recognizing neutralization reaction equation
[ ] Determining correct salt formula from acid – base neutralization reaction
[ ] Solving for unknown in a neutralization problem using the titration equation
[ ] Determining pH of a solution from H^+ or H_3O^+ concentration
[ ] Determining H^+ or H_3O^+ concentration of a solution from pH
[ ] Comparing the level of H+ (or acidity) of two solutions with different pH values
[ ] Determining formula or name of a salt.
[ ] Determining formulas or names of substances that are electrolytes (or are nonelectrolytes)
[ ] Writing and determining names of binary acids from formulas
[ ] Writing and determining names of ternary acids from formulas

If you do not have a check next to a concept task, look it up or ask your teacher.

Topic 8 – Acids, Bases, and Salts

Concept Fact Review Questions

1. A solution of a base in the presence of an phenolphthalein will
   1) Turn pink
   2) Turn blue
   3) Turn Red
   4) Stay colorless

2. When a solution of an acid is tested with a pH paper, the result will be a pH
   1) Above 7, and the solution will conduct electricity
   2) Above 7, and the solution will not conduct electricity
   3) Below 7, and the solution will conduct electricity
   4) Below 7, and the solution will not conduct electricity

3. When a base is dissolved in water, it produces
   1) OH^- as the only negative ions in solution
   2) NH_4^+ as the only positive ions in solution
   3) CO_3^{2-} as the only negative ions in the solution
   4) H^+ as the only positive ions in solution

4. A sample of acidic solution contains
   1) Neither OH^- nor H_3O^+
   2) Equal number of OH^- ion to H_3O^+ ion
   3) A smaller amounts of H_3O^+ ions than OH^- ions
   4) Larger amounts of H_3O^+ ions than OH^- ions

5. A water solution conducts electrical current because the solution contains mobile
   1) Ions
   2) Molecules
   3) Atoms
   4) Electrons

6. As a solution of a base is added to an acidic solution, the pH of the solution
   1) Increases   2) Decreases   3) Remains the same

7. According to an "alternate theory" of acids and bases, H_2O will act as a base in a reaction if
   1) Donates OH^- to another species in the reaction
   2) Donates H^+ ion to another species in the reaction
   3) Accepts OH^- ion from another species in the reaction
   4) Accepts H^+ ion from another species in the reaction

8. What type of reaction occurs when equal molar of an acid and a base are combined?
   1) Combustion
   2) Neutralization
   3) Single replacement
   4) Hydrolysis

9. Which substances are always produced in a reaction between an acid and a base?
   1) Water
   2) Hydrogen gas
   3) Oxygen gas
   4) A Precipitate

10. Unlike an acid solution, an aqueous solution of a base
    1) Contains only OH^- ions
    2) Contains only H_3O^+ ion
    3) Contains less OH^- than H^+
    4) Contains more OH^- than H^+

Topic 8 – Acids, Bases, and Salts

Concept Task Review Questions

11. Which is a formula of Arrhenius acid?
    1) $CaCl_2$
    2) H_3PO_4
    3) CCl_4
    4) NH_3

12. According to Arrhenius theory, which list of compounds includes only bases?
    1) KOH, $Ca(OH)_2$, and CH_3OH
    2) $LiOH$, $Ca(OH)_2$, and $C_2H_4(OH)_2$
    3) KOH, $NaOH$, and $LiOH$
    4) $NaOH$, $Ca(OH)_2$, and CH_3COOH

13. Which solution will contain more hydroxide ions than hydrogen ions?
    1) $CaCl_2$
    2) C_2H_5OH
    3) $Mg(OH)_2$
    4) CH_3Cl

14. Which aqueous solution would have a pH of 3?
    1) $H_2O(l)$
    2) $KOH\ (aq)$
    3) $CH_3OH(aq)$
    4) $HNO_3(aq)$

15. Which compound when dissolved in water will turn blue litmus red?
    1) CH_3OH
    2) HBr
    3) $C_6H_{12}O_6$
    4) $Ca(OH)_2$

16. Which are true of aqueous solution of $Mg(OH)_2$?
    1) It contains more OH^- ion than H^+ ion, and is a nonelectrolyte
    2) It contains more OH^- ion that H^+ ion, and is an electrolyte
    3) It contains more H^+ than OH^-, and is a nonelectrolyte
    4) It contains more H^+ than OH^-, and is an electrolyte

17. An example of a nonelectrolyte is
    1) $C_6H_{12}O_6\ (aq)$
    2) $K_2SO_4\ (aq)$
    3) $NaCl\ (aq)$
    4) $HCl\ (aq)$

18. Which pH of a solution indicates the strongest base?
    1) 6
    2) 7
    3) 8
    4) 9

19. When phenolphthalein is added to a solution, the solution stays colorless. What could be the pH of this solution?
    1) 2
    2) 7
    3) 9
    4) 11

20. A solution with a pH of 13 is
    1) An electrolyte that will turn litmus red
    2) An electrolyte that will turn litmus blue
    3) A nonelectrolyte that will turn litmus red
    4) A nonelectrolyte that will turn litmus red

21. What is the hydrogen ion concentration of a solution that has hydroxide ion concentration of 1.0×10^{-9} moles per liter at $25°C$?
    1) $1 \times 10^{-9}\ M$
    2) $1 \times 10^{-7}\ M$
    3) $1 \times 10^{-5}\ M$
    4) $1 \times 10^{-14}\ M$

22. Which of these metals will not produce a reaction with sulfuric acid?
    1) Ca
    2) Au
    3) Zn
    4) Li

Topic 8 – Acids, Bases, and Salts

23. Which balanced equation represents a neutralization reaction?
    1) Mg + NiCl$_2$ -------→ MgCl2 + Ni
    2) 2 KClO$_3$ --------------------→ 2 KCl + 3 O$_2$
    3) BaCl$_2$ + Cu(NO$_3$)$_2$ ----→ Ba(NO$_3$)$_2$ + CuCl$_2$
    4) H$_2$SO$_4$ + 2LiOH --------→ Li$_2$SO$_4$ + 2H$_2$O

24. In the neutralization reaction:
    $$HC_2H_3O_2 + NH_4OH \longrightarrow NH_4C_2H_3O_2 + H_2O$$
    The salt is
    1) NH$_4$OH   2) HC$_2$H$_3$O$_2$ 3) NH$_4$C$_2$H$_3$O$_2$ 4) H$_2$O

25. If 20 ml of a 2.0 M KOH is exactly neutralized by 10 ml of HCl, the molarity of the HCl is
    1) 0.50 M   2) 2.0 M   3) 4.0 M   4) 1.0 M

26. How many milliliters of a 3.0 M HCl are neutralized by 60 ml of a 0.5 M of Ca(OH)$_2$?
    1) 40 ml   2) 30 ml   3) 20 ml   4) 60 ml

Constructed Response Questions

Base your answers to questions 27 through 29 on the information below.

A student was studying the pH difference in samples from two Adirondack streams. The student measured a pH of 4 in stream A and a pH of 6 in stream B.

27. Identify one compound that could be used to neutralize the sample from stream A.

27.

28. What is the color of bromthymol blue in the sample from stream A?

28.

29. Compare the hydronium ion concentration in stream A to the hydronium ion concentration in stream B.

29.

Base your answers to questions 30 through 31 on the information below.

In a titration, 3.00 M NaOH(aq) was added to an Erlenmeyer flask containing 25.00 millimeters of HCl(aq) and three drops of phenolphthalein until one drop of NaOH(aq) turned the solution a light-pink color. The following data were collected by a student performing this titration.

Initial NaOH(aq) buret reading: 14. 45 milliliters
Final NaOH(aq) buret reading: 32.66 milliliters

Write answers here.

30. What is the total volume of NaOH(aq) that was used in the titration?

30.

31. Show a correct numerical setup for calculating the molarity of HCl(aq).

31.

Topic 9 - Kinetics and equilibrium

Topic outline:

In this topic, you will learn about the following concepts:

- Kinetic
- Rate of reactions
- Factors that affect rate of reactions
- Energy and chemical reactions
- Exothermic and endothermic reactions
- Potential energy diagrams

- Equilibrium
- Physical equilibrium
- Chemical equilibrium
- Le Chatelier's principle
- Entropy
- Spontaneous reactions

Lesson 1 : Kinetics

Introduction

Kinetics is the study of rates and mechanisms of chemical reactions.

Rate is the speed at which a reaction is taking place.

Mechanism is a series of reactions that lead to final products of a reaction.

In this lesson, you will learn mostly about the rate of chemical reactions and factors that can affect reaction rates. You will also learn about the relationship between chemical reactions and energy.

1. Rate of reactions: Definitions and facts

Rate of reaction is the speed at which a chemical reaction or a physical change occurs.

Rate of a reaction can be measured in many different ways.

For examples, rate can be measured by

The number of moles of a reactant consumed (used up) per unit time.

The number of moles of a product produced per unit time.

Chemical and physical changes occur at different rates.
Many factors affect how fast a reaction will occur.

Below are list of factors that affect how fast a reaction will occur.

Concept Facts: Study to remember these factors

- Nature (or type) of the reactants
- Concentration (or amount) of the reactants
- Temperature (or heat) of the reactions
- Pressure (or volume) of gaseous reactants
- Adding of catalysts

Equal amount of solid X and Y are placed in water at the same time.

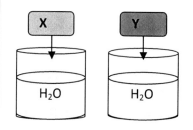

X and Y react with water, and are consumed as they react.

After 5 minutes, less of Y remained. Y reacts with (or is consumed in) water at a faster rate than X.

It is important to note that **not all** of these factors will affect how fast a reaction occurs. In one reaction, the nature of reactants may be the key factor in determining the rate of the reaction.
In a different reaction involving different substances, pressure may determine how fast the reaction will occur.

To understand how the above factors affect rate, it is important to learn about effective collisions, activation energy, and catalysts. On the next page you will learn what each terms means. You will also learn the relationship between these terms to the rate of chemical reactions.

Topic 9 - Kinetics and equilibrium

2. Effective collision: Definition and facts

Effective collision is when reacting particles collide with **sufficient (right amount of) kinetic energy** and at a **proper orientation (angle)**.

Collision theory states that for a chemical reaction to occur between reactants, there **must be effective collisions** between the reacting particles.

  This means: Reacting particles MUST collide (hit) with sufficient energy and at proper angle (orientation).

. Rate of a depends on how often (frequency of) effective collisions occur between particles

. Any factor that can change the frequency of effective collisions between reacting particles will change the rate of that reaction.

  For example: Any change made to a chemical reaction that increases frequency of (how often) effective collisions occurs between the reacting particles will cause the rate of the reaction to increase.

Reacting particles	Particles colliding	Result of collision
○ △	○△ ○△ Bad angle Insufficient energy **Ineffective collisions**	○ △ **No Product is formed**
○ △	○△ Proper angle and sufficient energy **Effective collision**	○△ **Product is formed**

3. Activation energy: Definition and facts

Concept Facts: Study to remember the followings about activation energy

Activation energy is the energy needed to start a chemical reaction.

. All chemical reactions, both endothermic and exothermic, require some amount of activation energy

. Chemical reactions that require small amounts of activation energy are faster (fast rate) than those that require higher amounts of activation energy.

. Any factor that can change the amount of activation energy for a reaction will change the rate of that reaction

For example: Any substance that can lower the activation energy for a reaction will increase (speeds up) the rate for that reaction.

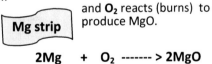 and O_2 reacts (burns) to produce MgO.

$$2Mg + O_2 \text{-------} > 2MgO$$

However, Mg strip must be lit with Bunsen burner or matches flame before it can burn and combines with O_2.

The flame provides the activation energy needed to start the reaction.

4. Catalysts: Definition and facts

A catalyst is any substance that can increase the speed (rate) of a reaction by lowering the activation energy for that reaction.

. A catalyst in a reaction provides alternate (lower activation energy) pathway for a reaction to occur faster

Topic 9 - Kinetics and equilibrium

5. Concentration and Rate of reaction: Facts and examples

A change in concentration (amount) of one or more reactants will affect the rate (speed) of certain chemical reactions.

Consider the reaction of metal Mg with the acid HNO_3 shown below:

$Mg + HNO_3 (aq) \longrightarrow MgCl_2 + H_2$

The rate of (how fast) H_2 gas is produced depends on the concentration of the acid.
The diagram below shows a comparison of this reaction in a 2 M HNO_3 and a 4 M HNO_3 solutions.

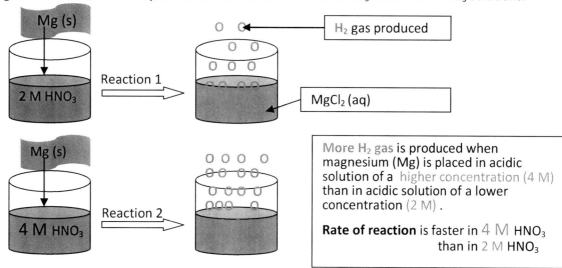

More H_2 gas is produced when magnesium (Mg) is placed in acidic solution of a higher concentration (4 M) than in acidic solution of a lower concentration (2 M).

Rate of reaction is faster in 4 M HNO_3 than in 2 M HNO_3

Relationship between concentration and rate of reaction is summarized below.

Concept Facts: Study to remember them.

When concentration of reactants is increased:
. Rate of reaction increases

   BECAUSE

. There will be more particles in the reaction to cause more effective collisions
   RECALL that increase in number of effective collisions means increase in rate of that reaction

6. Concentration and Rate: Determining in which reaction will occur the fastest

Concept Task: Be able to determine which solution concentration will produce a reaction with the fastest or the slowest rate.
 	
To determine which concentration of a solution will produce:
 	
  FASTEST reaction rate:
    LOOK for a solution of highest Molarity **(M)**
 	
  SLOWEST reaction rate:
    LOOK for a solution of lowest Molarity **(M)**
	Example 1
	Which concentration of hydrochloric acid solution would Zn metal react the fastest?
	
	1) 0.4 M 3) 0.2 M
	2) 0.3 M 4) 0.1 M
	
	Before choosing:
	
	Analyze: Fastest rate occurs in highest concentration solution.
	
	Answer: Choice 1

Topic 9 - Kinetics and equilibrium

7. Temperature and Rate of reaction: Facts and examples

A change in temperature one or more reactants will affect the speed (or rate) of some reactions.

In the diagrams below: Solutions A and B are placed in hot water baths of two different temperatures.

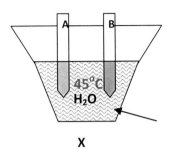
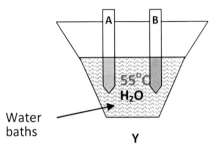

X   Water baths   Y

When solutions A and B are combined from each water bath, the reaction of A and B from **Y** will be **faster**. This is because the solutions in Y were raised to a higher temperature (55°C) than the solutions in water X (45°C).

Relationship between temperature and rate of reaction is summarized below.

Concept Facts: Study to remember this relationship

When temperature of reacting particles is increased:

.Rate of reaction will increase

BECAUSE

. Kinetic energy of the particles increases (**RECALL** that temperature is related to kinetic energy)

. Increase in kinetic energy (speed) of particles leads to an increase in number of effective collisions

. Increasing the number of effective collisions between particles always leads to an increase in the rate of the reaction

8. Temperature and Rate: Determining temperature in which a reaction will occur the fastest

Concept Task: Be able to determine which solution temperature of a solution will produce a reaction with fastest or slowest rate

To determine which temperature a reaction would occur with the:

FASTEST rate:

LOOK for the HIGHEST temperature

SLOWEST rate:

LOOK for the LOWEST temperature

Example 2
Which concentration and temperature of $AgNO_3$ solution will react the slowest with KI solution?

1) 0.1 M $AgNO_3$ at 30°C
2) 0.1 M $AgNO_3$ at 20°C
3) 0.2 M $AgNO_3$ at 30°C
4) 0.2 M $AgNO_3$ at 20°C

Before choosing:
THINK: SLOWEST rate occurs at :
   LOWEST concentration
   and
   LOWEST temperature.

Answer: Choice 2 because it has :
   LOWEST concentration (0.1 M)
   and
   LOWEST temperature (20°C)

Topic 9 - Kinetics and equilibrium

9. Pressure and Rate of reaction: Facts and examples

A change in pressure will affect the rate (speed) of a reaction when the reactants are gases.

In the diagrams below: **Gas ○ and Gas △** are reacting in a closed container.

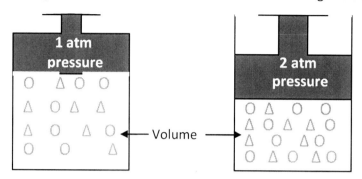

Lower Pressure

Slower reaction

Higher pressure = smaller volume, higher concentration of reactants.
Reacting particles are closer, and will collide more often, leading to an **increase in rate (faster speed)** of reaction.

Relationship between pressure and rate of a reaction is summarized below.

Concept Facts: Study to remember this relationship

When **pressure** of a reaction is **increased**:

. Rate of the reaction will increase

   BECAUSE

. The space (volume) in which the reaction is taking place will decrease

   As a result, concentration of the reactants will increase.

. This increase in concentration allows leads to an increase in the number of effective collisions between particles

. Increasing the number of effective collisions between particles always leads to an increase in the rate of the reaction

10. Pressure and Rate: Determining a pressure that reaction will occur the fastest or the slowest

Concept Task: Be able to determine which pressure will allow a gaseous reaction to occur at the fastest rate.

To determine which pressure a reaction would occur with the:

FASTEST rate:

   LOOK for HIGHEST (KPa or atm) **pressure**

SLOWEST rate:

   LOOK for LOWEST (KPa or atm) **pressure**

Example 3
Given the equation below:

$$N_2(g) + 3H_2(g) \longrightarrow 2NH_3(g)$$

Under which pressure would this reaction occur at the fastest rate?

1) 50 KPa   3) 60 KPa
2) 70 KPa   4) 80 KPa

Answer: Choice 4: 80 KPa is the highest of the four pressures that are given.

Topic 9 - Kinetics and equilibrium

11. Surface area and Rate of reaction: Facts and examples

Surface area is the amount of exposed area of a set mass of a solid substance.

A change in the surface area of a reacting solid will affect the rate (speed) of the reaction.

In the diagram below: A solid Zinc (Zn) is shown in three different forms.
Note the solid form with the most and the least surface area.

One big Piece
Least surface area

Smaller pellets

Powdered (grinded up)
Most surface area: Most exposed area for reaction to occur. Leads to increase in rate

If the Zn forms are each reacted in different beakers of 1 M HCl solution, the powdered zinc will react most vigorously (Fastest rate) with the acid.

Relationship between surface area and rate is summarized below:

Concept Facts: Study to remember this relationship.

When surface area **of a reacting solid** increases:

. Rate of reaction increases
   BECAUSE
. The number of exposed area for possible collision increases
. An increases in the exposed area leads to an increase in the number of effective collisions
. Increasing the number of effective collisions between particles always leads to an increase in the rate of the reaction.

12. Rate and surface area: Determining which form a solid will produce the fastest reaction

Concept Task: Be able to determine which solid form will produce a reaction with the fastest or slowest rate.

To determine which form of a solid will produce:

FASTEST reaction rate:
  LOOK for solid with the more surface area

SLOWEST reaction rate:
  LOOK for solid with least surface area

Example 4
Equation for a reaction is given below:

$Mg(s) + HCl(aq) \longrightarrow MgCl_2(aq) + H_2(g)$

Which form of Mg will produce hydrogen gas at the fastest rate?
1) 2 grams of magnesium ribbon
2) 2 grams of magnesium pieces
3) 2 grams of magnesium powder
4) 2 grams of magnesium pellets

Before choosing:
THINK: The more surface area a solid has, the faster it would react in a solution.

Answer: Choice 3: The powdered form of magnesium has the most surface area of the four forms given in the choices.

Topic 9 - Kinetics and equilibrium

13. Factors that affect rate of reaction: Summary

The list of factors that increase the rate of reactions is summarized below.

Concept Facts: Study to remember them:

NOTE the following as you study the factors below:

Left column lists *factors* that will *increase the reaction rate.*

Right column explains how each factor leads to an increase in reaction rate.

Factors that will increase reaction rate

1. *Increasing* **concentration** of reactants
2. *Increasing* **temperature** of the reactants
3. *Increasing* **pressure** on the reaction
4. *Increasing* **surface area** of reacting solid
5. *Addition of catalyst* to a reaction

Reasons why rate increases

Increases the number of reacting particles.
Increases the frequency of effective collisions between reacting particles.

Increases the kinetic energy of reacting particles.
Increases the frequency of effective collisions.

Decreases the volume of gaseous reactants.
Increases the concentration of gaseous reactants.
Increases the frequency of effective collisions.

Exposes more area for reactions to occur.
Increases the frequency of effective collisions.

Provides a lower activation energy (alternate) pathway for a reaction to occur.
Lowers activation energy.

6. **Nature of reactants:**

   Reactions of ionic solution are very fast (almost instantaneous) because no bond breaking is required.

   Reactions of molecular substances are slow because reaction requires breaking of strong covalent bonds. High activation energy is usually required for reactions involving molecular substances.

   Some metals, because of their nature, react faster than others in solutions.
   Sodium reacts more vigorously in water than Lithium because of the nature of sodium.

Topic 9 - Kinetics and equilibrium

Lesson 2 - Energy and chemical reactions

Introduction

Every chemical substance contains some amount of energy that is stored within the bonds of the substance. During chemical reactions, substances may release or absorb energy, as bonds are formed or broken.

In this lesson, you will learn the relationship between energy and chemical (or physical) changes.

14. Energy and reactions: Definitions and facts

To better understand the relationship between energy and chemical reactions, it is important for you know these terms. These terms will show up a lot in the next sets of notes.

Concept Facts: Study and remember them.

Potential energy is stored energy in chemical substances.
  Amount of potential energy in a substance depends on its **structure** and **composition.**

Potential Energy of reactants is the amount of potential energy stored in the bonds of the reactants.
  RECALL that reactants are substances that are present at the start of a chemical reaction.

Potential Energy of products is the amount of potential energy stored in the bonds of the products.
  RECALL that products are substances that remain at the end of a chemical reaction

Heat of reaction (Δ H) is the amount of energy absorbed or released during a reaction.

  ΔH of a reaction is the difference between the potential energy of products and of the reactants.

| ΔH = Energy of products − Energy of reactants |

  ΔH of a reaction can be negative or positive.

  − ΔH (negative heat of reaction) means that:
    . The **Products** of a reaction have **Less energy** than the reactants
    . The reaction is exothermic (releases heat)

  + ΔH (positive heat of reaction) means that:
    Products of a reaction have **more energy** than the reactants.
    The reaction is endothermic (absorbs heat).

Topic 9 - Kinetics and equilibrium

15. Exothermic and Endothermic reactions: Relating heat of reaction to type of reaction:

Some chemical reactions absorb energy, while others release energy. Reactions that release energy are exothermic. Reactions that absorb energy are endothermic. Since most chemical processes occur in some form of a liquid (water or aqueous) environment, measuring temperature of the liquid before and after a reaction is usually one way to tell if a reaction is exothermic or endothermic.

If heat was released during a reaction, the temperature of the liquid will be higher after the reaction.
If heat was absorbed during a reaction, the temperature of the liquid will be lower after the reaction.

In the next set of notes, you will learn more about exothermic and endothermic reactions, and how they each relate to the heat of reactions (ΔH).

16. Exothermic reactions and energy: Definitions and facts

Exothermic reactions occur when products formed from the reaction contain less energy than the reactants. If the products have less energy than the reactants, the reactants must have lost (or released) energy during the chemical change.

When heat energy is released to the surrounding area (such as a liquid) where the reaction is occurring, the temperature of the surrounding will go up (or increase.) **SEE DIAGRAM TO THE RIGHT.**

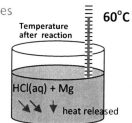

Concept Facts: Study and remember these facts about exothermic reactions.

In exothermic reactions:
- Products have less potential energy than the reactants
- Energy is released or lost, and the temperature of the surrounding area increases
- Heat of reaction, ΔH is always negative (-ΔH)
- Equation of an exothermic reaction always shows energy released to the right of the arrow

Example equation of an exothermic reaction

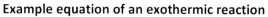

Mg + HCl ----------> MgCl$_2$ + H$_2$ + Energy

17. Endothermic reactions and energy: Definition and facts

Endothermic reactions occur when products formed from during a reaction contain more energy than the reactants. If products formed have more energy than the reactants, the substances must have gained (absorbed) energy during the chemical change.

When heat energy is absorbed from the surrounding area (such as a liquid) where the reaction is occurring, the temperature of the surrounding will go down (or decrease.) **SEE DIAGRAM TO THE RIGHT.**

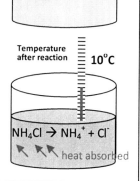

Concept Facts: Study to remember these facts about endothermic reactions.

In endothermic reactions:
- Products have more potential energy than the reactants
- Energy is absorbed, and the temperature of the surrounding area decreases
- Heat of reaction, ΔH, is always positive (+ΔH)
- Equation of an endothermic reaction always shows energy absorbed to the Left of the arrow

Example equation of an endothermic reaction

NH$_4$Cl(s) + Energy ---------> NH$_4^+$(aq) + Cl$^-$(aq)

Topic 9 - Kinetics and equilibrium

18. Exothermic and endothermic reactions: Relating change in temperature to type of reaction

Concept Task: Be able to determine certain information about energy of a reaction from the given temperature before and after the reaction.

Below, you are given information that will help you determine the correct answer.
Example questions related to this concept are also given. Study to learn how to answer similar questions.

If a question states or suggests that temperature after a reaction is higher:

LOOK for a choice in which the information given relate to exothermic reactions (Review Set 16).

Example 5

After a salt was dissolved in water, a student notices that the temperature of the water had gone up by 8°C. Which is the best explanation for this?

1) The dissolving of the salt is endothermic, which releases heat
2) The dissolving of the salt is endothermic, which absorbs heat
3) The dissolving of the salt is exothermic, which releases heat
4) The dissolving of the salt is exothermic, which absorbed heat.

Before choosing
Analyze and Think: Temperature of water increases by 8°C, therefore, heat must have been lost (or released) to the water.

Answer: Choice 3. Since heat was lost or released to water, the dissolving of the salt is an exothermic reaction.

If a question states or suggests that temperature after a reaction is lower:

LOOK for a choice in which the information given relate to an endothermic reactions (Review Set 17)

Example 6

A student noted this data for a reaction he conducted in a solution:

Initial temperature of solution: 23°C

Final temperature of solution: 18°C

Which is true of the reaction he conducted?

1) It is exothermic with $-\Delta H$
2) It is exothermic with $+\Delta H$
3) It is endothermic with $-\Delta H$
4) It is endothermic with $+\Delta H$

Before choosing:
Analyze and Think about the data:

Temperature of solution after reaction is lower. Reaction must had absorbed heat from the solution

Answer: Choice 4. Since heat was absorbed, the reaction is endothermic. And endothermic reactions have $+\Delta H$

Topic 9 - Kinetics and equilibrium

19. Exothermic and endothermic reactions: Determining type of reaction from an equation

Concept Task: Be able to determine information about energy of a reaction from a given equation.

If equation given has energy to the left:

Examples: CD + heat energy ---> C + D

 CD + 20 KJ ----------> C + D

LOOK for a choice relating to endothermic

If equation given has energy to the right:

Examples: A + B ------> AB + heat energy

 A + B ------> AB + + 90 KJ

LOOK for a choice relating to exothermic

Example 7

Given the reaction:

$$XW + energy \longrightarrow W$$

Which is true of this reaction?
1) The reaction is exothermic with $-\Delta H$
2) The reaction is exothermic with $+\Delta H$
3) The reaction is endothermic with $-\Delta H$
4) The reaction is endothermic with $+\Delta H$

Before choosing:

Analyze the equation: Since energy is on the left, the reaction is endothermic.

Answer: Choice 4. endothermic reactions have $+\Delta H$

Example 8

Given the reaction

$$H_2 + Br_2 \longrightarrow 2HBr + 73 KJ$$

The heat of reaction, ΔH, is
1) +73, because energy is released.
2) +73, because energy is absorbed.
3) -73, because energy is released.
4) -73, because energy is absorbed.

Before choosing:

Analyze equation: Since energy (73 KJ) is on the right, the reaction it is exothermic.

Answer: Choice 3; Since equation is exothermic, energy is released.
ΔH for all exothermic reaction must be negative. $-\Delta H$ (-73 KJ).

20. Exothermic and endothermic: Summary table

Below is a summary of exothermic an endothermic reactions. Use this table for a quick study, and comparisons of the two reactions.

Process	Potential Energy of reactants	Potential Energy of products	Energy change	Temperature of surrounding	Heat of reaction (ΔH)
Exothermic	Higher	Lower	Released	Increased	Negative ($-\Delta H$)
Endothermic	Lower	Higher	Absorbed	Decreased	Positive ($+\Delta H$)

Topic 9 - Kinetics and equilibrium

21. Reference Table I - heat of reaction: Reading and interpreting – ΔH of reaction

Reference Table I (below) lists equations for selected physical and chemical changes and their Δ H (heat of reaction) values.

NOTE the following about the Table.
  Some equations have - ΔH, and some have +ΔH.
On tests you may be asked to interpret information given on this table.

To the right of the table, one equation with a negative H (- ΔH) **value from the table is chosen and interpreted.** The same will be done on the next page for one equation with a positive ΔH (+Δ H).
Study the information underneath the selected equation to learn how to read and interpret all
  equations with -Δ H values.

Table I
Heats of Reaction at 101.3 kPa and 298 K

Reaction	ΔH (kJ)*
$CH_4(g) + 2O_2(g) \longrightarrow CO_2(g) + 2H_2O(\ell)$	–890.4
$C_3H_8(g) + 5O_2(g) \longrightarrow 3CO_2(g) + 4H_2O(\ell)$	–2219.2
$2C_8H_{18}(\ell) + 25O_2(g) \longrightarrow 16CO_2(g) + 18H_2O(\ell)$	–10943
$2CH_3OH(\ell) + 3O_2(g) \longrightarrow 2CO_2(g) + 4H_2O(\ell)$	–1452
$C_2H_5OH(\ell) + 3O_2(g) \longrightarrow 2CO_2(g) + 3H_2O(\ell)$	–1367
$C_6H_{12}O_6(s) + 6O_2(g) \longrightarrow 6CO_2(g) + 6H_2O(\ell)$	–2804
$2CO(g) + O_2(g) \longrightarrow 2CO_2(g)$	–566.0
$C(s) + O_2(g) \longrightarrow CO_2(g)$	–393.5
$4Al(s) + 3O_2(g) \longrightarrow 2Al_2O_3(s)$	–3351
$N_2(g) + O_2(g) \longrightarrow 2NO(g)$	+182.6
$N_2(g) + 2O_2(g) \longrightarrow 2NO_2(g)$	+66.4
$2H_2(g) + O_2(g) \longrightarrow 2H_2O(g)$	–483.6
$2H_2(g) + O_2(g) \longrightarrow 2H_2O(\ell)$	–571.6
$N_2(g) + 3H_2(g) \longrightarrow 2NH_3(g)$	–91.8
$2C(s) + 3H_2(g) \longrightarrow C_2H_6(g)$	–84.0
$2C(s) + 2H_2(g) \longrightarrow C_2H_4(g)$	+52.4
$2C(s) + H_2(g) \longrightarrow C_2H_2(g)$	+227.4
$H_2(g) + I_2(g) \longrightarrow 2HI(g)$	+53.0
$KNO_3(s) \xrightarrow{H_2O} K^+(aq) + NO_3^-(aq)$	+34.89
$NaOH(s) \xrightarrow{H_2O} Na^+(aq) + OH^-(aq)$	–44.51
$NH_4Cl(s) \xrightarrow{H_2O} NH_4^+(aq) + Cl^-(aq)$	+14.78
$NH_4NO_3(s) \xrightarrow{H_2O} NH_4^+(aq) + NO_3^-(aq)$	+25.69
$NaCl(s) \xrightarrow{H_2O} Na^+(aq) + Cl^-(aq)$	+3.88
$LiBr(s) \xrightarrow{H_2O} Li^+(aq) + Br^-(aq)$	–48.83
$H^+(aq) + OH^-(aq) \longrightarrow H_2O(\ell)$	–55.8

*Minus sign indicates an exothermic reaction.

Concept Task: Be able to interpret equations on
  Table I with - ΔH values

Equation with -ΔH:

FIND equation below on the Table I:

$$2C(s) + 3H_2(g) \longrightarrow C_2H_6(g) \quad \Delta H = -84 \text{ KJ}$$

This equation reads:

  2 moles of C and 3 moles of H_2 react to form 1 mole
  of C_2H_6 (ethane) by releasing 84 KJ (kilojoules) of
  heat energy.

Interpretations of negative Δ H (-84 KJ)

. The reaction is exothermic and releases heat energy

. The product C_2H_6 has less energy than the reactants
  C and H_2 (because ΔH is negative)

. The reaction will increase the temperature of the
  surrounding (because it releases heat)

Relating coefficient **to energy released:**

Since formation of *1 mole of C_2H_6* releases 84 KJ of
heat energy:

  Formation of 2 moles of C_2H_6 will release
    twice as much heat energy.

  Formation of 2 moles of C_2H_6 will release
    2(84 KJ) or 168 KJ of heat energy.

Incorporating negative ΔH (-84 KJ) **into the equation**

  $2C(g) + 3H_2(g) \longrightarrow C_2H_6 + 84KJ$

When ΔH is negative, the ΔH value (84 KJ) goes to
the RIGHT side of the equation as shown above.

Topic 9 - Kinetics and equilibrium

22. Reference Table I - Heat of reactions: Reading and interpreting + ΔH of reaction

Below, Reference Table I, which lists heat of reactions for selected reactions.

To the right of the table, an equation with a positive H (+ΔH) value from the table is chosen and interpreted. The same was done on the previous page for one equation with negative ΔH (-ΔH).

Study the information underneath the selected equation to learn how to read and interpret all equations with +ΔH values.

Table I
Heats of Reaction at 101.3 kPa and 298 K

Reaction	ΔH (kJ)*
$CH_4(g) + 2O_2(g) \longrightarrow CO_2(g) + 2H_2O(\ell)$	–890.4
$C_3H_8(g) + 5O_2(g) \longrightarrow 3CO_2(g) + 4H_2O(\ell)$	–2219.2
$2C_8H_{18}(\ell) + 25O_2(g) \longrightarrow 16CO_2(g) + 18H_2O(\ell)$	–10943
$2CH_3OH(\ell) + 3O_2(g) \longrightarrow 2CO_2(g) + 4H_2O(\ell)$	–1452
$C_2H_5OH(\ell) + 3O_2(g) \longrightarrow 2CO_2(g) + 3H_2O(\ell)$	–1367
$C_6H_{12}O_6(s) + 6O_2(g) \longrightarrow 6CO_2(g) + 6H_2O(\ell)$	–2804
$2CO(g) + O_2(g) \longrightarrow 2CO_2(g)$	–566.0
$C(s) + O_2(g) \longrightarrow CO_2(g)$	–393.5
$4Al(s) + 3O_2(g) \longrightarrow 2Al_2O_3(s)$	–3351
$N_2(g) + O_2(g) \longrightarrow 2NO(g)$	+182.6
$N_2(g) + 2O_2(g) \longrightarrow 2NO_2(g)$	+66.4
$2H_2(g) + O_2(g) \longrightarrow 2H_2O(g)$	–483.6
$2H_2(g) + O_2(g) \longrightarrow 2H_2O(\ell)$	–571.6
$N_2(g) + 3H_2(g) \longrightarrow 2NH_3(g)$	–91.8
$2C(s) + 3H_2(g) \longrightarrow C_2H_6(g)$	–84.0
$2C(s) + 2H_2(g) \longrightarrow C_2H_4(g)$	+52.4
$2C(s) + H_2(g) \longrightarrow C_2H_2(g)$	+227.4
$H_2(g) + I_2(g) \longrightarrow 2HI(g)$	+53.0
$KNO_3(s) \xrightarrow{H_2O} K^+(aq) + NO_3^-(aq)$	+34.89
$NaOH(s) \xrightarrow{H_2O} Na^+(aq) + OH^-(aq)$	–44.51
$NH_4Cl(s) \xrightarrow{H_2O} NH_4^+(aq) + Cl^-(aq)$	+14.78
$NH_4NO_3(s) \xrightarrow{H_2O} NH_4^+(aq) + NO_3^-(aq)$	+25.69
$NaCl(s) \xrightarrow{H_2O} Na^+(aq) + Cl^-(aq)$	+3.88
$LiBr(s) \xrightarrow{H_2O} Li^+(aq) + Br^-(aq)$	–48.83
$H^+(aq) + OH^-(aq) \longrightarrow H_2O(\ell)$	–55.8

*Minus sign indicates an exothermic reaction.

Concept Task: Be able to interpret equation on Table I with +ΔH

Equation with + ΔH :

FIND the equation below on the Table:

$NH_4Cl_{(s)} \longrightarrow NH_4^+{}_{(aq)} + Cl^-{}_{(aq)} \quad \Delta H = +14.78 \text{ KJ}$

This equation reads:

The dissolving of 1 mole of NH_4Cl (ammonium chloride) absorbs 14.78 KJ of heat energy

Interpretation of positive ΔH (+14.78 KJ)

. Dissolving NH_4Cl absorbs 14.78 KJ of heat energy

. The products (NH_4^+ and Cl^-) have more energy than the reactant $NH_4Cl_{(s)}$ (because ΔH is positive)

. The dissolving of NH_4Cl will decrease the temperature of the surrounding area (because heat is absorbed)

Relating coefficient to energy released:

Since the dissolving of 1 mole of NH_4Cl absorbs

14.78 KJ of heat energy:

  Dissolving of ½ (or 0.5) mole of NH_4Cl will absorb half as much heat energy.

  Dissolving of half a mole of NH_4Cl absorbs ½(14.78 KJ) or 7.39 KJ of heat energy.

Incorporating positive ΔH (+14.78 KJ) into the equation:

$NH_4Cl + 14.78 \text{ KJ} \longrightarrow NH_4^+ + Cl^-$

When ΔH is positive, the energy (+ΔH value) goes to the LEFT side of the equation as shown above.

Topic 9 - Kinetics and equilibrium

23. Potential Energy Diagram: Understanding potential energy diagrams

Potential energy diagram shows changes in heat energy of substances over a course of a reaction.

To understand potential energy diagrams, you will need to know the terms defined below. It is important to know these terms since they are parts of all potential energy diagrams.

Consider this equation:

$$A + B_2 \longrightarrow ABB \longrightarrow AB + B$$

Reactants   *Activated complex*   *Products*

Note the following three substances about the equation:

Reactants (A and B_2) are substances that are present at the beginning of a reaction

Products (AB and B) are substances formed at the end of a reaction

Activated complex (ABB) is a high energy intermediate substance that is formed during a reaction. Because of its high energy, activated complex is very unstable, and will always break down or rearrange itself to form a more stable *product*. Activated complex is not usually shown in a reaction equation. To understand the potential energy diagrams on the few pages, it is important to include the activated complex in this equation.

All of the above three substances are represented on all potential energy diagrams. As a result, all potential energy diagrams representing exothermic reactions look about the same, and all potential energy diagrams for endothermic reactions look about the same.

Example diagrams are shown below. The Exothermic diagram is drawn for the reaction that is given in the above equation.

24. Potential energy diagrams: Exothermic and endothermic diagrams

Below are example diagrams for exothermic and endothermic reactions:

Concept Task: Be able to recognize potential energy diagram for exothermic or endothermic reaction.

On the next page, these diagrams will be labeled with the important energy measurements that you need to know.

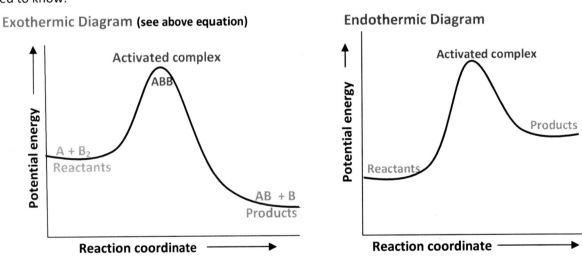

NOTICE the differences and similarities between the two potential energy diagrams.

NOTICE where reactants, activated complex, and products are labeled on the diagrams.

Topic 9 - Kinetics and equilibrium

25. Potential energy diagram: Identifying energy measurements

Concept Task: Be able to identify line measurements on potential energy diagrams.
Be able to draw potential energy diagrams for exothermic and endothermic reactions

Below are the same two diagrams from previous page.
The arrows represent the potential energy measurements.

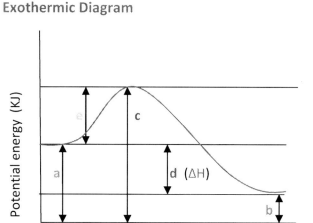
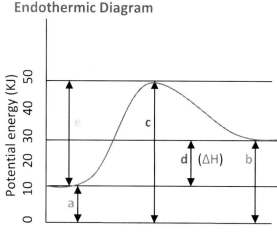

NOTE the followings about each diagram:

1. The y axis is potential energy.

2. The x axis is reaction coordinate (or progress of reaction).

3. Each curve shows potential energy of substances that are present at different times over the course of a reaction (starting with reactants, ending with products).

4. **Three potential energy measurements of substances are shown with arrows a, b and c.**
   These arrows are always drawn from the bottom of the diagram:

   (a) Potential energy of the reactants

   (b) Potential energy of the products

   (c) Potential energy of the activated complex

5. **Differences of two potential energies are shown with arrows d and e.**
   These arrows are always drawn between two energies of the diagram.

   (d) Heat of reaction, ΔH (Difference between the energy of products and the energy of reactants)

   (e) Activation energy (Difference between the energy of activated complex and the energy of reactants)

Topic 9 - Kinetics and equilibrium

26. Potential energy diagram: Catalyzed reaction diagram

RECALL that a catalyst is any substance added to a reaction **to increase the rate (speed) of the reaction.** Also **RECALL** that a catalyst speeds up reaction by lowering the activation energy (energy to start the reaction). The change (lowering) of activation energy by a catalyst can be represented on a potential energy diagram. On the graph below, a dotted curve is used to show the change of potential energy curve with the addition of a catalyst.

Concept Task: Be able to draw a change to potential energy diagram with addition of a catalyst

Below are diagrams without and with catalyst. Study and note the similarities and differences.

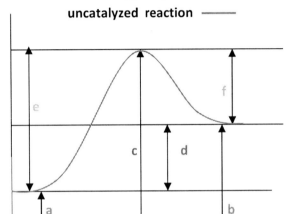

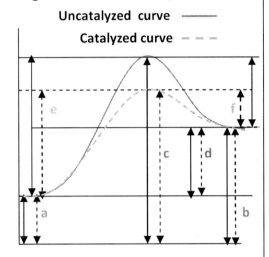

Measurements that changed with addition of a catalyst

NOTE (by the length of the dotted arrows) how these measurements have changed:

(c) The activated complex energy

(e) The activation energy for the forward reaction

(f) The activation energy for the reverse reaction

These three energy measurements, when measured to the green dotted curve (catalyzed), are **shorter** than when they are measured to the solid blue curve (uncatalyzed).

In another word, the addition of a catalyst lowers energy of activated complex (c) for the reaction. Therefore, the activation energies e and f (difference between energy of activated complex and energy of reactants) will also be lower with an addition of catalyst.

Measurements that do not change with addition of catalyst.

NOTE (by length of the arrows) that these measurements have not change.

(a) Potential energy of reactants

(b) Potential energy of products

(d) Heat of reaction, ΔH

These energy measurements to the green dotted curve (catalyzed) and to the solid blue curve (uncatalyzed) are the **same** length.

In another word, addition of catalyst does not change the heat energy of reactants (a) nor products (b). Therefore, (d), ΔH heat of reaction (difference between energy of products and of reactants) stays the same with or without a catalyst.

Topic 9 - Kinetics and equilibrium

27. Potential energy diagrams: Example questions

Below, example questions on potential energy diagram are given.
NOTE that questions are categorized by different concept tasks. Explanations of the correct choices are given for each question.
Study these examples to become familiar with questions relating to potential energy diagrams.

Concept Task: Be able to relate equation to potential energy diagrams

Example 9

Given the equation, $N_2 + O_2 + 183 \longrightarrow 2NO$
Which potential energy diagram best represents this reaction?

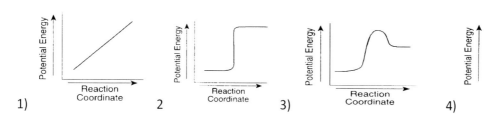

Before choosing:

Determine if equation given is exothermic or endothermic:
   Endothermic (energy is on the left)

LOOK for the endothermic curve:

Answer: Choice 3

Concept Task: Be able to relate potential energy diagrams to ▲H

Example 10

A potential energy for a reaction is shown below.

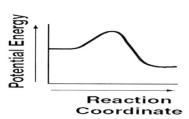

This reaction has
1) + ΔH, because heat is released
2) +ΔH, because heat is absorbed
3) – ΔH, because heat is released
4) – ΔH, because heat is absorbed

Before choosing:

Determine type of diagram given: Exothermic

Answer: Choice 3. Because in exothermic reactions:
   . ΔH is always negative (- ΔH)
   . Energy is always released

Concept Task: Be able to determine the energy measurements of a given potential energy diagram.

Example 11

Given the diagram below

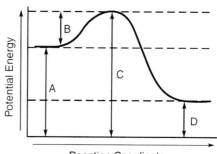

Which letter is correctly paired with the energy it measures?

1) A is heat of reaction
2) B is activation energy for forward reaction
3) C is activation energy for reverse reaction
4) D is energy of the activated complex

Answer: Choice 2.

Topic 9 - Kinetics and equilibrium

Lesson 3: Entropy

Introduction

During chemical and physical changes, particles of a substance can rearrange from one phase to another. Particles can become more or less organized depending on the type of change the substance have gone through during the change.

In this lesson, you will learn about entropy, which describe organization of a system.

28. Entropy: Definition and facts

Entropy is a measure of randomness or disorder of a system.

In chemistry, a system refers to any chemical or physical process that is taking place.

Entropy of chemical and physical systems is relative. That means, randomness or disorder of one system can only be described when compared to another system.

For example:

Water molecules in the liquid phase have a higher entropy than water molecules in the solid phase. However, water molecules in the liquid phase have a lower entropy than those in the gas phase.

Solid	Liquid	Gas
OOOOOOO	O O O	O O O
OOOOOOO	O O OO	O O O
OOOOOOO	O O O O	O O O
OOOOOOO	O O O	O O

Lowest entropy ------------------------------------> Highest entropy

Least random   Entropy increases   Most random
Least disorder   Randomness increases   Most disorder
                      Disorder increases

Entropy of a substance or a system changes as conditions such as temperature and pressure are changed.

Below are list of facts related to entropy

Concept Facts: Study and remember them

. Entropy (disorder) increases from solid to liquid to gas:

. Entropy (randomness) decreases from gas to liquid to solid:

. As temperature increases, so does the entropy of the system

. As pressure increases, entropy of the system decreases

. Entropy of free elements is higher than entropy of compounds

. A chemical reaction is more likely to occur if the change will lead to substances with higher entropy

Topic 9 - Kinetics and equilibrium

29. Entropy: Determining a chemical substance or temperature with highest or lowest entropy

Concept Task: Be able to determine which phase a substance has the highest or Lowest entropy.

For a phase with:

Highest entropy OR Most random
LOOK for a substance in the **gas phase**

Lowest entropy OR Least random
LOOK for a substance in the **solid phase**

Example 12
Which substance has particles that are most random?
1) $Hg(l)$ 3) $I_2(s)$
2) $CO_2(aq)$ 4) $O_2(g)$

Before choosing:
Analyze: Gas particles are usually the MOST random
LOOK for a Substance in the **gas** phase
Answer: Choice 4

Concept Task: Be able to determine which Temperature a substance has Highest or Lowest entropy

For Temperature with:

Highest entropy OR Most random
LOOK for **highest temperature**

Lowest entropy OR Least random
LOOK for **lowest temperature**

Example 13
Which of these substances will have particles that have the least entropy?
1) $CO_2(g)$ at $10°C$ 3) $SO_2(g)$ at $5°C$
2) $CO_2(g)$ at $15°C$ 4) $SO_2(g)$ at $20°C$

Answer: Choice 3: A substance at the lowest temperature will always have the Least entropy.

30. Entropy: Determining which change will lead to increase or decrease in entropy

Concept Task: Be able to determine which change equation is accompanied by an increase or a decrease in entropy

To determine equation showing:

Increase in entropy:
LOOK for a phase change
from Solid ---> Liquid --> Gas

LOOK for a chemical change that the reactants are changing
from solid ---> liquid ---> aqueous ----> gas

LOOK for a temperature change
from a Lower Temperature TO a Higher Temperature

Decrease in entropy:
LOOK for phase change
from Gas ---> Liquid --> Solid

LOOK for a chemical change that the reactants are changing
from Gas ---> aqueous ---> liquid ----> gas

LOOK for a temperature change
from High Temp TO Low Temp

Example 14
Which change is accompanied by an increase in entropy of the substance?

1) $Hg(l)$ ------> $Hg(s)$
2) $N_2(l)$ -------> $N_2(g)$
3) $I_2(g)$ --------> $I_2(s)$
4) $H_2O(g)$ ------> $H_2O(g)$

Answer: Choice 2 because a change from liquid to gas leads increase in randomness of the molecules

Example 15
Which temperature change of ethanol will lead to a decrease in randomness of its molecules?

1) $5°C$ to $-10°C$ 3) $0°C$ to $5°C$
2) $-10°C$ to $5°C$ 4) $-5°C$ to $0°C$

Answer: choice 1 because $5°C$ to $-10°C$ is a decrease in temperature. As temperature decreases, randomness (entropy) decreases

Topic 9 - Kinetics and equilibrium

Lesson 4: Equilibrium

Introduction:

Equilibrium refers to a state of balance between two opposing processes taking place at the same time (simultaneously). One example of two opposing process would be the freezing of water to ice and the melting of the ice back to water. Another example could be a reaction in which two elements are joining together to make a compound, and the compound that is being made, at the same time, is breaking up to re-make the same two elements.

In this lesson, you will learn about physical and chemical equilibrium.

31. Equilibrium: Definitions and facts

Equilibrium is a state of balance between two opposing (opposite) processes occurring at the same time.

Facts related to equilibrium are given below.

Concept Facts: Study to remember them.

When equilibrium is reached in a system:
- *Rate* of forward process is *equal* to rate of reverse process
- *Concentration* (or amount) of substances remains *constant*.

Equilibrium can only occur in a system in which changes that are taking place are *reversible*.

Equilibrium can only occur in a *closed system*. A closed system is a system in which nothing is allowed in or out.

A good example of a closed system would be a closed soda can. If a closed soda bottle is left undisturbed, equilibrium will be reached when the movements of carbon dioxide gas into and out of the liquid (inside the can) is occurring at the same rate.

Closed soda can — Equilibrium process will occur in this can.

Open soda can — Equilibrium process CANNOT occur in this can.

Equations showing a reversible process at equilibrium always contain a double ended arrow. (<------> or <======>)

Example of equilibrium equation:

$$N_2 + O_2 \underset{\text{Reverse}}{\overset{\text{Forward}}{\rightleftarrows}} 2NO$$

Interpretation: The reaction above is at equilibrium because the equation contains < ====== >.

At equilibrium:
- *Rate* of the forward and reverse reactions are *equal*.
- *Concentration* of N_2, O_2 and NO are all *constant*.

Topic 9 - Kinetics and equilibrium

32. Physical equilibrium: Examples, definitions, and facts

Physical equilibrium occurs in certain reversible physical changes.

RECALL that during a physical change, the composition of a substance does not change. Physical equilibrium, therefore, occurs in processes that do not lead to changes in the substance.

Examples of physical equilibrium are:
Phase equilibrium
Solution equilibrium

The next set of notes defines and gives examples of these two types of physical equilibrium.

33. Physical equilibrium – Phase equilibrium: Definitions, examples and facts

Phase equilibrium occurs in a CLOSED system in which phase changes are occurring.

RECALL that temperature is important to phase changes. So, at a specific temperature, a state of balance (equilibrium) can be reached between two opposing phase changes of a substance. The temperature at which a certain phase change equilibrium is reached, is different for different substances.

Phase changes that occur in water will be used to explain phase equilibrium.

Below are two phase equilibriums that occur with water.
NOTE: The temperature of water at which the equilibrium occurs is given.
Facts and equation related to each equilibrium are also given.

Concept Facts: Study to remember these information

Ice / water equilibrium: At 0°C or 273 K (melting and freezing point of water)

. Equilibrium exists between ice melting and liquid freezing
. The *rates* of melting and freezing are *equal*
. The *amounts* of ice and liquid water remain *constant*

$$H_2O(s) \underset{freezing}{\overset{melting}{<===========>}} H_2O(l) \quad \text{Ice/liquid water equilibrium equation}$$

Water /steam(vapor) equilibrium: At 100°C or 373 K (boiling point of water)

. Equilibrium exists between liquid evaporating and gas condensing
. The *rates* of evaporation and condensation are *equal*
. The *amounts* of liquid and gas remain *constant*

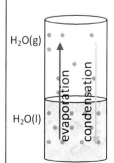

$$H_2O(l) \underset{condensation}{\overset{evaporation}{<============>}} H_2O(g) \quad \text{water/steam equilibrium equation}$$

Topic 9 - Kinetics and equilibrium

34. Physical equilibrium – Solution equilibrium: Definitions and facts

Solution equilibrium occurs in a CLOSED system in which a substance is dissolving in a liquid.

Below are two examples of solution equilibrium.
NOTE that facts and example equation for each equilibrium are given.

Concept Facts: Study to remember these information

Solid in liquid equilibrium: In a saturated solution
. Equilibrium exists between dissolved particles and undissolved particles
. *Rate* of dissolving of the solid is *equal* to the rate of crystallization of the particles
. *Amounts* of solid and ions remain *constant* in the solution

$$NaCl(s) \underset{crystallizing}{\overset{dissolving}{\rightleftharpoons}} Na^+(aq) + Cl^-(aq)$$ *solid in liquid equilibrium equation*

Gas in liquid equilibrium: In a gaseous solution
. Equilibrium exists between dissolved gas in the liquid and undissolved gas above the liquid.
. *Rate* of dissolving of the gas is *equal* to the rate of undissolving of the gas
. *Amounts* of undissolved gas (above liquid) and dissolved gas (in liquid) remain *constant*

$$CO_2(g) \rightleftharpoons CO_2(aq)$$ *solution equilibrium equation*

Solution equilibrium in a CLOSED soda can

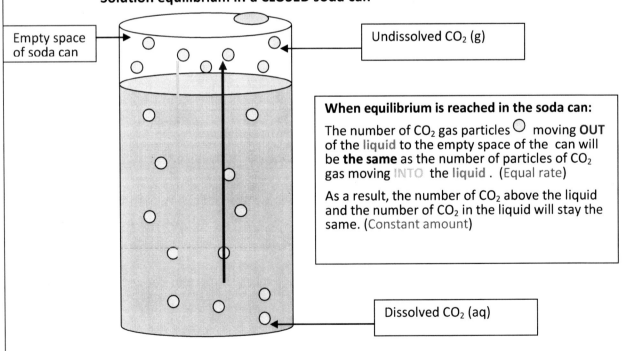

Empty space of soda can

Undissolved CO_2 (g)

When equilibrium is reached in the soda can:

The number of CO_2 gas particles ◯ moving **OUT** of the liquid to the empty space of the can will be **the same** as the number of particles of CO_2 gas moving INTO the liquid. (Equal rate)

As a result, the number of CO_2 above the liquid and the number of CO_2 in the liquid will stay the same. (Constant amount)

Dissolved CO_2 (aq)

Topic 9 - Kinetics and equilibrium

35. Chemical equilibrium: Understanding chemical equilibrium

Chemical equilibrium occurs in chemical reactions that are **reversible**.

RECALL that chemical changes lead to changes in composition of substances.

Chemical equilibrium, therefore, occurs in changes in which one or more substances are changing to other substances.

The note below explain more about reversible chemical reaction, and what is meant by a reactions at equilibrium. The note below is meant to give you a better understanding of chemical equilibrium and **Le Chatelier's principle that** will be discussed in the next few pages. It is important to KEEP IN MIND that the majority of questions on chemical equilibrium on tests, will test your understanding of Le Chatelier's principle. Understanding the notes below could lead to a better understanding of Le Chatelier's principle.

To explain more about chemical equilibrium, the following chemical equation will be use as an example.

Consider the following equation showing a reversible reaction taking place in a **closed system:**

$$N_2(g) + 3H_2(g) \underset{\text{Reverse reaction}}{\overset{\text{Forward reaction}}{\rightleftarrows}} 2NH_3(g)$$

At the start of the of the reaction, the reactants N_2 and H_2 will combine to produce NH_3 in the forward reaction. As NH_3 is being produced, the reverse reaction, in which NH_3 are decomposing to produce N_2 and H_2, will start. The speed (or rate) of this reverse reaction will be slow at first. As more and more NH_3 are being produced, the forward reaction will slow down, while the reverse reaction will speed up. Eventually, the forward and the reverse reactions will be occurring at the same rate (equal speed). This means that if at a given time period 10 molecules of NH_3 are being produced, there will be 10 other molecules of NH_3 breaking up to produce N_2 and H_2. When the rates of the reactions (forward and reverse) are equal, the reaction is said to have reach a state of equilibrium.

At equilibrium: The *rate* of forward is *equal* to the rate of reverse.
    The *concentrations* of N_2, H_2, and NH_3 will be *constant* (remain the same).

Topic 9 - Kinetics and equilibrium

36. Stress on equilibrium reaction: What is a stress?

Questions on chemical equilibrium usually deals with a given equilibrium reaction changing when a **stress** is introduced into the reaction at equilibrium.

What is a stress?
A stress on equilibrium reactions could be:
. Changing the concentration (By adding or removing substances)
. Changing the temperature (By adding or removing heat)
. Changing the pressure (By increasing or decreasing volume of gaseous reaction)
. Adding a catalyst

Le Chatelier's Principle states that when a stress is introduced into a reaction at equilibrium, the reaction will change by speeding up in one direction and slowing down in the other direction to bring back (reestablish) the reaction to an equilibrium state.

In the next few pages, different stresses to reactions will be discussed. You will also learn how to determine changes to a reaction when the different stresses are given in equilibrium questions.

37. Le Chatelier's Principle : Determining effect on reaction

When a change (stress) is made to a reaction at equilibrium, there will be changes to rates, shift, and concentration (amount) of the substances in the reaction.

On tests, you will be given an equilibrium reaction. You will be told what the change (stress) is in the reaction. You will be asked to choose the correct effect of the given stress on that reaction.

In the next set of notes, you will be given information on how to determine changes to a reaction, as concentration, temperature and pressure are changed on equilibrium reactions.

HOW TO STUDY the notes on the next page.

Each set deals with one kind of change (stress) to a reaction (ex. Change in temperature)

A Specific stress is given (ex. Stress 1: Increase in temperature...etc)

Under each stress :

A List (a –e) indicates how to determine change in rate, shift, and concentrations of the substances in the reaction.

Example equation showing a specific equilibrium reaction is given.

Result: Changes in rate, concentration and shift are determined using information on this List (a-e)

Topic 9 - Kinetics and equilibrium

38. Change in Concentration: Determining effect on shift, rates, and concentrations

Concept Task: Be able to determine the effect on an equilibrium reaction when the concentration of a substance is changed

IMPORTANT: When concentration of one of the substances in a reaction is changed, **ALWAYS NOTE,** The side (LEFT or RIGHT) in the equation where the substance is on.

Given below are two stresses of concentration:

STRESS 1: Increasing concentration

When a substance is added to a reaction to increase its concentration:
a) Rate increases toward opposite side of the change
b) Rate decreases toward the same side the substance
c) Concentration of other substances on the same side of the change decreases
d) Concentration of all substances on the opposite side of the change increases
e) Reaction will shift (speeds up) toward the opposite side of the change

Consider the reaction: $N_2 + 3H_2 \rightleftharpoons 2NH_3$

Add stress: Increase (↑) concentration of N_2
(**NOTE:** N_2 is on the LEFT, so the side of change is on the LEFT)

RESULT of increasing concentration of N_2
a) Rate of forward increases
b) Rate of reverse decreases
c) Concentration of H_2 decreases
d) Concentration of NH_3 increases
e) Shift of reaction is to the RIGHT

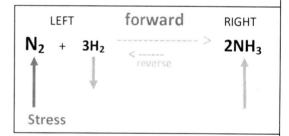

STRESS 2: Decreasing (↓) concentration
a) Rate increases toward the side of the change
b) Rate decreases toward the opposite side of the change
c) Concentration of other substances on the side of the change increases
d) Concentration of all substances on the opposite side of the change decreases
e) Reaction will shift (speeds up) toward the side of the change

Take this equation: $X + WY \rightleftharpoons XY + W$

Add stress: Decrease concentration of WY
(**NOTE:** WY is on the LEFT, so the side of the change is on the LEFT)

Result of decreasing concentration of WY
a) Rate of forward decreases
b) Rate of reverse increases
c) Concentration of XY and W decreases
d) Concentrations of X increases
e) Shift in reaction is to the LEFT

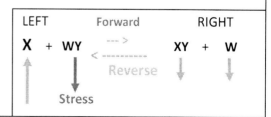

Topic 9 - Kinetics and equilibrium

39. Change in temperature: Determining effect on rate, shift, and concentration

Concept Task: Be able to determine the effect of adding or removing heat (changing temperature) on an equilibrium reaction:

IMPORTANT: When a question deals with adding or removing heat, heat will be written in the equation.
   Ex.   A   +   B   <----------->   AB   +   HEAT

ALWAYS NOTE: The side (LEFT or RIGHT) the heat energy is in the equation.
   Which direction (FORWARD or REVERSE) is exothermic, and which is endothermic

STRESS 1: Increasing temperature (Adding heat)
Favors endothermic (adding heat causes an increase in rate of endothermic reaction)

a) Rate increases toward the side without the heat (endothermic reaction increases)
b) Rate decreases toward the side with the heat (Exothermic reaction decreases)
c) Concentration of substances on the side with the heat decreases
d) Concentration of all substances on the side without heat increases
e) Reaction will shift (speeds up) toward side without heat

Consider the equation: HI + heat   <==========> H_2 + I_2

Add stress: Increase (↑) heat (temperature)
   (**NOTE: Heat on the left**: Forward is endothermic: Reverse is exothermic)

Result of increasing heat:
a) Rate of Forward increases
b) Rate of Reverse decreases
c) Concentration of HI decreases
d) Concentrations of H_2 and I_2 increases
e) Shift of reaction to the RIGHT

STRESS 2: Decreasing Temperature (Removing heat)
Favors exothermic reaction (removing heat causes the exothermic reaction to increase)

a) Rate increases Toward the side with the Heat (exothermic reaction increases)
b) Rate decreases Toward the side without the Heat (endothermic reaction decreases)
c) Concentration of substances on the side with the Heat increases
d) Concentration of all substances on the without Heat decreases
e) Reaction will shift (speeds up) Toward side with Heat

Consider the equation: HI + heat   <==============> H_2 + I_2

Add stress: Removing (↓) heat
   (**NOTE**: Heat on the left; Forward is endothermic; Reverse is exothermic)

Result of removing heat:
a) Rate of forward increases
b) Rate of Reverse decreases
c) Concentration of HI increases
d) Concentrations of H_2 and I_2 decreases
e) Shift of reaction toward the RIGHT

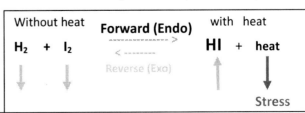

Topic 9 - Kinetics and equilibrium

40. Change in Pressure: Determining effects on rate, shift, and concentration

Concept Task: Be able to determine the effect of increasing or decreasing pressure (by changing volume) on an equilibrium reaction:

IMPORTANT: When an equilibrium question deals with change in pressure, you must consider the number of moles of substances on each side (LEFT and RIGHT) of the equation.

RECALL that to DETERMINE the total number of moles of substances in an equation:
You MUST ADD up all the coefficients of substances in the equation.

NOTE: The side (LEFT or RIGHT) of the equation that has the smaller and the greater number of moles

Given below are two stresses of pressure:
STRESS 1: Increasing pressure (Decreasing volume in gaseous reaction)

  a) Rate increases Toward the side of the smaller number of moles
  b) Rate decreases Toward the side of the greater number of moles
  c) Concentration of substances on the side of smaller number of moles increases
  d) Concentration of substances on the side of greater number of moles decreases
  e) Reaction will shift (speeds up) in the to direction of smaller number of moles
  f) None of the above will change if the number of moles on both sides are equal

Consider the equation: CH_4 + H_2O <===========> $3H_2$ + CO
Determine moles of substances: 1   +   1   3   +   1
Total moles: 2 moles   4 moles
NOTE: **LEFT:** Smaller number of moles   **RIGHT:** Greater number of moles

ADD stress: Increase in pressure:
Result of increasing pressure
  a) Rate of reverse increases (favors production of substances on side with lesser number of moles)
  b) Rate of forward decreases
  c) Concentration of CH_4 and H_2O increases
  d) Concentration of H_2 and CO decreases
  e) Shift of reaction to the LEFT

Consider the equation: $C_2(g)$ + $D_2(g)$ <----------------> 2 CD(g)
Determine number of moles: 1   +   1   2
Total moles: 2 moles   2 moles
NOTE: Equal number of moles on both sides

ADD stress: Increase or decrease pressure:
Change to reaction: NO effect on equilibrium concentrations
There will be no shift in equilibrium.

Topic 9 - Kinetics and equilibrium

41. Change in concentration by common ion effect: Determining effect on rate, shift, and concentration

Concept Task: Be able to determine the effect of adding a salt to a solution at equilibrium.

Common ion effect refers to a substance that will dissolve (ionize) in solution to produce the same ion that is already present in a solution.

When equilibrium questions deals with dissolving of salt, the equilibrium equation given will always look like the one below:

$$KNO_3 (s) \underset{\text{crystallization}}{\overset{\text{Dissolving}}{\rightleftharpoons}} K^+(aq) + NO_3^-(aq)$$

NOTE: The equation contains ions. The equation is showing equilibrium in a KNO_3 aqueous solution.
The rate of dissolving (forward) of ions is equal to rate of crystallization of ions (reverse).

The stress to these types of reactions will be the addition of a different solid (ex. **KCl**) to the solution. Addition of KCl will increase the amount (or concentration) of K^+ when it dissolved in the solution.

NOTE: The change to the reaction depends on the ion that is increased as a result of the added substance.

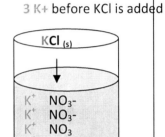

Below is an example stress by common-ion effect.

STRESS 1: Increasing concentration (By common effect)
  NOTE: The ion that is added and which side (LEFT or RIGHT) the ion is on in the equation given.

   a) Rate increases toward the opposite side of added ion (toward the solid)
   b) Rate decreases toward the same side as the added ion (toward aq)
   c) Concentration of other substances on the side of the added ion decreases
   d) Concentration of substances on the opposite side of the added ion increases
   e) Reaction shift toward the opposite side of the added ion (toward the solid)

Take this equation: $KNO_{3(s)} \rightleftharpoons K^+_{(aq)} + NO_3^-{}_{(aq)}$

Add stress: **Adding KCl (s) :** Will dissolve to give more K^+

Therefore: K^+ concentration will increase by addition of KCl (s)

Result **of adding KCl:**

a) Rate of Reverse increase
b) Rate of Forward decreases
c) Concentration of NO_3^- decreases
d) Concentration of $KNO_3(s)$ increases
e) Shift of reaction is to the Left

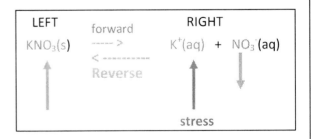

Topic 9 - Kinetics and equilibrium

42. Adding a catalyst: Determining effect on rate, shift, and concentration

When a catalyst is added to an equilibrium reaction, the following is true.

Concept Facts: Study and remember effect of catalyst on equilibrium reaction
1. The rate of BOTH forward and reverse increases (speeds up) equally

   As a result:

2. The addition of catalyst does not change (has no effect) on the equilibrium concentration
There will be NO shift in the reaction.

43. Example questions on equilibrium reactions: Determining effect of stress

In example questions 15 – 19 given below, you will be given an equilibrium reaction equation.
The question under each equation asks you to choose the correct change in the reaction when a given change (stress) is made to the reaction.

Each example question relates to each of the stresses discussed in the previous pages.
Study these example problems to become familiar with question on equilibrium reactions

Example 16: Determining effect of changing concentration:

Given the equilibrium reaction below:

$$2CO_2(g) \Longleftrightarrow O_2(g) + 2CO(g)$$

Which change in the reaction will occur if the concentration of CO is decreased?

1) Rate of forward will increase
2) Rate of reverse will increase
3) Concentration of O_2 will decrease
4) Concentration of CO_2 will increase

Answer: Choice 1: Decreasing concentration results in: (SEE SET 39 STRESS 2 list for GUIDE)

Rate increases TOWARD side of substance being removed.

CO is on the right. Reaction going right is forward. Forward reaction will increase

ALL other choices are incorrect changes to the reaction

Example 17: Determining effect of changing temperature

Given the following system at equilibrium:

$$2Cl + 2H_2O + energy \longleftrightarrow HCl + O_2$$

If the temperature of the system is increased, the concentration of O_2 will

1) Decrease, and equilibrium will shift to the right
2) Decrease, and equilibrium will shift to the left
3) Increase, and equilibrium will shift to the right
4) Increase, and equilibrium will shift to the left

Answer: Choice 3: Increasing heat results in : (See SET 40 STRESS 1 LIST for GUIDE)

Shift TOWARD side WITHOUT heat: Right side is WITHOUT heat: Shift is to RIGHT

Substances on side WITHOUT heat increase. O_2 concentration increases

All other choices are incorrect changes to the reaction.

Topic 9 - Kinetics and equilibrium

43 Cont.

Example 18: Determining the effect of increasing pressure
  Given the reaction:
  $$2SO_2(g) + O_2(g) <=======> 2SO_3(g) + Heat$$
  If pressure is increased on the reaction, there will be
  1) A decrease in concentration of SO_3
  2) An increase in concentration SO_2
  3) An increase in heat
  4) A shift in equilibrium to left

  Answer: Choice 3: Increasing pressure causes: (See Set 41 STRESS 1 List for Guide)
  Concentration of substances on side of smaller number of moles increases.
  SO_3 and Heat (on the RIGHT) are on side of smaller moles; they will increase

Example 19: Determining change by common-ion effects
  Given the reaction below at equilibrium:
  $$BaSO_4(s) <==========> Ba^{2+}(aq) + SO_4^{2-}(aq)$$

  The addition of H_2SO_4 will shift the equilibrium point
  1) Left, and increases the concentration of Ba^{2+}
  2) Left, and decreases the concentration of Ba^{2+}
  3) Right, and increase the concentration of $BaSO_4$
  4) Right, and decrease the concentration of $BaSO_4$

  Answer: Choice 2: Adding H_2SO_4 will Increase SO_4^{2-} on the RIGHT (SO_4^{2-} is the common ion)
  Increasing SO_4^{2-} on the RIGHT causes : (See Set 42 List for GUIDE)
  A Decrease concentration of the other ion on the RIGHT: Ba^{2+} will decrease
  A SHIFT toward opposite side of the ion added: Shift Toward LEFT

  ALL other choices are incorrect changes to the reaction

Example 20. Determining effect of addition of a catalyst
  Given the reaction below:
  $$2XY <------------------------> X_2 + Y_2$$

  What will happen when a catalyst is added to the system at equilibrium?
  1) The equilibrium concentration of XY will increase
  2) The equilibrium concentration of X will decrease
  3) The equilibrium rate of forward and reverse will decrease equally
  4) The equilibrium rate of forward and reverse will increase equally

  Answer: Choice 4. Catalyst speeds up both forward and reverse rate equally

  ALL other choices are incorrect changes to the reaction.

Topic 9 - Kinetics and equilibrium

44. Example questions on equilibrium: Determining stress that will cause a certain change in a reaction

Concept Task: Be able to determine stresses that will cause a certain change to a reaction

In the example question 20 – 22 given below, you will be given an equilibrium reaction equation.
The question under each equation asks you to choose a correct change (stress) that should be made to the reaction to produce the change that is given in the question.

These types of question are more common on exams.
Note the difference in these questions from the previous ones (examples 14 – 18)

Example 21: Determining a change that will cause an increase in rate of forward reaction
Given the equilibrium reaction below:

$$2SO_2(g) + O_2(g) \rightleftharpoons 2SO_3(g) + heat$$

Which change at equilibrium will cause the rate of forward reaction to increase?
1) Decreasing concentration of $SO_2(g)$
2) Decreasing concentration of $SO_3(g)$
3) Increasing temperature
4) Decreasing pressure

Answer: Choice 2. The reaction above will speed up to the right (rate forward increase) ONLY when:

On the LEFT side of equation	OR	On the RIGHT side of equation
. SO_2 is increased . O_2 is increased		. SO_3 is decreased . Heat is decreased
. Pressure is increased		

Example 22. Determining a change (stress) that will cause a decrease in concentration
Given the equilibrium reaction

$$H_2 + Cl_2 + energy \rightleftharpoons 2HCl$$

Which change will cause the concentration of H_2 to decrease?
1) Decreasing Cl_2
2) Decreasing pressure
3) Increasing temperature
4) Decreasing HCl

Answer: Choice 4: The amount of H_2 (on LEFT) will decrease only when:

On the LEFT (same side as H_2).	OR	On the RIGHT (opposite side of H_2)
. Cl_2 is increased. Temperature (heat) is increased		. HCl is decreased

Example 23: Determining a change (stress) that will cause a shift in a reaction
Given the reaction

$$2C_2(g) + D_4(g) \rightleftharpoons 4CD + 20 KJ$$

Which change in the reaction will cause the equilibrium reaction to shift left?
1) Increase in pressure
2) Decreasing heat
3) Increase in concentration of $C_2(g)$
4) Adding a catalyst

Answer: Choice 1. The above reaction will only shift LEFT when:

ON the LEFT	OR	ON the RIGHT
. C_2 or D_4 is decreased		.CD or heat is increased
.Pressure increase (**Note:** LEFT side has smaller number of moles)		

Topic 9 – Kinetics and Equilibrium

Check-A-list

Concept Terms

Below is a list of vocabulary terms from Topic 9. You should know the definition and facts related to each term.

Put a check in the box [V] next to a term if you know its definition and other facts related to the term.

[ ] Kinetics
[ ] Rate
[ ] Collision Theory
[ ] Effective collision
[ ] Catalyst
[ ] Activation energy
[ ] Potential energy
[ ] Potential energy of reactants
[ ] Potential energy of products
[ ] Heat of reaction
[ ] Activated complex
[ ] Potential energy of activated complex

[ ] Exothermic reaction
[ ] Endothermic reaction
[ ] Potential energy diagram
[ ] Equilibrium
[ ] Physical equilibrium
[ ] Phase equilibrium
[ ] Solution equilibrium
[ ] Ice/water equilibrium
[ ] Water/steam equilibrium
[ ] Stress
[ ] Le Chatelier's Principle
[ ] Entropy

If you do not have a check next to a term, look it up or ask your teacher.

Concept Tasks

Below is a list of concept tasks from Topic 9. You should know how to solve problems and answer questions related to each concept task.

Put a check in the box [V] next a concept task if you know how to solve problems and answer questions related to it.

[ ] Determining which solution concentration will have the fastest or the slowest rate of reaction
[ ] Determining which solution temperature will produce the fastest or the slowest rate of reaction
[ ] Determining which pressure will cause the fastest or the slowest rate of reaction
[ ] Determining which solid form (different surface area) will produce the fastest or the slowest rate
[ ] Determining energy information of a reaction based on temperature before and after a reaction
[ ] Determining energy information from a given reaction equation.
[ ] Interpreting Table I equation with -▲H value
[ ] Interpreting Table I equation with +▲H value
[ ] Recognizing correct potential energy diagram as exothermic or endothermic
[ ] Identify line measurements on potential energy diagrams.
[ ] Relating equation to potential energy diagram
[ ] Relating potential energy diagram to ▲H of a reaction
[ ] Determining which phase a substance has the Highest or Lowest entropy
[ ] Determining which temperature a substance has the Highest or Lowest entropy
[ ] Determining which change equation is accompanied by an increase or a decrease in entropy
[ ] Determining effect on equilibrium reaction when concentration of a substance is changed
[ ] Determining effect of adding or removing heat (changing temperature) on equilibrium reaction
[ ] Determining effect of increasing or decreasing pressure (changing volume) on equilibrium reaction
[ ] Determining effect of adding a different salt to a solution at equilibrium
[ ] Determining stresses that will cause a certain change to a reaction

If you do not have a check next to a concept task, look it up or ask your teacher.

Topic 9 – Kinetics and Equilibrium

Concept Facts Review Questions

1. Energy needed to start a chemical reaction is called
   1) Kinetic energy
   2) Activation energy
   3) Potential energy
   4) Ionization energy

2. For collision to be effective, reacting particles must collide with
   1) Sufficient kinetic energy only
   2) Proper orientation only
   3) Sufficient kinetic energy and proper orientation
   4) Sufficient potential energy and proper orientation

3. Adding a catalyst to a reaction will cause the rate of a reaction to
   1) Increase
   2) Decrease
   3) Remain the same

4. Increasing temperature will
   1) Increase reaction rate because of an increase in frequency of effective collisions
   2) Increase reaction rate because of a decrease in frequency of effective collisions
   3) Decrease reaction rate because of an increase in frequency of effective collisions
   4) Decrease reaction rate because of a decrease in frequency of effective collisions

5. When a catalyst is added to a reaction, the reaction rate is increased because the catalyst
   1) Increases activation energy
   2) Decreases activation energy
   3) Increases potential energy of the reactants
   4) Decreases potential energy of the reactants

6. Which best describes all endothermic reactions?
   1) They always release heat
   2) They always absorb heat
   3) They always occur spontaneously
   4) They never occur spontaneously

7. The heat of reaction (ΔH) is equal to
   1) Heat of products − Heat of reactants
   2) Heat of products + Heat of reactants
   3) Heat of products × Heat of reactants
   4) Heat of products ÷ Heat of reactants

8. When an exothermic process occurs in water, the temperature of the water will
   1) Increase because heat energy is given off by the reaction
   2) Increase because heat energy is absorbed by the reaction
   3) Decrease because heat energy is given off by the reaction
   4) Decrease because heat energy is absorbed by the reaction

9. Entropy measures which of the followings about a chemical system?
   1) Activation energy of the system
   2) Intermolecular forces of the system
   3) Energy change of the system
   4) Disorder of the system

10. A system is most likely to undergo a reaction if the system after the reaction has
    1) Lower energy and lower entropy
    2) Lower energy and higher entropy
    3) Higher energy and higher entropy
    4) Higher energy and lower entropy

11. At equilibrium, the rates at which the forward and the reverse processes are occurring are
    1) Equal
    2) Constant
    3) Increasing
    4) Decreasing

12. Increasing temperature on equilibrium reactions favors
    1) Exothermic reaction, only
    2) Endothermic reaction, only
    3) Both exothermic and endothermic reaction
    4) Neither exothermic nor endothermic reaction

Topic 9 – Kinetics and Equilibrium

Concept Task Review Questions

13. At which temperature would a reaction between zinc and hydrochloric acid occur at the slowest speed?
    1) 25°C 2) 50°C 3) 75°C 4) 100°C

14. Given the reaction
    $$CuSO_4(s) \longleftrightarrow Cu^{2+}(aq) + SO_4^{2-}(aq)$$
    The $CuSO_4(s)$ dissolves more rapidly when it is powdered because the increased in surface area allows for
    1) Increased exposure of solute to solvent
    2) Increased solute solubility
    3) Decreased exposure of solute to solvent
    4) Decreased solute solubility

15. Based on the nature of the reactants in each equation, which reaction at 25°C will occur at the fastest rate?
    1) $KI(aq) + AgNO_3(aq) \longrightarrow AgI(s) + KNO_3(aq)$
    2) $C(s) + O_2(g) \longrightarrow CO(g)$
    3) $2SO_2(g) + O_2(g) \longrightarrow 2SO_3(g)$
    4) $NH_3(g) + HCl(g) \longrightarrow NH_4Cl(s)$

16. Given the reaction:
    $$I + I \longrightarrow I_2 + energy$$
    This reaction has
    1) $+\Delta H$ because the products have less energy than the reactants
    2) $+\Delta H$ because the products have more energy than the reactants
    3) $-\Delta H$ because the products have less energy than the reactants
    4) $-\Delta H$ because the products have more energy than the reactants

17. Given the chemical change
    $$2H_2O(l) + 572\ KJ \longleftrightarrow 2H_2(g) + O_2(g)$$
    This reaction
    1) Is endothermic and releases 572 KJ of heat energy
    2) Is endothermic and absorbs 572 KJ of heat energy
    3) Is exothermic and releases 572 KJ of heat energy
    4) Is exothermic and absorbs 572 KJ of heat energy

18. Based on Reference Table I, the formation of 1 mole of which substance releases the greatest amount of heat energy?
    1) C_2H_2 2) NO 3) C_2H_6 4) NH_3

19. Given the reaction
    $$A + B \longrightarrow C + energy$$
    Which diagram below best represents the Potential energy change for this reaction?

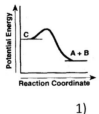
1)
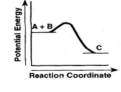
2)
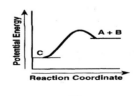
3)
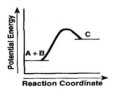
4)

20. A potential energy diagram for a chemical reaction is given below.

According to Reference Table I, which reaction could be represented by this potential energy diagram?
1) 2C₂(s) + 3H₂(g) -------> C₂H₆(g)
2) 2C(s) + 2H₂(g) ------> C₂H₄(g)
3) N₂(g) + O₂(g) -----> 2NO(g)
4) NH₄Cl(s) ----------------> NH₄⁺(aq) + Cl⁻(aq)

21. Given the equilibrium reaction below
$$N_2O_4 + 58.1 \text{ KJ} \longleftrightarrow 2 NO_2(g)$$
If the concentration of NO₂(g) is increased
1) The rate of forward reaction will increase, and equilibrium will shift to right
2) The rate of forward reaction will increase, and equilibrium will shift to left
3) The rate of reverse reaction will increase, and equilibrium will shift right
4) The rate of reverse reaction will increase, and equilibrium will shift left

22. Given the equilibrium reaction below
$$C_2(g) + D_2(g) \longleftrightarrow 2CD(g) + \text{energy}$$
Which change will cause the equilibrium point to shift to the left?
1) Increasing pressure
2) Increasing the amount of D₂ (g)
3) Adding heat
4) Addition of catalyst

Constructed Response Questions

Base your answer to questions 23 through 26 on the potential energy diagram below.

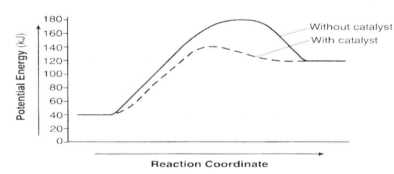

23. Explain, in terms of the function of catalyst, why the curves on the potential energy diagram for the catalyzed and uncatalyzed reactions are different.

24. What is the activation energy for the forward reaction with the catalyst?

25. What is the heat of reaction for the reverse reaction without catalyst?

26. What is the heat of the activated complex for the reaction without catalyst?

Topic 10 - Organic Chemistry

Topic outline

In this topic, you will learn about the following concepts:

. Properties of organic compounds
. Classes of organic compounds
. Hydrocarbon compounds
. Functional group compounds
. Naming and drawing organic compounds
. Isomers
. Organic reactions
. Substitution, addition, fermentation, combustion saponification, polymerization

Lesson 1 – Characteristics of carbon and organic compounds

Introduction:

Organic compounds are compounds of the element carbon. Bonding properties of carbon makes it possible for a carbon atom to bond with other carbon atoms and other nonmetal atoms, to form enormous number of organic compounds that can range from one to several hundreds carbon atoms in length. Properties of organic compounds are due, in part, to the chemical properties of a carbon atom. In this lesson, you will learn about general properties of carbon and organic compounds.

1. Properties of carbon and of organic compounds: Definitions and facts

Chemical and bonding properties of carbon atoms:

Concept Facts: Study to remember them
. A carbon atom has four valance electrons
. A carbon atom MUST form four (4) covalent bonds by sharing its four valance electrons
. A carbon atom can form a single, double or triple covalent bond
. A carbon atom bonds easily with other carbons atoms, as well as other nonmetal atoms such as H, N, and O, S and the halogens

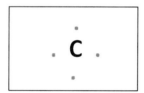

Lewis electron-dot symbol for a bonded carbon atom
4 dots = 4 valance electrons

General properties of organic compounds :

Concept Facts: Study to remember these properties of organic compounds

. Organic compounds are molecular (covalent) substances. That means they contain ONLY nonmetal atoms
. Bonding between atoms in molecules of organic compounds are all covalent bonds
. General shape of basic organic molecule is tetrahedral
. Most are nonpolar or slightly polar.
. Molecules of organic substances are held together by weak intermolecular forces
. Most have very low melting and low boiling points (due to weak intermolecular force)
. Reactions of organic compounds are generally slower than those of inorganic compounds.
   Reactions of organic involve breaking strong covalent bonds holding the atoms together.
.Most are nonelectrolytes (do not conduct electricity well)
   Organic acids are weak electrolytes.
. Most are insoluble in water (because they are nonpolar)
. Most decompose easily under heat (because they are molecular)

These properties vary by the different classes of organic compounds.

Topic 10 - Organic Chemistry

2. Names of organic compounds: Relating number of Carbon atoms to names

Name prefix **(name beginning)** of organic compounds is determined by the **number of carbon** atoms in the formula.

Name ending of a compound depends on the **class of organic compound** that the substance belongs.

For examples: In the name **Prop**ane

> Prefix: Prop indicates a three (3) Carbon atom molecule
>
> Name ending: -ane indicates that propane belongs to a class of organic compound known as alkane.

Below, a table of prefixes and a table summarizing name endings of substances from the different classes of organic compounds.

Name prefixes: Reference Table P

Number of Carbon	Prefix
1	meth
2	eth
3	prop
4	but
5	pent
6	hex
7	hept
8	oct
9	non
10	dec

Name endings of compounds

Classes of compound	Name ending
Alkanes	- ane
Alkenes	- ene
Alkynes	-yne
Alcohols	-ol
Ethers	ether
Aldehydes	-al
Ketones	-one
Organic acids	-oic
Esters	-oate
Amines	-amine
Amides	-amides

NOTE: Halides are named with the *halogen* name at the beginning.
Ex. *Chloro*butane

Concept Task: Be able to relate an organic compound name to the number of carbon atoms in the compound.

Use information on Table P

Example 1
How many carbon atoms are in a molecule of a compound whose IUPAC name is pentanone?

1) 1   3) 3
2) 5   4) 7

Answer: Choice 2 *Pent (in pent*anone) is prefix for 5 carbons
(SEE TABLE P TO THE LEFT)

Example 2
Which is a correct name for an organic compound containing seven carbon atoms?

1) Butanol   3) Hexanal
2) Pentene   4) Heptanoic acid

Answer: Choice 4 . A seven carbon compound will start with the prefix **Hept:** (SEE TABLE P)

Concept Task: Be able to relate name ending of a substance to class of organic compound.

Example 3.
Which compound is an organic acid?

1) Pentanone   3) Hexanoic
2) Methanal   4) Propanamide

Answer: Choice 3

You will learn more of these name endings as each class of compound is discussed in the next few sets.

Topic 10 - Organic Chemistry

3. Bonding in organic compounds: Describing bonding in organic compounds

A carbon atom has four (4) valance electrons.
LOOK on the Periodic Table for Carbon (atomic number 6)

```
12.001
   C
   6
 2 – 4
```

RECALL that valance electrons are the electrons in the outer most electron shell of an atom.
.Valance electrons can be found as the last number in the electron configuration of an atom.
Because of its four valance electrons, each carbon atom MUST form four covalent bonds.

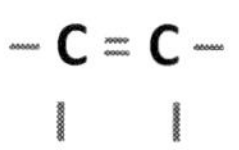

$$-\underset{|}{\overset{|}{C}}- \qquad -\underset{|}{C}=\underset{|}{C}- \qquad -C\equiv C-$$

Each C atom in the three structures shown above have four (covalent) bonds **around it.**
The four covalent bonds can be formed with other carbon atoms and with other nonmetal atoms.

Concept Task: Be able to identify a correctly drawn organic compound structure

Correctly drawn structures of organic compounds must show each carbon atom with **exactly four bonds**.
Any organic compound structure drawn with more or less than four bonds around any of the carbon is an incorrectly drawn structure.

Below are four possible organic structures.

Count the number of covalent bonds (–) around each **C** atom and note:

Structures with More or Less than four bonds around any of the carbon atoms are incorrect structures.

Structures with exactly four bonds around each carbon atom are correctly drawn.

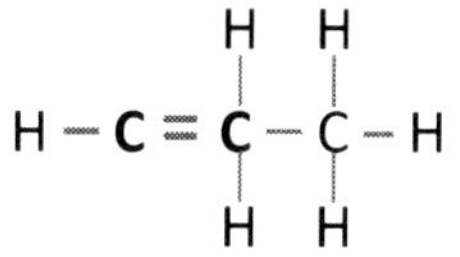

$$H-C\equiv C-\underset{H}{\overset{H}{C}}-H \text{ with extra H's} \qquad\qquad H-\underset{}{C}=\underset{H}{\overset{H}{C}}-\underset{H}{\overset{H}{C}}-H$$

Incorrect organic structure   **Correct organic structure**
The Left **C** atom only has 3 bonds   All **C** atoms have exactly 4 bonds
The middle **C** atom has 5 bonds

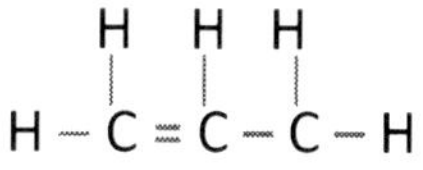

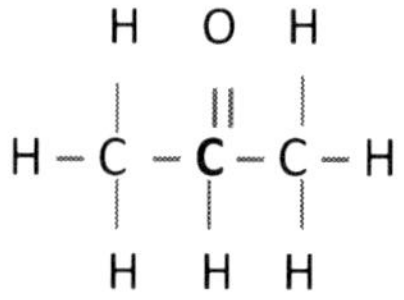

$$H-\underset{H}{\overset{H}{C}}-\underset{H}{\overset{O}{\underset{||}{C}}}-\underset{H}{\overset{H}{C}}-H \qquad\qquad H-\underset{H}{\overset{H}{C}}-\overset{O}{\underset{||}{C}}-\underset{H}{\overset{H}{C}}-H$$

Incorrect organic structure   **Correct organic structure**
The second **C** atom has 5 bonds   All **C** atoms have exactly 4 bonds

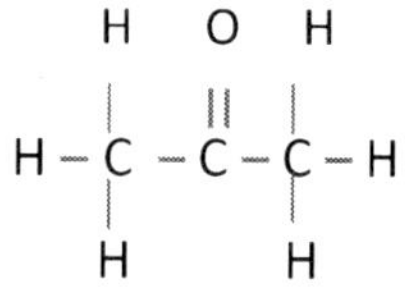

To determine correctly drawn organic structure:
JUST count the bonds around the carbons.
Correct structure must have 4 bonds for each C atom.
CORRECT structure must have exactly 4 bonds around each carbon atom

Topic 10 - Organic Chemistry

Lesson 2 – Classes of organic compounds

Introduction:

As mentioned, there are enormous number of organic compounds. The study of organic compounds is easy because organic compounds are classified into different groups. Compounds that belong in the same group share the following things in common: General formula, structural formula, molecular formula, and name ending.

Homologous series are groups of related organic compound in which each member of the class differ from the next member by a set number of atoms. Compounds belonging to the same homologous series always share the same general formula, same molecular name ending, and similar molecular formula.

In this lesson, you will learn about several different classes of organic compounds in two sections:

I. Hydrocarbons   II. Functional group compounds

I. Hydrocarbons

4. Hydrocarbons: Definitions and facts

Hydrocarbons are a classes of organic compounds that are composed of just two elements:

Hydrogen (H) and carbon (C)

The bonding between carbon atoms in hydrocarbon molecule could be a single, double or triple covalent.

Depending on the bond type found between the carbon atoms, hydrocarbons can be classified as saturated or unsaturated.

Saturated hydrocarbon (Alkanes)

Saturated hydrocarbons are hydrocarbons in which the bonding between the carbon atoms are all single covalent bonds.

A single covalent bond between two carbon atoms is formed when each of the carbon atom shares one (1) electron.

Since each carbon shares one electron, a single covalent bond is formed by 1 pair of electrons (or 2 total electrons).

Alkanes are classified as saturated hydrocarbons

1 pair (2 total) electrons

C •   • C

C •—• C

A single covalent bond

Unsaturated hydrocarbons. (Alkenes and Alkynes)

Unsaturated hydrocarbons are hydrocarbons that contain multiple (double or a triple) covalent bond between C atoms.

A double covalent bond is formed between two carbon atoms when each carbon atom share two (2) electrons.

Since each atom shares two electrons, a double covalent bond contains 2 pairs of electrons (total of 4 electrons.)

Alkenes are unsaturated hydrocarbons with a double bond.

A triple covalent bond is formed between two carbon atoms when the each shares three (3) electrons. Since each share three electrons, a triple covalent bond contains 3 pairs of electrons (6 total electrons).

Alkynes are unsaturated hydrocarbons with a triple bond.

Two pairs (4 total) electrons

C :   : C

C ═══ C

A double covalent bond

Three pairs (6 total) electrons

C ⋮   ⋮ C

C ≡≡≡ C

A triple covalent bond

Topic 10 - Organic Chemistry

5. Alkanes: Definitions, facts, and examples

Alkanes are saturated hydrocarbon in which all members share the following characteristics:

Concept Facts: Know these information about the alkanes.

Examples

General formula:

$$C_nH_{2n+2}$$

CH_4 C_3H_8

NOTE: In these molecular formulas of alkanes, the number of **H atoms is** two more than twice (2n+2) the number of C atoms (n)

Structural formula:

All **single** covalent bonds

H–C(H)(H)–H   H–C(H)(H)–C(H)(H)–C(H)(H)–H

In these structural formulas of the the alkanes, all the C – C and C – H bonds are single covalent.

IUPAC name ending: -*ane* :   Meth*ane*   Prop*ane*

In these molecular names of the alkanes, the name prefix for each is related to the number of carbon, and the name ending is - *ane*

SEE Reference Table Q for more information on Alkanes

6. Alkanes (saturated) hydrocarbon: Determining names, formulas and structures of Alkanes

Concept Task: Be able to determine or recognize a name of an alkane (saturated) hydrocarbon

To determine the correct name of an alkane:
  LOOK for a name ending with –*ane*

Example 4
Which name represents an alkane?
1) Octane   3) Propanal
2) Octene   4) Propanol
Answer: Choice 1

Concept Task: Be able to determine or recognize a formula of an alkane (saturated) hydrocarbon

To determine the correct formula of an alkane:
  LOOK for a formula that fits general the formula of C_nH_{2n+2}
  (The number of H atoms MUST BE 2 more than twice the number of C atoms (n)

Example 5
Which formula represents an alkane?
1) $C_{10}H_{10}$ 3) $C_{11}H_{22}$
2) $C_{10}H_{20}$ 4) $C_{11}H_{24}$
Answer: Choice 4

Example 6
Which structure is correct for an alkane?

1) H–C(H)(H)–C(H)(H)–OH
2) H–C(H)(H)–C(H)(H)–C(H)(H)–C(H)(H)–H
3) H\H C=C H/H
4) H–C≡C–C(H)(H)–H

Concept Task: Be able to determine or recognize a structure of alkane (saturated) hydrocarbon

To determine the correct structure of an alkane:
  LOOK for a structure containing all single (-) bonds.
  (Structure must have the correct number of bonds (4 bonds) around each C atom)

Answer: Choice 2

USE Reference Table Q to help you answer questions on Alkanes

Topic 10 - Organic Chemistry

7. Alkenes: Definitions, facts, and examples

Alkenes are unsaturated hydrocarbon in which all members share the following characteristics:

Concept Facts: Know these information about alkenes

Examples

General formula:

C_nH_{2n}

C_2H_4 C_3H_6

NOTE:
In these two molecular formulas of alkenes, the number of H atoms in each formula is twice (2n) the number of C atoms (n)

Structural formula:

One double

Covalent bond

$$\begin{array}{cc} H & H \\ | & | \\ C & = C \\ | & | \\ H & H \end{array}$$

$$\begin{array}{ccc} H & H & H \\ | & | & | \\ C & = C - C - H \\ | & & | \\ H & & H \end{array}$$

In these structural formulas of the alkenes, there is one double covalent bond(=) between two of the C atoms in each structure.

Name ending:

-ene :

Eth*ene*   Prop*ene*

In these molecular names of the alkenes, the name prefix (beginning) is related to the number of carbon atoms, and the name ending is - ene

SEE Reference Table Q for more information on Alkenes

8. Alkenes (unsaturated) hydrocarbons: Determine names, formulas and structures of alkenes

Concept Task: Be able to determine or recognize a name of alkene (unsaturated) hydrocarbon

To determine the correct a name of an alkene:
LOOK for a name ending with –*ene*

Example 7
Which name represents an alkene?
1) heptyne   3) Ethane
2) Pentanol   4) Pentene

Answer: Choice 4

Concept Task: Be able to determine or recognize a formula of an alkene (unsaturated) hydrocarbon

To determine the correct formula of an alkene:
LOOK for a formula that fits the general formula of C_nH_{2n}
(The number of H atoms MUST BE EXACTLY twice the number of C atoms (n)

Example 8
Which formula represents an alkene?
1) C_5H_{10} 3) C_8H_{18}
2) C_5H_{12} 4) C_8H_{14}

Answer: Choice 1

Concept Task: Be able to determine or recognize a structure of an alkene (unsaturated) hydrocarbon

To determine the correct structure of an alkene:
LOOK for a structure containing one double (=) bond.
(Structures must have the correct number of bonds (4 bonds) around each C atom)

Example 9
Which structure is correct for an alkene?

1) H—C=C—H

2) $\begin{array}{ccc} H & H & H \\ | & | & | \\ H-C-C-C-H \\ | & | & | \\ H & H & H \end{array}$

3) H—C(=O)—H (with O double bonded, H single)

4) $\begin{array}{cccc} H & H & H \\ | & | & | \\ C=C-C-C-H \\ | & | & | & | \\ H & H & H & H \end{array}$

Answer: Choice 4

USE Reference Table Q to help you answer questions on Alkenes

Topic 10 - Organic Chemistry

9. Alkynes: Definitions, facts, and examples

Alkynes are unsaturated hydrocarbon in which all members share the following characteristics:

Concept Facts: Know these information about alkynes

General formula:

$$C_nH_{2n-2}$$

Examples: C_2H_2, C_3H_4

NOTE: In these molecular formulas of alkynes, the number of H atoms is two less than twice (2n-2) the number of C atoms (n) in each formula.

Structural formula:
one triple
Covalent bond

$H-C\equiv C-H$ $H-C-C\equiv C-H$ (with H's on first C)

In these structural formulas of the alkynes, there is one **triple** ($\equiv$) covalent bond between two C atoms in each formula.

Name ending:

-yne :   Eth**yne**   Prop**yne**

In these molecular names of the alkynes, the name prefix is related to the number of carbon, and the name ending is - yne

SEE Reference Table Q for more information on Alkynes

10. Alkynes (unsaturated) hydrocarbons: Determine names, formulas and structures of alkynes

Concept Task: Be able to determine or recognize a name of an alkyne (unsaturated) hydrocarbon

To determine the correct name of an alkyne:
LOOK for a name ending with *–yne*

Example 10

Which name represents an alkyne?

1) heptanol   3) hexane
2) Pentanoic   4) Octyne

Answer: Choice 4

Concept Task: Be able to determine or recognize a formula of an alkyne (unsaturated) hydrocarbon

To determine the correct molecular formula of an alkyne:
LOOK for a formula that fits the general formula C_nH_{2n-2}
(The number of H atoms MUST BE 2 LESS than twice the number of C atoms (n))

Example 11

Which formula could be an alkyne?

1) C_8H_{10} 3) C_8H_{18}
2) C_8H_{14} 4) C_8H_{16}

Answer: Choice 2

Concept Task: Be able to determine or recognize a structure of an alkyne (unsaturated) hydrocarbon

To determine the correct structure representing an alkyne:
LOOK for a structure containing one triple ($\equiv$) bond.
(Structure must have the correct number of bonds (4 bonds) around each C atom)

USE Reference Table Q to help you answer questions on Alkynes

Example 12

Which structure is correct for an alkyne?

1) $H-C=C-C-C-H$ (with H's)   3) $N\equiv N$

2) $H-C-C-C\equiv C-H$ (with H's)   4) $O=C=O$

Answer: Choice 2

Copyright © 2010 E3 Scholastic Publishing. All Rights Reserved.

Topic 10 - Organic Chemistry

II. Organic compounds with functional groups

11. Functional Group: Definitions and facts

A functional group is an atom (other than hydrogen) or a group of atoms that replaces one or more hydrogen atom of a hydrocarbon compound.

The element commonly found in most functional groups is oxygen (O). Nitrogen (N) and halogens (F, Cl, Br, or I) are also found in a functional group. Since functional group compounds contain elements other than carbon and hydrogen, they are **not** classified as hydrocarbons.

The attached functional group to a hydrocarbon chain changes the physical and chemical properties of the hydrocarbon. Properties (characteristics) of compounds with functional groups are related to those of the functional group.

Classes of organic compounds containing a functional group that will be discussed in this section include:

Halides, alcohols, ethers, aldehydes, ketones, organic acids, esters, amines and amides.

Just as with the hydrocarbons, members of each class share similar characteristics such as general formula, molecular and structural formula, and a name ending.

Below, a table summarizing the classes of compounds with functional group is given.

Notes for each class of compound is further explained on the next few pages.

Study each class separately, and pay attention to the example formula, structure, and name given for each class.

12. Functional Group Compounds: Summary   Also See Reference Table R

	Class of compound	Functional group	How functional group attaches to hydrocarbon chain (R)	Example of formula
1.	Halide	-Halogen	R-Halogen	$CH_3CH_2CH_2Br$
2.	Alcohol	-OH	R-OH	$CH_3CH_2CH_2OH$
3.	Ether	-O-	R-O-R'	$CH_3OCH_2CH_3$
4.	Aldehyde	$-\overset{O}{\overset{\|\|}{C}}-H$	$R-\overset{O}{\overset{\|\|}{C}}-H$	$CH_3CH_2\overset{O}{\overset{\|\|}{C}}-H$
5.	Ketone	$-\overset{O}{\overset{\|\|}{C}}-$	$R-\overset{O}{\overset{\|\|}{C}}-R'$	$CH_3\overset{O}{\overset{\|\|}{C}}CH_2CH_2CH_3$
6.	Organic Acid	$-\overset{O}{\overset{\|\|}{C}}-OH$	$R-\overset{O}{\overset{\|\|}{C}}-OH$	$CH_3CH_2\overset{O}{\overset{\|\|}{C}}-OH$
7.	Ester	$-\overset{O}{\overset{\|\|}{C}}-O-$	$R-\overset{O}{\overset{\|\|}{C}}-O-R'$	$CH_3CH_2\overset{O}{\overset{\|\|}{C}}OCH_3$
8.	Amine	$-\overset{R'}{\overset{\|}{N}}-$	$R-\overset{R'}{\overset{\|}{N}}-R''$	$CH_3CH_2NH_2$
9.	Amide	$-\overset{O}{\overset{\|\|}{C}}-NH$	$R-\overset{O}{\overset{\|\|}{C}}-\overset{R'}{\overset{\|}{N}}H$	$CH_3CH_2\overset{O}{\overset{\|\|}{C}}-NH_2$

Topic 10 - Organic Chemistry

13. Halides (halocarbons) : Definitions, facts, and examples

Halides (aka halocarbons) are classes of organic compounds in which the functional group is one or more halogen atoms (F, Cl, Br, or I).   RECALL that halogens are elements in Group 17.

The following are general characteristics shared by halide compounds.

SEE Reference Table R for more information on Halides

Functional group
- Halogen

General formula:
R – X   (Where R is a hydrocarbon chain and X is an attached halogen)

Example formulas and names of three halide compounds are given below:

Molecular formula:	C_2H_5F	$CH_3CHBrCH_2CH_3$	$CH_2BrCHBrCH_3$
Structural formula:	H H | | H – C – C – H | | H F	H H H H | | | | H – C – C – C – C – H | | | | H Br H H	Br Br H | | | H – C – C – C – H | | | H H H
IUPAC Molecular name:	Fluoroethane	2-bromobutane	1,2-dibromopropane
NOTE how the IUPAC names relate to formulas.	Fluoro : The halide contains Fluorine (F). ethane: The chain is 2 C atoms long, and contains all single bonds.	bromo: The halogen is a bromine atom (Br). 2: The Br is on the 2nd C atom. butane: There are 4 C atoms, all single bonds between the C atoms.	dibromo: There are two (di) Br atoms attached 1,2- : The two Br atoms are bonded to 1st and 2nd C atoms. Propane: The C chain is 3 C long and single bonded.

14. Halides: Determining formula, name and structure of halides

Concept Task: Be able to determine or recognize names of halides.

To determine the correct name of a halide:
  LOOK for a name containing a halogen prefix.
    Ex. flour-   bromo- , etc

Example 13
Which name represents a halide?
1) 2-butene   3) Iodomethane
2) methyl proponaote   4) hexanol

  Answer: Choice 3. Iodomethane contains the halogen, iodine.

Concept Task: Be able to determine or recognize a formula of a halide.

To determine the correct formula of a halide
  LOOK for a formula containing one of the halogens (A Group 17 element: F Cl Br I)

Example 14
Which molecular formula represents a halide?
1) CH_3CH_2OH 3) $HClO_3$
2) CH_2Cl_2 4) CH_3CHN_2

  Answer: Choice 2

Use Reference Table R to help you answer questions related to halides

Topic 10 - Organic Chemistry

15. Alcohols: Definitions and facts of alcohols and alcohols functional group

Alcohols are classes of organic compounds with hydroxyl (-OH) as the functional group.

The followings are general characteristics shared by members of the alcohol family:

Concept Facts: Study to remember them

SEE Reference Table R for more information on alcohols

Functional group:	General formula:	Name ending:
-OH (hydroxyl)	R – OH	-ol

Example formulas and names of three alcohol compounds are given below:

Molecular formula:	C_2H_5OH	$CH_3CH(OH)CH_2CH_3$	$CH_2(OH)CH_2CH_2(OH)$

Structural formula:	H H
	   | |
	H – C – C – OH
	   | |
	H H
		H OH H H
		| | | |
		H – C – C – C – C – H
		| | | |
		H H H H
			H H H
			| | |
			H – C – C – C – H
			| | |
			OH H OH

IUPAC Molecular names:	**Ethan**ol	**2-butan**ol	**1,3- propane**diol

NOTE how the IUPAC names relate to formulas.	**Ethan-:** There are **2 C** atoms in the chain **-ol :** Indicates that the formula is an alcohol (OH).	**2** : Indicates that the OH is on a second **C** atom **Butan-:** 4 C atoms chain	**diol:** Two OH groups **1,3:** The Two **OH** are on Carbon **1** and **3** **Propane:** There are **3 C** atoms in the chain

16. Alcohols: Determining name and formulas of alcohols

Concept Task: Be able to determine or recognize a name of an alcohol **To determine the correct name of an alcohol:** LOOK for a name ending with -ol	**Example 15** *Which IUPAC name is of a compound of alcohol?* 1) 2-butanal 3) heptane 2) methanoic 4) octanol **Answer: Choice 4.**
Concept Task: Be able to determine or recognize a formula or structure of an alcohol **To determine the correct formula of an alcohol:** LOOK for a formula containing one or more OH attached to a hydrocarbon chain	**Example 16** *Which molecular formula represents an alcohol?* 1) CH_3CH_2OH 3) NH_4OH 2) CH_3CHO 4) $CH_3CH_2CH_2COOH$ **Answer: Choice 1**

Use Reference Table R to help you answer questions related to alcohols

Topic 10 - Organic Chemistry

17. Types of alcohols: Monohydroxyl alcohols: Definitions, facts, and examples

Monohydroxyl alcohols contain only **ONE –OH** functional group attached to a hydrocarbon chain.
   NOTE: Prefix **mono-** always means **1 (one)**
   Depending on which number C atoms in a chain the one OH is attached to, a monohydroxyl alcohol may also be described as primary, secondary or tertiary alcohol.

A. Primary alcohols:
   A primary alcohol is a monohydroxyl alcohol in which the one OH
   is attached to a carbon that is bonded to one other carbon atom
   . The OH is always on the end carbon atom
   . Names of primary alcohols usually DO NOT contain any number. (ex. butanol)
      If the name contains a number, it MUST be the number 1 (one)   (ex. 1 – butanol)

Concept Task: Be able to identify names and formulas of primary alcohols

Study examples below to learn how to identify names, formulas and structures of primary alcohols

Ethanol	CH_3CH_2OH	H-C-C-OH structure
1-butanol	$OHCH_2CH_2CH_2CH_3$	H-C-C-C-C-H structure

B. Secondary alcohol
   A secondary alcohol is a monohydroxyl alcohol in which the one OH
   is attached to a C atom that is bonded to two other C atoms.
      . The OH is never at the end carbon
      . Names of secondary alcohols will always contain a number greater than 1 (ex. 3-pentanol)
      . The number indicates which carbon atom the -OH is bonded to.

Concept Task: Be able to identify names and formulas of secondary alcohols
Study examples below to learn how to identify names, formulas and structures of secondary alcohols

2-propanol	$CH_3CH(OH)CH_3$	structure
3-Pentanol	$CH_3CH_2CH_2CH(OH)CH_2CH_3$	structure

C. Tertiary alcohol
   A tertiary alcohol is a monohydroxyl alcohol in which the one OH is attached to a carbon that is
   bonded to three other carbon atoms
   . Name of a tertiary alcohol will always contain two of the same number.
   . Numbers indicate the position of the methyl group and OH group.

Concept Task: Be able to identify names and formulas of tertiary alcohol
Study examples to the right to learn how to identify tertiary alcohols

   Example of a tertiary alcohol is given to the right.
   NOTE how the OH is on a middle C atom. The middle C atom is
      bonded (–) to three other C atoms

2-methyl-2-propanol

Topic 10 - Organic Chemistry

18. Types of alcohols: Dihydroxy alcohols : Definitions, facts and examples

Dihydroxy alcohols contain TWO OH functional groups attached to a hydrocarbon chain.
  NOTE: Prefix **Di-** always means **2**
  Names of dihydroxy alcohols have TWO numbers and end with –*diol*   (see examples below)

Below are examples names and structure to two dihydroxy alcohols.
As you study, pay attention to similarities in names and formulas between the two dihydroxy.

   1,2-ethane*diol*   1,3 – Propane*diol*

```
   H   H                              H   H   H
   |   |                              |   |   |
H– C – C –H                       H – C – C – C – H
   |   |                              |   |   |
  OH  OH                             OH   H  OH
```

19. Types of alcohols : Trihydroxy alcohols: Definitions, facts and examples

Trihydroxy alcohols contain THREE OH functional groups attached to a hydrocarbon chain.
  NOTE: Prefix Tri- means 3
  . Names of trihydroxy alcohols have three numbers and end with –*triol*   (see example below)

Example (and the most common) trihydroxy alcohol is given below.

   1,2,3-Propane*triol*   H   H   H
   (Glycerol) | | |
                                 H – C – C – C – H
                                     | | |
                                    OH OH OH

20. Types of alcohols: Determining name, molecular and structural formulas of alcohol

Example 17
Which IUPAC name is of a primary alcohol ?
1) 2-butanal   2) 2-butanol   3) 1-chloropropane   4) heptanol

  Answer: Choice 4.

Example 18
Which molecular formula represents a dihydroxy alcohol?
1) $CH_3CHOHCH_2OH$ 2) NH_4OH 3) CH_3CHO 4) $CH_3CH_2CH_2COOH$

  Answer: Choice 1

Topic 10 - Organic Chemistry

21. Ethers: definitions, facts, and examples

Ethers are classes of organic compounds containing the functional group $-O-$

SEE Reference Table R for more information on ethers

The followings are general characteristics shared by members of the ether family:
Study to remember them

Functional group:

$-O-$

General formula:

$R - O - R'$

Naming:

Name must include prefixes for the two hydrocarbon chains

Examples formulas and names of two ether compounds are given below.
As you study, pay attention to similarities in names and formulas between the two ethers.

Molecular formula: CH_3OCH_3 $CH_3CH_2OCH_3$

Molecular structure:

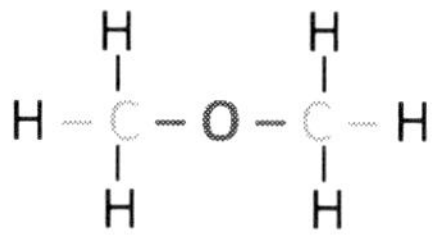

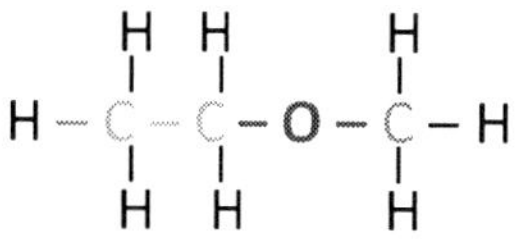

```
    H       H                H  H      H
    |       |                |  |      |
H - C - O - C - H        H - C -C -O - C - H
    |       |                |  |      |
    H       H                H  H      H
```

IUPAC name: Methyl Methyl ether   Methyl ethyl ether
(dimethyl ether)

NOTE how the IUPAC names relate to formulas.	Methyl: The hydrocarbon chain is 1 C atom long		Methyl: The shorter carbon chain (always named first) is 1 C atom long
	dimethyl: There are two methyl groups		ethyl: The longer carbon chain (named second) is 2 C atoms long.

22. Ethers: Determining molecular and structural formula of ethers

Concept Task: Be able to determine molecular or structural formula of an ether.

To determine if a molecular or structural formula is an ether
LOOK for the functional group $-O-$ between the C chains.

Example 19

Which molecular formula represents a member of the ether family?

1) $CH_3OCH_2CH_2CH_3$ 3) HCHO
2) $CH_3COOCH_2CH_3$ 4) $CH_2(OH)_2$

Answer: Choice 1

Use Reference Table R to help you answer questions related to **ethers**

Topic 10 - Organic Chemistry

23. Aldehydes: Definitions, facts, and examples

Aldehydes are classes of organic compounds that contain the functional group $-\overset{\overset{O}{\|}}{C}-H$ or $-CHO$

Compounds from aldehyde family share the following characteristics:
Study and remember them:

SEE Reference Table R for more information on aldehydes

Functional group:
$-\overset{\overset{O}{\|}}{C}-H$

General formula:
$R-\overset{\overset{O}{\|}}{C}-H$ or $R-CHO$

Name ending:
-al

Example formulas and names of two compounds of aldehydes are given below:
As you study, pay attention and note similarities in names and formulas between the two aldehydes.

Molecular formula: HCHO $CH_3CH_2\overset{\overset{O}{\|}}{C}-H$

Structural formula:

$H-\overset{\overset{O}{\|}}{C}-H$

$H-\overset{\overset{H}{|}}{\underset{H}{C}}-\overset{\overset{H}{|}}{\underset{H}{C}}-\overset{\overset{O}{\|}}{C}-H$

IUPAC molecular name: Methan**al**   Propan**al**
common name: (formaldehyde)

NOTE how the IUPAC names relate to formulas.	**Met:** indicates that the formula has **one C** atom. **al:** indicates that the formula is an aldehyde	**Prop:** Three C atoms **al:** indicates that the formula is an aldehyde

24. Aldehydes. Determining names, molecular and structural formulas of aldehydes

Concept Task: Be able to determine or recognize names of aldehydes

To determine the correct name of an aldehyde
LOOK for a name ending with -al

Example 20
Which IUPAC name is a compound of aldehyde?
1) Butanol   3) Butanal
2) Butanoate   4) Butanoic
Answer: Choice 3.

Concept Task: Be able to determine or recognize formulas of aldehydes

To determine the correct molecular or structural formula of an aldehyde

LOOK for a formula containing $-CHO$ or $\overset{\overset{O}{\|}}{C}-H$
attached to a hydrocarbon chain

Example 21
Which structure represents an aldehyde?

1) $\overset{H}{\underset{H}{}}C=C\overset{H}{\underset{H}{}}$ 3) $H-\overset{\overset{O}{\|}}{C}-OH$

2) $H-\overset{\overset{H}{|}}{\underset{H}{C}}-C\overset{H}{\underset{=O}{}}$ 4) $\overset{H}{\underset{O}{}}\diagdown O-H$

Answer: choice 2

Use Reference Table R to help you answer questions related to **aldehydes**

Topic 10 - Organic Chemistry

25. Ketones: Definitions, facts, and examples

Ketones are classes of organic compounds containing the functional group $-\overset{\overset{O}{\|}}{C}-$

Compounds from ketone family share the following characteristics:
Study to remember them :

SEE Reference Table R for more information on ketones

Functional group

$-\overset{\overset{O}{\|}}{C}-$ OR $-CO-$

General formula:

$R-\overset{\overset{O}{\|}}{C}-R'$

Name ending:

-one

Example formulas and names of two compounds of ketones are given below:
As you study, pay attention and note similarities in names and formulas between the two.

Molecular formula: CH_3COCH_3 $CH_3CH_2CH_2\overset{\overset{O}{\|}}{C}CH_3$

Structural formula:

IUPAC molecular name: Propanone   2 – Pentanone
(Other names)   (Acetone)

Nail polish remover (acetone)

NOTE how the IUPAC names relate to formulas.	**Prop-** : The Carbon chain (including functional group C) is **3 C** atoms long. **-one**: Formula contains $-\overset{\overset{O}{\|}}{C}-$ Formula is of a Ketone	**2** : The functional group C is a 2nd C atom in the chain **Pen-** : Indicates there are a total of **5 C** atoms in the chain

26. Ketones. Determining names, molecular and structural formulas of ketones

Concept Task: Be able to determine or recognize names of ketones **To determine which name is of a ketone** LOOK for a name ending with -one	**Example 22** Which IUPAC name is of a compound of ketone? 1) Chloropentane 3) 3- hexanol 2) Pentanoate 4) 3- hexanone **Answer: Choice 4.**
Concept Task: Be able to determine or recognize formulas of ketones **LOOK** for a formula containing $-CO-$ or $-\overset{\overset{O}{\|}}{C}-$ between two hydrocarbon chains.	**Example 23** Which structure represents a ketone? 1) $CH_3CH_2CH_2COCH_3$ 3) CH_3COOH 2) $CH_3CH_2OOCH_3$ 4) $CH_3CH(OH)CH_3$ **Answer: choice 1**

Use Reference Table R to help you answer questions related to ketones

Topic 10 - Organic Chemistry

27. Organic acids: Definitions, facts, and examples

Organic acids are classes of organic compounds with the functional group $-\overset{\overset{O}{\|}}{C}-OH$ or $-COOH$

. Organic acids are one of few organic compounds that ionize (is soluble) in water
. Organic acids are **weak electrolytes**, therefore, can conduct electricity
. Organic acids have the same properties of acids discussed in Topic 8 (acid - base topic)
  RECALL that acids (including organic acids) will change litmus to red, and phenolphthalein will be colorless.

SEE Reference Table R for more information on organic acids

Organic acid compounds also share the following characteristics:

Functional group	General formula:	Name ending:
$-\overset{\overset{O}{\|}}{C}-OH$	$R-\overset{\overset{O}{\|}}{C}-OH$ or $R-COOH$	-oic

Examples of formulas and names of two compounds of organic acids are given below:
As you study, pay attention to similarities in names and formulas between the two organic acids.

Molecular formula:	HCOOH	CH₃COOH
Structural formula:	$H-\overset{\overset{O}{\|}}{C}-OH$	$H-\overset{\overset{H}{\|}}{\underset{H}{C}}-\overset{\overset{O}{\|}}{C}-OH$
IUPAC name: (Other names)	Methanoic acid	Ethanoic acid (Acetic acid, Vinegar)

NOTE how the IUPAC names relate to formulas.	**Met:** indicates that the formula has **one C** atom. **oic:** indicates that the formula is an organic acid	**Eth:** indicates that there are **two C** atoms in the chain

28. Organic acids: Determining names, molecular and structural formulas of organic acids

Concept Task: Be able to determine or recognize names of organic acids **To determine which name is of an organic acid** **LOOK** for a name ending with -oic **Concept Task:** Be able to determine or recognize formulas of ketones **To determine which molecular or structural formula is an organic acid** **LOOK** for a formula containing the $-COOH$ or $-\overset{\overset{O}{\|}}{C}-OH$ attached to a hydrocarbon chain	**Example 24** Which substance is an organic acid? 1) Butanoic 3) Iodomethane 2) Methylamine 4) heptanone **Answer: Choice 1.** **Example 25** Which molecular formula is organic acid? 1) CH₃COCH₃ 3) CH₃CH₂COOH 2) CH₃COOCH₃ 4) OHCH₂CH₂OH **Answer: Choice 3**

Use Reference Table R to help you answer questions related to organic acids.

Topic 10 - Organic Chemistry

29. Esters: Definitions, facts, and examples

Esters are groups of organic compounds that have the functional group
$$-\overset{\overset{\displaystyle O}{\|}}{C}-O-$$

Ester compounds are generally responsible for characteristic smells of fruits and flowers, as well as scents of colognes and perfumes.

Esters can be synthesized (made) by combining an organic acid with an alcohol.

The smells of bananas and strawberries are due to compounds of esters.

Compounds of esters share the following general characteristics.

Functional group	General formula:	Name ending:
$-\overset{\overset{\displaystyle O}{\|}}{C}-O-$	$R-\overset{\overset{\displaystyle O}{\|}}{C}-O-R'$ or R-COO-R'	-oate

SEE Reference Table R for more information on esters

Examples formulas and names of two compounds of esters are given below:
As you study, pay attention and note similarities in names and formulas between the two.

Molecular formula:	CH₃COOCH₃	CH₃CH₂COOCH₂CH₃
Structural formula:	H—C—C—O—C—H (with H's)	H—C—C—C—O—C—C—H (with H's)
IUPAC name	Methyl ethanoate	Ethyl propanoate

NOTE how the IUPAC names relate to formulas.	Methyl: 1 C atom to the right of O – (always named first) ethan: 2 C atoms to the left of – O (always named second). oate: Name indicates an ester	Ethyl: 2 C atoms to the right of O – (always named first) Propan: 3 C atoms to the left of – O (always named second). oate: Name indicates an ester

30. Esters: Determining names, molecular and structural formulas of esters

Concept Task: Be able to determine or recognize names of esters To determine which name is of an ester LOOK for a name ending with -oate	**Example 26** Which substance is an ester? 1) 1,2 ethandiol 3) Pentanal 2) Ethyl ethanoate 4) heptanoic **Answer: Choice 2**
Concept Task: Be able to determine or recognize formulas of esters To determine which molecular or structural formula is of an ester LOOK for a formula containing the – COO – or $-\overset{\overset{\displaystyle O}{\|}}{C}-O$ attached to a hydrocarbon chain	**Example 27** Which formula is of an ester? 1) CH₃CH₂COOH 3) CH₃CH₂CHO 2) CH₃COOCH₂CH₃ 4) CH₃COCH₃ **Answer: choice 2**

Use Reference Table R to help you answer questions related to esters

Topic 10 - Organic Chemistry

31. Amines: Definitions, facts, and examples

Amines are groups of organic compounds that have the functional group - N -

Compounds of amines share the following characteristics: Study to remember them.

Functional group:	General formula:	Name ending:
- N -	R - N(R') - R''	- amine
		SEE Reference Table R for more information on amines

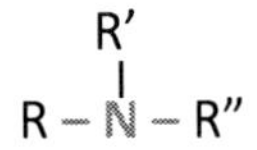

Example formulas and names of two compounds of amines are given below:

As you study, pay attention to similarities in names and formulas between the two amines.

Molecular formula: CH_3NH_2 2-$CH_3 CH(NH_2)CH_2CH_3$

Structural formula:

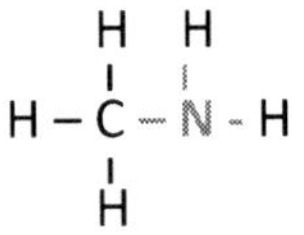

H H
| |
H - C - N - H
|
H

Methanamine

H H
 \ /
  N
H | H H
| | | |
H - C - C - C - C - H
| | | |
H H H H

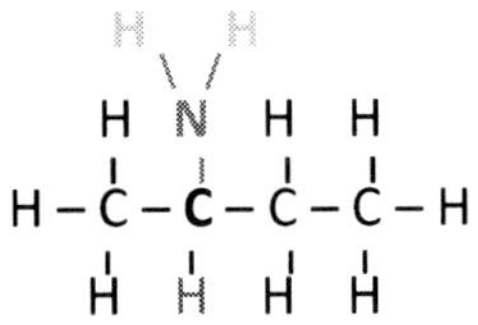

2-butanamine

NOTE how the IUPAC names relate to formulas.	**Meth:** 1 C atom in the formula **amine:** indicates formulas contain –N– group.	**2** – indicate that the -N- group is on **carbon number 2** of the hydrocarbon chain.

32. Amides: Definitions, facts and examples

Amides are groups of organic compounds that have the functional group

$$-\overset{O}{\underset{}{C}}-NH$$

Compounds of amides share the following characteristics:

Functional group:	General formula:	Name ending:
$-\overset{O}{C}-NH$	$R-\overset{O}{C}-NH$ with R'	- amide
		SEE Reference Table R for more information on amides

Example of a formula and name of a compound of an amide are given below:

Molecular formula: CH_3CONH_2

Structural formula:

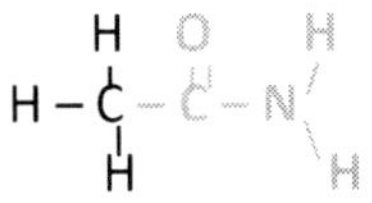

H O H
| || /
H - C - C - N
| \
H H

IUPAC name: Ethanamide

Topic 10 - Organic Chemistry

33. Amino acids: Definitions, facts, and examples

Amino acids are groups of organic compounds that have the functional group

$$\begin{array}{c} NH_2 \\ | \\ -C-COOH \end{array}$$

Amino acids functional group is composed of two functional groups:
An amine group, – N – , and an acid group, -COOH

Amino acids are joined together in a polymerization chemical reactions to make proteins.

A Protein can be made with as little as two amino acids, but most are composed of 10 or more amino acids in a chain.

Lesson 3 - Isomers
34. Isomers: Definitions and facts

Isomers are organic compounds with the same number of atoms, but different structural arrangement of their atoms.

Concept facts: Study to remember these facts related to isomers:
. Isomers have the same molecular formula (same percent composition, same ratio of atoms)
   BUT
   Different structural formulas (different arrangement of the atoms)

. Compounds that are isomers have different structures, different names, and also different properties

. Every hydrocarbon with four or more carbon atoms have at least one isomer

. As the number of carbons in a formula increases, the number of possible isomers also increase
   Ex. A hydrocarbon formula with 5 C atoms has more isomers than a formula with 4 C atoms.

In this lesson, you'll learn examples of isomers from the different classes of organic compounds.

On the next page you'll see examples of formulas, structures, and names of isomers from different classes of organic compounds. Study the examples below and on the next page to learn more about isomers.

Concept Task: Be able to determine formulas
                 of compounds that are isomers.

To determining formulas that are isomers:
  LOOK for formulas that have the same number of atoms

Example 28 :
Which compound is an isomer of CH_3CH_2OH?

1) CH_3COOH 3) CH_3OCH_3
2) $CH_3CH_2CH_3$ 4) CH_3COOCH_3

Before Choosing:
  Count the atoms in the formula (CH_3CH_2OH) given in the question:
    CH_3CH_2OH has :   2 C   6 H   1 O

  Answer: Choice 3 because:
    CH_3OCH_3 also has: 2 C   6 H   1 O

Concept Task: Be able to determine or
    recognize names of compounds
    that are isomers

Example 29:
Which compounds are isomers?
1) 1 - propanol and 1- butanol
2) 1 - propanol and 2- propanol
3) Methanoic acid and ethanoic acid
4) Butane and butyne

Before Choosing:
  Draw correct structure or write correct formula for both names of each choice.
  Count atoms in both formulas that you drew.

Answer: Choice 2 because:
  1-propanol and 2-propanol will have the same number of C , H and O atoms. Both names have a formula of C_3H_7OH.

Topic 10 - Organic Chemistry

35. Alkane isomers: Example formulas and names

Isomers of Alkanes usually have different arrangements of carbon chain with the structures having one or more side chains (alkyl group)
. The first formula of an alkane with isomer is C_4H_{10} (butane).
. The number of possible isomers increases as the number of carbon atoms of the alkane increases.

Examples below show two Alkanes (butane and pentane) and their isomers.
NOTE: For each molecular formula, the condense formula, structural formula and name of the isomer are given
As you study each alkane below, note the similarity in number of atoms of the isomers, as well as the differences in the structural arrangements of their atoms.

Alkyl is a hydrocarbon group with 1 less hydrogen than the corresponding alkane:
Ex. CH_4 (methane, an alkane)
CH_3 (methyl, an alkyl)
C_2H_6 (ethane, an alkane)
C_2H_5 (ethyl, an alkyl)

Butane (C_4H_{10}) isomers

Molecular formula	C_4H_{10}	C_4H_{10}
Condensed formula:	$CH_3CH_2CH_2CH_3$	$CH_3CH(CH_3)CH_3$
Structural formula	H-C-C-C-C-H (with H's)	H-C-C-C-H with CH₃ branch
IUPAC name	Butane	2-methyl propane (methyl propane)

Butane and 2-methyl propane are isomers BECAUSE they have:
.Same molecular formula, BUT Different structural formula
NOTE: Butane and 2-methyl propane are different compounds with different properties

Pentane (C_5H_{12}) isomers

Molecular formulas	C_5H_{12}	C_5H_{12}	C_5H_{12}
Condensed formula:	$CH_3CH_2CH_2CH_2CH_3$	$CH_3CH_2(CH_3)CHCH_3$	$CH_3(CH_3)C(CH_3)CH_3$
Structural formula:	(straight chain)	(branched)	(double branched)
IUPAC name	Pentane	2-methyl butane	2,2-dimethyl propane

Pentane, 2-methyl butane and 2,2-dimethyl propane are isomers.
Same molecular formula, BUT different structural formulas.

Topic 10 - Organic Chemistry

36. Isomers of alkenes and alkynes: Facts and examples

Isomers of alkenes and alkynes typically have the multiple (double or triple) bonds being placed between different carbon atoms in the structure.

. The first alkene formula with an isomer is C_4H_8 (butene)

. The first alkyne formula with an isomer is C_4H_6 (butyne)

The number of alkene and alkyne isomers increases as the number of C atoms increases.

Examples below show one alkene (butene) and one alkyne (butyne) and their isomers.

NOTE: For each molecular formula, the condense formula, structural formula and name of the isomer are given

As you study each alkane below, note the similarity in number of atoms of the isomers, as well as the differences in the structural arrangements of the their atoms.

Alkene isomer: Butene (C_4H_8) isomers

Molecular formula	C_4H_8	C_4H_8
Condensed formula:	$CH_2CHCH_2CH_3$	$CH_3CHCHCH_3$
Structural formula	H−C=C−C−C−H (with H's)	H−C−C=C−C−H (with H's)
IUPAC name	butene (1-butene)	2-butene

Butene and 2-butene are isomers because they have:
the same molecular formula, BUT, different structures.
NOTE: Butene and 2-butene are different compounds with different properties.

Alkyne isomer: Butyne (C_4H_6) isomers

Molecular formula	C_4H_6	C_4H_6
Condensed formula	CH_3CH_2CCH	CH_3CCCH_3
Structural formula	H−C−C−C≡C−H (with H's)	H−C−C≡C−C−H (with H's)
IUPAC name	Butyne (1-butyne)	2-butyne

1-Butyne and 2-butyne are isomers.

Topic 10 - Organic Chemistry

37. Isomers of functional group compounds: Example formulas and names

Isomers of compounds with functional groups usually involve the functional group being attached to different carbon atoms. In some cases, a compound from one functional group may be an isomer of a compound from a different functional group class. For example, a monohydroxy alcohol and an ether of the same number of carbon atoms are always isomers.

Below are examples of functional group compounds and their isomers.

Halide isomers:

Molecular formula	$C_3H_6F_2$	$C_3H_6F_2$	$C_3H_6F_2$	$C_3H_6F_2$
Condensed formula:	$CHF_2CH_2CH_3$	$CH_2FCHFCH_3$	$CH_3CF_2CH_3$	$CH_2FCH_2CH_2F$
Structural formula:	(structure)	(structure)	(structure)	(structure)
IUPAC name:	1,1-difluoropropane	1,2-difluoropropane	2,2-difluoropropane	1,3-difluoropropane

All four compounds are isomers. Same molecular formula, different structural formulas

Alcohol and ether isomers:

Molecular formula	C_3H_8O	C_3H_8O	C_3H_8O
Condensed formula:	$CH_3CH_2CH_2OH$	$CH_3CH(OH)CH_3$	$CH_3OCH_2CH_3$
Structural formula:	(structure)	(structure)	(structure)
IUPAC name:	1-propanol	2-propanol	Methyl ethyl ether

All three compounds are isomers. Same molecular formula, different structural formulas

Ketone isomers

Molecular formula	$C_5H_{10}O$	$C_5H_{10}O$
Condensed formula	$CH_3COCH_2CH_2CH_3$	$CH_3CH_2COCH_2CH_3$
Structural formula:	(structure)	(structure)
IUPAC name:	2-pentanone	3-pentanone

Both compounds are isomers. Same molecular formula, different structural formulas

Topic 10 - Organic Chemistry

Lesson 4: Drawing and naming organic compounds

You have seen several examples of names, formulas and structures from different classes of organic compounds.

In this section you will learn how to draw and name organic compounds.

38. Naming organic compound from structures.

Concept Task: Be able to name a given structural or condense formula of an organic compound.

When naming an organic structure:
- **Determine the class** of organic compound from its bond type or functional group in the structure
- **Determine the correct name** prefix from the number of C atoms in the carbon chain
  For ester and ether compounds, be sure to name both carbon chains
- **Determine the correct name ending** of the compound from the class
- **Take into consideration** the position of a side chain, a double or triple bond, or an attached functional group when naming a given structure.

Below, structural formulas of compounds from several classes of organic compounds are given.
The steps listed above will be use to name the structural formulas.
Study how these structural formulas are named so you can do the same for other organic structures.

Example 30. Name this structure:

$$H-\underset{\underset{H}{|}}{\overset{\overset{H}{|}}{C}}-\underset{\underset{H}{|}}{\overset{\overset{H}{|}}{C}}-\underset{\underset{H}{|}}{\overset{\overset{H}{|}}{C}}-\underset{\underset{H}{|}}{\overset{\overset{H}{|}}{C}}-\underset{\underset{H}{|}}{\overset{\overset{H}{|}}{C}}-\underset{\underset{H}{|}}{\overset{\overset{H}{|}}{C}}-H$$

To name:

Determine class of organic compound from bond type:	*Alkane*: all single (–) bonds in structure
Determine the name Prefix from number of C atoms:	*Hex-*: prefix for 6 C atoms in structure
Recall name ending from the class you had determined:	*-ane* : name ending for an alkane
Name the structure by combining prefix and name ending	**Hex**ane

---

Example 31: Name this structure:

$$H-\underset{\underset{H}{|}}{\overset{\overset{H}{|}}{C}}-\underset{\underset{H}{|}}{\overset{\overset{H}{|}}{C}}-\underset{\underset{H}{|}}{\overset{\overset{H}{|}}{C}}-\underset{\underset{H}{|}}{\overset{\overset{H}{|}}{C}}-\underset{\underset{H}{|}}{\overset{\overset{H}{|}}{C}}-\underset{\underset{H}{|}}{\overset{\overset{CH_3}{|}}{C}}-\underset{\underset{H}{|}}{\overset{\overset{H}{|}}{C}}-H$$

To name:

Determine class of organic compound from bond type:	*Alkane*: all single (–) bonds in structure
Determine the name of the side chain (CH_3)	*Methyl* : CH_3 has 1 C atom: met- prefix for 1 C
Determine which **C atom** the side chain (methyl) is on: Count from both directions: Use lowest number C. Methyl in on **Carbon number 2** (NOT number 6)	$\overset{CH_3}{\underset{7}{C}}-\underset{6}{C}-\underset{5}{C}-\underset{4}{C}-\underset{3}{C}-\underset{2}{C}-\underset{1}{C}-$ $\overset{1\ 2\ 3\ 4\ 5\ 6}{}$ 2 – *methyl* (CH_3 on **carbon number 2**)
Determine prefix from number of C atoms in long chain	*Hept -* : there are 7 C atoms in the long chain
Recall name ending from the class you had determined:	*ane -* : name ending for an alkane
Name structure by combining side chain, prefix, and ending	**2-methyl hept**ane

Copyright © 2010 E3 Scholastic Publishing. All Rights Reserved.

Topic 10 - Organic Chemistry

38. cont.

Example 32: *Name this structure:*	H H H H H
	  | | | | |
	H – C – C = C – C – C – H
	  | | | |
	  H H H H

To name:
Determine class of organic compound from bond type:
Determine the name Prefix from number of C atoms:
 	
Determine the position of the double bond
  Count bonds between C atoms :
  Count from both directions.
      Use lowest bond position
 	
Recall name ending from the class you had determined:
 	
Name the structure by prefix and name ending:
	Alkene : One double (=) bond in structure
	Pent - : Prefix for a 5 C atom structure
	
	   1 2 3 4
	– C – C = C – C – C –
	   4 3 2 1
	
	2 – pent : Double bond (=) in position **2**
	  (between **2nd** and **3rd C atom**)
	
	- ene : name ending for an alkene
	
	**2 - pent*ene*

Example 33: *Name this structure:*	Br H Br H H
	  | | | | |
	H – C – C – C – C – C – H
	  | | | | |
	  H H H H H

To name:
Determine class of compound from attached Br atoms
Determine first part of name from:
  Position of Br on the chain, and the name of halogen
  Count in one direction. Start with lowest C atom
 	
Determine second part of name from:
  number of C atoms and bond type
 	
Name the structure by combining 1st and 2nd parts of names
	Halide: Br is a halogen functional group
	
	1,3 – dibromo : 2 Bromine atoms on **Carbon 1** and **carbon 3**
	(Remember *di* means 2)
	
	Pentane : 5 C atoms in chain, all single bonds
	
	1,3-*dibromo*pentane

Example 34: *Name this structure:*	H H H OH
	  | | | |
	H – C – C – C – C – H
	  | | | |
	  H H H OH

To name:
Determine class of compound with OH groups:
 	
Determine position of OH groups by:
  Counting which **C** atom the OH are on.
  (Count from both directions. Use the lowest number)
 	
Determine name of carbon chain from number of C atoms and bond type.
Recall name ending of alcohols with 2 OH groups
Name structure by combining names:
	Alcohol : OH is a functional group of alcohols
	          OH
	   1 2 3 4
	– C – C – C – C –
	   4 3 2 1
	                  OH
	
	1, 1 - : Two OH groups, BOTH on **Carbon 1**
	
	Butane - : 4 C atoms in chain, all single bonds
	
	-diol (two OH group ending)
	
	1,1 - butane*diol*

Topic 10 - Organic Chemistry

38. cont.

Example 35: Name this structure:	H H H H H H H–C–C–C–C–O–C–C–H H H H H H H

To name:	
Determine class from –O– functional group:	*Ether* : –O– is a functional group for ethers
Determine first name from shorter C chain:	*Ethyl* : 2 C atom after –O–, eth is prefix for 2 C
Determine second name from Longer C chain:	*Butyl* : 4 C atoms before –O–, But is prefix for 4 C
	NOTE: Ethers are named with –yl (alkyl group) ending
Name structure by combining both alkyl names: The shorter chain name MUST always be first.	***Ethyl butyl ether***

Example 36: Name this structure:	H H O H H–C–C–C–O–C–H H H H

To name:	
Determine class from $-\overset{\overset{O}{\|\|}}{C}-O-$ functional group	*Ester* : $-\overset{\overset{O}{\|\|}}{C}-O-$ is functional group for esters.
Determine First part of name from: Number of C atoms after O–	*Methyl* : after O–, there is a 1 C atom chain) NOTE: First name of ethers are named with -yl
Determine second part of name from : Number of C atoms before –O	*Propane–* : before –O, there is a 3 C atom chain
Add ending of esters (-oate) to second name	*Propanoate* : oate is name ending of ethers
Name structure by combining first and second names	***Methyl propanoate***

Example 37: Name this structure:	H H H O H–C–C–C–C–OH H H H

To name	
Determine class from $-\overset{\overset{O}{\|\|}}{C}-OH$ functional group	*Organic acid* : $-\overset{\overset{O}{\|\|}}{C}-OH$ is organic acids group
Determine prefix from number of C atoms (including functional group carbon)	*But-* : Prefix for 4 C atoms)
Recall name ending of organic acids	*-oic* : (name ending of organic acids)
Name structure by combining prefix and name ending	***Butanoic acid***

Copyright © 2010 E3 Scholastic Publishing. All Rights Reserved.

Topic 10 - Organic Chemistry

39. Drawing structures from names :

Concept Task: Be able to draw organic compound structure from a given name.

When drawing a structure of organic compound from a given name

Determine the class of organic compound from name ending (**Use Table R** to determine the correct class).
Knowing the class of compound will tell you the type of bonding or functional group your structure should have.

Draw the carbon chain first if you are drawing a hydrocarbon (alkane, alkene and alkynes), halide or alcohol compound. (**Use Table P** to determine the correct number of C atoms to draw based on the prefix of the name that is given.
Second, draw bonds between carbon atoms of the chain you drew.
For an halide or alcohol, bond the correct functional group to the correct C atom in the chain.

Draw the functional group first if you are drawing a compound from all other functional groups.
(**Use Table R** to draw the correct functional group based on the name ending or class)
Second, draw the correct carbon chain (or chains) to the functional group that you drew.

Make sure of the followings for your completed structure:
. The side chain or functional group MUST be on the correct C atom ⎫
. The double or triple bond MUST be in the right bond position ⎬ As given by a number (or numbers) in the name.
. EACH C atoms should have EXACTLY Four (4) bonds
. NEVER bond hydrogen atoms to each other

Example 38 Draw the structure for:	**Heptane**
Step 1: Determine the number of carbon (C) atoms from the beginning (prefix) of the name. **Hept**ane = **7 C** atoms *Draw* 7 C atoms (Carbon chain)	C C C C C C C
Step 2: Determine type of bonding between C atoms from ending of the name. Hept**ane**: Alkane : All single (–) bonds *Draw* single bonds (–) between all C atoms	C – C – C – C – C – C – C
Step 3: Add H atoms to complete the structure. *How many H atoms to add?* heptanes is an alkane: A 7 C atom alkane has 16 H (2n + 2). C_7H_{16} is formula of heptane. *Where and how to add the 16 H atoms?* . Bond H atoms to C atoms with single bonds . Be sure that EACH C atom has **EXACTLY FOUR (4) b**onds **DO NOT BOND H atoms to each other**	H H H H H H H | | | | | | | H – C – C – C – C – C – C – C – H | | | | | | | H H H H H H H **Heptane** (C_7H_{16})

Topic 10 - Organic Chemistry

39. cont.

Example 39: Draw the structure for:	2 - pentene
Step 1: *Determine* the number of carbon (C) from beginning (prefix) of the name. **Pent**ene = **5 C** atoms *Draw* 5 C atoms	C C C C C
Step 2: *Determine* the type of bonding between C atoms from name ending Pent*ene* : Alk*ene* : One *double* (=) bond *Determine* the position of double bond: **2** in name suggest (=) in bond position **2** *Draw* one double bond (=) in position **2**. *Draw* single bonds (−) between the other C atoms.	$\quad$ 1 2 3 4 C − C = C − C − C OR C − C − C = C − C $\qquad\qquad\qquad\qquad\qquad\quad$ 4 3 2 1
Step 3: *Add H atoms* to complete the structure *How many H atoms to add?* Pentene is an alkene (C_nH_{2n}) A 5 C atom alkene has 10 H atoms (2n). C_5H_{10} is the formula of pentene *Where and how to add the 10 H atoms?* . Bond H atoms to C atoms. . Be sure that EACH C atom has **EXACTLY FOUR (4) b**onds **DO NOT BOND H atoms to each other**	H H H H H $\qquad\qquad$ H H $\qquad$ H | | | | | $\qquad\qquad\quad$ | | $\qquad$ | H − C − C = C − C − C − H OR H − C − C − C = C − C − H | $\qquad\quad$ | | $\qquad\qquad\qquad$ | | | | | H $\qquad\quad$ H H $\qquad\qquad\qquad$ H H H H $\qquad$ 2 - Pentene $\qquad\qquad\qquad$ 2 - Pentene $\qquad\qquad$ (C_5H_{10})

Example 40: Draw *the structure for:*	2,4- *dimethyl* hexane	
Step 1: *Determine* how many C atoms for the long chain from the second part of the name **Hex**ane: **6** C $\quad\quad$ *Draw* **6 C** atoms	C C C C C C	
Step 2: *Determine* side chain and its position on the carbon chain. **2,4-dimethyl:** Two CH_3 (methyl) side chains on Carbon **2** and **4** *Bond two* CH_3(methyl) to carbon **2** and **4**	$\quad\quad CH_3 \quad\quad CH_3$ $\quad\quad$ | $\quad\quad\quad$ | C C C C C C 1 2 3 4 5 6	H | H − C − H | C 2 You can draw out the methyl groups (CH_3) on Carbon **2** and **4** as shown.
Step 3: *Determine* the bond type from name ending. Hexane: alkane : All single bonds (−) *Draw* single (−) bonds between C atoms	$\quad\quad CH_3 \quad\quad CH_3$ $\quad\quad$ | $\quad\quad\quad$ | C − C − C − C − C − C	
Step 4: *Add H atoms* to complete structure . Bond H atoms to C atoms. . Be sure that EACH C atom has **EXACTLY FOUR (4) b**onds **DO NOT BOND H atoms to each other.**	H CH_3 H CH_3 H H | | | | | | H − C − C − C − C − C − C − H | | | | | | H H H H H H **2,4-***dimethyl* **hexane** $\quad$ (C_8H_{18})	

Topic 10 - Organic Chemistry

39. cont

Example 41: Draw structure for :	3-fluoro, 2-methyl butane
Step 1: Determine the number of C atoms in long chain **But**ane: 4 C atoms: Draw 4 C atoms	C C C C
Step 2: Determine and draw side chains. 3-fluoro : F (fluorine) atom on **Carbon 3** 2-methyl: CH₃ (methyl) on **Carbon 2** Draw and bond the side chains.	$\quad\quad CH_3$ C C C C or C C C C $\quad\quad\quad\quad F$ $\quad\quad\quad F\;CH_3$
Step 3: Determine and draw bond between C atoms: Butane: Alkane: All single bonds Draw single bonds (–) between all C atoms	$\quad\quad CH_3$ C – C – C – C or C – C – C – C $\quad\quad\quad F$ $\quad\quad\quad F\;CH_3$
Step 4: Add H atoms to complete the structures . Bond H atoms to C atoms. . Be sure that EACH C atom has **EXACTLY FOUR (4)** bonds	H CH₃ H H H F CH₃ H H – C – C – C – C – H or H – C – C – C – C – H H H F H H H H H 3 –fluoro, 2-methyl butane ($C_5H_{11}F$)

Example 42: Draw structure for	propyl ethanoate
Step 1. Determine and draw functional group Ethanoate: Name ending: -oate: Ester Draw $-\overset{O}{\underset{\|\|}{C}}-O-$ (functional group of esters)	$\quad\;\; O$ $\quad\;\; \|\|$ $-C-O-$
Step 2: Determine and draw hydrocarbon chain to the left and right of – O – Propyl (3 C atoms): Draw 3 C to the Right ethanoate (2 C atoms including functional group C) to the left; Draw 1 more C atom to the left	$\quad\quad O$ $\quad\quad \|\|$ C – C – O – C – C – C
Step 3: Draw single bonds (–) between C atoms .Bond H to C atoms to complete structure .Be sure no C atom has more or less than 4 bonds.	H O H H H H – C – C – O – C – C – C – H H H H H propyl ethanoate

Example 43: Draw structure for	3- heptanone
Step 1: Determine and draw functional group Heptanone: Name ending –one: ketone Draw $-\overset{O}{\underset{\|\|}{C}}-$ (ketone functional group)	$\quad O$ $\quad \|\|$ $-C-$
Step 2: Determine number of C atoms Hept : 7 C atoms (including – C –) Draw 6 more C atoms: Be sure the – C – is the **3ʳᵈ C** atom from either end Add H atoms to complete structure	H H H H O H H H – C – C – C – C – C – C – C – H H H H H H H 3 - heptanone

Topic 10 - Organic Chemistry

Lesson 5: Reactions of Organic compounds

Introduction:

There are many kinds of organic reactions. An organic compound can react with other organic compounds, or with inorganic compounds to form a wide range of organic products.

As mentioned in Lesson 1 of this topic, organic reactions are generally slower than reactions of inorganic compounds. This is due to the fact that organic reactions involve the breaking of strong covalent bonds within the organic molecules.

In this lesson, you'll learn about the different types of organic reactions.

As you study the different types of organic reactions, note the followings:

. The reaction name is given and defined

. The main organic reactants and products are given

. General equation of the reaction is given

. Example equations for the different reactions are also given.

Study each reaction separately and note the differences between the reactions.

40. Substitution: Definitions, facts, and example

Substitution reactions typically involve the removing of a hydrogen atom from an alkane and replacing it with a halogen. The main organic product in a halogen substitution is a halide.

Organic reactant	*Organic product*
Alkane (saturated hydrocarbon)	Halide (with 1 halogen attached)

Example substitution reactions is shown below.

Study these examples to learn how to recognize other substitution reactions.

NOTE the followings about the example reaction:

The general equation shows the type of substances involved in any substitution reaction.

The example equations are given in three different ways: By molecular and structural formulas, and by the names of the substances.

General equation: Alkane   +   Halogen   ------>   Halide   +   Acid

Example equations: C_3H_8 + F_2 ----------> C_3H_7F +   HF

$$\underset{\text{Propane}}{H-\underset{\underset{H}{|}}{\overset{\overset{H}{|}}{C}}-\underset{\underset{H}{|}}{\overset{\overset{H}{|}}{C}}-\underset{\underset{H}{|}}{\overset{\overset{H}{|}}{C}}-H} + \underset{\text{Fluorine}}{F-F} \longrightarrow \underset{\text{Fluoropropane}}{H-\underset{\underset{H}{|}}{\overset{\overset{H}{|}}{C}}-\underset{\underset{H}{|}}{\overset{\overset{H}{|}}{C}}-\underset{\underset{H}{|}}{\overset{\overset{H}{|}}{C}}-F} + \underset{\text{Hydrogen Fluoride}}{H-F}$$

Topic 10 – Organic Chemistry

41. Organic reaction summary

Use this table for a quick a review of organic reactions.

Organic Reaction	Reactants	Products
1. Substitution	Alkane Halogen (saturated hydrocarbon)	1 – Halide Acid
2. Addition **Hydrogenation Addition**	Alkene Hydrogen (unsaturated hydrocarbon)	Alkane
Halogenation Addition	Alkene Halogen	1,2 – Halide (A two halogens halide)
3. Saponification	Fat Base	1,2,3-propanetriol Soap (glycerol)
4. Fermentation	$C_6H_{12}O_6$ (sugar)	C_2H_5OH CO_2 (ethanol alcohol) (Carbon dioxide)
5. Combustion	Hydrocarbon O_2	Carbon dioxide Water
6. Esterification	Organic Acid Alcohol	Ester Water
7. Polymerization **Condensation Polymerization**	Alcohol Alcohol (monomers)	Ether Water (polymer)
	Amino acid Amino acid (monomers)	Protein Water (polymer)
Additional Polymerization	$n(CH_2=CH_2)$ (ethene monomers)	$(-CH_2-CH_2-)_n$ (polyethylene polymer)
8. Cracking	$C_{14}H_{30}$ (large long chain)	C_7H_{16} C_7H_{14} (smaller shorter chains)

Topic 10 - Organic Chemistry

42. Addition reactions: Definitions, facts and examples

Addition reactions usually involve the breaking of a double or a triple bond in an unsaturated hydrocarbon, and adding hydrogen (or halogen) atoms to the free electrons.

RECALL that alkenes (double bond) and alkynes (triple bond) are unsaturated hydrocarbons. Therefore, an **addition** is organic reaction in which the organic reactant is either an alkene or an alkynes.

In addition reactions, one of the multiple bonds of an alkene (or an alkyne) is broken. The two free electrons from the broken bond is then covalently bonded with hydrogen atoms or halogens atoms.

Below are two types of addition reactions.

Example equations for both types of addition reactions are also given.

Hydrogen addition (hydrogenation)

In an hydrogen addition, hydrogen atoms are added to a double or a triple bond. In these types of reactions, unsaturated hydrocarbons (alkene) is changed to a saturated hydrocarbon (alkane).

Main organic reactants	*Main organic products*
Alkene (unsaturated)	Alkane (saturated)

Example of a hydrogenation addition reaction is shown by the equations below.
Study to learn how to recognize other hydrogen addition reactions.

General equation: Alkene + Hydrogen ---------> Alkane

Example equations: C_3H_6 + H_2 ---------> C_3H_8

$$H-\overset{H}{\underset{H}{C}}-\overset{H}{C}=\overset{H}{C}-H \quad + \quad H-H \quad ---------> \quad H-\overset{H}{\underset{H}{C}}-\overset{H}{\underset{H}{C}}-\overset{H}{\underset{H}{C}}-H$$

Propene   hydrogen   **Propane**

Halogen addition (Halogenation)

In a halogenation, halogen atoms are added to a double or a triple bond. In these types of reactions, an unsaturated hydrocarbon (alkene) can be changed to a halide compound with two attached halogen atoms.

Organic reactant	*Organic product*
Alkene	Halide (with 2 halogen atoms attached)

Example of a Halogenation addition reaction is shown by equations below.
Study to learn how to recognize other halogen addition reactions.

General equation: Alkene + halogen ---------> Halide

Example equation: C_3H_6 + Br_2 ---------> $C_3H_6Br_2$

$$H-\overset{H}{C}=\overset{H}{\underset{H}{C}}-\overset{H}{\underset{H}{C}}-H \quad + \quad Br-Br \quad ---------> \quad H-\overset{H}{\underset{Br}{C}}-\overset{H}{\underset{Br}{C}}-\overset{H}{\underset{H}{C}}-H$$

Propene   Bromine   **1,2-dibromopropane**

Topic 10 - Organic Chemistry

43. Fermentation reaction: Definition, facts, and example

Fermentation is an organic process of making ethanol (an alcohol) from sugar.
. CO_2 (carbon dioxide) and water are also produced
. Enzyme, which acts as a catalyst, is required for this process

A fermentation reaction is shown below:
Study to remember this fermentation equation (The only one you need to know).

$$C_6H_{12}O_6 \xrightarrow{\text{enzyme}} 2C_2H_5OH + CO_2$$

Sugar   ethanol (an alcohol)   carbon dioxide

$$H-\underset{\underset{H}{|}}{\overset{\overset{H}{|}}{C}}-\underset{\underset{H}{|}}{\overset{\overset{H}{|}}{C}}-OH$$

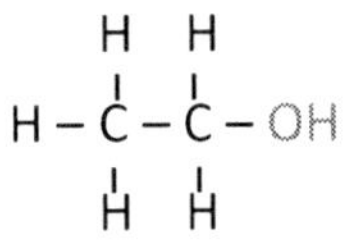

44. Saponification: Definitions, facts, and example:

Saponification is organic process of making soap. Glycerol, a tertiary alcohol, is also produced during saponification process.

Organic reactant: *Organic product*
Fat   Glycerol (an alcohol)

Saponification equation is shown below:
Study to remember this saponification equation:

Fat + Base --------> Soap + Glycerol

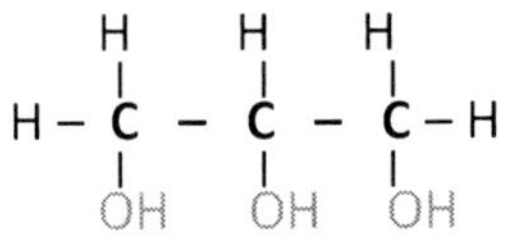

$$H-\underset{\underset{OH}{|}}{\overset{\overset{H}{|}}{C}}-\underset{\underset{OH}{|}}{\overset{\overset{H}{|}}{C}}-\underset{\underset{OH}{|}}{\overset{\overset{H}{|}}{C}}-H$$

1,2,3-propanetriol (Glycerol)
(an alcohol)

45. Combustion (oxidation): Definition, facts, and example

Combustion is the process of burning organic compounds (fuel) in the presence of oxygen.
Carbon dioxide (CO_2) and water (H_2O) are the two main products of combustion reactions.

Examples combustion reaction equation is shown below.
Study to learn how to recognize other combustion equations.

General equation: Organic compound + Oxygen -------> Carbon dioxide + water

Example equation: C_8H_{18} + O_2 --------> CO_2 + H_2O
Octane (car fuel)

Topic 10 - Organic Chemistry

46. Esterification: Definitions, facts, and examples

Esterification is the process of making an ester by reacting an organic acid with a primary alcohol.

During esterification processes, water is formed from H+ ion of the acid and the OH (hydroxyl) group of the alcohol

Organic reactants	*Organic product*
Organic acid and alcohol	Ester

Example of esterification reaction equations are given below.
Study to learn how to recognize other esterification reactions.
 Pay attention to the color of atoms in structures to help you see and understand how the products are formed from the reactants.

General equation: Organic acid + Alcohol ---------- > Ester + Water

Example equation: CH_3COOH + $OHCH_2CH_2CH_3$ --------- > $CH_3COOCH_2CH_2CH_3$ + H_2O

```
     H O                   H H H                H O       H H H
     | ||                  | | |                | ||      | | |
 H – C – C – OH   +   OH – C – C – C – H ----> H – C – C – O – C – C – C – H   +  HOH
     |                     | | |                |         | | |
     H                     H H H                H         H H H
```

Ethanoic acid   propanol   propyl ethanoate   water

47. Polymerization: Definitions, facts, and examples

Polymerization is a process of joining small organic molecules to make a molecule of a longer chain.
 Monomers are small unit molecules that are being joined together by covalent bonds.
 A Polymer is the large unit molecule formed by joining many (poly) monomers together in polymerization reactions.

Two types of polymerization reaction are discussed below.

Condensation polymerization

In condensation polymerization, monomers with OH group are joined together as water is removed.
 . **Ethers and proteins** are substances commonly produced by condensation polymerization

Condensation polymerization reactions are given below:

General equation: Monomer + Monomer -------------- > Polymer + water

              (alcohol monomers)   (ether polymer)
Example equation: CH_3OH + $HOCH_2CH_3$ ---------------- > $CH_3OCH_2CH_3$ + H_2O

```
     H                   H H                  H     H H
     |                   | |                  |     | |
 H – C – OH    +    HO – C – C – H  ------> H – C – O – C – C – H   +  HOH
     |                   | |                  |     | |
     H                   H H                  H     H H
```

Methanol   Ethanol   Methyl Ethyl ether   water

Topic 10 - Organic Chemistry

47. cont.

Addition polymerization
In addition polymerization, double bonded unsaturated monomers are joined together to create a longer and larger hydrocarbon polymer.

Addition polymerization is ALWAYS represented as shown below.

$$n(-CH_2=CH_2) \longrightarrow (CH_2-CH_2)_n$$

n and n represent several repeated units of the molecule.

monomers (several individual small units) Polymer (one long unit)

Substances produced by polymerization reactions.
Below are some familiar polymers produced by natural and synthetic polymerization processes. Study and remember them:

Natural polymers: Protein, starch, cellulose

Synthetic polymers: Nylon, plastic, polyethylene, and polyvinyl

Organic reactions: Example question

On tests, you may be asked different types of questions related to organic reactions. Questions ranges from recalling facts as stated in the notes to predicting organic reactant or product of a given reaction.

How well you can answer each question depends on several factors, including how well you know names, structures, and formulas of organic compounds taught in the previous lesson.

Below are example questions on organic reactions.

48. Organic reactions: Determining organic reactants and products

Concept Task: Be able to identify reactant or product of a given organic reaction

Example 44
Which substance can undergo a substitution reaction with an iodine molecule to form a halide?

1) Propanal   2) Methyl ethanoate   3) Propyne   4) Pentane

Before choosing:
  Determine class of compound that usually involve in substitution reactions: *Alkane*
  Choose a name of an alkane: *-ane ending*
Answer: Choice 4. Pentane is an alkane.

Example 45.
Which compound is likely formed from a reaction between C_6H_{12} and Cl_2?

1) $C_6H_{12}Cl$ 2) $C_6H_{12}Cl_2$ 3) $C_5H_{12}Cl$ 4) $C_5H_{12}Cl_2$

Before choosing:
  Determine type of reaction from reactants: C_6H_{12} (alkene) + Cl_2 (halogen) : *Halogen addition*
  Determine main product of halogen addition: *halide with two halogen atoms*
  NOTE: Number of C and H atoms remain the same in halogen addition.
Answer: Choice 2. $C_6H_{12}Cl_2$. Same number of C, H and Cl atoms as the reactants.

Topic 10 - Organic Chemistry

48. cont.

Example 46:

Which structure represents a product of a polymerization reaction between two alcohol molecules?

1) $H-\underset{\underset{H}{|}}{\overset{\overset{H}{|}}{C}}-\underset{\underset{H}{|}}{\overset{\overset{H}{|}}{C}}-\underset{\underset{H}{|}}{\overset{\overset{H}{|}}{C}}-\overset{\overset{O}{\|}}{C}-OH

2) $\underset{\underset{H}{|}}{C}=\underset{\underset{H}{|}}{\overset{\overset{H}{|}}{C}}-\underset{\underset{H}{|}}{\overset{\overset{H}{|}}{C}}-H$

3) $H-\underset{\underset{H}{|}}{\overset{\overset{H}{|}}{C}}-O-\underset{\underset{H}{|}}{\overset{\overset{H}{|}}{C}}-H$

4) $H-\underset{\underset{H}{|}}{\overset{\overset{H}{|}}{C}}-\overset{\overset{O}{\|}}{C}-O-\underset{\underset{H}{|}}{\overset{\overset{H}{|}}{C}}-H$

Before choosing:
    Determine type of reaction two alcohols will likely undergo: Condensation polymerization
    Determine type of compound formed from condensation polymerization of alcohols: Ether
        (LOOK back at notes on condensation polymerization)
    Choose structure of an ether: - O - functional group (**Use Table R**)

Choose: Choice 3.

Example 47.
Pentanoic acid will likely undergo esterification reaction with which substance?
  1) Methanal   2) Methanol   3) Propyne   4) Propanone

Before choosing:
    Consider what organic substances are the reactants in esterification reactions:
              Organic acid   and   Alcohol
    Since pentanoic acid is an organic acid, the other reactant must be an alcohol:
CHOOSE: Choice 2 : Methanol is an alcohol

49. Organic reactions: Determining type of reaction from equation

Concept Task: Be able to determine or recognize organic reaction name from a given equation

Example 48.
  Consider the equation:
            C_5H_{10} + H_2 --------> C_5H_{12}
  This reaction can be best described as
  1) Hydrogen addition   2) Hydrogen substitution   3) polymerization   4) Combustion

Before choosing
    Consider what are the organic reactants and products: C_5H_{10} (alkene) -----> C_5H_{12} (alkane)
    Determine type of reaction from general equation: Alkene (reactant) ----> Alkane (product)

Answer: Choice 1. Hydrogen addition involves the adding of H atoms to a double bond of an
                      alkene and changing it to an alkane.

Example 49.
  The organic reaction: CH_3COOH + CH_3OH ----> CH_3COOCH_3 + H_2O *can be described as*
  1) Addition polymerization   2) Substitution   3) Saponification   4) Esterification

Correct: Choice 4. The reaction produces CH_3COOCH_3: This is an ester because it contains -COO- group.
        (confirm that this is an ester functional group using **Reference Table R**)

Topic 10 - Organic Chemistry

50. Organic reactions: Determining missing reactant or product from equation

Concept Task: Be able to determine reactant or product of an incomplete organic reaction.

Example 50
Given the incomplete reaction below:

$$C_4H_{10} + F_2 \longrightarrow HF + X$$

What is the missing organic product X?

1) C_4H_8F 2) $C_4H_8F_2$ 3) C_4H_9F 4) $C_4H_9F_2$

You can answer this question by considering conservation of atoms: Atoms on both sides must be equal

$$C_4H_{10} + F_2 \longrightarrow HF + X$$

Before choosing: Determine:

Atoms On the LEFT (from C_4H_{10} and F_2)	Atoms On the RIGHT (from HF)	Missing atoms (from X)
4 C		4 C
10 H	1 H	9 H
2 F	1 F	1 F

Answer: Choice 3. C_4H_9F contains same number of atoms as the missing atoms

You could have also predict the correct product by knowing that:
. The reaction is a substitution reaction
. The product of a substitution reaction is a halide with 1 halogen attached (C_4H_9F)

Example 51.
Given the equation:

$$CH_3CH_2CH=CHCH_3 + Br_2 \longrightarrow X$$

Product X must be
1) 1,2-dibrompentane   2) 2,3-dibromopentane   3) bromopentane   4) bromopentene

Before choosing:
Consider the type of reaction, and the product that will be formed (Use your notes):

$$CH_3CH_2CH=CHCH_3 + Br_2 \longrightarrow X$$

Halogen addition: Alkene   +   halogen $\longrightarrow$ halide (two halogens attached) as product

Consider correct answer from choices 1 and 2.
The halogens (Br atoms) must attached to the double bonded C atoms.

$$CH_3CH_2CH=CHCH_3 + Br \longrightarrow CH_3CH_2\underset{Br}{C}H\underset{Br}{C}HCH_3$$

Answer: Choice 2. The product must be **2, 3** – because the double bonded C atoms are carbon **2 and 3**

Example 52.
Given the incomplete reaction

H H H   H H H   H H H
| | | | | | | | |
H – C – C – C – OH   +   X   --------→   H – C – C – C – O – C – C – C – H
| | | | | | | | |
H H H   H H H   H H H

Which structure represents the organic reactant X ?

1) H–C(H)(H)–C(H)–C(=O)–OH   2) H–C(H)–C(O)(H)–C(H)–H   3) HO–C(H)–C(H)–C(H)(H)–H   4) H–C(H)(O)–C–O–C(H)–H

Answer: Choice 3. The product is an ether. Ethers are formed by joining alcohols together.
Reactant X MUST BE another alcohol. **Choice 3 has OH** (alcohols functional group)

Topic 10 - Organic Chemistry

Check-A-list

Concept Terms

Below is a list of vocabulary terms from Topic 10. You should know the definition and facts related to each term.

Put a check in the box [v] next to a term if you know its definition and other facts related to the term.

- [ ] Homologous Series
- [ ] Hydrocarbon
- [ ] Saturated hydrocarbon
- [ ] Unsaturated hydrocarbon
- [ ] Alkane
- [ ] Alkene
- [ ] Alkyne
- [ ] Alkyl
- [ ] Single covalent bond
- [ ] Double covalent bond
- [ ] Triple covalent bond
- [ ] Halide
- [ ] Alcohol
- [ ] Monohydroxy alcohol
- [ ] Primary alcohol
- [ ] Secondary alcohol
- [ ] Tertiary alcohol
- [ ] Dihydroxy alcohol
- [ ] Trihydroxy alcohol
- [ ] Ether
- [ ] Aldehyde
- [ ] Ketone
- [ ] Organic acid
- [ ] Ester
- [ ] Amine
- [ ] Amide
- [ ] Amino acid
- [ ] Substitution
- [ ] Addition
- [ ] Fermentation
- [ ] Saponification
- [ ] Combustion
- [ ] Esterification
- [ ] Polymerization
- [ ] Addition polymerization
- [ ] Condensation polymerization

If you do not have a check next to a term, look it up or ask your teacher.

Concept Tasks

Below is a list of concept tasks from Topic 10. You should know how to solve problems and answer questions related to each concept task.

Put a check in the box [v] next a concept task if you know how to solve problems and answer questions related to it.

- [ ] Relating number of Carbon atoms to organic compounds names
- [ ] Determining and recognizing correctly drawn organic compound structures
- [ ] Determining names, formulas and structures of Alkanes (saturated hydrocarbons)
- [ ] Determining names, formulas and structures of alkenes (unsaturated hydrocarbons)
- [ ] Determining names, formulas and structures of alkynes (unsaturated hydrocarbons)
- [ ] Determining names, formulas and structures of halides
- [ ] Determining names, formulas and structures of alcohols
- [ ] Determining names, formulas and structures of primary, secondary, and tertiary alcohols
- [ ] Determining names, formulas and structures of ethers
- [ ] Determining names, formulas and structures of aldehydes
- [ ] Determining names, formulas and structures of ketones
- [ ] Determining names, formulas and structures of organic acids
- [ ] Determining names, formulas and structures of esters
- [ ] Determining names, formulas and structures of amines
- [ ] Determining names, formulas and structures of amides
- [ ] Determining names, formulas and structures of amino acids
- [ ] Determining and recognizing formulas of compounds that are isomers.
- [ ] Determining and recognizing names of compounds that are isomers
- [ ] Naming structural and condense formulas of organic compounds
- [ ] Drawing organic compounds structures from names or formulas.
- [ ] Identify a reactant or a product of a given organic reaction
- [ ] Determining or recognizing organic reaction name from equation
- [ ] Determine missing reactant or product in an incomplete reaction

If you do not have a check next to a concept task, look it up or ask your teacher.

Topic 10 - Organic Chemistry

Concept Fact Review Questions

1. A compound that is classified as organic must contain the element
   1) Carbon
   2) Nitrogen
   3) Oxygen
   4) Hydrogen

2. Compared with the rate of an inorganic reaction, the rate of organic reaction is usually
   1) Faster, because organic compounds are ionic substances
   2) Faster, because organic compounds are molecular substances
   3) Slower, because organic compounds are ionic substances
   4) Slower, because organic compounds are molecular substances

3. A series of hydrocarbons in which each member of a group differs from the preceding member by one carbon is called
   1) A periodic series
   2) A homologous series
   3) An Actinide series
   4) A lanthanide series

4. The total number of electrons shared between two adjacent carbon atoms in a saturated hydrocarbon is
   1) 1
   2) 2
   3) 3
   4) 4

5. Which series of hydrocarbons may contain unsaturated molecules?
   1) Alkane and benzene series
   2) Alkyl and alkene series
   3) Alkene and alkyne series
   4) Alkane and alkyne series

6. Each molecule of butane will contain a total of how many carbon atoms?
   1) 2
   2) 4
   3) 6
   4) 8

7. The total number of pair of electrons found between two carbon atoms in a single bond is
   1) 1 pair
   2) 2 pairs
   3) 3 pairs
   4) 4 pairs

8. As the length of the chain of carbon atoms in molecules of alkene series increases, the number of double bonds per molecule
   1) Increases
   2) Decreases
   3) Remains the same

9. The general formula for all alkyne molecules is
   1) C_nH_{2n}
   2) C_nH_{2n+2}
   3) C_nH_{2n-2}
   4) C_nH_{2n+6}

10. Which functional group is found in all alcohols?
    1) –OH
    2) – COOH
    3) –CHO
    4) – O –

11. Which IUPAC name ending is common for class of organic compound called aldehyde?
    1) –yl
    2) –al
    3) –ol
    4) –one

12. Which is true of organic acids?
    1) They are non electrolyte
    2) They are weak electrolytes
    3) They are turn litmus blue
    4) They turn phenolphthalein pink

12. Two isomers must have the same
    1) Percent composition
    2) Arrangement of atoms
    3) Physical properties
    4) Chemical properties

13. The formation of large molecules from smaller molecules is an example of
    1) Saponification
    2) Decomposition
    3) Substitution
    4) Polymerization

14. What type of organic reaction describes the burning of a hydrocarbon in the presence of oxygen?
    1) Addition
    2) Decomposition
    3) Combustion
    4) Substitution

Topic 10 - Organic Chemistry

Concept Task Review Questions

15. Each molecule of butane will contain a total of how many carbon atoms?
    1) 2 2) 4 3) 6 4) 8

16. Given the organic structure below,

    H H
    | |
    H—C—C—OH
    | |
    H H

    Which IUPAC name is possible for a compound with this structure?
    1) Methane 2) Ethanol 3) Propene 4) Butanol

17. Which two formulas are of compounds belonging to alkane series?
    1) C_4H_6 and C_4H_8
    2) $C_{11}H_{22}$ and $C_{11}H_{24}$
    3) C_2H_4 and C_4H_6
    4) C_8H_{18} and C_9H_{20}

18. Which set of IUPAC names are of compounds that are classified as alkenes?
    1) Methyl and ethyl
    2) Ethene and decene
    3) Ethane and pentene
    4) Ethyne and ethane

19. Which is an IUPAC name of a secondary alcohol?
    1) 1,2,-ethandiol 2) Propanol 3) 1,2,3-propanetriol 4) 2-butanol

20. The formula of which compound represents an alcohol?
    1) CH_3CHO 2) CH_3CH_2OH 3) CH_3COOH 4) CH_3COOCH_3

21. A formula of which compound is an organic halide?
    1) $CH_3CH_2NH_2$
    2) CH_3OCH_3
    3) $CH_3CH_2CH_2Br$
    4) HCl

22. A compound of which IUPAC name represents an aldehyde?
    1) Pentane 2) Butanoic 3) Propanol 4) Hexanal

23. The structure 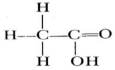 is classified as an organic acid because it contains

    1) –OH groups 2) –COOH group 3) – C – C – bonds 4) C = O bond

24. Which IUPAC name is of a compound that is an ester?
    1) Pentanone 2) Pentanoate 3) Ethanal 4) Ethanoic

25. The structure of which compound contains the functional group –C – O –
    1) Dimethyl ether 2) Propanone 3) Methyl Butanoate 4) Ethanoic acid

26. The condensed formula that represents methyl propanoate is
    1) $CH_3CH_2COOCH_3$ 2) CH_3CH_2CHO 3) CH_3COOH 4) CH_3CHO

27. Which two condensed formulas are isomers of each other?
    1) $CH_3CH_2CH(Cl)CH_3$ and $CH_3CH(Cl)CH_2CH_3$
    2) CH_2CH_2 and CH_3COCH_3
    3) $CH_3CH_2CH_3$ and CH_2CHCH_3
    4) $CH_3CH(OH)CH_3$ and $CH_3CH(OH)CH_2CH_3$

28. Given the reaction below:
$$C_4H_8 + Br_2 \longrightarrow C_4H_8Br_2$$
What type of reaction is represented by the equation.
1) Combustion   2) Substitution   3) Polymerization   4) Addition

29. Which organic reaction is represented by the equation below?
$$n(CH_2=CH_2) \longrightarrow (-CH_2-CH_2-)n$$
1) Condensation polymerization
2) Addition polymerization
3) Esterification
4) Substitution

30. Which formula correctly represents a compound formed from a reaction between C_2H_4 and Br_2?
1) Bromoethene
2) 1,2-dibromoethane
3) Bromoethane
4) 1,2-dibromoethene

31. Given the equation
$$C_2H_6 + F_2 \longrightarrow X + HF$$
What is the name of compound X produced?
1) Ethene   2) Flouroethane   3) 1,2-difluoroethane   4) Fluropropane

Constructed Response Questions

Base your answers to questions 32 and 33 on the information below.

A thiol is very similar to an alcohol, but a thiol has a sulfur atom instead of an oxygen atom in the functional group. One of the compounds in a skunk's spray is 2-butene-1-thiol. The formula of this compound is shown below.

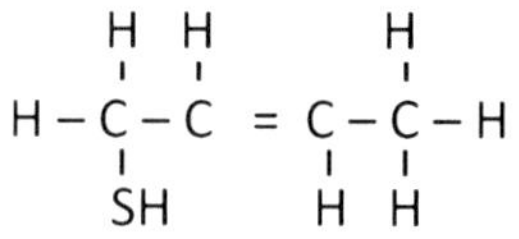

```
    H  H      H
    |  |      |
H - C - C  =  C - C - H
    |         |   |
    SH        H   H
```

32. Explain, in terms of electron configuration, why oxygen and sulfur atoms form compounds with similar molecular structures.   32

33. Explain, in terms of composition, why this compound is a thiol.   33.

Given the structural formula below.

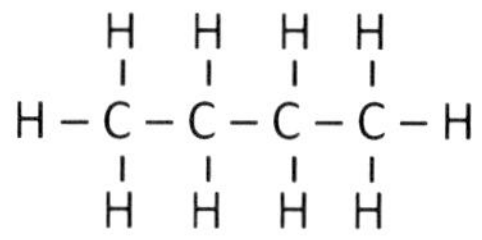

```
    H  H  H  H
    |  |  |  |
H - C - C - C - C - H
    |  |  |  |
    H  H  H  H
```

34. Draw a structural formula for an isomer of butane

Answer questions 35 and 36 based on the equation below

_____ $C_6H_{12}O_6$ _____ C_2H_5OH + _____ CO_2

35. Identify the type of reaction represented.   35.

36. What is the IUPAC name of the organic product?   36.

Topic 11 - Redox and Electrochemistry

Topic outline

In this topic, you will learn about the following concepts:
. Oxidation numbers

.Redox reactions
  . Oxidation
  . Reduction
  . Half-reactions
  . Balancing redox equations
  . Writing half-reaction equations

.Electrochemistry
  . Electrochemical cells
  . Anode, Cathode, salt bridge
  . Voltaic cells
  . Electrolytic cells
  . Electrolytic reductions
  . Electroplating

Lesson 1 – Oxidation Numbers

Introduction:

Most chemical reactions involve the losing and gaining of electrons by substances in the reaction. The losing and gaining of electrons in these reactions occur simultaneously (at the same time).

Oxidation is a loss of electrons by a substance in a reaction.

Reduction is a gain of electrons by a substance in a reaction.

Redox are chemical reactions in which Reduction and oxidation are occurring at the same time.

A redox reaction occurs when substances in the reaction compete for electrons. Some substances compete to lose electrons, others compete to gain electrons. Since electrons are negatively charge, substances that loss and gained electrons undergo changes in oxidation state s(Oxidation numbers). In another word, substances in redox reactions become more positively charge or more negatively charge depending if they had lost or gained electrons.

These changes in oxidation numbers (charges) of substances in redox reaction equations are used to determine which substance had lost and which one had gained electrons.

A complete understanding of oxidation numbers is the key to understanding redox reactions, as well as being able to correctly answer questions related to redox reaction.

In this lesson, you will learn about oxidation numbers.

1. Oxidation numbers: Understanding oxidation numbers

Oxidation number is the charge an atom has (or appears to have) when it had lost or gained electrons.

Oxidation number of an atom can be 0, - (negative) or + (positive).

Examples of oxidation numbers are given below:

    The neutral atom K or K^0 has oxidation number of 0

    The ion O^{2-} has an oxidation number of -2

    The ion Al^{3+} has an oxidation number of +3

The followings are facts about oxidation numbers.

Concept Facts: Study to remember.

    In all compounds, the sum of all oxidation numbers must equal zero.
        Example: In the compound Na_2SO_4, the sum of oxidation numbers of Na, S and O is Zero (0).

    In polyatomic ions the sum of all oxidation numbers must equal the charge of the ion. (See Table E).
        Example: In the polyatomic ion CO_3^{2-}, the sum of oxidation numbers of C and O is equal to -2.

Copyright © 2010 E3 Scholastic Publishing. All Rights Reserved.

Topic 11 - Redox and Electrochemistry

2. Oxidation numbers: Rules for assigning oxidation numbers

Oxidation numbers can be assigned to each element and ions in formulas and equations.
However, oxidation numbers must be assigned according to rules.
Below, a table of rules for assigning oxidation number to elements is formula.

Concept Facts: Use this table as a guide. Most oxidation numbers are on the Periodic Table.
However, pay attention to and note those that cannot be found on the Periodic Table.

NOTE: **LEFT column** gives categories of elements in formulas and equations.
MIDDLE column gives the common oxidation number to assign elements in each category.
RIGHT column gives certain cases (exceptions) when the element from the category cannot have that common oxidation number.

Category of element	Common oxidation states	Example formulas
Free element	0	Na Zn O_2 Cl_2
Simple ion	Charge on the ion	Na^+ Zn^{2+} O^{2-} Cl^-
Group 1 element In ALL compounds (see Periodic Table)	+1	NaCl Li_2O
Group 2 element In ALL compounds (see Periodic Table)	+2	$MgCl_2$ CaO
Hydrogen		
In most compound (see Periodic Table)	+1	HCl H_2O H_2SO_4
In metal hydrides compounds	-1	LiH CaH_2
Oxygen		
In most compound (see Periodic Table)	-2	H_2O CO_2 $HClO_3$
In OF_2 (a compound with fluorine)	+2	OF_2
In Peroxides compounds	-1	H_2O_2 N_2O_2
Group 17 halogen		
In MOST compounds (see Periodic Table)	-1	NaCl MgBr CaI_2
In compounds in which a halogen is between other elements or is a first element. (see Periodic Table)	Positive +	$NaBrO_3$ ClO_3

$$\underset{\text{Free element}}{\overset{0}{O_2}} + \underset{\text{Simple ion}}{\overset{+2}{Ca^{2+}}} + \underset{\substack{\text{Group 1}\\\text{element in a}\\\text{compound}\\\text{Hydrogen in}\\\text{metal hydride}}}{\overset{+1\ -1}{NaH}} + \underset{\substack{\text{Group 2}\\\text{element in a}\\\text{compound}}}{\overset{+2}{CaBr_2}} \longrightarrow \underset{\substack{\text{Hydrogen in a}\\\text{compound}}}{\overset{+1}{H_2O}} + \underset{\substack{\text{Halogen between}\\\text{other elements}\\\text{Oxygen in a}\\\text{compound}}}{\overset{+5\ -2}{NaBrO_3}} + \underset{\substack{\text{Halogen in a}\\\text{compound}}}{\overset{-1}{NaBr}}$$

Topic 11: Redox and Electrochemistry

3. Oxidation numbers: Determining oxidation number of atoms with multiple positive charges.

Some elements have multiple oxidation numbers. You can see this among the transition elements, halogens, nitrogen, sulfur, etc. The oxidation number assigned to these elements in compounds depends on the oxidation numbers of the other elements in the compound. This can be done using a math.

Mn 25 — +2, +3, +4, +7

RECALL that the sum of all oxidation numbers in a neutral compound must equal zero.

Below, three formulas are given: PCl_2 $LiMnO_4$ K_2SO_4.

Note that phosphorous (**P**), manganese (**Mn**) and sulfur (**S**) each has multiple oxidation numbers (LOOK on the Periodic Table to confirm this fact.)

The oxidation number of **P** in PCl_2 depends on the total charge from Cl.

  .Oxidation number of **P** must add to the total charge from Cl to equal Zero

The oxidation number of **Mn** in $LiMnO_4$ depends on the total charges from Li and O.

  .Oxidation number of **Mn** must add to the total charge from Li and O to equal Zero.

The oxidation number of **S** in K_2SO_3 depends on the total charges from K and O.

  .Oxidation number of **S** must add to the total charges of K and O to equal zero

Concept Task: Be able to determine oxidation numbers of elements in a neutral formula

The steps below show how to determine oxidation number of **P** in PCl_2, of **Mn** in $LiMnO_4$ and of **S** in K_2SO_4. Study these steps to learn how to determine the oxidation numbers of elements in other neutral formulas.

As you study the steps below, KEEP IN MIND that you are learning how to determine the charge of an element that will allowed the charges in the formula to add up to Zero.

	Example 1	*Example 2*	*Example 3*
Step 1: Assign oxidation numbers to the first and last element in formula according to the rules.	-1 PCl_2	$+1 \quad -2$ $Li\,MnO_4$	$+1 \quad -2$ K_2SO_3
Step 2: Determine the total charge so far for the compound: BY Multiplying the charge you assigned by the subscript of that element. Set total charge to equal 0	$-2 = 0$ -1 PCl_2	$+1 \quad -8 = 0$ $+1 \quad -2$ $LiMnO_4$	$+2 \quad -6 = 0$ $+1 \quad -2$ K_2SO_3
Step 3: Determine the oxidation number of P, N and S in each compound Find the charge of P, N and S that you need to add to total charges to equal Zero in each formula. You JUST have to think of the Positive number you need so all the charges in the formula **add up to Zero**	$+2 \quad -2 = 0$ -1 PCl_2 **P** must have a +2 charge	$+1 \quad +7 \quad -8 = 0$ $+1 \quad -2$ $LiMnO_4$ **Mn** must have a +7 charge	$+2 \quad +4 \quad -6 = 0$ $+1 \quad -2$ K_2SO_3 **S** must have a +4 charge

These charges allowed the sum of all charges in each formula to add up to Zero (0)

Topic 11 - Redox and Electrochemistry

4. Oxidation numbers: Determining oxidation number of an atom in polyatomic ions.

RECALL that in neutral compounds, the sum of the oxidation numbers is equal to zero.
BUT in polyatomic ions, the sum of the oxidation numbers of atoms is equal to the charge of that ion.

Examples: In polyatomic ion NH_4^+ : The sum of oxidation numbers of N and H is equal to +1.
In polyatomic ion CO_3^{2-} : The sum of oxidation numbers of C and O is equal to -2.
Symbols of polyatomic ions are on Reference Table E.

Concept Task: Be able to determine the oxidation numbers of the elements in a polyatomic ion.

Below two polyatomic ions are given:
The steps below show how to determine the oxidation number of **N** in NH_4^+ and of **C** in CO_3^{2-}
Study these steps to learn how to determine the oxidation numbers of elements in other polyatomic ions.

	Example 4 NH_4^+	*Example 5* CO_3^{2-}
Step 1: Assign oxidation number to last element according to the rules	-1 NH_4^+	-2 CO_3^{2-}
Step 2: Determine the total (-) charge in the ion BY Multiplying subscript by charge you assigned. Set the total charge to equal charge of ion	-4 = +1 -1 NH_4	-6 = -2 -2 CO_3
Step 3: Determine + charge of the first element needed to add to total – charge so the sum is equal to the charge of the ion	+5 - 4 = +1 N H_4	+4 - 6 = -2 CO_3
	Oxidation number of N in NH_4^+ is +5	**Oxidation number of C in CO_3^{2} is +4**

The oxidation number allows the sum of all charges in each ion to equal the charge of the ion.

5. Oxidation number: Example questions on determining oxidation number in formulas

Below, four example questions relating to oxidation number of an element in a formula are given
Study explanation of the correct choice for each question to learn how to answer similar questions.

Example 6
What is the oxidation number of H in H_2?
1) 0   2) +1   3) -   4) +2

Answer: Choice 1. H_2 is a free element
(See Oxidation number rules table)

Example 7
What is the oxidation number of O in $HClO_3$?
1) -6   2) -2   3) 0   4) 3

Answer: Choice 2: O is in a compound.
Oxidation number of O in compounds is -2. (See Table of oxidation number rules or Your Periodic Table).

Example 8
What is the oxidation number of Cr in K_2CrO_4?
1) 0   2) +1   3) +6   4) +8

Before choosing: Do the math (the Sum must **equal 0**)
K is +1 : Total + charge = 2(+1) = +2
O is -2 : Total – charge = 4(-2) = -8
For charges to add up to 0; **Cr** must be +6
Answer: Choice 3

Example 9
What is the oxidation number of **Cl** in ClO_2^- ?
1) -2   2) -1   3) +3   4) +4

Before choosing: Do the math (sum must equal -1)
O is -2 : Total – charge = 2(-2) = -4
For sum of charges to equal -1, **Cl** must be +3
Answer: Choice 3

Topic 11 - Redox and Electrochemistry

Lesson 2 – Oxidation and reduction (redox)

Introduction

As mentioned earlier, redox reactions involve the losing (oxidation) and the gaining (reduction) occurring simultaneously.

In this lesson, you will learn more about redox, as well as oxidation and reduction.

6. Redox reaction: Types of equation that represent redox

Redox reaction falls into three major categories:
  Synthesis, decomposition, and single replacement.

⬅️ **LOOKING BACK: Topic 5:** You learned about these different types of reactions.

Example equations showing these types of reactions are given below.

Synthesis:	$N_2 + O_2 \longrightarrow 2NO$
Decomposition:	$CaCO_3 \longrightarrow Ca + CO_3$
Single replacement	$Cu + AgNO_3 \longrightarrow CuNO_3 + Ag$
Simplified redox	$Cu + Ag^+ \longrightarrow Cu^{2+} + Ag^+$

The above equations, and similar equations, represent redox because:
 . Two elements in each equation are showing a change in oxidation number.
 . Therefore, electrons are lost and gained in each reaction

NOTE: The equations below are **NOT** redox reactions.

Double replacement:	$KI + AgNO_3 \longrightarrow AgI + KNO_3$
Ions combining:	$Na^+ + Cl^- \longrightarrow NaCl$
Ionization:	$H_2O \longrightarrow H^+ + OH^-$

These three equations, and those like them, are NOT redox because:
 . None of the elements in each equation is showing a change in oxidation number.
 . Therefore, no electron is lost nor gained in any of the reactions

7. Redox equations: Determining which equation is a redox reaction

Concept Task: Be able to recognize equations that are REDOX

Use one of the following three methods to determine which equation is a redox.

  . **LOOK** for equation with at least one free element (Quickest and easiest)
  . **LOOK** for equation that is showing synthesis, decomposition, or single replacement.
  . **Determine** for which equation has two elements changing oxidation numbers

Example 10
Which equation represents a redox reaction?
1) $AgNO_3 + LiBr \longrightarrow AgBr_2 + LiNO$
2) $KI \longrightarrow K^+ + I^-$
3) $4Na + O_2 \longrightarrow 2Na_2O$
4) $Na^+ + SO_4^{2-} \longrightarrow Na_2SO_4$

Answer: Choice 3:
  This equation shows a synthesis reaction.
  The equation also has an element (Na or O) that is a free element on one side, but in a compound on the other side.

Example 11
Which equation represents an oxidation-reduction reaction?
1) $2AgNO_3 + Cu \longrightarrow Cu(NO_3)_2 + 2Ag$
2) $3O_2 \longrightarrow 2O_3$
3) $H_3PO_4 + KOH \longrightarrow K_3PO_4 + H_2O$
4) $H^+ + Cl^- \longrightarrow HCl$

Answer: Choice 1:
  This equation represents a single replacement reaction.
  The equation also has a single element, Cu, on one side, but combined as $Cu(NO_3)_2$ on the other side.

Topic 11 - Redox and Electrochemistry

8. Oxidation and Reduction: Definitions and facts

RECALL that Redox reactions involve oxidation and reduction.

The following are definitions and facts related to oxidation and reduction:

Concept Facts: Study to remember these oxidation and reductions facts

Oxidation: Loss of Electron is Oxidation **(LEO)**

．Oxidation is the loss of electrons by a substance in a redox reaction

Oxidized substance (aka reducing agent)

． The substance (or species) that is losing (or transferring) its electrons

．Oxidation number of an oxidized substance always increases after a redox reaction

NOTE: As an atom or an ion loses a negative particle (electrons), it will become more positive.

Reduction: Gained of Electron is Reduction **(GER)**

．Reduction is the gained of electrons by a substance in a redox reaction

Reduced substance (aka is oxidizing agent)

． The substance that is gaining (or accepting) electron

． Oxidation number of a reduced substance always decreases after the reaction

NOTE: As an atom or an ion gains a negative particle (electrons), it will become more negative.

9. Half-reaction: Example oxidation-half and reduction-half equations

Half-reaction equation shows either the oxidation portion or the reduction portion of a redox.

． A correct half reaction must show conservation of atoms, mass, and charge

Consider the redox reaction equation: $2Na + Cl_2 \longrightarrow 2NaCl$

Oxidation-half equation will show the losing of
electrons by a substance in the redox reaction $2Na^0 \longrightarrow 2Na^+ + 2e^-$
(see the equation to the right)

Reduction-half equation will show the gaining of
Electrons by a substance in the reaction. $Cl_2^0 + 2e^- \longrightarrow 2Cl^-$
(see the equation to the right)

NOTE the difference between the two half equations.
In both equations, atoms and charges are equal on both sides of the equation.

Topic 11 - Redox and Electrochemistry

10. Half-reaction equation: Interpreting Half-reaction equations

Half-equations provide several information about the changes that a substance is going through in a redox reaction.

Concept Task: Be able to describe and interpret half-reaction equations

Below, **two half-reaction** equations are given. One has electrons on the left and the other on the right. Each half-equation is interpreted by describing changes the substance is going through.
Study to learn how to interpret and describe half-reaction equations

Equation with electrons on the LEFT :
(Reduction-half equation)

$$C^0 + 4e^- \longrightarrow C^{4-}$$

C^0 atom gains 4 electrons to become C^{4-} ion

C^0 oxidation number decreases from 0 to -4

C^0 is the reduced substance, and also the oxidizing agent.

Equation with electrons on the RIGHT:
(Oxidation-half equation)

$$Sb^{3+} \longrightarrow Sb^{5+} + 2e^-$$

Sb^{3+} loses 2 electrons to become Sb^{5+}

Sb^{3+} oxidation number increases from +3 to +5

Sb^{3+} is the oxidized substance, and also the reducing agent.

11. Half-reaction equation: Determining if half-reaction equation represents oxidation or reduction

Concept Task: Be able to recognize oxidation half-reaction equations.

To determine which equation is showing **oxidation**

LOOK for equation with :

Electrons on the RIGHT

And

Oxidation number that is increasing.

NOTE: The sum of atoms and charges MUST be equal on both sides of the equation.

Concept Task: Be able to recognize reduction half-reaction equations

To determine which equation is showing **Reduction**

LOOK for equation with:

Electrons on the LEFT

AND

Oxidation number that is decreasing

NOTE: The sum of atoms and charges MUST be equal on both sides of the equation.

Example 12

Which of equation is showing oxidation?

1) $F_2^0 \longrightarrow 2F^- + 2e^-$
2) $Ca^0 \longrightarrow Ca^{2+} + 2e^-$
3) $Ca^{2+} + 2e^- \longrightarrow Ca^0$
4) $2F^- + 2e^- \longrightarrow F_2^0$

Answer: Choice 2: This equation is correct because:

. Electrons that are lost are to the RIGHT of arrow

. Atoms of Ca on both sides are equal.
    1 Ca on LEFT and 1 Ca on RIGHT

. Total charges on both sides are equal
    0 Total Charge on the LEFT.
    0 Total charge on the RIGHT ($Ca^{2+} + 2e^- = 0$)

Example 13

Which half-reaction correctly represents reduction?

1) $Al(s) \longrightarrow Al^{3+}(aq) + 3e^-$
2) $H_2(g) + 2e^- \longrightarrow 2H^+(aq)$
3) $I_2(s) \longrightarrow 2I^-(aq) + 2e^-$
4) $Cu^{2+}(aq) + e^- \longrightarrow Cu^+(s)$

Answer: Choice 4.

This equation is correct because:

Oxidation number of Cu^{2+} decreases, and

electrons gained are to the LEFT of the arrow.

Topic 11 - Redox and Electrochemistry

12. Oxidation and Reduction: Determining oxidation and reduction based on oxidation number changes

Concept Task: Be able to determine which oxidation number change represents oxidation or reduction.

To determine which oxidation number change represents:

OXIDATION or LOSS of electrons
  LOOK for a change that is increasing
    Ex.   +2 --------------------- > + 3

REDUCTION or GAIN of electrons
  LOOK for a change that is decreasing
    Ex.   +2 ------------------- > +1

Concept Task: Be able to determine which oxidation number change represents the greatest number of electrons lost or gained.

To determine which oxidation number change represents:

GREATEST number of electrons LOST or GAINED
  LOOK for Greatest difference in numbers

LEAST number of electrons LOST or GAINED
  LOOK for Least difference in numbers

Difference = High oxidation – Low oxidation number

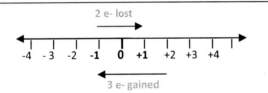

Make and use a scale like this to see differences between two oxidation numbers.

Example 14
Which change in oxidation number represents reduction?

1) +1 ------- > 2+   3) -1 -------- > 0
2) -2 --------- > -1   4) 0 ------- > -1

Answer: Choice 4 :
This choice is correct because the change from 0 to -1 is decreasing.

Example 15
Which change in oxidation number represents the greatest number of electrons lost?

1) +2 to +1   3) -1 to +1
2) +2 to -1   4) -1 to 0

Before choosing:
THINK: When electrons are lost, oxidation number increases: Choice 3 and 4 show an increase. (Consider Choosing choice 3 or 4))

Determine the change with the greatest difference between the oxidation numbers.
  Choice 3: $(+1 - (-1)) = 2$
  Choice 4: $(0 - (-1)) = 1$

Answer: Choice 3: A change of -1 to +1 represents the greatest number of electrons lost of the four choices.

Also see the scale to the left

13. Oxidation and reduction: Determine number of electrons lost or gained

Concept Task: Be able to determine how many electrons were lost or gained based on a changed in oxidation numbers.

If the oxidation number of a substance given in a question goes from low to high:

Electrons were LOST, and the substance is oxidized.
Number of electron LOST = The difference between oxidation numbers

If the oxidation number of a substance given in a question goes from high to low:

Electrons were Gained, and the substance is reduced
Number of electron gained = The difference between oxidation numbers

Example 16
When Cr^{4+} changes to Cr^{2+}, there will be
1) 6 electrons gained
2) 6 electrons lost
3) 2 electrons gained
4) 2 electrons lost

Correct: Choice 3.
Cr goes from Cr^{4+} (high state) to Cr^{2+} (low state).
Therefore, *Electrons are gained.*

Number of electrons gained = 2 (which I s the difference between +4 and +2)

Topic 11 - Redox and Electrochemistry

14. Redox equations

In the last few sections you learned about oxidation and reduction separately. In the next few sections, you will apply what you had learned about oxidation and reduction to learn more about, and understand redox reactions. How well you understand redox, and be able to answer questions about any given redox equation, depends largely on your understanding of oxidation, reduction, and oxidation number concepts you had learned.

RECALL that REDOX reactions involve REDuction and OXidation.

15. Redox equations: Two forms of redox equations.

Redox equations can be given in two different forms. On tests, you may be given any of these two forms of equation.

Two ways of representing redox reactions are given below:
NOTE how **EQUATION 1** is written differently from **EQUATION 2**.

$$\text{REDOX EQUATION 1:} \quad Fe^{3+} + Ni^{0} \longrightarrow Fe^{+} + Ni^{2+}$$

$$\text{REDOX EQUATION 2:} \quad Mg + H_2SO_4 \longrightarrow MgSO_4 + H_2$$

BOTH equations represent redox reactions because each equation has two substances changing their oxidation state. Again, this means that electrons are lost and gained in each reaction.
When answering questions about a given redox equation, one of the main things to consider about the equation is the oxidation number change of the substances.

In EQUATION 1, the oxidation numbers are already assigned to the elements in the equation.
Fe^{3+}, Fe^{+}, Ni^{0} and Ni^{2+} have oxidation of $+3$, $+1$, 0, and $+2$ respectively.
The oxidation number changes can be easily identified.
$$Fe^{3+} \text{ changes to } Fe^{+}$$
and
$$Ni^{0} \text{ changes to } Ni^{2+}$$

In EQUATION 2, oxidation numbers are not assigned to the elements. The oxidation numbers and the oxidation number changes of the substances (Mg, H, S, and O) are not immediately seen.
In order to see oxidation number of each element and the oxidation number changes, you will first need to assign oxidation numbers to the elements in the equation. The oxidation number you assigned to each element must be done according to the rules. The oxidation number you assigned each element must be correct. Assigning incorrect oxidation number to any of the elements in the equation could lead to several incorrect answers to questions about the redox equation.

Below are some common questions you may be asked to answer from a given redox equation.
1. What is the oxidation number change of the substances
2. How many electrons are lost or gained
3. Which substance is being oxidized (or loss electrons)
4. Which substance is being reduced (or gained electrons)
5. Which substance is the reducing agent
6. Which substance is the oxidizing agent
7. What is correct oxidation-half equation
8. What is correct reduction-half equation

You will learn how to figure out the answer to each of these questions in the next few sections.

Topic 11 - Redox and Electrochemistry

16. Redox equations: Interpreting redox equations

In this section of the notes, you will learn to interpret redox reaction equations. How well you can answer the eight questions listed on the previous page depends on how well you can interpret a given redox equation. As you study the interpretation of the two equations below, **KEEP IN MINE** that a lot of the information given for each redox equation was previously mentioned in notes on oxidation and reduction half-reactions.

17. Redox equation: Interpretation of Redox EQUATION 1

Below, EQUATION 1 (from previous page) is interpreted.
NOTE that for this equation: Oxidation number changes of two elements are described
Oxidation number change is interpreted (explanation given in parenthesis)
Half-reaction equations for oxidation and reduction are written.

EQUATION 1

$$Fe^{3+} + Ni^{0} \longrightarrow Fe^{+} + Ni^{2+}$$

Describing oxidation number change of iron (Fe)

Fe^{3+} oxidation number changes from $+3 \longrightarrow +1$

Fe^{3+} oxidation number decreases from $+3$ to $+1$

Interpreting oxidation number decrease of Fe^{3+} to Fe^{1+}

Fe^{3+} is reduced or had gained electrons (because its oxidation number decreases)

Fe^{3+} is the reduced substance and the oxidizing agent (they are one and the same)

Fe^{3+} has gained 2 electrons (number of electrons gained is the difference between the oxidation
numbers: $+3 - +1 = 2$)

Half-reaction equation for reduction of Fe^{3+}

$Fe^{3+} + 2e^{-} \longrightarrow Fe^{+}$ (electrons gained must always appear to the LEFT of the arrow)

Describing oxidation number change of nickel (Ni)

Ni^{0} oxidation number changes from $0 \longrightarrow +2$

Ni^{0} oxidation number increases from 0 to $+2$

Interpreting oxidation number increase of Ni^{0} to Ni^{2+}

Ni^{0} is oxidized or had lost electrons (because its oxidation number increases)

Ni^{0} is the oxidized substance and the reducing agent (They are one and the same)

Ni^{0} has lost 2 electrons (number of electrons lost is the difference between the two oxidation
numbers: $+2 - 0 = 2$)

Half-reaction equation for oxidation of Ni^{0}

$Ni^{0} \longrightarrow Ni^{2+} + 2e^{-}$ (electrons lost must always appear to the RIGHT of the arrow)

Topic 11 - Redox and Electrochemistry

18. Redox reaction: Interpreting redox EQUATION 2

Below, EQUATION 2 (from two pages back) is interpreted.
NOTE that for this equation: Oxidation numbers are assigned to each element according to rules.
Oxidation number changes of two elements are described.
Oxidation number changes is interpreted (explanation given in parenthesis)
Half-reaction equations for oxidation and reduction are written.

EQUATION 2

$$Mg + H_2SO_4 \longrightarrow MgSO_4 + H_2$$

Assign oxidation number to each element in equation (according to rules)

$$\overset{0}{Mg} + \overset{+1}{H_2}\overset{+6}{S}\overset{-2}{O_4} \longrightarrow \overset{+2}{Mg}\overset{+6}{S}\overset{-2}{O_4} + \overset{0}{H_2}$$

NOTE: After oxidation numbers are assigned correctly, **Mg** and **H** are the ONLY two substances that show changes in their oxidation numbers. These changes are described and interpreted.

Describing oxidation number change of Mg^0

Mg^0 oxidation number changes from a $0 \longrightarrow +2$
Mg^0 oxidation number increases from 0 to $+2$

Interpreting oxidation number increase of Mg^0 to Mg^{2+}

Mg^0 is oxidized or has lost electrons   (because its oxidation number increases)
Mg^0 is also the reducing agent   (because a reducing agent is the same as the oxidized substance)
Mg^0 has lost 2 electron   (number of electrons lost is the difference between the
   oxidation numbers: $2 - 0 = 2$)

Oxidation half equation for Mg^0

$Mg^0 \longrightarrow Mg^{2+} + 2e^-$ (electrons lost must always appear to the RIGHT of the arrow)

Describing Oxidation number change of H^{+1}

H^{+1} oxidation number changes from $+1 \longrightarrow 0$
H^{+1} oxidation number decreases from $+1$ to 0

Interpreting oxidation number decrease of H^+ to H_2^0

H^+ is reduced or had gained electrons   (because its oxidation decreases)
H^+ is also an oxidizing agent   (because an oxidizing agent is the same as the reduced substance)
H^+ (each) has gained 1 electron   (number of electrons gained is the difference between the two
   oxidation numbers: $+1 - 0 = 1$)

Reduction half equation for H^+

$H^+ + 1e^- \longrightarrow H_2^0$

Balanced reduction half for H^+

$2H^+ + 2e^- \longrightarrow H_2^0$ (electrons gained must always appear to the LEFT of the arrow)

Topic 11 - Redox and Electrochemistry

19. Redox equations: How to determine oxidized and reduced substance
How to determine reducing and oxidizing agent

Concept Task: Be able to determine in a redox equation the followings:
oxidized substance, reduced substance, oxidizing agent and reducing agent.

To determine which substance is oxidized, lost electrons, or is a reducing agent
Choose the substance to the **LEFT** of arrow with the SMALLER charge.

To determine which substance is reduced, gained electron, or is an oxidizing agent
Choose the substance to the **LEFT** of arrow with the BIGGER charge.

See example multiple choice questions on the next set

Consider the equation below:

$$3Mg^0 + 2Al^{3+} \longrightarrow 3Mg^{2+} + 2Al^0$$

Mg^0 has a SMALLER charge than Al^{3+}.	Al^{3+} has a LARGER charge than Mg^0	Substances (Mg^{2+} and Al^0) to the RIGHT of arrow in redox equations are the results of substances losing and gaining electrons. Therefore, these substances are neither oxidized nor reduced, and they can never be oxidizing nor reducing agent either.
Therefore: Mg^0 is oxidized Mg^0 has lost (2) electrons Mg^0 is also the reducing agent Mg^0 oxidation number increases from 0 to +2	**Therefore:** Al^{3+} is reduced Al^{3+} has gained (3) electron. Al^{3+} is also the oxidizing agent Al^{3+} oxidation number decreases from +3 to 0	

20. Redox Equation: Determining oxidized and reduced substance

Example multiple choice questions are given below.

Example 17: *Given the equation*

$$Br_2 + 2I^- \longrightarrow 2Br^- + I_2$$

Which substance is the oxidizing agent?
1) Br_2 2) I^- 3) Br^- 4) I_2

THINK: Oxidizing agent (Reduced substance) is the substance LEFT of ARROW with the BIGGER charge

Answer: Choice 1: Br_2^0 charge of 0 is BIGGER or HIGHER than I^- charge of -1
Br_2 is the reduced substance, and also the oxidizing agent.
(Br_2^0 is reduced from 0 to a lower oxidation state of -1)

Example 18
Given the equation below:

$$Ca + FeSO_4 \longrightarrow CaSO_4 + Fe$$

Which of these species is oxidized?
1) Fe^{2+} 2) Fe 3) Ca 4) Ca^{2+}

Before choosing a choice:

Assign correct oxidation numbers: $Ca^0 + Fe^{2+}(SO_4)^{2-} \longrightarrow Ca^{2+}(SO_4)^{2-} + Fe^0$

NOTE: Ca^0 and Fe^{2+} are the two substances that are LEFT of the arrow.
One is losing electrons (is oxidized), and one is gaining electrons.

RECALL: The one with the SMALLER charge is oxidized

Answer: Choice 2: Ca^0 charge of 0 is LOWER or SMALLER than Fe^{2+} charge of +2
(Ca is oxidized) to a higher oxidation state of +2)

Topic 11 - Redox and Electrochemistry

21. Redox equations: Determining the correct oxidation and reduction half equations

RECALL that in redox reactions, one substance is oxidized, and one is reduced.

Half-reaction equation are written to show the oxidation and reduction reactions that occur in a given redox reactions.

Concept Task: Be able to determine the correct oxidation-half and reduction- half equation in a given redox equation

NOTE: In last Concept Task, you had learn how to determine the correct oxidized and reduced substance. In this Concept Task, you are determining the correct oxidation-half or reduction-half equation.

RECALL that:

In Oxidation-half equation: Electrons lost are to the RIGHT of the arrow AND oxidation number increases. Study example question 12 below

In Reduction-half equation: Electrons gained are to the LEFT of arrow AND oxidation number decreases. Study example question 13 below.

22. Redox equation: Example questions on determining the correct half-reaction equation

Example 19

Given the redox equation below

$$Br_2^0 + 2I^- \longrightarrow 2Br^{-1} + I_2^0$$

Which half-equation represents oxidation that occurs?

1) $Br_2^0 \longrightarrow 2Br^{-1} + 2e^-$
2) $2I^- \longrightarrow I_2 + 2e^-$
3) $Br_2 + 2e- \longrightarrow 2Br^-$
4) $2I^- + 2e^- \longrightarrow I_2$.

Answer: Choice 2. This equation is the ONLY one correctly showing oxidation-half because:

. It is the only choice that is showing oxidation number increasing

. Electrons are on the right, and atoms and charges are equal on both sides.

Example 20

Given the equation below:

$$Ca + FeSO_4 \longrightarrow CaSO_4 + Fe$$

Which of these equations represents the reduction that occurs?

1) $Ca^{2+} \longrightarrow Ca^0 + 2e-$
2) $Fe^0 \longrightarrow Fe^0 + 2e-$
3) $Ca^0 + 2e- \longrightarrow Ca^{2+}$
4) $Fe^{2+} + 2e- \longrightarrow Fe^0$

Before choosing:

Assigning oxidation numbers to elements and consider the oxidation number changes.

Assign correct oxidation numbers: $Ca^0 + Fe^{2+}(SO_4)^{2-} \longrightarrow Ca^{2+}(SO_4)^{2-} + Fe^0$

Consider the element that is showing a decrease in oxidation number.

RECALL that a reduced substance has a lower oxidation state on the right:

Fe^{2+} is the reduced substance because its oxidation state decreases to Fe^0 (a lower state).

LOOK at choice 4. This equation is the only equation showing Fe^{2+} changing to Fe^0

Answer: Choice 4

Topic 11 - Redox and Electrochemistry

23. Redox equations: Writing correct half-reaction equation for oxidation and reduction

Concept Task: Be able to write the correct half-reaction equation for a given redox reaction

NOTE that on the previous pages, you learned how to choose the correct oxidation and reduction half equation to a redox reaction in multiple choice test questions. In this section, you will learn how to actually write out the correct oxidation and reduction equations to a given redox in short answer type questions. Knowing how to choose the correct half-equation on a multiple choice question does not necessarily means you can actually write out these equations correctly on a short answer type test. However, you can use the skills you will learn in this section to help you on multiple choice tests.

In the next two sets, two redox equations are given.
For each equation:
Steps to writing the correct half-reaction equations for both oxidation and reduction are given.

As you study the steps in each equation, keep in mind the purpose of going through these steps.
The purpose of these steps is to teach you how to write two perfectly balanced half-equations:
One will be for oxidation, the other will be for reduction.

24. Redox equations: Steps to writing correct half-reaction equations for oxidation and reduction

Example 21
Given the equation

$$Ca^0 + Fe^{2+} \longrightarrow Ca^{2+} + Fe^0$$

Write the correct balanced oxidation half-reaction and reduction half-reaction equations.

Step 1: LOOK at the redox equation given
Write BOTH changes of the two elements as so:
$$Ca^0 \longrightarrow Ca^{2+}$$
$$Fe^{2+} \longrightarrow Fe^0$$

Step 2: Add electrons (VERY IMPORTANT):
To each equation, **add electron** to
the side with **higher oxidation** number
$$Ca^0 \longrightarrow Ca^{2+} + e^-$$
$$Fe^{2+} + e^- \longrightarrow Fe^0$$

Step 3: Adjust number of electrons to equalize charges
The number of electrons you add to each
equation should be equal to the difference
between the two charges
$$Ca^0 \longrightarrow Ca^{2+} + 2e^-$$
$$Fe^{2+} + 2e^- \longrightarrow Fe^0$$

Check each equation to be sure charges and atoms
are equal on both sides of the arrow.

Step 4. Identify the half-reactions equations
If a question asked for *oxidation* half equation: Choose: $Ca^0 \longrightarrow Ca^{2+} + 2e^-$

If a question asked for *reduction* half equation: Choose: $Fe^{2+} + 2e^- \longrightarrow Fe^0$

NOTICE that the number of electrons lost (2e-) is equal to the number of electrons gained (2e-).

Topic 11 - Redox and Electrochemistry

24. Cont.

Example 22
Given the redox reaction below:

$$Mg(s) + 2AgCl(aq) \longrightarrow MgCl_2(aq) + 2Ag(s)$$

What is the correct half-reaction equations for oxidation and reduction that occurs?

Step 1: Assign the correct oxidation number to each element according to the rules: (See Pg 262)

$$Mg^0(s) + 2Ag^+Cl^-(aq) \longrightarrow Mg^{+2}Cl_2^-(aq) + 2Ag^0(s)$$

Step 2: LOOK at the equation with assigned oxidation numbers:
Write out changes as shown in the equation:

$$Mg^0 \longrightarrow Mg^{2+}$$
$$2Ag^+ \longrightarrow 2Ag^0$$

NOTE: Cl^- DID NOT change its oxidation state.
Half-equation cannot be written for Cl^-

Step 3: Add electrons (VERY IMPORTANT):
To each equation, **add e-** to the side with a **higher charge.**

$$Mg^0 \longrightarrow Mg^{2+} + e^-$$
$$2Ag^+ + e^- \longrightarrow 2Ag^0$$

Step 4: Adjust number of electrons to equalize the charges
The number of electrons you add to each equation should be the difference between the two charges

$$Mg^0 \longrightarrow Mg^{2+} + 2e^-$$
$$2Ag^+ + 2e^- \longrightarrow 2Ag^0$$

Check to make sure charges and atoms are equal in both equations.

Step 5: Identify this equation as: Oxidation half: $\quad Mg^0 \longrightarrow Mg^{2+} + 2e^-$

Identify this equation as: Reduction half: $\quad 2Ag^+ + 2e^- \longrightarrow 2Ag^0$

25. Oxidation and reduction: Summary   Concept Facts: Study to remember

Below, a summary of oxidation and reduction. Use this table for a quick review and comparisons of the half-reactions of redox.

Half-reaction	Electrons are	Oxidation number	Example equation

Oxidation
  Oxidized substance
  Reducing agent
	Lost	Increases	$Zn \longrightarrow Zn^{2+} + 2e^-$

Reduction
  Reduced substance
  Oxidizing agent
	Gained	Decreases (reduces)	$Si + 4e^- \longrightarrow Si^{4-}$

Topic 11 - Redox and Electrochemistry

Lesson 3 - Electrochemistry

Introduction

Electrochemistry is the study of relationships between redox chemical reactions and electrical energy.

RECALL from lesson 1 that redox reactions involve the losing and gaining of electrons. When a substance in a redox reaction is oxidized, the electrons that are lost goes to the substance that is reduced (gains the electrons). If a redox reaction system is set up so that there are paths for the electrons and the ions to flow, electrical current can be produced.

Battery is a good example of a system that is set up to produce electrical energy from a redox reaction.

In Topic 9, you learned how exothermic chemical reactions release energy, and endothermic reactions absorb energy in the form of heat.

In this lesson of topic 11, you will learn how certain redox chemical reactions can produce (release) electrical energy, while other redox reactions require the use of (absorb) electrical energy for a reaction to occur.

26. Electrochemical cells: Definitions and facts

For a redox reaction to produce or use electrical energy, the reaction must occur in an electrochemical cell.

An electrochemical cell is any device in which chemical energy can be converted to electrical energy or electrical energy to chemical energy.

There are two types of electrochemical cells.

The note below defines the two electrochemical cells, and summarizes key facts about each cell.

Diagrams to the right show example of these two cells.

Concept Facts: Study to remember facts on voltaic and electrolytic cells

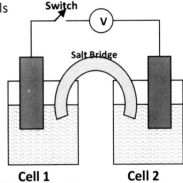

Voltaic Cell is an electrochemical cell in which spontaneous redox reaction occurs to produce electrical energy.

  Facts about voltaic cells.
  - Redox reaction is spontaneous and exothermic
  - Chemical energy is converted to electrical energy
  - Electrical energy produced is due to flow of electrons
  - Oxidation and reduction occurs in two separate cells
  - A salt bridge connects the two half cells and allows ions to flow
  - **Battery** is a type of voltaic cell

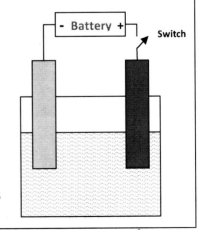

Electrolytic Cell is an electrochemical cell in which electrical energy is used to force a nonspontaneous redox reaction.

  Facts about electrolytic cells.
  - Redox reaction is nonspontaneous and endothermic
  - Electrical energy is converted to chemical energy
  - Uses battery or external electrical current as a source of energy needed to start the redox reaction
  - Both oxidation and reduction occurs in one (same) cell
  - Electrolytic reduction, electroplating of metals, and electrolysis of water use electrolytic cells

Topic 11 - Redox and Electrochemistry

27. Anode, cathode, and salt bridge: Definitions and facts

RECALL that redox reactions involve oxidation (loss of electrons) and reduction (gained of electrons).
The oxidation and reduction reactions that occur in electrochemical cells take place at specific sites.

Electrodes are sites on the electrochemical cells where oxidation and reduction take place.
Anode and **Cathode** are the two electrodes on all electrochemical cells.
Anode and **Cathode** on electrochemical cells are usually labeled with – (negative) and + (positive) signs.
The type of electrochemical cell determines which electrode is positive and which electrode is negative.

Anode and Cathode are defined below.
Concept Facts: Study to remember information related to anode, cathode and salt bridge
. Keep in mind the similarities and differences between these two electrodes.

Anode: (Oxidation)
Anode is the electrode where oxidation occurs in both the voltaic and electrolytic cells.
Anode, therefore, is the site on any electrochemical cell where *electrons are lost.*

   The sign for anode in voltaic and electrolytic cells are as follows.
   Voltaic cells – **A**node is **N**egative (-)
   Electrolytic cells – **An**ode is **P**ositive (+)

Cathode: (Reduction)
Cathode is the electrode where reduction occurs in both the voltaic and the electrolytic cells
Cathode is, therefore, the site on any electrochemical cell where *electrons are gained.*

   The sign for anode in voltaic and electrolytic cells are as follows.
   Voltaic cells – **C**athode is **P**ositive (+)
   Electrolytic cells – **C**athode is **N**egative (-)

Salt bridge: (Permit ions flow)
Salt bridge is a connection between the two half-cells of a voltaic cell.
Salt bridge allows for the migration (movement) of ions between the two half-cells of a voltaic cell.
Salt bridge is not present in electrolytic cells.

28. Codes to remembering your facts.

You had learned many facts about oxidation and reduction. You are now learning signs of anode and cathode in voltaic and electrolytic cells. You need to keep your facts straight.
Below are some codes that may help you keep some facts straight.
Concept Facts: Study to remember if you think they will be helpful.

LEO :	Loss of Electrons is Oxidation	VAN:	Voltaic Anode is Negative
GER:	Gain of Electrons is Reduction.	VCP:	Voltaic Cathode is Positive
An Ox:	Anode is for Oxidation	APE:	Anode is Positive in Electrolytic
Red Cat:	Reduction is at Cathode	CEN:	Cathode in Electrolytic is Negative

Topic 11 - Redox and Electrochemistry

29. Electrochemical cells: Questions about electrochemical cells

There are several questions that could be asked of any cell diagram.
Given a cell diagram, you could be asked to identify any of the following.

1. The oxidized substance (the reducing agent)
2. The reduced substance (the oxidizing agent)
3. The Anode
4. The Cathode
5. The positive electrode
6. The negative electrode
7. The salt bridge
8. Direction of electrons flow
9. Direction of ions flow
10. Electrode that loses mass
11. Electrode that gains mass
12. Equation for oxidation half-reaction (at anode)
13. Equation for reduction half-reaction (at cathode)

How well you answer questions depends on your understanding of the cell diagrams. It may also depend on how much information is given in the diagram. In some cell diagrams, a redox equation of the reaction that is occurring in that cell is also given. The redox equation could be used to answer several of the above questions without even considering the diagram.

The next set of notes give examples of the two cell diagrams, and instructions on how you can identify the items listed above.

30. Voltaic cells: Diagram and its components

RECALL that a voltaic cell is set up so the redox reaction taking place can produce electrical energy.

Concept Task: Be able to identify components of a voltaic cell

Given below is a typical diagram of a voltaic cell.
Study the and note following components of a voltaic cell:
   Cell 1 and Cell 2, Anode and Cathode, Salt bridge, external conductor (wire), and voltmeter.

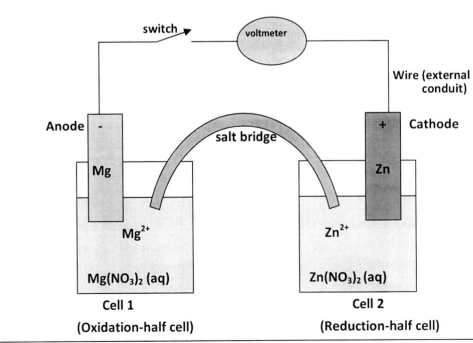

NOTE:

On tests, components of a cell diagram may not be labeled for you. It will be up to you to use information given in a question to correctly label (or determine) the different components of the cell diagram.

In the next few page, you will learn how to determine these information on a given voltaic cell diagram.

Topic 11 - Redox and Electrochemistry

31. Voltaic cell: How to answer test questions.

Concept Task: Be able to answer questions related to a given voltaic cell

Below, information on how to determine several answers on test questions when a voltaic cell diagram is given.

Note the following about the information provided.

The Left column of the notes below the diagram list items that you could be asked to identify from a given voltaic cell diagram.

The middle column indicates what to look for in the diagram to help you identify these items.
　　NOTE: The information in the middle column relies on your ability to correctly identify:
　　　　The MOST and the LEAST active of the metals (as well as their ions in the given diagram.)
　　Use Table J to identify the most and least active metals.
　　The metal closer to the top is the most active of the two metals.
　　The metal closer to the bottom is the less active of the two metals.

The right column identifies these items from the voltaic cell diagram given below.

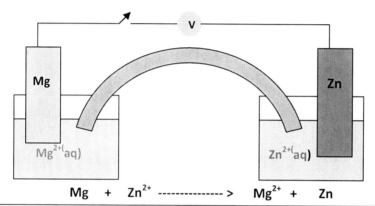

$Mg + Zn^{2+} \longrightarrow Mg^{2+} + Zn$

An equation of the redox reaction is sometimes given below a diagram.

You can use the equation to answer most of the questions.

To determine in any voltaic cell:	LOOK for :	In above diagram
1. The oxidized substance 　The reducing agent 　The substance that loses electrons	The more active of the two metals ON TABLE J, the metal closer to top	Mg
2. The reduced substance 　The oxidizing agent 　The substance that gains electrons	The ion of less active of the two metals ON Table J, the ion of metal closer to bottom	Zn^{2+}
3. The Anode 　The positive electrode 　The substance or object that loses mass	The more active of the two metals ON TABLE J, the metal closer to top	Mg
4. The Cathode 　The negative electrode 　The substance or object that gains mass	The less active of the two metals ON Table J, the metal closer to bottom	Zn
5. The oxidation equation at Anode 　The equation for lost of electrons	MORE active of the metal ------> its ion + e- 　　　　$Mg \longrightarrow Mg^{2+} + 2e-$	
6. The reduction equation at Cathode 　The equation for gained of electrons	Ion of LESS active metal + e- -------> LESS active metal 　　　　$Zn^{2+} + 2e- \longrightarrow Zn$	

Copyright © 2010 E3 Scholastic Publishing. All Rights Reserved.　　　　279

Topic 11 - Redox and Electrochemistry

32. Voltaic cell: How does a voltaic cell works to produce electrical (current) energy?

Concept Task: Be able to describe how a voltaic cell works.

The note below describes how the voltaic cell diagram below will operate to produce electrical current. **Study** this description to learn how to describe other voltaic cells.

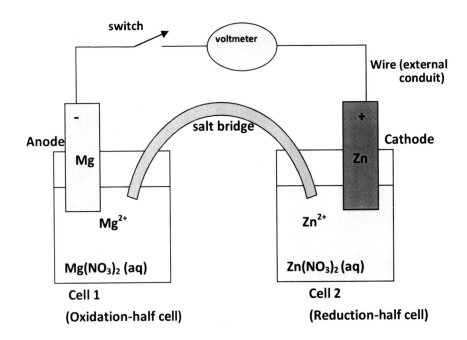

Describing how the voltaic cell works:

RECALL that redox chemical reactions taking place in all voltaic cells is spontaneous. That means:

When the switch is closed:

In Cell 1: The MORE active of the two metals, Mg, will be oxidized by losing its electrons.
. In voltaic cells, the MORE active (Mg) of the two metals is also the Anode (- electrode)
The electrons lost by Mg (the anode) will travel through the wire to Cell 2.
The Oxidation-half reaction at the anode: Mg ----------> Mg^{2+} + $2e^-$

In Cell 2: The ion of the less active metal, Zn^{2+} will be reduced by gaining electrons lost by Mg.
.In voltaic cells, the ion of the LESS active of the two metals (Zn^{2+}) is always reduced.
. In voltaic cells, the LESS active of the two metals (Zn) is the Cathode (+ electrode)
Number of electrons gained by Zn^{2+} is the same as number of electrons lost by Mg.
The reduction-half reaction at the Cathode: Zn^{2+} + $2e^-$ -------> Zn

The wire (external conduit) carries electrons from Mg (anode or oxidation site) to Zn (cathode or reduction site).

. **Electrical current or energy produced** is the flow of electrons from the anode to cathode

The voltmeter registers the amount of electrical current (electrical energy) produced by the reaction.

The salt bridge allows ions in the solution to flow back and forth between Cell 1 and Cell 2 to maintain neutrality. This is necessary for a voltaic cell to operate.

Topic 11 - Redox and Electrochemistry

33. Electrolytic cells: Diagram and its components

RECALL that an electrolytic cell is set up so that electrical current from an external source (battery) will force a nonspontaneous chemical reaction to occur within the cell.

Diagrams of electrolytic cells vary slightly depending on what type of a reaction is taking place in the cell.

RECALL that electrolytic cell can be set up for electrolysis, electrolytic reduction, or electroplating reactions.

Concept Task: be able to identify components of electrolytic cells.

Below two diagrams of electrolytic cells are shown.

As you study the two electrolytic cell diagrams, note these two common similarity among them:
. Reaction occurs is ONE Cell (Both oxidation and reduction occurs in the same container)
. External power source (battery) is always used to provide the electrical energy needed.

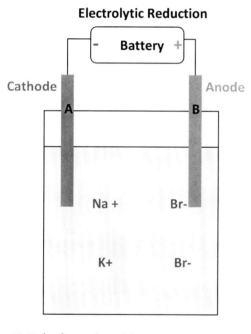

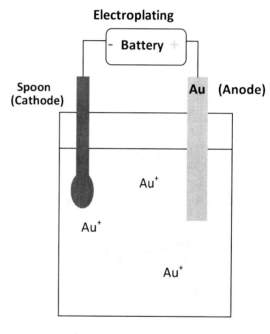

NaBr(aq) + electricity ------> Na + Br$_2$ Au$^+$ + electricity ------> Au

On the next two pages, the reaction that occurs in these cells will be described.

You will also learn how to answer questions from information provided in a given electrolytic cell diagram.

NOTE:

On tests, components of an electrolytic cell diagram may not be labeled for you. It will be up to you to use information given in a question to correctly label (or determine) the different components of the cell diagram.

Copyright © 2010 E3 Scholastic Publishing. All Rights Reserved.

Topic 11 - Redox and Electrochemistry

34. Electrolytic reduction diagram: How to answer test questions

Electrolytic Reduction is a reaction by which very reactive metals are obtained from their fused salts.
In electrolytic reduction, an ion of a very reactive metal is reduced (gained electrons) to form the element.

Concept Task: Be able to answer questions related to an electrolytic reduction cell diagram.

Below, you are given an electrolytic cell diagram that shows the electrolytic reduction of sodium (Na).
. The equation below the diagram shows the redox reaction taking place in the cell

The table below the diagram tells you how to identify and answer questions related to electrolytic reduction diagram.
Note the following about the information provided below.

The Left column lists items that you could be asked to identify from a given electrolytic reduction diagram.

The middle column shows what to look for in the diagram to help you identify these items in questions.
    The information in the middle column relies on your ability to correctly identify:
    Metal and nonmetal atoms, as well as their ions in the diagram

The right column identifies these items from the electrolytic reduction cell diagram given below.

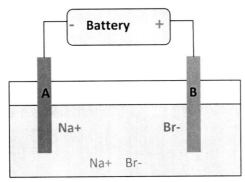

NOTE:

Group 1 and **Group 2** metals, as well as **Fluorine** are very reactive elements. These elements are not found in nature in their free states because of their high reactivity. These elements have to be obtained through electrolytic reduction of compounds (fused salt) containing the element.

$2NaBr$ + electricity --------> $2Na(s)$ + $Br_2(g)$

How to determine:	LOOK for:	in above diagram
1. The oxidized substance The reducing agent The substance that loses electrons	The nonmetal negative (-) ion:	Br^-
2. The reduced substance The oxidizing agent The substance that gains electrons	The metal positive (+) ion:	Na^+
3. The Anode (site for Oxidation) The electrode losing mass	Metal connected to + end of battery:	Positive electrode **Metal B**
4. The Cathode (site for Reduction) The electrode gaining mass	Metal connected to – end of battery:	Negative electrode **Metal A**
5. The Oxidation equation at Anode Equation showing the lost of electrons	- nonmetal ion ---> nonmetal element + e- $2Br^-$ ---------> Br_2 + $2e^-$	
6. The Reduction equation at Cathode Equation showing the gained of e-	+ metal ion + e- ---------> metal atom Na^+ + e^- ---------> Na	

Topic 11 - Redox and Electrochemistry

35. Electrolytic reduction cell diagram: How does it work?

Concept Task: Be able to describe how an electrolytic reduction cell works.

The note below describes how the electrolytic cell diagram on the last page works to produce sodium (Na). **Study** this description to learn how to describe other electrolytic cell diagrams.
LOOK BACK to the diagram on the last page as you study the notes below.

Note the followings about the diagram from the last page.

At the positive (+) end of the battery
Metal B connects to the positive (+) end of the battery.
   RECALL: **A**node is **P**ositive in **E**lectrolytic cells (**APE**).
Metal B, therefore, acts as the Anode (site for Oxidation, site where electrons will be lost)

At the negative (-) end of the battery
Metal A connects to the negative (-) end of the battery.
   RECALL: **C**athode in **E**lectrolytic is **N**egative (**CEN**)
Metal A, therefore, acts as the Cathode (site for Reduction, site where electrons will be gained)

NOTE that the solution in which both metal A and B are submerged contains the Na+ and Br- ions. The ions are from molten (melted) NaBr salt (fused compound).

The Br- ions will migrate (move toward) the positive (+) anode
   RECALL: Opposites attracts (Br- attracts + metal B anode)

The Na+ ions will migrate (move toward) the negative (-) cathode
   RECALL: Opposites attracts (Na+ attracts - metal A cathode)

Describing the reaction in the electrolytic reduction cell.
RECALL that the reaction in this electrolytic cell is non-spontaneous (will not occur by itself).

The Battery provides electrical energy needed for this non-spontaneous endothermic reaction to occur.
When the switch is closed, electrical energy from the battery will force the following reactions to occur.

At the Anode (+):   Electrical energy will force Br- to lose electrons (oxidized) and change to Br_2.
(Metal B)   The equation for the oxidation of Br- (at anode): $2Br^- \longrightarrow Br_2 + 2e^-$

At the Cathode (-): Electrical energy will force Na+ to gain electron (reduced) and change to Na.
(Metal A)   The equation for the reduction of Na+ (at cathode): $Na^+ + e^- \longrightarrow Na$

Na, sodium, a very reactive Group 1 metal, is found in nature only as a fused compound (ex. NaBr, NaCl), NOT as free element Na.

Through the process of electrolytic reduction, the element sodium (in its free state) can be obtained, stored, and sold.

Topic 11 - Redox and Electrochemistry

36. Electroplating cell diagram: How to answer questions.

Electroplating is a process in which a thin layer of a metal is coated onto a surface of another object.
In electroplating process, the ion of a metal element is reduced, and the metal is coated to a surface of another object.

Concept Task: Be able to answer questions related to electroplating cell diagrams.

Below, you are given an electroplating cell diagram that shows the electroplating of a spoon with gold.
. **The table** below the diagram tells you how to identify and answer questions related to any electroplating cell diagram.
Note the following about the information provided below.
  The Left column of the notes below list items that you could be asked to identify from a given electroplating cell diagram.
  The middle column tells you what to look for in a diagram to help you identify these items in questions.
  The right column identifies these items from the electroplating cell diagram given below.

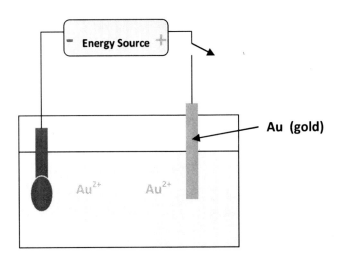

To determine:	LOOK for:	In above diagram
1. The oxidized substance The substance that loses electrons	The metal connected to + end of battery:	Au
2. The reduced substance The substance that gains electrons	The ion of the metallic element in the solution:	Au^{2+}

3. The Anode (site of oxidation)
   The positive electrode
   The metal or object that loses mass
	The metal element connected to + end of battery:	Au

4. The Cathode (site of reduction)
   The negative electrode
   The metal or object that gains mass
	The object connected to – end of the battery:	Spoon

5. The Oxidation equation at Anode
   Equation showing the lost of electrons
	Metal element --------> Metal ion + e^-
	   Au --------> Au^{2+} + e^-	

6. The Reduction equation at Cathode
   Equation showing the gained of e-
	Metal ion + e^- ----> Metal element
	   Au^{2+} + e^- ----> Au	

Topic 11 - Redox and Electrochemistry

37. Electroplating: How does it work

Concept Task: Be able to describe how an electroplating works

The note below describes how the electroplating diagram on the last page works to produce a gold spoon. **Study** this description to learn how to describe other electroplating cell diagrams.
LOOK BACK to the diagram on the last page as you study the notes below

Note the followings about the diagram from the last page.

At the positive (+) end of the battery
The metal (Au, gold) that will be coated unto another object always connects to the positive (+).
  RECALL: **A**node is **P**ositive in **E**lectrolytic cells (**APE**)
The metal (Au) acts as the anode (site for oxidation).

At the negative (-) of the battery:
The object (spoon) to be plated is *always* connected to the negative (-) end of the battery.
  RECALL: **C**athode in **E**lectrolytic cell is **N**egative (**CEN**)
The object (spoon) to be electroplated *always* acts as the cathode (site for reduction**)**.

Describing the reaction in the electroplating cell
Recall that the reaction in this electroplating cell is nonspontaneous (will not occur by itself).

The Battery provides electrical energy needed for the nonspontaneous endothermic reaction to occur.

When the switch is closed, electrical energy from the battery will force the following reactions to occur.

At the anode: The metal Au (the anode) loses electrons (is oxidized) and changes to Au^{2+} ion.
  (Au metal)   *Recall:* Anode is site for Oxidation   (AnOX)
      The equation for oxidation of Au (the anode):   Au --------> Au^{2+} + 2e-

In the solution: The Au^{2+} will move toward, and be attracted to, the - cathode (the spoon)

At the Cathode : The gold ion (Au^{2+}) gains electrons (is reduced) and changes back to gold (Au).
  (spoon)   *Recall:* Reduction occurs at Cathode (RedCat)
      The equation for reduction of Au^{2+} (at cathode): Au^{2+} + 2e- ------> Au

Since the changing of Au^{2+} ion to Au (gold) is occurring at the cathode (the spoon), the gold is coated onto (electroplates) the spoon. And you'll have a gold spoon.

Topic 11 - Redox and Electrochemistry

38. Electrochemical cells: Summary of the the two cells

Below, a summary of voltaic and electrolytic cells. Use this table for a quick review and comparisons of the two electrochemical cells.

Concept Facts: Study to remember

		Voltaic	Electrolytic
	Diagrams		
Differences	Example redox equation	$Pb + Cu^{2+} \longrightarrow Pb^{2+} + Cu$	$H_2O + electricity \longrightarrow H_2 + O_2$
	Type of reaction	Spontaneous redox Exothermic	Non-spontaneous redox Endothermic
	Energy conversion	Chemical to electrical energy	Electrical to chemical energy
	Anode (site for oxidation)	Negative (-) electrode	Positive (+) electrode
	Cathode (site for reduction)	Positive (+) electrode	Negative (-) electrode
	Half-Reactions occur in	Two separate cells	One cell
	Salt bridge present?	Yes (connects the two cells) (permits ions flow)	No
	Usages and examples	Battery	Electroplating Electrolytic reduction Electrolysis
Similarities	Oxidation (losing of electrons) at	Anode (-) (loses mass)	Anode (+) (loses mass)
	Reduction (gaining of electrons) at	Cathode (+) (gains mass)	Cathode (-) (gains mass)
	Electrode flow from	Anode to Cathode	Anode to Cathode

Topic 11 - Redox and Electrochemistry

39. Electrochemical cell diagrams: Example questions

Three example questions on electrochemical cells are given below.

Answer questions 23 and 24 based on the electrochemical cell diagram below.

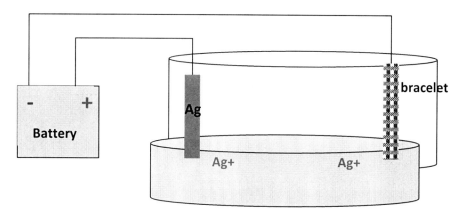
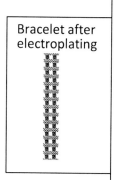

Bracelet after electroplating

Example 23

Which substance or object serves as the cathode in this cell diagram?

1) Battery   2) Ag   3) Ag^+ 4) Bracelet

Answer: Choice 4. The cathode is always the object connected to the negative end of a battery in electrolytic (electroplating) cells.

Example 24.

When the switch is closed, what will occur in this cell?

1) The bracelet will be oxidized, and Ag will gain mass
2) The bracelet will be reduced, and Ag will gain mass
3) Ag will be oxidized, and the bracelet will gain mass
4) Ag will be reduced, and the bracelet will gain mass

Answer: Choice 3: In electroplating cells, the metal at the (+) end of a battery is oxidized. The object to be electroplated, connected to (−) end of battery, always gains mass.

Answer questions 25 and 26 based on the electrochemical cell diagram below.

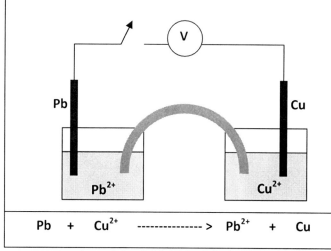

$Pb + Cu^{2+} \longrightarrow Pb^{2+} + Cu$

Example 25.

Which species is reduced in the reaction that occurs in this cell?

1) Pb   2) Pb^{2+} 3) Cu   4) Cu^{2+}

Answer: Choice 4. According to the equation, Cu^{2+} shows a decrease in oxidation state (is reduced) to Cu^0.

Example 26.

When the switch is closed, electrons will travel from

1) Pb to Pb^{2+} 3) Pb to Cu
2) Cu to Cu^{2+} 4) Cu to Pb

Answer: Choice 3. Electrons always travel from the Anode (a more active Pb) to the cathode (a lesser active Cu)

Topic 11 - Redox and Electrochemistry

Lesson 4 – Spontaneous reactions

Introduction

Spontaneous reaction is a reaction that will take place (occur) under a specific set of conditions.

In the acid-base Topic 8, you learned that certain metals will react "spontaneously" with acids to produced hydrogen gas.

In kinetics and equilibrium Topic 9, you learned that a reaction is spontaneous if the reaction will lead to a lower energy and higher entropy products.

Recall: Systems in nature tend to go in the directions of higher entropy (greater disorder) and lower enthalpy (lower energy.)

In this lesson, You will learn how to use the Activity Series Reference Table J to predict which reactions will occur spontaneous.

40. Spontaneous reactions: Determining spontaneous reactions using Activity Series Table J

Recall that a single replacement reaction is a redox reaction. A single replacement reaction will occur spontaneously when a **single (free) element reactant** is more reactive than the similar element in the compound it is replacing.

Example 20

Consider the following single replacement reaction:

   Fe + ZnCl$_2$ --------> FeCl$_2$ + Zn

According to the redox equation, **Fe** is replacing Zn.

Is this redox reaction spontaneous ?

To determine: Use Reference Table J .

   The reaction is spontaneous if: Fe is more reactive (Higher up) than Zn

   The reaction is nonspontaneous if: Fe is less reactive (Lower down) than Zn

   According to Table J, Fe is less reactive (lower down) than Zn :

   The above reaction is nonspontaneous (will not occur.)

Example 21:

Consider the following single replacement reaction:

   Cl$_2$ + SnBr$_2$ -------> MgCl$_2$ + Br$_2$

According to the equation, **Cl$_2$** is replacing Br$_2$.

The reaction is spontaneous (will occur) because **Cl$_2$** is more reactive (higher up) than Br$_2$ (lower than). See Table J.

To determine if a reaction is spontaneous:

   The single element **MUST BE** more reactive than (above) the element of the compound it is replacing.

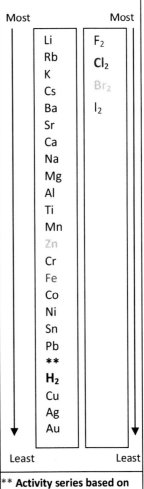

** Activity series based on Hydrogen standard

Topic 11 – Redox and Electrochemistry

Check-A-list

Concept Terms

Below is a list of vocabulary terms from Topic 11. You should know the definition and facts related to each term.

Put a check in the box [V] next to a term if you know its definition and other facts related to the term.

[ ] Oxidation number
[ ] Redox
[ ] Oxidation
[ ] Reduction
[ ] Oxidized substance
[ ] Reduced substance
[ ] Oxidizing agent
[ ] Reducing agent
[ ] Half-reaction
[ ] Spontaneous reactions

[ ] Electrochemical cell
[ ] Voltaic cell
[ ] Electrolytic cell
[ ] Electrolytic reduction
[ ] Electrolysis
[ ] Electroplating
[ ] Electrode
[ ] Anode
[ ] Cathode
[ ] Salt bridge
[ ] Battery

If you do not have a check next to a term, look it up or ask your teacher.

Concept Tasks

Below is a list of concept tasks from Topic 11. You should know how to solve problems and answer questions related to each concept task.

Put a check in the box [V] next a concept task if you know how to solve problems and answer questions related to it.

[ ] Determine oxidation numbers of elements in a neutral formula
[ ] Determining oxidation numbers of elements in polyatomic ions
[ ] Recognizing equations that are REDOX
[ ] Describing and interpreting half-reaction equation for oxidation and reduction
[ ] Recognizing half-reaction equation for oxidation
[ ] Recognizing half-reaction equation for reduction
[ ] Determining oxidation number change for oxidation
[ ] Determining oxidation number change for reduction
[ ] Determining oxidation number change showing greatest or least number of electrons lost or gained
[ ] Determining number of electrons lost or gained based on a change in oxidation number.
[ ] Determining oxidized substance (reducing agent, substance losing electrons) in redox equation
[ ] Determining reduced substance (oxidizing agent, substance gaining electrons) in redox equation
[ ] Recognizing the correct oxidation half-reaction equation for a given redox
[ ] Recognizing the correct reduction half-reaction equation for a given redox reaction
[ ] Writing oxidation and reduction half-equation for a given redox reaction
[ ] Identifying components of a voltaic cell
[ ] Answering question related to voltaic cells
[ ] Describing how a voltaic cell works
[ ] Identifying components of an electrolytic cell
[ ] Answering questions related to electrolytic reduction cell diagram
[ ] Answering questions related to electroplating cell diagrams
[ ] Describing how an electrolytic reduction cell works
[ ] Describing how an electroplating cell
[ ] Determining spontaneous and nonspontaneous reactions using Table J

If you do not have a check next to a concept task, look it up or ask your teacher.

Topic 11 – Redox and Electrochemistry

Concept Fact Review Questions

1. Which particles are gained and lost during a redox reaction?
   1) Protons
   2) Electrons
   3) Neutrons
   4) Positrons

2. Which statement correctly describes a redox reaction?
   1) The oxidation half-reaction and the reduction half-reaction occur simultaneously
   2) The oxidation half-reaction occurs before the reduction half-reaction
   3) The oxidation half-reaction occurs after the reduction half-reaction
   4) The oxidation half-reaction occurs spontaneously but the reduction half

3. The sum of all oxidation numbers of atoms in a chemical formula must equal
   1) -1
   2) 0
   3) 1
   4) 2

4. In an oxidation-reduction chemical reactions, reduction is a
   1) Gain of protons
   2) Loss of protons
   3) Gain of electrons
   4) Loss of electrons

5. What kind of reaction occurs in a voltaic cell?
   1) Non-spontaneous oxidation-reduction
   2) Spontaneous oxidation-reduction
   3) Non-spontaneous oxidation, only
   4) Spontaneous reduction, only

6. Which is true of the anode in any electrochemical cell?
   1) The anode is the site for oxidation
   2) The anode is the site for reduction
   3) The anode is the site for both oxidation and reduction
   4) The anode is the site where protons are lost and gained

7. An electrolytic cell is different from a voltaic cell because in an electrolytic cell
   1) A redox reaction occurs
   2) A spontaneous reaction occurs
   3) An electrical current is produced
   4) An electrical current causes a chemical reaction

8. The negative electrode in a chemical (voltaic) cell is the
   1) Cathode, where electrons are gained
   2) Cathode, where electrons are lost
   3) Anode, where electrons are gained
   4) Anode, where electrons are lost

9. An electrochemical cell setup consists of two half cells connected by an external conductor and a salt bridge. The function of the salt bridge is to
   1) Block a path for the flow of electrons
   2) Block a path for the flow of ions
   3) Provide a path for the flow of electrons
   4) Provide a path for the flow of ions

10. What type of a chemical reaction occurs in all electrochemical cells?
    1) Neutralization
    2) Double replacement
    3) Redox
    4) Hydrolysis

Topic 11 – Redox and Electrochemistry

Concept Tasks Review questions

11. What is the oxidation number of nitrogen in HNO_3?

    1) +5 2) +4 3) -3 4) -1

12. What is the oxidation of hydrogen in LiH?

    1) 0 2) +1 3) +2 4) -1

13. What is the oxidation number of Cr in the polyatomic ion, $Cr_2O_7^{2-}$?

    1) +7 2) +6 3) -2 4) +2

14. In which substance does bromine has oxidation number of +3
    1) KBrO
    2) $KBrO_3$
    3) $KBrO_2$
    4) $KBrO_4$

15. Which equation represents oxidation – reduction reaction?
    1) $SO_2 + H_2O \rightarrow H_2SO_3$
    2) $SO_3^{2-} + 2H^+ \rightarrow H_2SO_4$
    3) $O_2 + 2H_2 \rightarrow 2H_2O$
    4) $OH^- + H^+ \rightarrow H_2O$

16. In which oxidation number change would a species is a redox reaction gains the most number of electrons?

    1) +3 to -1
    2) +6 to +3
    3) 0 to +4
    4) +3 to +7

17. Which half-reaction equation correctly represents a reduction reaction?
    1) $Li^0 + e^- \rightarrow Li^+$
    2) $Na^0 + e^- \rightarrow Na^+$
    3) $Br_2^0 + 2e^- \rightarrow 2Br^-$
    4) $Cl_2^0 + e^- \rightarrow 2Cl^-$

18. Consider the half-reaction equation below?
    $$Li^0 \rightarrow Li + e^-$$

    The Li^0 is

    1) Oxidized, and becomes the reducing agent
    2) Oxidized, and becomes the oxidizing agent
    3) Reduced, and becomes the reducing agent
    4) Reduced, and becomes the reducing agent

19. Given the oxidation-reduction reaction equation below:
    $$Na + H_2O \rightarrow NaOH + H_2$$
    Which substance is oxidized?

    1) H_2 2) O^{2-} 3) H^+ 4) Na

20. Given the following redox reaction
    $$Mg + 2HBr \rightarrow MgBr_2 + H_2$$
    Which equation correctly represents the oxidation that occurs?
    1) $2H^+ \rightarrow H_2 + 2e^-$
    2) $Mg^0 \rightarrow Mg^{2+} + 2e^-$
    3) $2H^+ + 2e^- \rightarrow H_2$
    4) $Mg^0 + 2e^- \rightarrow Mg^{2+}$

Topic 11 – Redox and Electrochemistry

21. Given the cell diagram below.

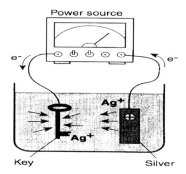

The reaction occurring in this cell is described as
1) Non-spontaneous, taking place in a voltaic cell
2) Non-Spontaneous, taking place in an electrolytic cell
3) Spontaneous, taking place in a voltaic cell
4) Spontaneous, taking place in an electrolytic cell

22. Given the reaction:

$$Mg(s) + FeSO_4(aq) \rightarrow Fe(s) + MgSO_4(aq)$$

The reaction would most likely occur in
1) A voltaic cell, and will produce energy
2) An electrolytic cell, and will produce energy
3) A voltaic cell, and will absorb energy
4) An electrolytic cell, and will absorb energy

Answer questions 23 – 24 based on the electrochemical cell below

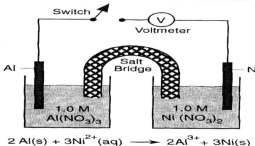

$$2\,Al(s) + 3Ni^{2+}(aq) \rightarrow 2Al^{3+} + 3Ni(s)$$

23. Which is true of the electrochemical cell when the switch is closed?
   1) Electrons will flow from Ni^{2+} to Ni
   2) Electrons will flow from Al^{3+} to Al
   3) Electrons will flow from Ni to Al
   4) Electrons will flow from Al to Ni

24. Which particles in this electrochemical cell undergoes reduction?
   1) Al^{3+} 2) Al   3) Ni^{2+} 4) Ni

25. Based on Reference Table J, which ion is most easily reduced?
   1) Sr^{2+} 2) Mg^{2+} 3) Ca^{2+} 4) Ba^{2+}

26. Referring to the Activity Series on Reference Table J, which reaction will not occur spontaneously under standard conditions?
   1) Sn + 2HF ----------> SnF_2 + H_2
   2) Mg + 2HF ----------> MgF_2 + H_2
   3) Ba + 2HF ----------> BaF_2 + H_2
   4) 2Cu + 2HF ----------> CuF_2 + H_2

Copyright © 2010 E3 Scholastic Publishing. All Rights Reserved.

Topic 11 – Redox and Electrochemistry

Constructed Response Questions

Base your answers to questions 27 through 29 on the diagram and balanced equation below, which represents the electrolysis of molten NaCl.

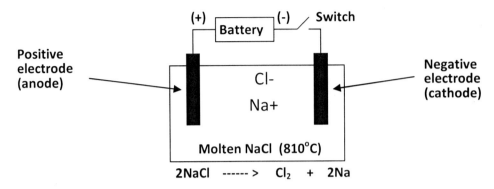

2NaCl ------> Cl₂ + 2Na

27. Write the balance half-reaction for the reduction that occurs in this electrolytic cell.

    27.

28. What is the purpose of the battery in this electrolytic cell?

    28.

29. When the switch is closed, which electrode will attract the sodium ions?

    29.

Base your answers to questions 30 and 31 on the equation below.

$$4\ Al(s) + 3O_2(g) \longrightarrow 2\ Al_2O_3\ (s)$$

30. Write a balance oxidation half-reaction equation for this reaction.

    30.

31. What is the oxidation number of oxygen in Al_2O_3?

    31.

Base your answers to questions 32 and 33 on the unbalanced redox reaction below.

__Cu(s) + __ AgNO₃(aq) -----> __ Cu(NO₃)₂(aq) + __ Ag(s)

32. Balance the redox equation using the smallest whole number coefficients.

33. Write half-reaction equations for oxidation and reduction that occur in the above reaction.

    33. Oxidation half:

        Reduction half:

Topic 12 - Nuclear Chemistry

Topic outline

In this topic, you will learn the following concepts:

- Transmutations
- Nuclear stability
- Nuclear equations
- Nuclear particles and radiations
    - Alpha particle
    - Beta particles
    - Positron
    - Neutron
    - Gamma rays
- Separation of particles
- Balancing nuclear equations
- Natural transmutation
    - Alpha decay
    - Beta decay
    - Positron emission
- Artificial transmutation
- Nuclear energy
    - Fission
    - Fusion
- Half life
- Radioisotopes usages and wastes

Lesson 1 – Nuclear transmutations

Introduction:

Nuclear chemistry is the study of changes that occur in the nucleus of atoms.

LOOKING back: Topic 3: **Atomic structure**, you had learned about the nucleus of the atom.

RECALL the following important facts about the nucleus, and about particles found in the nucleus:

- Protons and neutrons are found in the nucleus of an atom
- The number of protons determines the identity (Atomic number) of the atom.
- The number of neutrons determines the (Mass number) of the atom.

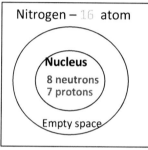

Nitrogen – 16 atom
Nucleus
8 neutrons
7 protons
Empty space

Any change to the nucleus of an atom likely involves changes to the number of protons and/or neutrons.
Any change to the nucleus of an atom will always change that atom to become different atom.

Transmutation is the changing (converting) of one atom to another by nuclear changes.

In this lesson, you will learn about the different types of nuclear changes, and ways of representing them by nuclear equations.

1. Nuclear transmutations: Ways a nucleus can change to another

Nuclear transmutation occurs when one nucleus is changed into another.
There are several ways that a nucleus of an atom can be changed to become a different nucleus.

For examples:

- A nucleus can release a particle (proton, neutron, alpha, positron, and/or electron)
- A nucleus can absorb a particle
- A nucleus can absorb one particle, and release another
- A nucleus can split into smaller nuclei
- A nucleus can join with another nucleus to form a larger nucleus.

Any of the above changes to the nucleus of an atom will result in the formation of a different atom.
Nuclear equations can be used to show a change of one nucleus to another.

Topic 12 - Nuclear Chemistry

2. Nuclear equation: Definition, facts and examples

Nuclear equations are used to show changes taking place during nuclear changes (nuclear reaction).
RECALL that information about a nucleus of an atom can be represented using a nucleus symbol.

⬅ **LOOKING BACK: Topic 3 - Atomic structure:** You learned about nucleus symbols

Below, the nucleus symbol for the atom of strontium (Sr) is given.

$$^{90}_{38}Sr$$

- 90 = mass number = number of protons + neutrons (in nucleus)
- Sr = symbol of the element strontium
- 38 = Atomic number = number of protons (in nucleus)

Nucleus symbols are used in nuclear change equations.
You will be seeing a lot of these symbols in this topic

Below, an example of a nuclear equation is shown below.
NOTE the clear difference in equations showing the three types of changes.

Nuclear change equation: $\quad ^{90}_{38}Sr \quad \text{--------->} \quad ^{86}_{36}Rn \quad + \quad ^{4}_{2}He$

Chemical change equation: $\quad KClO_3(s) \quad \text{---------->} \quad 2KCl(s) \quad + \quad O_2(g)$

Physical change equation: $\quad CO_2(s) \quad \text{------------>} \quad CO_2(g)$

In this topic, you will learn only nuclear equations.

3. Nuclear equation: Determining which equation is showing nuclear change or transmutation

Concept Task: Be able to recognize a nuclear Change equation **To determine which equation is showing a nuclear change or transmutation:** **LOOK** for an equation that uses nucleus symbols	**Example 1** *Which of the these equation represents a nuclear change?* 1) $H^+ + OH^- \text{---}> H_2O$ 2) $H_2O + Na \text{------->} NaOH + H_2$ 3) $NaCl(s) \text{--------->} Na^+(aq) + Cl^-(aq)$ 4) $^{4}He + ^{12}C \text{--->} ^{16}N + ^{0}n$ **Answer: Choice 4.** Equation contains nucleus symbols

Topic 12: Nuclear Chemistry

4. Nuclear chemistry particles and radiations: Definitions and facts

During nuclear transmutations and radioactivity, particles are absorbed and released by the nucleus. The change (or transmutation) depends on the type of particles absorbed and / or released.
Radiation (or radioactivity) describes particles and energy related to nuclear changes.

Particles and radiations most commonly involve in nuclear changes are given below.

Concept Facts: Study to remember the information given for each particle.

Alpha particle: $^{4}_{2}He$ or α

Alpha particle is similar to a helium nuclei.
Alpha particle has a mass of 4 amu and a charge of +2
Alpha particles have the lowest penetrating power of all radiations

Beta particle: $^{0}_{-1}e$ or β

Beta particle is similar to a high speed electron.
Beta particle has a mass of 0 and a charge of -1.

Positron: $^{0}_{+1}e$

Positron is commonly known as an electron catcher
Positron has a mass of 0 and a charge of +1.

Gamma radiation: $^{0}_{0}\gamma$

Gamma radiation is similar to a high energy x-ray.
Gamma radiation has a mass of 0 and a charge of 0.
Gamma radiation has the highest penetrating power of all radiations.

Neutron: $^{1}_{0}n$

Neutron has a mass of 1 amu and a charge of 0

Concept facts: Study to remember the following terms:

Accelerator is a device that moves charged particles to a high speed.
Only charged particles (alpha, beta, and positron) can be accelerated.

Penetrating power refers to the strength of a particle to go through an object.

Alpha particle (α) has the weakest penetrating power. It can be stopped by a sheet of paper.

Gamma radiation (γ) has the strongest penetrating power
Gamma rays can only be stopped by a lead metal.

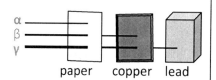

Summary table of Common Nuclear particles and radiations:

Nuclear Particle	Symbol	Mass	Charge	Penetrating power	Able to be accelerated
Alpha	$^{4}_{2}He$, α	4 amu	+2	Low (weakest)	Yes
Beta	$^{0}_{-1}e$, $-\beta$	0 amu	-1	Medium	Yes
Positron	$^{0}_{+1}e$, $+\beta$	0 amu	+1	Medium	Yes
Gamma	$^{0}_{0}\gamma$	0 amu	0	High (strongest)	No
Neutron	$^{1}_{0}n$	1 amu	0	------	No

NOTE: On **Reference Table O,** you can find name, notation, and symbol of each particle.

Topic 12: Nuclear Chemistry

5. Separation of nuclear particles: Facts and example

An electric or magnetic field can be used to separate particles and radiations that are released from a radioactive source during nuclear decays.

An electric field contains two charged plates; A positive and a negative charged plates as shown below.

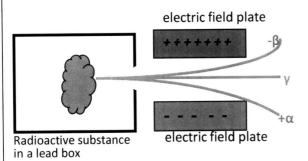

As the particles are released from a source:

. Negative (-) particles will attract (deflected) toward the positive plates (+) of the electric field

. No charge particles will be unaffected (not deflected) by the electric field, and will go straight through

. Positive (+) particles will attract (deflected) toward the negative plates (-) of the electric field.

The paths of these particles can be followed and traced by a detector.

6. Nucleus stability: Relating ratio of neutrons to protons to nucleus stability

Most elements are stable (do not undergo spontaneous decay) in their natural state.
A few of the elements have no stable isotopes. These elements are unstable and spontaneously decay in their natural state.

What determines if an element in their natural state is stable or unstable?

. The ratio of neutrons to protons in the nucleus determines stability of elements in the natural state.
. The lower the ratio of neutrons to protons, the more stable the element.
. The higher the ratio of neutrons to protons, the more unstable is the element
. Elements with 1 : 1 ratio of neutrons to protons are the most stable

Elements with atomic number less 83 are all stable because they have a low neutron to proton ratio. Their ratio is within the "belt of stability".

Elements with atomic number 83 and above are all unstable (have no stable isotopes) because they have a high neutron to proton ratio. These elements in their natural state spontaneously decay through natural transmutation.

Below is a comparison of ratio of protons and neutrons of two atoms

NOTE that the isotope names and symbols are given, followed by the nucleus diagram showing the number of protons and neutrons. Note the ratio difference between the two atoms.

Silicon – 28   or $^{28}_{14}$Si

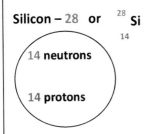

Low ratio of neutrons to protons
    1   :   1

All natural isotopes of silicon are stable.

Francium – 223   or $^{223}_{87}$Fr

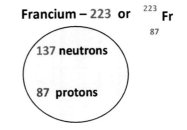

High ratio of neutrons to protons
    1.5   :   1

No stable isotopes of francium exist in nature.

Topic 12: Nuclear Chemistry

7. Transmutations: Types of transmutations

RECALL that transmutation is the changing (converting) of one atom to a different atom. A transmutation can be natural or artificial.

Natural transmutation is when a single unstable radioactive nucleus spontaneously changes by decaying (breaking down).

. Alpha decay, Beta decay, and positron emission are all types of natural transmutation.

. Elements with atomic number 83 and above spontaneously decay by natural transmutation in their natural states

. Element with atomic number 82 and below *must* be made radioactive first (by artificial transmutation) before they can spontaneously decay

Artificial transmutation is when a stable nonradioactive nucleus absorbs a particle to form an unstable (radioactive) nucleus.

For example: Nitrogen (atomic number 7) is naturally stable. (Low neutron to proton ratio)

If a radioactive isotope of Nitrogen is needed for medical studies, artificial transmutation process can be used to create a radioactive nitrogen.

Both types of transmutations and their examples are discussed on the next page.

8. Decay mode: Determining decay mode of radioisotopes

Decay mode refers to the type of radiation that a radioisotope will release as it decays.

Reference Table N shows selected radioisotopes, and their decay modes.

A radioisotope is any radioactive isotope of an element.

A radioisotope can be described as one of the followings depending on its decay mode.

An alpha emitter is a radioisotope that decays by releasing an alpha particle (α, $^{4}_{2}He$)
  Ex. Francium – 220 and uranium – 238 are both alpha emitters.

A beta emitter is a radioisotope that decays by releasing a beta particle ($-\beta$, $^{0}_{-1}e$)
  Ex. Cobalt – 60 and Strontium – 90 are both beta emitters.

A positron emitter is a radioisotope that decays by releasing a positron ($+\beta$, $^{0}_{+1}e$)
  Ex. Iron – 53 and Neon – 19 are both positron emitters

Concept Task: Be able to determine the decay mode of a radioisotope	Example 2
To determine which radioisotope is an alpha, beta, or positron emitter	*Which radioisotope decays by releasing a particle with a mass of 4 ?* 1) ^{32}P 2) ^{14}C 3) ^{239}Pu 4) ^{3}H
	Before choosing: Consider the particle released: Alpha particles have a mass of 4.
LOOK at Reference Table N (see next page)	**Answer: Choice 3.** ^{239}Pu is an alpha emitter

Topic 12: Nuclear Chemistry

9. Alpha decay – A natural transmutation: Definitions, facts and equation.

Alpha decay is when a radioactive nucleus spontaneously breaks down to emit an alpha particle.

An alpha particle symbol is $^{4}_{2}He$

Example of Alpha Decay equation: $^{238}_{92}U \longrightarrow\ ^{4}_{2}He + ^{234}_{90}Th$

| | Alpha emitter (Unstable radioactive nucleus) | Alpha particle emitted | New atom |

When a radioactive nucleus emits an alpha particle, atomic information such as the atomic number and the mass number of the new element can be compared to the radioactive element.

Below is the comparison for the alpha decay equation given above.

	Radioactive atom $^{238}_{92}U$	New atom formed after decay $^{234}_{90}Th$
Mass number	238	234
Number of protons (atomic #)	92	90
Number of neutrons (mass # - atomic #)	146	144

As you can see, after the decay, the mass number is four less than the original mass number of the radioactive atom. The atomic number and the number of neutrons are both two less that of the radioactive atom. These will always be the case in all alpha decay.

After an Alpha decay, the followings are always true:

Concept Facts: Study to remember.

. Mass number is decreased by 4
. Number of protons (Atomic number) is decreased by 2
. Number of neutrons is decreased by 2

10. Alpha Decay: Determining which equation represents alpha decay

Concept Task: Be able to recognize alpha decay equations.

To determine which equation represents alpha decay

LOOK for equation that shows one radioisotope LEFT of arrow and an alpha particle ($^{4}_{2}He$) on the **RIGHT**

Example 3
Which of the following equations represents an alpha decay?

1) $^{19}_{10}Ne \longrightarrow\ ^{19}_{11}Na + ^{0}_{-1}e$

2) $^{228}_{89}Ac \longrightarrow\ ^{228}_{88}Ra + ^{0}_{+1}e$

3) $^{232}_{90}Th \longrightarrow\ ^{4}_{2}He + ^{228}_{88}Ra$

4) $^{220}_{87}Fr + ^{4}_{2}He \longrightarrow\ ^{224}_{89}Ac$

Answer: Choice 3. $^{4}_{2}He$ is on the **RIGHT**

Topic 12: Nuclear Chemistry

11. Beta Decay – A natural transmutation: Definitions, facts, and example

A **beta decay** is when a radioactive nucleus spontaneously breaks down to emit (release) a beta particle.

A beta particle symbol is $_{-1}^{0}e$

Example of beta decay equation: $_{6}^{14}C \longrightarrow\ _{-1}^{0}e\ +\ _{7}^{14}N$

- Beta emitter (Unstable radioactive nucleus)
- beta particle emitted
- New element (stable)

When a radioactive nucleus emits a beta particle, the atomic information such as the atomic number and the mass number of the new element can be compared to that of the radioactive element.

Below is the comparison for the beta decay equation shown above.

	Radioactive nucleus $_{6}^{14}C$	New element formed after decay $_{7}^{14}N$
Mass number (nucleons)	14	14
Number of protons (atomic #)	6	7
Number of neutrons (mass # - atomic #)	8	7

As you can see, after the decay, the mass number of the new element is the same as the original mass number of the radioactive atom. The atomic number is one more than that of the radioactive atom. The number of neutrons is one less than that of the radioactive atom. These will always be the case in all beta decay.

After a beta decay, the followings are always true.

Concept Facts: Study to remember.

. Mass number remains the same
. Number of protons (Atomic number) is increased by 1
. Number of neutrons is decreased by 1

12. Beta decay: Determining which equation represents a beta decay

Concept Task: Be able to recognize beta decay equations.

To determine which equation represents a beta decay

LOOK for equation that shows one radioisotope left of the arrow and a beta particle ($_{-1}^{0}e$) on the right

Example 4
Which of the following equations represents and alpha equation?

1) $_{10}^{19}Ne \longrightarrow\ _{11}^{19}Na\ +\ _{-1}^{0}e$

2) $_{89}^{228}Ac \longrightarrow\ _{88}^{228}Ra\ +\ _{+1}^{0}e$

3) $_{90}^{232}Th \longrightarrow\ _{2}^{4}He\ +\ _{88}^{228}Ra$

4) $_{87}^{220}Fr\ +\ _{2}^{4}He \longrightarrow\ _{89}^{224}Ac$

Answer: Choice 1. $_{-1}^{0}e$ is on the **RIGHT**

Topic 12: Nuclear Chemistry

13. Positron emission - A natural transmutation: Definition, facts, and examples

A **positron emission** occurs when an atom emits (releases) a positron as it decays.
The positron that is released is from a proton being converted to a neutron.

A positron symbol is $^{0}_{+1}e$

Example of positron emission equation: $^{37}_{20}Ca \longrightarrow\ ^{0}_{+1}e\ +\ ^{37}_{19}K$

A positron emitter (Radioactive nucleus)   positron emitted   New element (stable)

When a radioactive nucleus emits a positron, the atomic information such as the atomic number and the mass number of the new element can be compared to the radioactive element.

Below is the comparison for the positron emission equation shown above.

	Radioactive nucleus $^{37}_{20}Ca$	New element formed after decay $^{37}_{19}K$
Mass number (nucleons)	37	37
Number of protons (atomic #)	20	19
Number of neutrons (mass # - atomic #)	17	18

As you can see, after the decay, the mass number of the new element is the same as the original mass number of the radioactive atom. The atomic number is one less than that of the radioactive atom. The number of neutrons is one more than that of the radioactive atom. These will always be the case in all positron emission.

After a positron emission, the followings are always true.

Concept Facts: Study to remember.

. Mass number remains the same
. Number of protons (Atomic number) is decreased by 1
. Number of neutrons is increased by 1

14. Positron emission: Determining equation of a positron emission

Concept Task: Be able to recognize positron emission equations.	**Example 5** *Which incomplete nuclear equation represents a positron emission by a radioactive nucleus?*
To determine which equation represents a positron emission **LOOK** for equation that shows one radioisotope left of the arrow and a positron ($^{0}_{+1}e$) on the right	1) $^{20}_{10}Ne \longrightarrow\ ^{20}_{9}F\ +\ ^{0}_{+1}e$ 2) $^{232}_{90}Th \longrightarrow\ ^{4}_{2}He\ +\ ^{228}_{88}Ra$ 3) $^{228}_{89}Ac\ +\ ^{0}_{+1}e \longrightarrow\ ^{228}_{90}Th$ 4) $^{220}_{87}Fr\ +\ ^{4}_{2}He \longrightarrow\ ^{224}_{89}Ac$ **Answer: Choice 1.** $^{0}_{+1}e$ is on the **RIGHT**

Topic 12: Nuclear Chemistry

15. Artificial transmutation: Definitions, facts, and examples

Artificial transmutation occurs when a stable non radioactive nucleus is bombarded (hit) with a high speed particle, and is changed (transmuted) into an unstable radioisotope.

Example of Artificial transmutation equation:

$$^{4}_{2}He + ^{9}_{4}Be \longrightarrow ^{12}_{6}C + ^{1}_{0}n$$

accelerated high speed particles — stable and non-radioactive — unstable radioisotope — neutron released

The unstable radioisotope can decay through alpha, beta or positron emission.

Concept Task: Be able to recognize artificial Transmutation equations

LOOK for equation with TWO particles on the LEFT and TWO particles on the RIGHT

Example 6

Which equation is showing an artificial transmutation?

1) $^{228}_{89}Ac \longrightarrow ^{228}_{88}Ra + ^{0}_{+1}e$

2) $^{232}_{90}Th \longrightarrow ^{4}_{2}He + ^{228}_{88}Ra$

3) $^{14}_{7}N + ^{1}_{0}n \longrightarrow ^{15}_{8}O + ^{0}_{-1}e$

4) $^{220}_{87}Fr + ^{4}_{2}He \longrightarrow ^{224}_{89}Ac$

Answer : Choice 3

Lesson 2 – Nuclear energy through fission and fusion

Introduction

During certain nuclear processes, it is known that the mass of the new atom (product) is usually slightly less than that of the reactants. This phenomenon is called **the mass defect.** The relationship between the missing mass and the tremendous amount of energy produced from nuclear reactions is given by this well known equation:

$$E = mc^2$$

Where E is energy produced

m is the mass defect (missing mass)

c is the speed of light

Concept Facts: Study to remember the relationship between mass and energy during nuclear reactions.

According to the above equation, it can be concluded that during a nuclear reaction:

. Energy is converted from mass (or mass is converted to energy)

. Energy released is extremely high in comparison to an ordinary chemical reaction

Fission and fusion reactions are two types of nuclear reactions that can produce such high energy.

In this lesson, you will learn more about nuclear fission and fusion reactions.

Topic 12: Nuclear Chemistry

16. Fission – Nuclear energy reaction: Definition, fact, and example

Fission is a form of a nuclear reaction in which a large nucleus is split into smaller nuclei.

The diagram and the equation below are showing a nuclear fission reaction. In the reaction, a neutron is hitting and splitting a large uranium nucleus to produce two smaller nuclei fragments. Three neutrons and tremendous amount of energy and radiation are also produced.

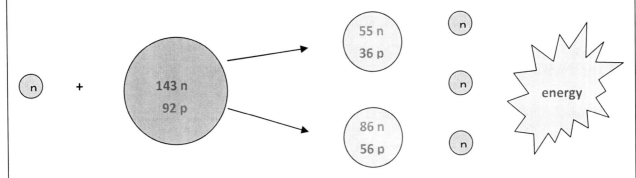

$^{1}_{0}n$ +	$^{235}_{92}U$	---------->	$^{91}_{36}Kr$ +	$^{142}_{56}Ba$ +	$3\,^{1}_{0}n$
neutron (slow moving)	A large fissionable (split able) nucleus		Two smaller nuclei		neutrons released

Example of a fission equation: All fission equations look similar.

The following are facts about all fission reactions:

Concept Facts: Study to remember.

. A large fissionable (splitable) nucleus absorbs slow moving neutrons
  . The large nucleus is split into smaller fragments, with released of more neutrons

.Tons of nuclear energy is released. Energy is converted from mass
  .Energy released is less than that of fusion reactions

. In nuclear power plants, fission process is well controlled.
  . Energy produced is used to produce electricity

. In nuclear bombs, fission process is uncontrolled
  . Energy and radiations released are used to cause destructions

. Nuclear wastes is also produced
  . Nuclear wastes are dangerous and poses serious health and environmental problems
  . Nuclear wastes must be stored and disposed of properly

Concept Task: Be able to recognize fission reaction equations

NOTE: ALL fission equations LOOK like the one above.

STUDY the equation to learn how to recognize other fission equations

Topic 12: Nuclear Chemistry

17. Fusion - Nuclear energy reaction: Definitions facts, and examples

Fusion is a form of nuclear reaction in which small nuclei are joined (fused) to create a larger nucleus.

The fusion diagram and equation below are showing nuclear fusion reaction. In the reaction, two small hydrogen nuclei are joining together to produce a larger helium nucleus. Tremendous amount of energy are produced.

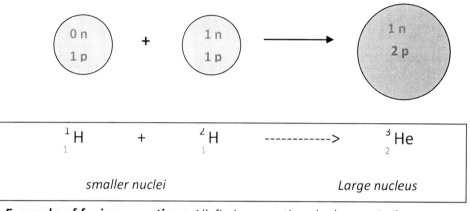

$$^{1}_{1}H + ^{2}_{1}H \longrightarrow ^{3}_{2}He$$

smaller nuclei   *Large nucleus*

Example of fusion equation: All fission equations look very similar.

During fusion reactions, the following are true:

Concept Facts: Study to remember.
. Two small nuclei are brought together under extreme high temperature and high pressure
. The two nuclei fused (joined) to create a slightly larger nucleus

.Tons of nuclear energy is released. Energy is converted from mass
.Energy released is much greater than that of fission reaction

. Fusion produces no nuclear waste, unlike fission
. Fusion reactions occur exclusively in the sun

. High temperature and high pressure are required for fusion reaction to occur.
. High temperature and pressure are necessary to overcome the repelling of two positive nuclei that are to be joined (fused) together.

RECALL: The nucleus is positively charge. In fusion, two positively charge nuclei must be brought (joined) together. Opposites attract, BUT similar charges repel. Therefore, extreme amount of energy and pressure are needed to make two positive charged nucleus join together.

Concept Task: Be able to recognize fusion reaction equations.

NOTE: ALL fusion equations LOOK like the one above.

STUDY the equation to learn how to recognize other fusion equations.

Topic 12 - Nuclear Chemistry

18. Nuclear equations : Summary Table

Below is a summary of the five types of nuclear processes discussed in the last few pages.
Use this table for a quick studying, and for comparing the five nuclear reactions.

Important facts to remember

Nuclear process and equation	Mass number after decay	Protons (atomic number) after decay	Neutrons after decay
Alpha decay (natural transmutation) $$^{226}_{88}Ra \longrightarrow {}^{222}_{86}Rn + {}^{4}_{2}He$$	↓ 4	↓ 2	↓ 2
Beta decay (natural transmutation) $$^{14}_{6}C \longrightarrow {}^{14}_{7}N + {}^{0}_{-1}e$$	same	↑ 1	↓ 1
Positron emission (natural transmutation) $$^{226}_{88}Ra \longrightarrow {}^{226}_{87}Fr + {}^{0}_{+1}e$$	same	↓ 1	↑ 1
Artificial Transmutation $$^{40}_{19}Ar + {}^{1}_{1}H \longrightarrow {}^{40}_{19}K + {}^{1}_{0}n$$	Bombarding nucleus with high speed particles		
Fission (nuclear energy) $$^{235}_{92}U + {}^{1}_{0}n \longrightarrow {}^{142}_{56}Ba + {}^{91}_{36}Kr + 3{}^{1}_{0}n$$	Nucleus splits into smaller nuclei. Mass is converted to energy. More energy then chemical reaction. *Problems:* Produces dangerous radioactive wastes.		
Fusion (nuclear energy) $$^{2}_{1}H + {}^{2}_{1}H \longrightarrow {}^{4}_{2}He + energy$$	Nuclei join to make a larger nucleus. Mass is converted to energy. Energy is more than fission. Produce no radioactive waste. *Problems:* High energy and High pressure to overcome repelling nuclei		

Topic 12: Nuclear Chemistry

19. Balancing a nuclear equation: Be able to balance a nuclear equation

A **nuclear equation** is balanced when the sum of masses (top numbers) and sum of charges (bottom numbers) are equal on both sides of the equation:

Example of a balanced nuclear equation is demonstrated below:

$$^{222}_{86}Rn \longrightarrow\ ^{4}_{2}He\ +\ ^{218}_{84}Po$$

The equation above is balanced because:
The mass number on the left (222) is equal to the sum of the masses on the right (4 + 218 = 222).
The charge on the left (86) is equal to the sum of charges on the right (2 + 84 = 86)

An **unbalanced nuclear equation** is usually given as an incomplete equation in which a particle is missing. An example of an unbalance nuclear equation is given below:

$$X\ +\ ^{0}_{-1}e \longrightarrow\ ^{37}_{17}Cl$$

Concept Task: Be able to determine the missing particle in an incomplete nuclear equation

Example 7: What particle is X in the above equation?

Think it through: Top (mass) number of X MUST add to 0 to equal 37.
Bottom (charge) number of X must add to -1 to equal 17.

$$^{37}_{18}X\ +\ ^{0}_{-1}e \longrightarrow\ ^{37}_{17}Cl$$

$$^{37}_{18}Ar$$

See Periodic Table (Atomic number of Argon)

20. Decay equation: Writing a balance decay equation

On Reference Table N, you are given radioisotope symbols and their decay mode.

Concept task: Be able to write a balance nuclear equation for a radioisotope if its decay mode is known.

Below, a balance nuclear decay equation is written for two radioisotopes from Reference Table N. Study the steps to learn how to do the same for any radioisotope whose decay mode is known.

Example 8: Write a balanced nuclear equation for plutonium – 239 and iodine – 131.

	Step 1: Write Nuclide symbol (Use Table N)		*Step 2: Write* Decay mode symbol (Use Table N and O)		*Step 3 : Determine missing* Top #, bottom #, and atom's symbol
Plutotonium-239	$^{239}_{94}Pu$	----->	$^{4}_{2}He$	+	$^{235}_{92}U$
Iodine-131	$^{131}_{53}I$	----->	$^{0}_{-1}e$	+	$^{131}_{52}Te$

Topic 12: Nuclear Chemistry

Lesson 3 – Half-life

Introduction:

Half-life is the length of time it takes for a radioactive substance to decay to half its original mass. **RECALL** that during a radioactive decay, the radioactive substance is converted to a different substance. As a radioactive substance decays, there'll be less and less of the radioactive substance remaining, while more of the new substance will form. There will come a time during the decaying process when exactly **half of the original mass** (or atoms) of the radioactive substance remains unchanged. The time (number of seconds, minutes, hours, or years) it takes for the substance to decay to **half its original mass** is described as the half-life of the substance.

For example : (see diagrams to the right)
10 grams (original mass) sample of a radioactive element is present at the beginning of a decay. After three days, only 5 grams (half of 10 grams) of the radioactive substance remained. The **half-life** of this radioactive substance is three days.

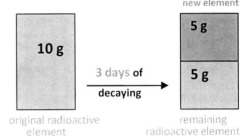

Concept Facts: Study and remember the following facts about half-life.
. Decaying of a radioisotope substance is at a constant rate (constant half-life)
. Temperature, pressure, and amount do not change the half-life of a substance
. Each radioisotope has its own half-life

In this lesson, you will learn how to solve half-life related problems.

21. Half-life of selected radioisotopes:

Reference Table N:

This table shows a list of selected radioisotopes, their decay mode, and their half-life.

In the next few sections, you will learn how to solve half life problems.

You will need to LOOK back at this table to get the half life of a radioisotope that you need in solve half-life problems.

In the next few pages, you will find detailed step-by-step instructions on solving different half-life related problems.

Keep in mind of the following:
. If you have a very clear understanding of half-life, you can solve many half-life problems with very little set up. It is very important that you read and study the definition of half-life given above to get a very clear understanding of this concept.
. If you are still having problem solving a half-life related question, then take your time to locate similar question in the next few pages, and study how the problem is solved. Follow the same steps to determine answer to your question.

Table N
Selected Radioisotopes

Nuclide	Half-Life	Decay Mode	Nuclide Name
^{198}Au	2.69 d	β^-	gold-198
^{14}C	5730 y	β^-	carbon-14
^{37}Ca	175 ms	β^+	calcium-37
^{60}Co	5.26 y	β^-	cobalt-60
^{137}Cs	30.23 y	β^-	cesium-137
^{53}Fe	8.51 min	β^+	iron-53
^{220}Fr	27.5 s	α	francium-220
^{3}H	12.26 y	β^-	hydrogen-3
^{131}I	8.07 d	β^-	iodine-131
^{37}K	1.23 s	β^+	potassium-37
^{42}K	12.4 h	β^-	potassium-42
^{85}Kr	10.76 y	β^-	krypton-85
^{16}N	7.2 s	β^-	nitrogen-16
^{19}Ne	17.2 s	β^+	neon-19
^{32}P	14.3 d	β^-	phosphorus-32
^{239}Pu	2.44×10^4 y	α	plutonium-239
^{226}Ra	1600 y	α	radium-226
^{222}Rn	3.82 d	α	radon-222
^{90}Sr	28.1 y	β^-	strontium-90
^{99}Tc	2.13×10^5 y	β^-	technetium-99
^{232}Th	1.4×10^{10} y	α	thorium-232
^{233}U	1.62×10^5 y	α	uranium-233
^{235}U	7.1×10^8 y	α	uranium-235
^{238}U	4.51×10^9 y	α	uranium-238

ms = milliseconds; s = seconds; min = minutes;
h = hours; d = days; y = years

Topic 12: Nuclear Chemistry

22. Number of half-life periods: Determining the number of half-life periods

Number of half-life period is the number of times a radioactive substance decays in half to go from one mass to another.

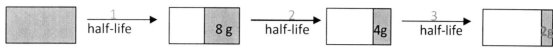

Original mass — 3 half-life periods — Remaining mass

In all half-life problems, the number of half-life periods must be known in order to solve the problem. Determining the number of half-life periods depends on the information that is given in the question.

A. If the original mass and the remaining mass are known (or given) in a question:

Concept Task: Be able to determine the number of half-life periods

Example 9

How many half-life periods does it takes for a radioactive substance to decay from the original mass of 12 grams to the remaining mass of 0.75 grams.

1) 2   2) 4   3) 8   4) 16

Before choosing a choice:
Analyze question: Question is basically asking how many times 12 g has to be cut in half to get to 0.75 g.

Identify known factors: Original mass = 12 g   Remaining mass = 0.75 g

Choose a method to solve: There are two methods to determine number of half-life periods from masses.

Method 1: USING arrows: Each arrow represents one half-life period (or the cutting in half of the number)	Method 2: Dividing original mass by 2 until you get to remaining mass. Each division sign (÷) represents one half-life period (or cutting in half of the number)
12 g ----> 6 g ----> 3g ----> 1.5 ----> 0.75 g Start here Stop here	$12 \div 2 = 6 \div 2 = 3 \div 2 = 1.5 \div = 0.75$
Four arrows = Four half-life periods: It takes four cuts of 12 grams in half to get to 1.5 g	Four divide signs = Four half-life periods It takes four halves of 12 g to get to 1.5 g.
Answer: Choice 2	**Answer: Choice 2**

B. IF the length of time and the half-life are known (given) in the question:

Concept Task: Be able to calculate the number of half-life periods from the length of time and half-life.

Equation below can be used to calculate number of half-life periods

$$\text{Number of half-life periods} = \frac{\text{Length of time}}{\text{Half-life}}$$

Example 10

The half-life of a radioisotope is 15 minutes. In 75 minutes, how many half-life periods would the substance have gone through?

1) 1125   2) 5   3) 0.2   4) 90

Identify the known factors: Half-life = 15 minutes   Length of time = 75 minutes

$$\text{Number of half-life period} = \frac{\text{Length of time}}{\text{Half-life}} = \frac{75 \text{ minutes}}{15 \text{ minutes}} = 5$$

Answer: Choice 2

Topic 12: Nuclear Chemistry

23. Length of time of decay: Calculating the length of time from known information

If certain information are known about the decaying of a substance, **the length of time** it takes for a substance to go from one mass to another can be calculated.

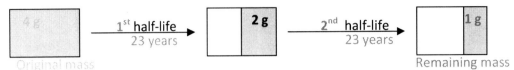

Total Length of time = 46 years

Below are some ways you can calculate length of time from information given in a half-life problem.

A. If the half-life and the number of half-life periods are given in a question:

Concept Task: Be able to calculate the total length of time of decaying

The equation below can be used to calculate the length of time.

Length of time = Half-life x number of half-life periods

Example 11

Approximately how long will it take for a radioactive ^{42}K to undergo 6 half-life periods?
1) 42.0 hours   2) 7.0 hours   3) 74.4 hours   4) 2 hours

Before choosing:
Identify the known: Get the half-life from the Table: Half of ^{42}K = 12.4 hours
Number of half-life periods = 6 half-life periods

Use equation above (if necessary) to solve
Length of time = Half-life x number of half-life periods
Length of time = 12.4 x 6 = **74.4 hours**

Answer: Choice 3.

B. If half-life, original mass and remaining mass are known

Concept Task: Be able to calculate the length of time of decaying.
Study how the example problem below is solved in two steps.

Example 12

How long will it take for potassium – 42 to decay from 100 grams to 12.5 grams?
1) 37.2 hours   2) 3 hours   3) 8.1 hours   4) 155 hours

Before choosing:
Identify known factors:
Original mass = 100 grams
Remaining mass = 12.5 grams
Half-life of potassium – 42 = 12.4 hours (From the Table N)

Solve in two steps:
First: Determine half-life period from masses
100 g ------> 50 g --------> 25g ---------> 12.5
Three arrows = 3 half-life periods

Second: Calculate length of time using equation given above
Length of time = half-life x number of half-life periods
Length of time = 12.5 x 3 = **37.2 hours**

Answer: Choice 1

Topic 12: Nuclear Chemistry

24. Half-life: Calculating half-life of unknown substance

Recall that Half-life of a substance is the time it takes for a radioisotope to decay to half its original mass. Half-life of selected radioisotopes are listed on Reference Table N. However, you may be asked to calculate half-life of a radioisotope that is not listed on Table N.

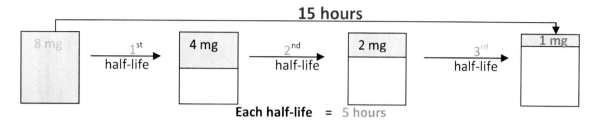

Each half-life = 5 hours

A. If length of time and number of half-life periods are given in a question:

Concept Task: Be able to calculate half-life of the radioactive decay

Equation below can be used to calculate of half-life a radioisotope

$$\text{Half-life} = \frac{\text{Length of time}}{\text{Half-life periods}}$$

Example 13
What is the half-life of an unknown radioisotope if takes 12 years for the radioisotope to undergo 5 half-life periods?

1) 60 years   2) 0.4 years   3) 17 years   4) 2.4 years

Before choosing
Identify known factors: Length of time = 12 years   Half-life periods = 5

Solve using equation: $\text{Half-life} = \frac{\text{Length of time}}{\text{Half-life periods}} = \frac{12}{5} = 2.4 \text{ years}$

Answer: choice 4

B. If the length of time, original mass and remaining mass are given in a question:

Concept Task: Be able to calculate half-life of the radioactive decay

Example 14
An unknown substance decays from 64 grams to 2 grams in 1.5×10^3 years. What is the half-life of this substance?

1) 1.28×10^2 years   2) 3.00×10^2 years   3) 3.00×10^3 4) 2.34×10^1 years

Before choosing:
Identify known factors: Original mass = 64 grams   Remaining mass = 2 grams
Length of time = 1.5×10^3 years (1500 years)
(use calculator)

Solve in two steps:
First: Find number of half-life periods from original and remaining mass

64 g -------> 32 g -------> 16 g -------> 8 g -------> 4 g -------> 2 g
Five arrows = 5 half-life periods

Second: Calculate half-life using equation given above.

$\text{Half-life} = \frac{\text{Length of time}}{\text{half-life periods}} = \frac{1500}{5} = 300 = 3.00 \times 10^2 \text{ yrs.}$

Answer: Choice 2

Copyright © 2010 E3 Scholastic Publishing. All Rights Reserved.

Topic 12: Nuclear Chemistry

25. Original mass: Determining original mass of a substance

Original mass of a radioisotope is the mass that was present at the beginning of a decay process.

 $\xrightarrow[\text{period}]{1^{st} \text{ half-life}}$ 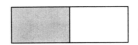 $\xrightarrow[\text{period}]{2^{nd} \text{ half-life}}$

Original mass = 400 g   Remaining mass

Below are some ways you can use to calculate the original mass from the information given.

A. If the number of half life periods and the remaining mass are given in a question:

Concept Task: Be able to calculate the original mass.

Study how the example problem below is solved using two different methods.

Example 15
After 6 half-life periods, 15 grams of an unknown radioisotope remains. What was the original mass of the unknown radioisotope?
1) 960 g   2) 120 g   3) 2.5 g   4) 90 g

Before choosing:
Identify the known: Remaining mass = 15 g   Number of half-life periods = 6

Method 1: Solve by multiplying remaining mass by 2 six times:

$15 \times 2 = 30 \times 2 = 60 \times 2 = 120 \times 2 = 240 \times 2 = 480 \times 2 = 960$ grams

Answer: Choice 1

Method 2: Solve by using arrows backward starting with remaining mass (each arrow back represents the doubling of the mass

960 < ----- 480 < -------- 240 < ---------- 120 < -------- 60 < ------- 30 < -------- 15 g

STOP here to get the Original mass prior to 6 half-life periods (6 arrows)

Answer: Choice 1

START here with the remaining mass. Double each mass as you go left)

B. If the length of time, half-life and remaining mass are given in a question:

Concept Task: Be able to calculate the original mass

Study how the example problem below is solved in two steps.

Example 16
After 24 day of decaying, a 5 grams sample of ^{131}I remains unchanged. What amount of the ^{131}I was present at the beginning of the decay?
1) 4.8 g   2) 120 g   3) 40 g   4) 655 g

Before choosing:
Identify known information: Length of time   = 24 days
                                   Half-life of ^{131}I = 8.07 days (Use the Table)
                                   Remaining mass   = 5 grams

First: Determine number of half-life periods using equation:

$$\text{Number of half-life periods} = \frac{\text{Length of time}}{\text{Half-life}} = \frac{24}{8.07} = 3$$

Second: Determined the original mass: Multiply the remaining mass by 2 three times

$5 \times 2 = 10 \times 2 = 20 \times 2 = 40$ g

Answer: Choice 3

Topic 12: Nuclear Chemistry

26. Remaining mass: Determining the remaining mass of a radioisotope

Remaining mass of a radioisotope is the mass that is present after a certain number of half-life periods.

32 g (Original mass) → 16 g → 8 g → X g (4 g = Remaining mass)

Below are some ways you can use to calculate the original mass from information given.

A. If the number of half life periods and the original mass are given in a question:

Concept Task: Be able to calculate the remaining mass
Study how the example problem below is solved using two different methods.

Example 17
After 4 half-life periods, how many grams of a 12 mg sample of a radioisotope will remain unchanged?
1) 12 mg   2) 0.75 mg   3) 0.33 mg   4) 48 mg

Before choosing:
Identify the known: Original mass = 12 mg   Number of half-life periods = 4

Method 1: Solve by diving original mass by 2 four times:
12 ÷ 2 = 6 ÷ 2 = 3 ÷ 2 = 1.5 ÷ 2 = 0.75 g (mass remaining after 4 halves)
Answer: Choice 2

Method 2: Solve by using arrows starting with original mass: (each arrow forward represents the cutting in half or one half-life periods: You need 4 arrows)

12 mg ------> 6 ------> 3 ------> 1.5 ------> 0.75 mg

START here with the original mass

STOP here to get the remaining mass after 4 half-life periods

Answer: Choice 2

B. If the length of time, half-life and original mass are known in a question:

Concept Task: Be able to calculate the remaining mass
Study how the example problem below is solved in two steps.

Example 18
In approximately 8×10^3 years, how many grams of 100 grams sample of Radon – 226 will remain unchanged?
1) 3.125 g   2) 50.0 g   3) 80.0 g   4) 250 g

Before choosing:
Identify known information: Length of time = 8×10^3 years (8000 years)
Half-life of ^{226}Rn = 1.6×10^3 (1600) years   (SEE Table N)
Original mass = 100 grams

First: Determine number of half-life periods using equation:

$$\text{Number of half-life periods} = \frac{\text{Length of time}}{\text{Half-life}} = \frac{8000}{1600} = 5$$

Second: Find remaining mass: Divide original mass by 2 five times (cut original mass by half 5 times)

100 ÷ 2 = 50 ÷ 2 = 25 ÷ 2 = 12.5 ÷ = 6.25 ÷ 2 = 3.125 g
Original mass   **Answer: Choice 1**   (mass remaining)

Topic 12: Nuclear Chemistry

27. Fraction remaining: Using and determining fraction remaining after a decayed period.

Fraction remaining expresses the remaining mass of a radioisotope in terms of ratio.

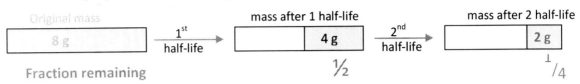

Below are some ways you can calculate fraction remaining from information given.

A. If the number of half-life period of decaying is given in a question:

Concept Task: Be able to determine the fraction remaining of the radioisotope.

Equation below can be used to calculate fraction remaining

$$\text{Fraction remaining} = \frac{1}{2^n}$$

n = number of half-life periods

Example 19
What fraction of Au-198 will remain unchanged after 4 half-life periods?
a) $1/8$ 2) $1/2$ 3) $1/16$ 4) $1/4$

Before choosing:
Identify information given: Number of half-life periods (n) = 4

Use above equation to solve: $\text{Fraction remaining} = \frac{1}{2^n} = \frac{1}{2^4} = \frac{1}{2 \times 2 \times 2 \times 2} = \frac{1}{16}$

Answer: Choice 3

NOTE: For any radioactive decay, there will always be $1/16^{th}$ of the original substance remaining after 4 half-life periods.

B. If Length of time and half-life of a substance are given in a question:

Concept Task: Be able to determine the fraction remaining of a radioisotope.

The equation below can be used to calculate the fraction remaining

$$\text{Fraction remaining} = \frac{1}{(2)^{t/T}}$$

t = Length of time
T = Half-life of the substance
t/T = n = number of half-life periods

Reference Table T equation

Example 20
What fraction of ^{19}Ne will remain unchanged after 86 seconds:
1) $1/32$ 2) $1/5$ 3) $1/2$ 4) $1/16$

Before choosing
Identify information given:
t = Length of time = 86 sec   T = Half-life of ^{19}Ne = 17.2 sec   (SEE Reference Table N)

Solve using equation :
$\text{Fraction remaining} = \frac{1}{2^{t/T}} = \frac{1}{2^{86/17.2}} = \frac{1}{2^5} = \frac{1}{2 \times 2 \times 2 \times 2 \times 2} = \frac{1}{32}$

Answer: Choice 1

Topic 12: Nuclear Chemistry

28. Fraction remaining: Using fraction remaining and length of time to determine isotope symbol

Given the length of time of decay and fraction the remaining of a radioisotope, you can determine which isotope on Reference Table N is going through decay.

Concept Task: Be able to determine the name or symbol of radioisotope from the half-life information

Example 21
Which of these radioisotopes will only have $1/16^{th}$ of its original mass remaining after about 112 years?

1) Cobalt-60   2) Cesium 37   3) Krypton-85   4) Strontium-90

Before choosing:
Determine known: Fraction remaining = $1/16^{th}$ Length of time = **112 years**

To determine the correct radioisotope from Table N, you need to first determine the half-life of the radioisotope based on information from the question. Once you know the half life, you can find a radioisotope with the same half-life on Reference Table N.

Step 1: Determine the number of half-life periods from the fraction remaining:

$$\text{Fraction remaining} = \frac{1}{16} = \frac{1}{2}^n \quad n = 4$$

Step 2. Determine the half-life of the radioisotope from the half-life equation below

$$\text{Half-life} = \frac{\text{Length of time}}{n \text{ (number of half-life periods)}} = \frac{112}{4} = 28 \text{ years}$$

Step 3: LOOK on Reference Table N for a radioisotope with a half-life of approximately 28 years.

Answer: Choice 4 : Half-life of strontium-90 is 28.1 years

Topic 12: Nuclear Chemistry

29. Isotope symbol: Determining correct isotope symbol from Reference Table N

Given certain information about the decay process of a radioisotope, you can identify which radioisotope on Table N the information is referring to:

Concept Task: Be able to determine which radioisotope decays to the greatest or least extent.

To identify which radioisotope:

Decays to the greatest extent in a given time period
  LOOK for radioisotope with the shortest Half-life

Decays to the least extent in a given time period
  LOOK for radioisotope with the Longest half-life

Use Reference Table N

Concept Task: Be able to determine which radioisotope has the greatest or smallest percentage remaining after a given time period

To determine which radioactive sample has:

Greatest (or most) amount (or percentage) remaining after a given period:
  LOOK for radioisotope with LONGEST half-life and MOST mass

Least (smallest) amount (or percentage) remaining in a given time period
  LOOK for radioisotope with SHORTEST half-life and LEAST mass

---

Example 22
Which 10 grams of these radioisotope will decay to the greatest extent in 50 years?
1) Kr-85   3) Cs-137
2) H-3   4) Sr-90

Before choosing:
LOOK on Table N for half-life of each radioisotope:
Choose the one with the shortest half-life:

Answer: Choice 1. Kr-85 has the shortest half-life

Example 23
Which sample will have the greatest amount of its isotope remaining after 60 seconds?
1) 5 g of ^{19}Ne
2) 10 g of ^{19}Ne
3) 5 g of ^{220}Fr
4) 10 g of ^{220}Fr

Before choosing:
LOOK on Table N for the half-lives of Fr and Ne.

CHOOSE the one with longest half-life and greatest mass:

Answer: Choice 4. Fr-220 has a longer half-life than Ne-19
There be more of a 10 g of Fr-220 remaining than of a 5 g.

Topic 12: Nuclear Chemistry

30. Half-life data and graphs: Interpreting data table and graph of a decay.

The decaying process of a radioisotope can be represented with graphs, diagrams and data tables.

Concept Task: Be able to interpret the half-life information represented on data tables and graphs:

Below are examples of data table and graph of a decaying of a radioisotope.
The graph and data are both showing the mass of a radioisotope remaining as it decays over time (days).

NOTE that graph (B) corresponds to data table (A).

A. Data table of a decay.

Time (days)	Mass of radioisotope sample remaining (g)
0	160
4	120
8	80 (half original mass)
12	60
16	40
20	30
24	20
28	15
32	10

B. Graph of a decay

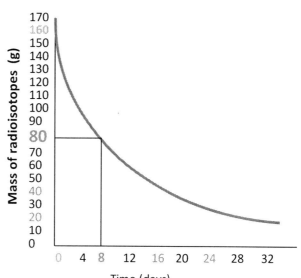

Information from data and graph shown above is interpreted below.

Determining mass from the data and graph.

Original mass	= mass at time Zero	= 160 g
½ the original mass	= mass after 1 half-life period	= 80 g
$1/4^{th}$ original mass	= mass after 2 half-life periods	= 40 g
$1/8^{th}$ original mass	= mass after 3 half-life periods	= 20 g

Determining time from the data and graph

Half-life = time when (80 g), ½ original mass, remained = 8 days
Two half-life periods = Time when (40 g), $1/4^{th}$ original mass, remained = 16 days
Three half-life periods = Time when (20 g), 1/8th of original mass, remained = 24 days

Determining which radioisotope from the data and graph:

LOOK for a radioisotope on Table N with the half-life of about 8 days: = Iodine - 131

Topic 12: Nuclear Chemistry

31. Radioisotope application: Definitions, facts and examples

Some of the radioisotopes listed on Reference Table N have common usages in areas such as medicine, research, geological (rocks) and archeological (fossil) dating.

Note the following definitions and facts related to common applications of radioisotopes.

Tracer is a radioisotope that is used to follow the path of a chemical reaction

  Radioisotope tracers in medical treatments and diagnoses must have a short half-life and be quickly eliminated from the body.

  Radioisotopes tracers for dating usually have very long half-life

The Table below gives a list of radioisotopes and their common applications.
Concept Facts: Study to remember.

Radioisotope name	Radioisotope symbol	Common application	Field of application
Iodine-131	^{131}I	Thyroid disorder; diagnosis and treatment	Medical
Technetium-99	^{99}Tc	Cancer tumor diagnosis	Medical
Cobalt-60	^{60}Co	Cancer treatment	Medical
Iron-56	^{56}Fe	Blood disorder treatment	Medical
Carbon-14 (alone)	^{14}C	Tracer for chemical reactions	Research
Carbon-14 and Carbon-12	^{14}C ^{12}C	Fossilized dating	Archeological dating
Uranium – 238 and Lead - 206	^{238}U ^{206}Pb	Rock dating	Geological dating

32. Radioisotope waste: Facts and examples

Wastes and radiations produced from nuclear reactors are highly dangerous to life on earth.
Prolong and high dose exposure to radiation can cause serious health issues, and sometimes death.
  . **Radiation** from nuclear power must be well contained to protect humans and other living things.
Nuclear waste are equally dangerous because they are highly radioactive.
  . Nuclear wastes have to be stored in safe areas to protect the public from being exposed to them.

Below are a list of some nuclear wastes:

Solid wastes (Highly radioactive):
  ^{90}Sr (strontium-90)
  ^{137}Cs (cesium-137)

Gaseous Wastes:
  ^{222}Rn (radon-22)
  ^{85}Kr (Krypton-85)
  ^{16}N (Nitrogen-16)

Topic 12: Nuclear Chemistry

Check-A-list

Concept Terms

Below is a list of vocabulary terms from Topic 12. You should know the definition and facts related to each term.

Put a check in the box [v] next to a term if you know its definition and other facts related to the term.

[ ] Transmutation
[ ] Natural transmutation
[ ] Artificial transmutation
[ ] Alpha particle
[ ] Beta particle
[ ] Gamma ray
[ ] Positron
[ ] Neutron

[ ] Alpha decay
[ ] Beta decay
[ ] Positron emission
[ ] Fission
[ ] Fusion
[ ] Half-life
[ ] Radioisotope
[ ] Tracer

[ ] Accelerator
[ ] Penetrating power
[ ] Separation of particles

If you do not have a check next to a term, look it up or ask your teacher.

Concept Tasks

Below is a list of concept tasks from Topic 12. You should know how to solve problems and answer questions related to each concept task.

Put a check in the box [v] next a concept task if you know how to solve problems and answer questions related to it.

[ ] Recognizing a nuclear change equation
[ ] Determining the decay mode of a radioisotope
[ ] Recognizing natural transmutation equations
[ ] Recognizing alpha decay equations
[ ] Recognizing beta decay equations
[ ] Recognizing positron emission equations
[ ] Recognizing artificial transmutation equations
[ ] Recognizing fission equations.
[ ] Recognizing fusion equations.
[ ] Recognizing a nuclear reaction in which mass is converted to energy
[ ] Determining the missing particle in an incomplete nuclear equation
[ ] Calculating number of half-life periods from original and remaining mass
[ ] Calculating number of half-life periods from length of time and half-life
[ ] Calculating length of time of decaying from half-life and half-life periods
[ ] Calculating length of time of decaying from half-life and original and remaining masses
[ ] Calculating half-life of a radioisotope from length of time and half-life periods
[ ] Calculating half-life of a radioisotope from length of time, original and remaining masses
[ ] Calculate original mass from number of half-life periods and remaining mass
[ ] Calculate original mass from length of time, half-life, and remaining mass
[ ] Calculate remaining mass from number of half-life periods and original mass
[ ] Calculate remaining mass from length of time, half-life, and original mass
[ ] Calculating fraction remaining from number of half-life period
[ ] Calculating fraction remaining from length of time and half-life
[ ] Determining name or symbol of radioisotope from half-life information
[ ] Determining a radioisotope that decays to the greatest or least extent
[ ] Determining a radioisotope that has the greatest or the smallest percentage remaining
[ ] Interpreting data and graph of a decay

If you do not have a check next to a concept task, look it up or ask your teacher.

Topic 12: Nuclear Chemistry

Concept Fact Review Questions

1. Which process converts an atom from one element to another when the nucleus of an atom is bombarded with high-energy particles?
   1) Artificial transmutation
   2) Addition polymerization
   3)) Natural transmutation
   4) Condensation polymerization

2. Spontaneous decay of certain elements in nature occurs because these elements have
   1) Disproportionate ratio of electrons to protons
   2) Disproportionate ratio of neutrons to protons
   3) High reactivity with oxygen
   4) Low reactivity with oxygen

3. The energy released by a nuclear reaction results primarily from
   1) Breaking of bonds between atoms
   2) Formation of bonds between atoms
   3) Conversion of mass into energy
   4) Conversions of energy into mass

4. An electron has a charge identical to that of
   1) A positron
   2) A beta particle
   3) An alpha particle
   4) A proton

5. Which list is showing the particles arranged in order of increasing penetrating power?
   1) Gamma------> Beta ----------> Alpha
   2) Beta ------- > Gamma ------- > Alpha
   3) Alpha-------- > Beta ----------- > Gamma
   4) Gamma ------> Alpha -------- > Beta

6. Which nuclear emission moving through an electric field would be attracted toward a positive electrode?
   1) Proton
   2) Gamma radiation
   3) Beta Particle
   4) Alpha particle

7. When an alpha particle is emitted by an atom, the atomic number of the atom
   1) Increases by 2
   2) Decreases by 2
   3) Increases by 4
   4) Decreases by 4

8. As a radioactive isotope emits a positron, the atomic number of the atom
   1) Decreases
   2) Increases
   3) Remains the same

9. Which best describes what occurs in a fusion reaction?
   1) Light nuclei join to form heavier nuclei
   2) Heavy nuclei split into lighter nuclei
   3) Energy is converted to mass
   4) Electron is converted to energy

10. One benefit of nuclear fission reaction is
    1) Nuclear reaction meltdowns
    2) Storage of waste materials
    3) Biological exposure
    4) Production of energy

11. Which nuclear process is a type of natural transmutation?
    1) Alpha decay
    2) Artificial transmutation
    3) Fission
    4) Fusion

12. Diagnostic injections of radioisotopes used in medicine normally have
    1) Short half-lives and are quickly eliminated from the body
    2) Short half-lives and are slowly eliminated from the body
    3) Long half-lives and are quickly eliminated from the body
    4) Long half-lives and are slowly eliminated from the body

Topic 12: Nuclear Chemistry

Concept Task Review Question

13. Which Group 18 element is naturally radioactive and has no known stable isotope?
    1) Ar
    2) Rn
    3) Xe
    4) Kr

14. Which notation of a radioisotope is correctly paired with the notation of its emission particle?
    1) $^{37}_{19}K$ and $^{0}_{-1}e$
    2) $^{222}_{86}Rn$ and $^{4}_{2}He$
    3) $^{16}_{7}N$ and $^{1}_{1}p$
    4) $^{99}_{43}Tc$ and $^{0}_{+1}e$

15. A nuclear change resulting in a release of an alpha particle is shown in which equation?
    1) $^{252}_{98}Cf \longrightarrow {}^{248}_{96}Cm + {}^{4}_{2}He$
    2) $^{19}_{10}Ne \longrightarrow {}^{19}_{11}Na + {}^{0}_{-1}e$
    3) $^{220}_{87}Fr + {}^{4}_{2}He \longrightarrow {}^{224}_{89}Ac$
    4) $^{228}_{89}Ac \longrightarrow {}^{228}_{88}Ra + {}^{1}_{1}p$

16. Fission reaction is represented by which nuclear equation?
    1) $^{238}_{92}U + {}^{4}_{2}He \longrightarrow {}^{241}_{94}Pu + {}^{1}_{0}n$
    2) $^{14}_{7}N + {}^{1}_{0}n \longrightarrow {}^{14}_{6}C + {}^{1}_{1}H$
    3) $^{235}_{92}U + {}^{1}_{0}n \longrightarrow {}^{87}_{35}Br + {}^{146}_{57}La + 3\,{}^{1}_{0}n$
    4) $^{2}_{1}H + {}^{1}_{1}H \longrightarrow {}^{3}_{2}He$

17. Given the nuclear reaction
    $$^{60}_{27}Co \longrightarrow {}^{0}_{-1}e + {}^{60}_{28}Ni$$
    The reaction is an example of
    1) Fission
    2) Natural transmutation
    3) Fusion
    4) Artificial transmutation

18. Which particle is represented by X in the nuclear equation below?
    $$^{75}_{33}As + X \longrightarrow {}^{78}_{35}Br + {}^{1}_{0}n$$
    1) $^{1}_{1}H$
    2) $^{1}_{0}n$
    3) $^{0}_{+1}e$
    4) $^{4}_{2}He$

19. Exactly how much time elapse before 16 grams of potassium-42 decays, leaving 2 grams of the original isotope?
    1) 99.2 hours
    2) 24.8 hours
    3) 37.2 hours
    4) 49.6 hours

20. A radioactive isotope of an element decays from 20 grams to 5 grams in 8 minutes. What is the half-life of this radioisotope?
    1) 15 minutes
    2) 20 minutes
    3) 10 minutes
    4) 4 minutes

21. The half-life of a radioisotope is 20.0 minutes. What is the total amount of a 10 g sample of this isotope remaining after 1 hour minutes?
    1) 5.00 g
    2) 3.33 g
    3) 2.50 g
    4) 1.25 g

22. Approximately what fraction of an original ^{60}Co sample remains unchanged after 21 years?
    1) $1/2$
    2) $1/4$
    3) $1/8$
    4) $1/16$

23. Which radioisotope sample will have the greatest amount remaining after 10 years?
    1) 2.0 g of Au-198
    2) 2.0 g of K-42
    3) 4.0 g of P-32
    4) 4.0 g of Co-60

24. Radioactive dating of the remains of organic materials can be done by comparing the ratio of which two isotopes?
    1) Uranium-235 to Uranium-238
    2) Carbon-14 to Carbon-12
    3) Nitrogen-14 to Nitrogen-16
    4) Hydrogen-2 to Hydrogen-3

Topic 12: Nuclear Chemistry

Constructed Response Questions

Base your answers to questions 25 through 27 on the nuclear equation shown below.

$$^{235}_{92}U + ^{1}_{0}n \longrightarrow ^{142}_{56}Ba + ^{91}_{36}Kr + 3^{1}_{0}n + energy$$

25. State the type of nuclear reaction represented by the equation.

    25. _____

26. The sum of the masses of the products is slightly less than the sum of the masses of the reactants. Explain this loss of mass.

    26. _____

27. This process releases greater amount of energy than an ordinary chemical reaction does. Name another type of nuclear reaction that releases greater energy than an ordinary chemical reaction.

    27. _____

Base your answers to questions 28 to 30 on the information and Table below.

Some radioisotopes used tracers to make it possible for doctors to see the images of internal body parts and observe their functions. The table below lists information about three radioisotopes and their body part each radioisotope is used to study.

Medical uses of Some Radioisotopes

Radioisotope	Half-life	Decay Mode	Body Part
^{24}Na	15 hours	Beta	Circulatory system
^{59}Fe	44.5 days	Beta	Red blood cells
^{131}I	8.1 days	Beta	Thyroid

28. It could take up to 60. hours for a radioisotope to be delivered to the hospital from the laboratory where it is produced. What fraction of an original sample of ^{24}Na remains unchanged after 60 hours?

    28. _____

29. Complete the equation for the nuclear decay of the radioisotope used to study red blood cells. Include both atomic number and the mass number for each missing particle.

    29. ^{59}Fe $\longrightarrow$ _____ + _____

30. A patient at a clinic was injected with 100 mg sample of Iodine-131 during a routine thyroid functions test. How much of the original iodine-131 will remain in the patient's body after approximately 48 hours?

    30. _____

Reference Tables

Table A : Standard temperature and Pressure

Name	Value	Unit
Standard Pressure	101.3 kPa 1 atm	kilopascal atmosphere
Standard Temperature	273 K 0°C	kelvin degree Celsius

Table B : Physical Constants for Water

Heat of Fusion	333.6 J/g
Heat of Vaporization	2259 J/g
Specific Heat Capacity of H_2O (ℓ)	4.2 J/g•K

Table C : Selected Prefixes

Factor	Prefix	Symbol
10^3	kilo-	k
10^{-1}	deci-	d
10^{-2}	centi-	c
10^{-3}	milli-	m
10^{-6}	micro-	μ
10^{-9}	nano-	n
10^{-12}	pico-	p

Table D : Selected Units

Symbol	Name	Quantity
m	meter	length
kg	kilogram	mass
Pa	pascal	pressure
K	kelvin	temperature
mol	mole	amount of substance
J	joule	energy, work, quantity of heat
s	second	time
L	liter	volume
ppm	part per million	concentration
M	molarity	solution concentration

Reference Tables

Table E: Selected Polyatomic ions

Formula	Name	Formula	Name
H_3O^+	hydronium	CrO_4^{2-}	chromate
Hg_2^{2+}	dimercury (I)	$Cr_2O_7^{2-}$	dichromate
NH_4^+	ammonium	MnO_4^-	permanganate
$C_2H_3O_2^-$ / CH_3COO^-	acetate	NO_2^-	nitrite
		NO_3^-	nitrate
CN^-	cyanide	O_2^{2-}	peroxide
CO_3^{2-}	carbonate	OH^-	hydroxide
HCO_3^-	hydrogen carbonate	PO_4^{3-}	phosphate
$C_2O_4^{2-}$	oxalate	SCN^-	thiocyanate
ClO^-	hypochlorite	SO_3^{2-}	sulfite
ClO_2^-	chlorite	SO_4^{2-}	sulfate
ClO_3^-	chlorate	HSO_4^-	hydrogen sulfate
ClO_4^-	perchlorate	$S_2O_3^{2-}$	thiosulfate

Table F : Solubility Guideline for Aqueous solutions

Solubility Guidelines

Ions That Form Soluble Compounds	Exceptions
Group 1 ions (Li^+, Na^+, etc.)	
ammonium (NH_4^+)	
nitrate (NO_3^-)	
acetate ($C_2H_3O_2^-$ or CH_3COO^-)	
hydrogen carbonate (HCO_3^-)	
chlorate (ClO_3^-)	
perchlorate (ClO_4^-)	
halides (Cl^-, Br^-, I^-)	when combined with Ag^+, Pb^{2+}, and Hg_2^{2+}
sulfates (SO_4^{2-})	when combined with Ag^+, Ca^{2+}, Sr^{2+}, Ba^{2+}, and Pb^{2+}

Ions That Form Insoluble Compounds	Exceptions
carbonate (CO_3^{2-})	when combined with Group 1 ions or ammonium (NH_4^+)
chromate (CrO_4^{2-})	when combined with Group 1 ions or ammonium (NH_4^+)
phosphate (PO_4^{3-})	when combined with Group 1 ions or ammonium (NH_4^+)
sulfide (S^{2-})	when combined with Group 1 ions or ammonium (NH_4^+)
hydroxide (OH^-)	when combined with Group 1 ions, Ca^{2+}, Ba^{2+}, or Sr^{2+}

Reference Tables

Table G: Solubility Curves

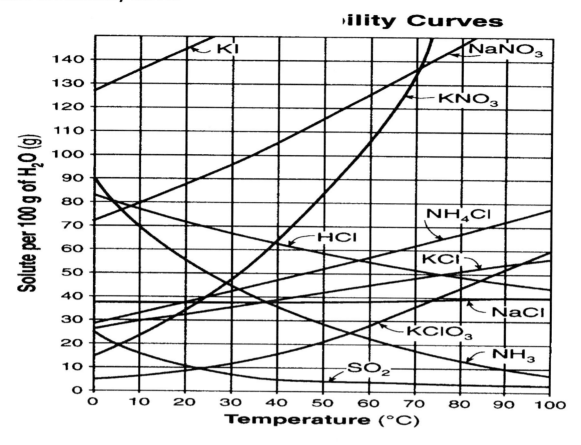

Table H : Vapor Pressure of Four Liquids

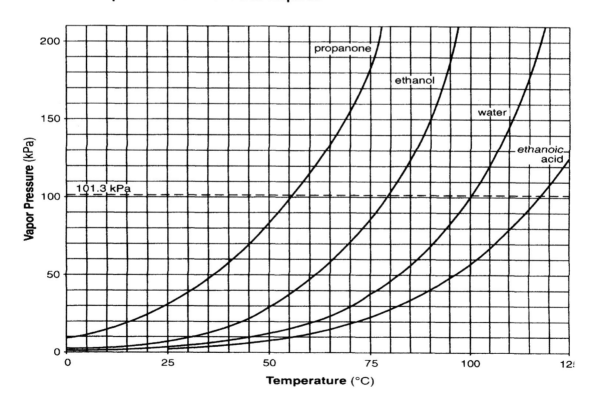

RT-3

Reference Tables

Table I: Heat of Reactions at 101.3 kPa and 298 K

Heats of Reaction at 101.3 kPa and 298 K

Reaction	ΔH (kJ)*
$CH_4(g) + 2O_2(g) \longrightarrow CO_2(g) + 2H_2O(\ell)$	–890.4
$C_3H_8(g) + 5O_2(g) \longrightarrow 3CO_2(g) + 4H_2O(\ell)$	–2219.2
$2C_8H_{18}(\ell) + 25O_2(g) \longrightarrow 16CO_2(g) + 18H_2O(\ell)$	–10943
$2CH_3OH(\ell) + 3O_2(g) \longrightarrow 2CO_2(g) + 4H_2O(\ell)$	–1452
$C_2H_5OH(\ell) + 3O_2(g) \longrightarrow 2CO_2(g) + 3H_2O(\ell)$	–1367
$C_6H_{12}O_6(s) + 6O_2(g) \longrightarrow 6CO_2(g) + 6H_2O(\ell)$	–2804
$2CO(g) + O_2(g) \longrightarrow 2CO_2(g)$	–566.0
$C(s) + O_2(g) \longrightarrow CO_2(g)$	–393.5
$4Al(s) + 3O_2(g) \longrightarrow 2Al_2O_3(s)$	–3351
$N_2(g) + O_2(g) \longrightarrow 2NO(g)$	+182.6
$N_2(g) + 2O_2(g) \longrightarrow 2NO_2(g)$	+66.4
$2H_2(g) + O_2(g) \longrightarrow 2H_2O(g)$	–483.6
$2H_2(g) + O_2(g) \longrightarrow 2H_2O(\ell)$	–571.6
$N_2(g) + 3H_2(g) \longrightarrow 2NH_3(g)$	–91.8
$2C(s) + 3H_2(g) \longrightarrow C_2H_6(g)$	–84.0
$2C(s) + 2H_2(g) \longrightarrow C_2H_4(g)$	+52.4
$2C(s) + H_2(g) \longrightarrow C_2H_2(g)$	+227.4
$H_2(g) + I_2(g) \longrightarrow 2HI(g)$	+53.0
$KNO_3(s) \xrightarrow{H_2O} K^+(aq) + NO_3^-(aq)$	+34.89
$NaOH(s) \xrightarrow{H_2O} Na^+(aq) + OH^-(aq)$	–44.51
$NH_4Cl(s) \xrightarrow{H_2O} NH_4^+(aq) + Cl^-(aq)$	+14.78
$NH_4NO_3(s) \xrightarrow{H_2O} NH_4^+(aq) + NO_3^-(aq)$	+25.69
$NaCl(s) \xrightarrow{H_2O} Na^+(aq) + Cl^-(aq)$	+3.88
$LiBr(s) \xrightarrow{H_2O} Li^+(aq) + Br^-(aq)$	–48.83
$H^+(aq) + OH^-(aq) \longrightarrow H_2O(\ell)$	–55.8

*Minus sign indicates an exothermic reaction.

Table J: Activity Series **

Activity Series**

Most Metals	Nonmetals Most
Li	F_2
Rb	Cl_2
K	Br_2
Cs	I_2
Ba	
Sr	
Ca	
Na	
Mg	
Al	
Ti	
Mn	
Zn	
Cr	
Fe	
Co	
Ni	
Sn	
Pb	
**H_2	
Cu	
Ag	
Au	
Least	Least

**Activity Series based on hydrogen standard

Reference Tables

Table K: Common (Arrhenius) Acids

Formula	Name
$HCl(aq)$	hydrochloric acid
$HNO_3(aq)$	nitric acid
$H_2SO_4(aq)$	sulfuric acid
$H_3PO_4(aq)$	phosphoric acid
$H_2CO_3(aq)$ or $CO_2(aq)$	carbonic acid
$CH_3COOH(aq)$ or $HC_2H_3O_2(aq)$	ethanoic acid (acetic acid)

Table L: Common Bases

Formula	Name
$NaOH(aq)$	sodium hydroxide
$KOH(aq)$	potassium hydroxide
$Ca(OH)_2(aq)$	calcium hydroxide
$NH_3(aq)$	aqueous ammonia

Table M: Common Acid-base indicators

Indicator	Approximate pH Range for Color Change	Color Change
methyl orange	3.2–4.4	red to yellow
bromthymol blue	6.0–7.6	yellow to blue
phenolphthalein	8.2–10	colorless to pink
litmus	5.5–8.2	red to blue
bromcresol green	3.8–5.4	yellow to blue
thymol blue	8.0–9.6	yellow to blue

Table N: Selected radioisotopes

Nuclide	Half-Life	Decay Mode	Nuclide Name
^{198}Au	2.69 d	β^-	gold-198
^{14}C	5730 y	β^-	carbon-14
^{37}Ca	175 ms	β^+	calcium-37
^{60}Co	5.26 y	β^-	cobalt-60
^{137}Cs	30.23 y	β^-	cesium-137
^{53}Fe	8.51 min	β^+	iron-53
^{220}Fr	27.5 s	α	francium-220
^{3}H	12.26 y	β^-	hydrogen-3
^{131}I	8.07 d	β^-	iodine-131
^{37}K	1.23 s	β^+	potassium-37
^{42}K	12.4 h	β^-	potassium-42
^{85}Kr	10.76 y	β^-	krypton-85
^{16}N	7.2 s	β^-	nitrogen-16
^{19}Ne	17.2 s	β^+	neon-19
^{32}P	14.3 d	β^-	phosphorus-32
^{239}Pu	2.44×10^4 y	α	plutonium-239
^{226}Ra	1600 y	α	radium-226
^{222}Rn	3.82 d	α	radon-222
^{90}Sr	28.1 y	β^-	strontium-90
^{99}Tc	2.13×10^5 y	β^-	technetium-99
^{232}Th	1.4×10^{10} y	α	thorium-232
^{233}U	1.62×10^5 y	α	uranium-233
^{235}U	7.1×10^8 y	α	uranium-235
^{238}U	4.51×10^9 y	α	uranium-238

ms = milliseconds; s = seconds; min = minutes; h = hours; d = days; y = years

Table O: Symbols Used in Nuclear Chemistry

Name	Notation	Symbol
alpha particle	$^4_2$He or $^4_2\alpha$	α
beta particle (electron)	$^0_{-1}$e or $^0_{-1}\beta$	β^-
gamma radiation	$^0_0\gamma$	γ
neutron	$^1_0$n	n
proton	$^1_1$H or $^1_1$p	p
positron	$^0_{+1}$e or $^0_{+1}\beta$	β^+

Table P: Organic Prefixes

Prefix	Number of Carbon Atoms
meth-	1
eth-	2
prop-	3
but-	4
pent-	5
hex-	6
hept-	7
oct-	8
non-	9
dec-	10

Table Q: Homologous Series of Hydrocarbons

Name	General Formula	Examples	
		Name	Structural Formula
alkanes	C_nH_{2n+2}	ethane	H H | | H−C−C−H | | H H
alkenes	C_nH_{2n}	ethene	H　　　H 　\\　　/ 　　C=C 　/　　\\ H　　　H
alkynes	C_nH_{2n-2}	ethyne	H−C≡C−H

n = number of carbon atoms

Reference Tables

Table R: Organic Functional Groups

Class of Compound	Functional Group	General Formula	Example
halide (halocarbon)	—F (fluoro-) —Cl (chloro-) —Br (bromo-) —I (iodo-)	$R-X$ (X represents any halogen)	$CH_3CHClCH_3$ 2-chloropropane
alcohol	—OH	$R-OH$	$CH_3CH_2CH_2OH$ 1-propanol
ether	—O—	$R-O-R'$	$CH_3OCH_2CH_3$ methyl ethyl ether
aldehyde	$-\overset{\overset{O}{\|\|}}{C}-H$	$R-\overset{\overset{O}{\|\|}}{C}-H$	$CH_3CH_2\overset{\overset{O}{\|\|}}{C}-H$ propanal
ketone	$-\overset{\overset{O}{\|\|}}{C}-$	$R-\overset{\overset{O}{\|\|}}{C}-R'$	$CH_3\overset{\overset{O}{\|\|}}{C}CH_2CH_2CH_3$ 2-pentanone
organic acid	$-\overset{\overset{O}{\|\|}}{C}-OH$	$R-\overset{\overset{O}{\|\|}}{C}-OH$	$CH_3CH_2\overset{\overset{O}{\|\|}}{C}-OH$ propanoic acid
ester	$-\overset{\overset{O}{\|\|}}{C}-O-$	$R-\overset{\overset{O}{\|\|}}{C}-O-R'$	$CH_3CH_2\overset{\overset{O}{\|\|}}{C}OCH_3$ methyl propanoate
amine	$-\overset{\|}{N}-$	$R-\overset{\overset{R'}{\|}}{N}-R''$	$CH_3CH_2CH_2NH_2$ 1-propanamine
amide	$-\overset{\overset{O}{\|\|}}{C}-\overset{\|}{N}H$	$R-\overset{\overset{O}{\|\|}}{C}-\overset{\overset{R'}{\|}}{N}H$	$CH_3CH_2\overset{\overset{O}{\|\|}}{C}-NH_2$ propanamide

R represents a bonded atom or group of atoms.

Table S: Properties of Selected Elements

Table S
Properties of Selected Elements

Atomic Number	Symbol	Name	Ionization Energy (kJ/mol)	Electro-negativity	Melting Point (K)	Boiling Point (K)	Density** (g/cm^3)	Atomic Radius (pm)
1	H	hydrogen	1312	2.1	14	20	0.00009	208
2	He	helium	2372	—	1	4	0.000179	50
3	Li	lithium	520	1.0	454	1620	0.534	155
4	Be	beryllium	900	1.6	1551	3243	1.8477	112
5	B	boron	801	2.0	2573	3931	2.340	98
6	C	carbon	1086	2.6	3820	5100	3.513	91
7	N	nitrogen	1402	3.0	63	77	0.00125	92
8	O	oxygen	1314	3.4	55	90	0.001429	65
9	F	fluorine	1681	4.0	54	85	0.001696	57
10	Ne	neon	2081	—	24	27	0.0009	51
11	Na	sodium	496	0.9	371	1156	0.971	190
12	Mg	magnesium	736	1.3	922	1363	1.738	160
13	Al	aluminum	578	1.6	934	2740	2.698	143
14	Si	silicon	787	1.9	1683	2628	2.329	132
15	P	phosphorus	1012	2.2	44	553	1.820	128
16	S	sulfur	1000	2.6	386	718	2.070	127
17	Cl	chlorine	1251	3.2	172	239	0.003214	97
18	Ar	argon	1521	—	84	87	0.001783	88
19	K	potassium	419	0.8	337	1047	0.862	235
20	Ca	calcium	590	1.0	1112	1757	1.550	197
21	Sc	scandium	633	1.4	1814	3104	2.989	162
22	Ti	titanium	659	1.5	1933	3580	4.540	145
23	V	vanadium	651	1.6	2160	3650	6.100	134
24	Cr	chromium	653	1.7	2130	2945	7.190	130
25	Mn	manganese	717	1.6	1517	2235	7.440	135
26	Fe	iron	762	1.8	1808	3023	7.874	126
27	Co	cobalt	760	1.9	1768	3143	8.900	125
28	Ni	nickel	737	1.9	1726	3005	8.902	124
29	Cu	copper	745	1.9	1357	2840	8.960	128
30	Zn	zinc	906	1.7	693	1180	7.133	138
31	Ga	gallium	579	1.8	303	2676	5.907	141
32	Ge	germanium	762	2.0	1211	3103	5.323	137
33	As	arsenic	944	2.2	1090	889	5.780	139
34	Se	selenium	941	2.6	490	958	4.790	140
35	Br	bromine	1140	3.0	266	332	3.122	112
36	Kr	krypton	1351	—	117	121	0.00375	103
37	Rb	rubidium	403	0.8	312	961	1.532	248
38	Sr	strontium	549	1.0	1042	1657	2.540	215
39	Y	yttrium	600	1.2	1795	3611	4.469	178
40	Zr	zirconium	640	1.3	2125	4650	6.506	160

Reference Tables

Atomic Number	Symbol	Name	Ionization Energy (kJ/mol)	Electro-negativity	Melting Point (K)	Boiling Point (K)	Density** (g/cm^3)	Atomic Radius (pm)
41	Nb	niobium	652	1.6	2741	5015	8.570	146
42	Mo	molybdenum	684	2.2	2890	4885	10.220	139
43	Tc	technetium	702	1.9	2445	5150	11.500	136
44	Ru	ruthenium	710	2.2	2583	4173	12.370	134
45	Rh	rhodium	720	2.3	2239	4000	12.410	134
46	Pd	palladium	804	2.2	1825	3413	12.020	137
47	Ag	silver	731	1.9	1235	2485	10.500	144
48	Cd	cadmium	868	1.7	594	1038	8.650	171
49	In	inidium	558	1.8	429	2353	7.310	166
50	Sn	tin	709	2.0	505	2543	7.310	162
51	Sb	antimony	831	2.1	904	1908	6.691	159
52	Te	tellurium	869	2.1	723	1263	6.240	142
53	I	iodine	1008	2.7	387	458	4.930	132
54	Xe	xenon	1170	2.6	161	166	0.0059	124
55	Cs	cesium	376	0.8	302	952	1.873	267
56	Ba	barium	503	0.9	1002	1910	3.594	222
57	La	lanthanum	538	1.1	1194	3730	6.145	138
			Elements 58–71 have been omitted.					
72	Hf	hafnium	659	1.3	2503	5470	13.310	167
73	Ta	tantalum	728	1.5	3269	5698	16.654	149
74	W	tungsten	759	2.4	3680	5930	19.300	141
75	Re	rhenium	756	1.9	3453	5900	21.020	137
76	Os	osmium	814	2.2	3327	5300	22.590	135
77	Ir	iridium	865	2.2	2683	4403	22.560	136
78	Pt	platinum	864	2.3	2045	4100	21.450	139
79	Au	gold	890	2.5	1338	3080	19.320	146
80	Hg	mercury	1007	2.0	234	630	13.546	160
81	Tl	thallium	589	2.0	577	1730	11.850	171
82	Pb	lead	716	2.3	601	2013	11.350	175
83	Bi	bismuth	703	2.0	545	1833	9.747	170
84	Po	polonium	812	2.0	527	1235	9.320	167
85	At	astatine	—	2.2	575	610	—	145
86	Rn	radon	1037	—	202	211	0.00973	134
87	Fr	francium	393	0.7	300	950	—	270
88	Ra	radium	—	0.9	973	1413	5.000	233
89	Ac	actinium	499	1.1	1320	3470	10.060	—
			Elements 90 and above have been omitted.					

*Boiling point at standard pressure
**Density at STP

Reference Tables

Table T: Important Formulas and Equations

Density	$d = \dfrac{m}{V}$	d = density m = mass V = volume
Mole Calculations	number of moles = $\dfrac{\text{given mass (g)}}{\text{gram-formula mass}}$	
Percent Error	% error = $\dfrac{\text{measured value} - \text{accepted value}}{\text{accepted value}} \times 100$	
Percent Composition	% composition by mass = $\dfrac{\text{mass of part}}{\text{mass of whole}} \times 100$	
Concentration	parts per million = $\dfrac{\text{grams of solute}}{\text{grams of solution}} \times 1\,000\,000$ molarity = $\dfrac{\text{moles of solute}}{\text{liters of solution}}$	
Combined Gas Law	$\dfrac{P_1 V_1}{T_1} = \dfrac{P_2 V_2}{T_2}$	P = pressure V = volume T = temperature (K)
Titration	$M_A V_A = M_B V_B$	M_A = molarity of H⁺ M_B = molarity of OH⁻ V_A = volume of acid V_B = volume of base
Heat	$q = mC\Delta T$ $q = mH_f$ $q = mH_v$	q = heat H_f = heat of fusion m = mass H_v = heat of vaporization C = specific heat capacity ΔT = change in temperature
Temperature	K = °C + 273	K = kelvin °C = degrees Celsius
Radioactive Decay	fraction remaining = $\left(\dfrac{1}{2}\right)^{\frac{t}{T}}$ number of half-life periods = $\dfrac{t}{T}$	t = total time elapsed T = half-life

The Reference Tables are copyrighted materials of NYS Education Department.

Glossary

A

Absolute Zero
　　0K or -273°C; the temperature at which all molecular movements stop.

Accelerator
　　a device which gives charged particles sufficient kinetic energy to penetrate the nucleus.

Acid, Arrhenius
　　a substance that produces H+ (hydrogen ion, proton) or H_3O+ (hydronium) ion as the positive ion is solutions.

Acid , Alternate Theory
　　a substance that donates H+ (hydrogen ion, proton) in acids-base reactions.

Activation energy
　　minimal amount of energy needed to start a reaction.

Addition reaction
　　organic reaction that involves the adding of hydrogen atoms (or halogen atoms) to a double or a triple bond.

Addition polymerization
　　the joining of monomers (small unit molecules) with double bonds to form a polymer (a larger unit) molecule.

Alcohol
　　an organic compound containing the hydroxyl group (-OH) as a functional group.

Aldehyde
　　an organic compound containing the $-\overset{\overset{O}{\|}}{C}-H$ as the functional group.

Alkali metal
　　an element in Group 1 of the Periodic Table.

Alkaline Earth metal
　　an element in Group 2 of the Periodic Table.

Alkane
　　a saturated hydrocarbon with all single bonds and a general formula of CnH_{2n+2}

Alkene
　　an unsaturated hydrocarbon with a double bond and a general formula of CnH_{2n}

Alkyl group
　　a hydrocarbon group (found as a side chain) that contains one less H atom than an alkane with the same number of C atoms.

Alkyne
　　an unsaturated hydrocarbon with a triple (≡) bond and a general formula of CnH_{2n-2}

Allotropes
　　two or more different forms of the same element that have different formulas, structures, and properties.

Alloy
　　a homogeneous mixture of a metal with another element (often another metal.)

Alpha decay
　　a nuclear decay that releases an alpha particle.

Alpha particle
　　a helium nuclei, $^{4}_{2}He$

Amide
　　an organic compound formed from a reaction of organic acid with an amine.

Amine
　　an organic compound that has $-\overset{|}{N}-$ (nitrogen) as its functional group.

Copyright © 2010 E3 Scholastic Publishing. All Rights Reserved.

Glossary

A cont.

Amino acid
an organic compound containing an amine (-NH$_2$-) and a carboxyl (-COOH) functional group.

Amphoteric
a species that can act either as an acid or as a base in acid-base reactions.

Anode
an electrode (site) where oxidation occurs in electrochemical (voltaic and electrolytic) cells.
In voltaic cells, the anode is negative.
In electrolytic cells, the anode is positive.

Aqueous solutions
a homogeneous mixture made with water as the solvent.

Artificial Transmutation
converting (transforming) a stable element to a radioactive unstable element by bombarding (hitting) the stable nucleus with a high energy particle.

Asymmetrical molecule
a molecule that has a polarized structure because of an uneven charge distribution.

Atom
the basic or the smallest unit of an element that can be involved in chemical reactions.

Atomic mass
the weighted average mass of an element's naturally occurring isotopes.

Atomic mass unit
one-twelfth (1/12th) the mass of a carbon-12 atom.

Atomic number
the number of protons in the nucleus of an atom.

Atomic radius (size)
half the distance between adjacent nuclei of identical bonded atoms.

Avogadro's law (hypothesis)
equal volume of all gases under the same pressure and temperature contain equal number of molecules.

Avogadro's number
Quantity of particles in one mole of a substance; 6.02×10^{23}

B

Base, Arrhenius
a substance that produces OH- (hydroxide) ion as the only negative ion in solutions.

Base, Alternate Theory
a substance that accepts H+ (hydrogen ion, protons) in acid-base reactions.

Battery
an electrochemical (voltaic) cell that produces electricity from a redox reaction.

Beta particle
a high-speed electron ($_{-1}^{0}e$) released from atomic nucleus during a nuclear decay.

Beta decay
a nuclear decay that releases a beta particle.

Binary compound
a chemical substance composed of two different elements chemically combined.

Boiling point
the temperature of a liquid at which the vapor pressure of the liquid is equal to the atmospheric pressure. Boiling point of water = 100°C

Boyle's Law
describes behavior of a gas at constant temperature: At constant temperature, volume of a gas varies indirectly with the pressure.

Glossary

C

Calorimeter
a device used in measuring heat energy change during a physical and a chemical process.

Catalyst
a substance that speeds up a reaction by providing an alternate, lower activation energy pathway.

Cathode
an electrode (site) where reduction occurs in electrochemical (Voltaic and electrolytic) cells.
In Voltaic cells, the cathode is Positive.
In Electrolytic cells, the cathode is Negative.

Charles' Law
describes behavior of gases at constant pressure: at constant pressure, the volume of a gas is directly proportional to its Kelvin (absolute) temperature.

Chemical bonding
the simultaneous attraction of two nuclei to electrons.

Chemical change
the changing of compositions of one or more substances during chemical reactions.

Chemical formula
expression of qualitative and quantitative composition of pure substances.

Chemical property
a characteristic of a substance based on its interaction with other substances.

Chemistry
the study of the composition, properties, changes, and energy of matter.

Coefficient
a number (usually a whole number) in front of a formula that indicates how many moles (or unit) of that substance.

Collision Theory
for a chemical reaction to occur, reacting particles must collide effectively.

Combustion
an exothermic reaction of a substance with oxygen to release energy.

Compound
a substance composed of two or more different elements chemically combined in a definite ratio
a substance that can be separated (decomposed) only by chemical methods.

Concentrated solution
a solution containing large amount of dissolved solute relative to amount of solvent.

Condensation
exothermic phase change of a substance from gas (vapor) to a liquid.

Condensation polymerization
the joining of monomers (small unit molecules) into a polymer (a large unit molecule) by the removal of water.

Conductivity
ability of an electrical current to flow through a substance.
Conductivity of electrolytes (soluble substances) in aqueous and liquid phase is due to mobile ions.
Conductivity of metallic substances is due to mobile valance electrons.

Covalent bond
a bond formed by the sharing of electrons between nonmetal atoms.

Cracking
the breaking of a large hydrocarbon molecule into smaller molecules.

Crystallization
a process of recovering a solute from a solution (mixture) by evaporation (or boiling).

Glossary

D

Decomposition
 a chemical reaction in which a compound is broken down into simpler substances.

Density
 mass per unit volume of a substance ; Density = $\dfrac{Mass}{Volume}$

Deposition
 an exothermic phase change by which a gas changes to a solid.

Diatomic molecules (element)
 a molecule consisting of two identical atoms.

Dilute solution
 a solution containing very little dissolved solute in comparison to the amount of solvent.

Dipole (aka polar)
 a molecule with positive and negative ends due to uneven charge distributions.

Distillation
 a process by which components of a homogeneous mixture can be separated by differences in boiling points.

Double covalent bond (=)
 the sharing of two pairs of electrons (four total electrons) between two atoms.

Double replacement
 a chemical reaction that involves the exchange of ions.

Dynamic equilibrium
 a state of a reaction by which the forward and reverse reactions are equal, while the concentration (amount) of substances remains constant.

Ductility
 ability (property) of a metal to be drawn into a thin wire.

E

Effective collision
 a collision in which the particles collide with sufficient kinetic energy, and at appropriate angle.

Electrochemical cell
 a system in which there is a flow of electrical current while a chemical reaction is taking place. Voltaic and Electrolytic cells are the two most common types of electrochemical cells.

Electrode
 a site at which oxidation or reduction can occur in electrochemical cells.
 Anode (Oxidation site) and Cathode (Reduction site) are two electrodes of electrochemical cells.

Electrolysis
 a process by which electrical current forces a nonspontaneous redox reaction to occur.
 Electrolysis of water: $2H_2O$ + electricity ------ > $2 H_2$ + O_2

Electrolyte
 a substances that dissolves in water to produce an aqueous solution that which conducts. electricity
 Conductivity of an electrolyte is due to its mobile ions in solutions.

Electrolytic cell
 an electrochemical cell that requires an electrical current to cause a nonspontaneous redox reaction to occur.

Electron
 a negatively charge subatomic particle found surrounding the nucleus (in orbital) of an atom.

Electron configuration
 distribution of electrons in electron shells (energy levels) of an atom.

Electron-dot diagram
 a diagram showing the symbol of an atom and dots equal to the number of valance electrons.

Glossary

E cont.

Electronegativity
a measure of atom's ability (tendency) to attract electrons during chemical bonding.

Electrolytic reduction
the use of electrolytic cell to force an ion to gain electrons and form a neutral atom.

Electroplating
the use of electrolytic cell to coat a thin layer of a metal into another surface.

Element
a substance composed of atoms of the same atomic number.
a substance that CANNOT be decomposed (broken down) into simpler substances.

Empirical formula
a formula showing atoms combined in the simplest whole number ratio.

Endothermic
a process that absorbs energy.
Products of endothermic reaction always have more energy than the reactants.

Energy
ability to do work; can be measured in joules or calories.

Entropy
a measure of the disorder or randomness of a system.
entropy increases from solid to liquid to gas.

Equilibrium
a state of a system by which the rate (speed) of opposing processes (reaction) are equal.

Ester
an organic compound with $-\overset{\overset{O}{\|}}{C}-O-$ ($-COO-$) as the functional group.

Esterification
an organic reaction between an alcohol and organic acid to produce an ester.

Ether
an organic compound with $-O-$ as the functional group.

Ethene
first member of the alkene hydrocarbons with a formula of C_2H_4

Ethyne
first member of the alkyne hydrocarbons with formula of C_2H_2 $H-C\equiv C-H$

Evaporation
an endothermic phase change by which a liquid changes to gas (vapor)

Excited state
a state of an atom in which electrons have "jumped" to higher electron shells (energy levels)

Exothermic
a process that releases energy.
Products of exothermic reactions always have less energy than the reactants.

F

Family (Group)
the vertical column of the Periodic Table.
Elements in the same family have same number of valance electrons and share similar chemical properties.

Fermentation
an organic reaction in which sugar is converted to alcohol (ethanol, C_2H_5OH) and carbon dioxide.

F cont.

Filtration
a process that is used to separate a liquid mixture that is composed of substances with different particle sizes.

Fission
the splitting of a large nucleus into smaller nuclei fragment in a nuclear reaction.
mass is converted to huge amounts of energy during fission.

Formula
symbols and subscripts used to represent the composition of a substance.

Formula mass
the total mass of all the atoms in one unit of formula.

Freezing (solidification)
an exothermic phase change by which a liquid changes to a solid.

Freezing point (solid/liquid equilibrium)
the temperature at which both solid and liquid phases of a substance can exist at equilibrium
the freezing point and melting point of a substance are the same.

Functional group
an atom or a group of atoms that replaces a hydrogen atom in a hydrocarbon.

Fusion (nuclear change)
the joining of two small nuclei to make a larger nucleus in a nuclear reaction.
Mass is converted to a tremendous amount of energy during fusion.

Fusion (melting) phase change
endothermic phase change by which a solid changes to a liquid.

G

Gamma ray
high-energy rays similar to X-ray that is released during nuclear decay.
a gamma ray has zero mass and zero charge ($^{0}_{0}\gamma$).

Gaseous phase
a phase of matter with no definite shape and no definite volume.

Geological dating
determining the age of a rock or mineral by comparing amounts of Uranium-238 to Lead-206 in a sample.

Gram-formula mass
a mass of one mole of a substance expressed in grams.
the total mass of all atoms in one mole of a substance.

Ground state
a state of an atom in which all electrons of the atom occupy the lowest available electron shell.

Group (family)
the vertical column of the Periodic Table.
elements in the same group have the same number of valance electrons and share similar chemical properties.

H

Haber process
a chemical reaction that produces ammonia from nitrogen and hydrogen.
$N_2 + 3H_2 \longrightarrow 2NH_3$ (Haber process equation).

Half-life
the length of time it takes for a sample of a radioisotope to decay to half its original mass (or atoms)

Glossary

H cont.

Half-reaction
a reaction that shows either the oxidation or the reduction part of a redox reaction.

Halide
a compound that contains a halogen (Group 17) atom.

Halogen
an element found in Group 17 of the Periodic Table.

Heat
a form of energy that can flow (or transfer) from one substance (or area) to another
Joules and calories are two units commonly used to measure the quantity of heat.

Heat of fusion
the amount of heat needed to change a unit mass of a solid to a liquid at its melting point.
Heat of fusion for water is 334 Joules per gram.

Heat of reaction (Δ H)
the amount of heat absorbed or released during a reaction.
the difference between the heat energy of the products and the heat energy of the reactants.
ΔH = heat of products − heat of reactants.

Heat of vaporization
the amount of heat needed to change a unit mass of a liquid to vapor (gas) at its boiling point.
Heat of vaporization for water is 2260 Joules per gram.

Heterogeneous
a type of mixture in which substances in the mixture are not uniformly or evenly mixed.

Homogeneous
a type of mixture in which substances in the mixture are uniformly and evenly mixed.
Solutions are homogenous mixtures.
Pure substances (compounds and elements) always have homogeneous properties.

Homologous series
a group of related compounds in which one member differs from the next member by a set number of atoms.

Hydrate
an ionic compound containing a set number of water molecules within its crystal structures.
$CuSO_4 \cdot 5H_2O$ is an example formula of a hydrate. This hydrates contains five moles of water.

Hydrocarbon
an organic compound containing only hydrogen and carbon atoms.

Hydrogen bond
the attraction of a hydrogen atom to oxygen, nitrogen, or fluorine atom of another molecule.
hydrogen bonding exists (or is strongest) in H_2O (water), NH_3 (ammonia), and HF (hydrogen fluoride).

Hydrogen ion (H^+)
a hydrogen atom that had lost its only electron. H+ is similar to a proton.
the only positive ion produced by all Arrhenius acids in solutions.

Hydrolysis
a reaction of a salt in water to produce a solution that is either acidic, basic, or neutral.

Hydronium ion (H_3O^+)
a polyatomic ion formed when H_2O (a water molecule) combines with H^+ (hydrogen ion).
ion formed by all Arrhenius acids in solutions.

Hydroxide ion (OH^-)
the only negative ion produced by Arrhenius bases in solutions.

Hydroxyl group (−OH)
a functional group found in compounds of alcohols.

Copyright © 2010 E3 Scholastic Publishing. All Rights Reserved.

Glossary

I

Ideal gas
a theoretical gas that posses all the characteristics described by the kinetic molecular theory

Immiscible liquids
two liquids that do not mix well with each other

Indicator
any substance that change color in the presence of a another substance.
an indicator can also be used to determine the completion of a chemical reaction.
acid-base indicators are used to determine if a substance is an acid or a base.

Inert gas (noble gas)
elements in Group 18 of the Periodic Table.

Insoluble
a solute substance with low solubility (doesn't dissolve well) in a given solvent.

Ion
a charged (+ or −) particle.

Ionic bond
a bond formed by the transfer of one or more electrons from one atom to another.
An ionic bond is formed by the electrostatic attraction of positive ion to a negative ion.

Ionic compound (substance)
compounds that are composed of positive and negative particles.
$NaCl$, $NaNO_3$, and ammonium chloride are examples of ionic substances.

Ionic radius
the size of an ion as measured from the nucleus to the outer energy level of that ion.

Ionization energy
the amount of energy needed to remove the most loosely bound valance electrons from an atom.

Isomers
organic compounds with the same molecular formula but different structural formulas.
isomers also have different properties.

Isotopes
atoms of the same element with the same number of protons but different number of neutrons.
atoms of the same element with the same atomic number but different mass numbers.

J

Joules
a unit for measuring the amount of heat energy.

K

Kelvin (K)
a unit for measuring temperature.
a Kelvin temperature unit is always 273 higher than the equivalent temperature in Celsius.
K = °C + 273

Ketone
an organic compound containing $-\overset{\overset{O}{\|}}{C}-$ ($-CO-$), a carbonyl group) as the functional group.

Kinetic energy
energy due to motion or movement of particles in a substance.
average kinetic energy of particles in a substance determines temperature of the substance.

Kinetic molecular theory (ideal gas law)
a theory that is used to explain behavior of gas particles.

Kinetics
the study of rates and mechanisms of reactions

Glossary

L

Law of conservation
  in a chemical reaction mass, atoms, charges, and energy are conserved (neither created nor destroyed).

Law of definite proportions
  atoms of a compound are in a fixed ratio.

Le Chatelier's principle
  a chemical or physical process will shift at equilibrium to compensate for added stress

Lewis electron-dot diagram
  a diagram showing the symbol of an atom and dots equal to the number of its valance electrons.

Liquid
  a phase of matter with definite volume but no definite shape (takes the shape of the container).

Luster
  a property that describes the shininess of a metallic element

M

Malleability
  ability (or property) of a metal to be hammered into a thin sheet.

Mass number
  the total number of protons and neutrons in the nucleus of an atom.

Matter
  anything that has mass and volume (occupied space).

Melting point (solid/liquid equilibrium)
  the temperature at which both the solid and the liquid phases of a substance can co-exist. The melting point of water is $0^{\circ}C$ or 273 K.

Metal
  an element that tend to lose electrons and form a positive ion during chemical reactions. the majority of the elements (about 75%) are metals.

Metallic bond
  a bond due to the attraction of valance electrons of a metallic atom to its positive nucleus. metallic bonding is described as "positive ions immersed in a sea of mobile electrons."

Metalloid
  an element with both metallic and nonmetallic properties (characteristics).

Mixture
  a physical (not chemically bonded) combination of two or more substances.
  a type of matter that can be separated by a physical method.
  a type of matter that can be either homogeneous or heterogeneous.

Molarity
  concentration of a solution expressed in moles of solute per liter of solution.

  $$\text{Molarity} = \frac{\text{moles of solute}}{\text{liter of solution}}$$

Mole
  a unit for measuring the number of particles (atoms, molecule, ions, electrons) in a substance.

Molecular formula
  a formula showing the actual composition (or ratio of atoms) in a substance

Molecule
  the smallest unit of a covalent (molecular) substance that has the same properties of the substance.
  a molecule could be one nonmetal atom (He, Ne) or a group of nonmetal atoms ($C_6H_{12}O_6$) covalently bonded

Copyright © 2010 E3 Scholastic Publishing. All Rights Reserved.

Glossary

M cont.

Molecular substance (covalent substance)
 a substance composed of molecules
 H_2O CO_2 O_2 NH_3 $C_6H_{12}O_6$ are a few examples of molecular substances.

Monomer
 an individual unit of a polymer.

Multiple covalent bond
 a double or a triple covalent bond formed by the sharing of more than two electrons.

N

Neutralization
 a reaction of an acid with a base to produce water and salt.

Neutron
 a subatomic particle with no charge found in the nucleus of an atom

Noble gas (inert gas)
 an element found in Group 18 of the Periodic Table

Nonmetal
 an element that tends to gain electrons and forms negative ions, or shares electrons to form a covalent bond.

Nonpolar covalent bond
 a bond formed by the equal sharing of electrons between two identical atoms (or of the same Electronegativity)

Nonpolar substance
 a substance whose molecules have symmetrical shape and even charge distribution

Nucleus
 the small, dense, positive core of an atom containing protons and neutrons.

O

Octet of electrons
 when an atom has a stable electron configuration with eight electrons in the valance shell.

Orbital
 a region in an atom where electrons are likely to be found (or located).

Organic acid
 a compound containing $-COOH$ or $\overset{\overset{O}{\|}}{C}-OH$ as its functional group.

Organic chemistry
 the study of carbon and carbon based compounds.

Oxidation
 the loss of electrons by an atom during a redox reaction.
 oxidation leads to an increase in oxidation state (number) of a substance.

Oxidized substance (Reducing agent)
 a substance that loss electrons in a redox reaction.
 a substance whose oxidation number (state) increases after a redox reaction

Oxidizing agent (Reduced substance)
 a substance that is reduced (gained electrons) in a redox reaction.
 a substance whose oxidation number (state) decreases after a redox reaction

Oxidation number/ Oxidation state
 a charge an atom has or appears to have during a redox reaction

Ozone
 O_3, an allotrope (a different molecular form) of oxygen

Glossary

P

Parts per million
concentration of a solution expressed as ratio of grams of solute per million n parts of a solution.

$$\text{Part per million (ppm)} = \frac{\text{grams of solute}}{\text{grams of solution}} \times 1\,000\,000$$

Percent composition
composition of a compound as the percentage by mass of each element compared to the total mass of the compound.

$$\text{Percent composition} = \frac{\text{mass of parts}}{\text{mass of whole}} \times 100$$

Period
the horizontal row of the Periodic Table
elements within a Period have the same number of occupied electron shells (or energy levels).

Periodic law
states that properties of elements are periodic functions of their atomic numbers.

pH
values that indicate the strength of an acid or a base. pH values ranges from 1 – 14.
pH values is determined from how much H^+ ions are in a solution.

Phase equilibrium
a state of balance when the rates of two opposing (opposite) phase changes are equal.

Physical change
a change that does not change the composition of a substance.
phase change and dissolving are examples of physical changes.

Physical properties
characteristics of a substance that can be observed or measured without changing the chemical composition of the substance

Polar covalent bond
a bond formed by the unequal sharing of electrons between two different nonmetal atoms.

Polyatomic ion
a group of two or more atoms with excess positive or negative charge (See Reference Table E).

Polymer
an organic compound composed of chains of monomers (smaller units).

Polymerization
an organic reaction by which monomers (small units molecules) are joined together to make a polymer (a larger unit molecule).

Position (electron catcher)
a positively charge particle similar in mass to an electron. $^{0}_{+1}e$

Positron decay (emission)
a nuclear decay that releases a positron

Potential energy
stored energy in chemical substances.
amount of potential energy depends on composition and the structure of a substance.

Potential energy diagram
a diagram showing the changes in potential energy of substances during a reaction.

Precipitate
a solid that forms out of a solution

Primary alcohol
an alcohol with –OH functional group attached to an end carbon

Glossary

P cont.

Product
a substance that remained (or formed) after a chemical reaction is completed.
products are placed to the right of an arrow in equations.

Proton
a subatomic particle with a positive charge found in the nucleus of an atom.
the number of protons in an atom is equal to the atomic number of the element.

Pure substances
a type of matter with the same composition and properties in all samples.
elements and compounds are pure substances.

Q

quanta
a specific amount of energy absorbed or released by an electron as it changes from one level to another.

Qualitative
indicates the type of atom in a chemical formula.

Quantitative
indicates the number of each atom in a formula.

R

Radioisotope
an unstable isotope of an element that is radioactive and can decay.

Rate
a measure of the speed (how fast) a reaction occurs.

Reactant
the starting substance in a chemical reaction.
reactants are shown (or placed) to the left of the arrow in equations.

Redox
a reaction that involves oxidation and reduction.

Reduction
the gaining of electrons during a redox reaction.
reduction leads to a decrease in oxidation number (state) of a substance

Reduced substance (oxidizing agent)
a substance that gained electron during a redox reaction
a substance whose oxidation number (state) decreases after a reaction

Reducing agent (oxidized substance)
the substance that is oxidized (loss electrons) in a redox reaction.
a substance whose oxidation number (state) increases after a redox reaction.

S

Saponification
an organic reaction that produces soap and glycerol (a trihydroxy alcohol).

Salt
a product of neutralization reaction.
an ionic substance.

Salt bridge
allows for ions to flow (migrate) between the two half cells of voltaic cells.

Glossary

S cont.

Saturated hydrocarbon
  alkane hydrocarbon with only single bonds between the carbon atoms.

Saturated solution
  a solution containing the maximum amount of dissolved solute possible at a given temperature.

Secondary alcohol
  an alcohol in which the –OH is bonded to a carbon atom that is already bonded to two other carbon atoms.

Single covalent bond
  a covalent bond formed by the sharing of just two electrons (or one pair of electrons)

Single replacement
  a reaction in which a more reactive element replaces the less reactive element of a compound.

Solid phase
  a phase of matter with definite shape and definite volume

Solubility
  a measure of the extent to which a solute will dissolve in a given solvent at a specified temperature.

Soluble
  a substance with high solubility.

Solute
  the substance that is being dissolved.
  when a salt dissolved in water, the solute is the salt.

Solution
  a homogeneous mixture of substances in the same physical state.

Solvent
  the substance (usually a liquid) that is dissolving the solute.
  water is the solvent in all aqueous solutions.

Spontaneous reaction
  a reaction that will occur under a given set of conditions
  a reaction that proceed in the direction of lower energy and greater entropy

Stress
  a change in temperature, pressure, concentration to a reaction at equilibrium.

Sublimation
  an endothermic phase change from solid to gas.

Subscript
  a whole number written next to a chemical symbol to indicate the number of atoms present.

Substitution reaction
  an organic reaction of an alkane with a halogen to produce a halide.
  a reaction in which a halogen atom replaces a hydrogen atom of an alkane (saturated) hydrocarbon.

Supersaturated solution
  a solution containing more solutes than would dissolve at that given temperature.

Symbol
  a one, two, or three-letter designation of an element.

Symmetrical molecule
  a molecule that has a nonpolarized structure due to an even charge distribution.

Synthesis
  a chemical reaction in which two or more substances combine to make one substance.

Glossary

T

Temperature
the measure of the average kinetic energy of particles in a substance
Temperature and average kinetic energy are directly related. As one increases, so does the other.

Tertiary alcohol
an alcohol in which the –OH is bonded to a carbon atom that is already bonded to three other carbon atoms.

Titration
a process used in determining the concentration of an unknown solution by reacting it with a solution of a known concentration.

Tracer
a radioisotope used to track a chemical reaction.

Transition element
an element found in Group 3 – 12 of the Periodic Table

Transmutation
the changing or converting of a nucleus of one atom into a nucleus of a different atom

Trihydroxy alcohol
an alcohol with three –OH (hydroxyl) groups

Triple covalent bond
a covalent bond resulting from the sharing of three pairs of electrons (six total electrons).

U

Unsaturated hydrocarbon
organic compound containing double or triple bonded carbon atoms.

Unsaturated solution
a solution containing less dissolved solute than can be dissolved at a given temperature.

V

Valance electrons
the electrons in the outermost electron shell (energy level) of an atom.

Vapor
a gas form of a substance that is normally a liquid at room temperature

Vapor pressure
the pressure exerted by vapor (evaporated particles) on the surface of the liquid

Vaporization (evaporation).
endothermic phase change of a substance from liquid to a gaseous state at its boiling point.

Voltaic cell
an electrochemical cell in which electrical energy is produced from a spontaneous redox chemical reaction.

W

Wave-mechanical model (electron-cloud model)
the current model of an atom that places electrons in orbital.
the orbital is describe as the probable location (region) of finding electrons in an atom.

Index

Absolute zero 10
Accelerator 293
Acids 166 – 184
    Arrhenius 166
    alternate theory 166
    binary 184
    formulas and names 167, 184
    neutralization reaction 175
    organic 238
    properties 165
    reaction with metals 172 – 174
    ternary 184
Activated complexes 202
Activation energy 190
Addition reaction 252, 253
Addition polymerization 252, 256
Alcohols 232 – 234
    in reactions 255
Aldehydes 236
Alkali metals 36, 38, 40
Alkaline earth metals 36, 38, 40
Alkalinity 168
Alkanes 227
    bonding in 226
    in reactions 251, 252
    isomers of 242
Alkenes 228
    bonding in 226
    in reactions 252, 253
    isomers of 243
Alkyl groups 242
Alkynes 229
    bonding in 226
    in reactions 253
    isomers of 243
Allotropes 45
Alpha decays 296, 302
Alpha emitters 295
Alpha particles 293
Amides 240
Amines 240
Amino acids 241
Anode 277
    in electrolytic cells 281
    in voltaic cells 278
Aqueous solutions 139
    properties 141
Arrhenius theories of
    acids 166
    bases 166
Artificial transmutation 295, 299, 302
Asymmetrical molecules 82 - 83
Atom 51
    historical scientists' models 49

Atomic mass 58
    on periodic table 37 – 37
    calculation of 59
Atomic mass unit 58
Atomic numbers 53
    on periodic table 36 – 37
    relating to other particles 54
    in isotope symbols 57
Atomic radii 42
    trend in 42
Avogadro's law (hypothesis) 21
Avogadro's number 121

Bases 166 – 184
    alternate theory 166
    Arrhenius theory 166
    formulas and names 167, 185
    neutralization reaction 175
    properties 165
Battery 276
Beta decay 297, 302
Beta emitter 295
Beta particles 293
Binary compounds 5, 102, 105
    formulas 103, 105
    naming 107
Bohr, Neil 49
Bohr's atomic diagrams 61
Boiling 157
Boiling points
    concentration effect on 160
    of solutions 159
    of water 10, 159
    on phase change diagrams 13
Bonding 73
    coordinate covalent 77
    covalent 75
    energy 74
    hydrogen 91, 93
    intermolecular 91 – 96
    intramolecular 75 – 78
    ionic 75
    metallic 77
    network 76
    nonpolar covalent 76
    polar covalent 76
    stability of atoms 73
    in water 91
Boyle's law 22, 26
Buckminsterfullerene 45

Index

Calorimeter 14
Carbon
    allotropes 45
    bonding in organic 223
    properties 223
Carbon – 12   314
Carbon – 14   314
Catalyst 190
    effect on reaction rate 190
    effect on equilibrium reaction 217
    on potential energy diagram 204
Cathode 277
    on electrolytic cells 281
    on voltaic cells 278
Celsius scale 10
    conversion to Kelvin 10
Charles' law 22, 26
Chemical bonds (see bonding)
Chemical equations 113
    balancing 115 – 117
    coefficients 11
    conservation 113
    mole ratio in 131
    mass – mass relationship in 135
    mole – mole relationship in 133
    volume – volume relationship 133
Chemical formulas 97
    counting atoms in 97
    ratio of ions 98
    empirical 99 – 100
    molecular 99 – 100
    structural 99
    naming 106 – 110
    writing 101 – 105
Chemical reactions
    types of 112 – 113
    of metal with acids 172 – 174
    of acids with bases 175
    endothermic 195 - 201
    exothermic 195 – 201
    and potential energy diagrams 202
    forward and reverse 208, 211
    Le Chatelier's principle 212
    Stress on 212 – 217
    of equilibrium 211
    rate of 189
    collision theory of 190
    activation energy 190
    organic 251 – 158

Chemical properties 27
Chemical changes 27, 112 – 113
Chemical symbols
    of elements 5, 36 – 37
    of compounds 5
    of mixtures 5
    of pure substances 1 – 2
Chemistry 1
Cobalt – 60   314
Coefficients   111
    mole ratio 131
    calculating 132 - 135
    conservations 113
    balancing 114 – 117
Collision theory 191
Combined gas laws 26
Combustion 252, 254
Compounds   2, 4
    binary 80, 102, 105, 107, 110
    diagrams of 6
    oxidation number of 262 – 263
    symbols of 5
Concentration 154
    at equilibrium 213
    effect on equilibrium reaction 208
    effect on rate 191
    molarity 154 – 155
    parts per million 156
    of hydrogen ion and pH 178 – 180
Condensation 9, 13
    calculating heat during 16
Condensation polymerization 252, 255
Conductivity 35
    of acids and bases 182
    of elements 34
    of ionic substances 79, 80
    of metallic substances 79, 80
    of molecular substances 79, 81
Conversion
    temperature 10
    pressure 24
    grams to mole 125 – 126
Cooling curves 12 – 13
Covalent bonds 75 – 78
    single 88, 226 – 227
    double 88 , 226, 228
    triple 88, 226, 229
Covalent compounds
    formulas 105
    naming 110
    properties 81
Cracking 252

Index

Dalton, John 49
Decomposition 112 – 113
Density 27
Deposition 9
Diamonds 76, 79
Diatomic molecules 39, 76, 82
    Lewis electron-dot diagrams 88- 89
Dipole molecules   (see polar molecules)
Distillation 7
Double covalent bond 88, 226, 227
Double replacement reactions 112 - 113
Ductile 33
Electricity
    in redox 276
Effective collision 190
    an reaction rate 195
Electrochemical cells 276 - 286
Electrodes 286, 277
Electrolysis 276
Electrolytes 182
Electrolytic cells 276, 281 – 286
Electrolytic reductions 281 – 283
    of Group 1 metals 38
Electron cloud model 49
Electron-dot diagrams 86 – 90
    of neutral atoms 86
    of ions 86
    of ionic compounds 87
    of diatomic 88
    of molecular compounds 88 - 89
Electronegativity 33, 44
    trend in 44
    in molecular polarity 85
Electrons 52
    in bonding 73
    configurations 61 – 64
    discovery 50
    in ion 69 – 70
    orbital 49
    in nuclear chemistry 293
    relating to other particles 54
Electroplating 276   281   284 – 385, 287
Elements 1, 4, 6
    on periodic table 36 – 37
Emission spectra 64 – 66
Empirical formulas 99 - 100
    in determining molecular formula 130

Endothermic
    in phase changes 9, 12
    in bonding 74
    in chemical reactions 196 – 201
    in potential energy diagrams 202 – 204
    related to equilibrium 214
    electrochemical cells   276, 286
Energy
    activation 190
    ionization 33, 35
    potential 196
    of reactions 196
    during phase change
    heat 14 – 17
    unit 14
Enthalpy 196
Entropy 206 – 207
Equilibrium 208 – 219
    physical 209 – 210
    chemical 211 – 219
Esterification 252, 255
Ester 239
Exothermic
    in phase changes 9, 12
    in bonding 74
    in chemical reactions 196 – 201
    in potential energy diagrams 202 – 204
    related to equilibrium 214
    electrochemical cells   276, 286
Excited states   63 – 64
    relating to spectral lines 65
Evaporation 9, 13
    heat during 16
    in separating mixtures 7

Families of elements (see Groups)
Fermentation   124
Filtration 7, 141
Fission 300, 302
Formula mass 124
    in moles calculation 125
    in mass calculation 126
    in percent composition 127 – 128
Formulas (see chemical formulas)
Freezing 9, 13
Freezing point 13
    of water 10
    in equilibrium 209
Functional groups 230 – 241
    Isomers of 244
Fusion
    phase change 9, 13, 16
    nuclear change 300, 302

Copyright © 2010 E3 Scholastic Publishing. All Rights Reserved.

Index

Gamma rays 293 – 294
    separation in electric field 294
Gases
    properties of 8
    Kinetic molecular theory 19
    real gases 18
    ideal gas 19
Gas laws calculations 22 – 26
Gay-Lussac's law 23, 26
Geological dating 314
Gold foil experiment 50
Gram formula mass (see formula mass)
Group 32, 36, 40
Ground state 64 – 65

Haber process equation 113, 211
Half-life 304
    in calculations 313
    relating to dating 314
Half-reaction 266 – 268
    Writing 274 – 275
Halides 230 - 231
    In organic reaction 251 - 253
Halogens 37 , 39
Heat 14
    unit of 14
    calculations 15 – 18
Heating curve 12 – 13
Heat of fusion 16 – 17
Heat of reaction 196 - 197
    endothermic reactions 197
    exothermic reactions
    potential energy diagrams 203 - 204
    tables of 200 – 201

Heat of vaporization 16 – 17
Heterogeneous mixture 3, 4
Homogeneous mixture 3, 4, 139 – 140
    separation 7, 141
Homologous series 226
Hydrates 126 – 127
    composition atoms 97
    formula mass of 124
    percent composition of 128 – 129
Hydrocarbon 226 – 229
    alkanes 227
    alkenes 228
    alkynes 229
    isomers of 242 – 243
Hydrogen bonding 91, 93

Hydrogen
    emission spectra 66
    isotopes of 60, 66
    in fusion nuclear reaction 301
    product of reactions 172
Hydrogen ion
    in acid definitions 166, 168
    relating to pH 169,   178 – 180
Hydronium (see hydrogen ion)
Hydroxide ion 160, 168
Hydroxyl group 232 – 234

Ideal gas 19
Immiscible liquids 141
Indicators 170
Inert gases (see noble gases)
Insoluble 141
    using Reference Table F 144 – 145
Intermolecular forces 91 – 93
    relating to boiling points 157 – 158
    relating to vapor pressure 157 – 158
Ionic bonds 75, 77 – 78
Ionic compounds 79 – 80
    as electrolytes 182
    formulas of 102 – 1054
    Lewis electron-dot 87
    naming 107 – 109
    properties 79 - 80
    ratio of ions 98
    reaction rate 195
Ionization energy 33, 35
    trend in 44 – 45
Ions 67
    compared to neutral atoms 68
    determining particles in 67
    ionic configuration 68, 70
Ionic radii 68
Ionic substances (see ionic compounds)
Isomers 241 – 244
Isotopes 55 – 56
    in atomic mass calculations 58 – 59
    in nucleus chemistry 292
    radioisotopes 295

Joules 14

Kelvin scale 10
    conversion to Celsius 10
Ketones 237
Kinetic energy 10
    in phase change diagram 13
Kinetic molecular theory 19
Kinetics 189

Index

Law of conservation 113 – 114
Law of definite proportion 2
Le Chatelier's principle 211 – 212
Lewis electron-dot (see electron-dot diagram)
Liquids 8
    Vapor pressure 157
    in aqueous solutions 139
Luster 33, 35

Malleable 33, 35
Mass
    conservation of 113
Mass defect 299
Mass number 53 – 54
    relating to other particles 54
Matter 1
    classifications 4
Melting (fusion) 9
Melting points 10, 13
Metallic bonds 77
Metalloids 34, 35
Metals 33 – 35
    in ionic compounds 102 – 104
    in compounds 75 – 78
Methyl orange indicator 170
Miscible liquids 141
Mixtures 3, 4, 139
    symbols of 140
    separation of 141
Molarity 154 – 155
Moles 121 – 122
    relation to mass 123 – 126
Molecular formulas 99
    relating to empirical formula 100
Molecular mass (see formula mass)
Multiple covalent bonds
    in oxygen and nitrogen 88
    in hydrocarbon 226
Molecular substances 79, 81
Molecules 81 – 84
    degree of polarity 82 – 85
    symmetry 82
Network solid 76, 79
Neutralization 175 – 176
    titration 177
Neutrons 52, 54 – 55
    in nuclear chemistry 293, 296 – 298, 300
Noble gas 40
Nonmetals 33 – 35
    in compounds 75

Nonpolar covalent bonding 76
Nonpolar substances 82
    Lewis electron-dots diagram 88
Nuclear chemistry 291 – 315
Nuclear particles 293
    separation of
Nuclear waste 314
Nucleus 51, 291
    stability 294
Octet 73
Orbital 49
Organic chemistry 223 – 260
Organic acids 183, 230, 238
    in reactions 252, 255
Organic compounds 226 – 229
    properties 223
    bonding in 225 – 226
Organic reactions 251 – 254
Oxidation 262, 266 – 268, 275
Oxidation numbers 261 – 264
Oxidized substances 266 – 267, 270 – 272, 275
Oxidizing agents 266 – 275
Ozone 45

Parts per million 156
Percent compositions 127
    of hydrates 128 – 129
Periodic law 32
    Periodic Table 36 – 37
Periods 32, 36 – 37
Periodic Trends 41 – 45
Phases of matter 8 – 9
    equilibrium 33
Phenolphthalein 170
pH 169
    relating to hydrogen ions 178 – 180
Physical changes 27, 111
Physical properties 27
    of elements 33, 35
Polar covalent 76 - 77, 84
    Lewis electron-dot diagrams 84
Polyatomic ions 100, 103
    in balancing equations 116
    in formulas 103
    in naming 107
    oxidation number of 264
    in ratio of ions in compounds 98

Polymerization 252 255 – 256
    condensation 255
    addition 256

Index

Positrons 293
Positron emitter 295
positron emission 298, 302
Potential energy 196
    in chemical reaction 196
    relating to phase changes 12 – 13
Potential energy diagrams 202 – 205
Precipitates 149
Pressures 19
    in behavior of gases 19
    in Avogadro's law 21
    in gas law calculations 22 – 23
    conversion between units 24
    effect on solubility 142
    effect on reaction rate 193
    effect on equilibrium reactions 215
Primary alcohols 233
Products 111 – 112
Propane 227
    in organic reactions 251, 253
Protein 241
    in organic reactions 255
Protons 51 – 52
    relating to atomic numbers 53
    determining from other particles 54
    in isotopes 55
Pure substances 1, 4
    symbols of 5
    diagrams of 6

Quanta 64
Qualitative composition 97 – 98
Quantitative composition 97 – 98

Radiations 293
Radioisotopes 295
    in radioactive dating 314
    in medical usages 314
    wastes 314
Rates
    of reactions 189, 195
    activation energy 190
    catalyst effect 190, 195
    concentration effect 191, 195
    pressure effect 193, 195
    surface area effect 194, 195
    temperature effect 192, 195
Reactants 111 – 112
Reactions (see chemical reactions)
Reactivity of metals 172 – 173

Redox 261 - 271
    equations 265, 269
    interpretations 270 – 271
Reducing agents 272, 266, 267
Reduction 262, 266 – 268, 275
Reduced substances 266 – 275
Reducing agent 266 – 267, 270 – 272, 275
Replacement reactions 112 – 113
    in acid – metal reactions 172
    in neutralization reactions 175
Rutherford, earnest 49
Rutherford's gold foil experiment 50

Salt bridge 277, 280, 286
Salts
    ionic substances 80
    solubility of 144
    solubility curves 147
    effect on physical properties 32 – 33
    products of neutralization 175 – 176
    electrolytes 182
    formulas of 181
Saturated hydrocarbons 226, 227, 251
Saturated solutions 146
    from solubility curves 148
    equilibrium 210
Single covalent bonds 226 – 227
Single replacements 112 – 113
Solid phase 8
    in phase change diagrams 12 – 13
Solubility 141
    temperature effects 142
    pressure effects 142
    nature of reactants 142
    solubility curves 147
Soluble 141, 144 – 145
Solutes 139
    amount to saturation 148 - 149
Solutions 139 – 162
    type of matter 3
    aqueous 139
    compare to water 159
    properties of 141
    descriptions of 146
    concentration of 154 – 156
Solvent 139

Index

Stock system of naming 104, 108
Stress on equilibrium 212 – 218
Spectral lines 64 – 66
Spectroscope 66
Stability
    in bonding 73
    of nucleus 294
Spontaneous reactions 288
STP 23
    in gas law calculations 26
State of matter (see phases of matter)
Substitution reaction 251, 252
Supersaturated solutions 146
    and precipitate (re-crystallization) 149
    using solubility curves 150
Symbols
    of elements and compounds 5
    of mixtures 5, 139, 140
Symmetrical molecules 82, 84, 89
Subatomic particles 51
Synthesis reactions 112 – 113

Technitium-90 314
Temperature 10
    Avogadro's law
    behavior of gases 19
    conversions 11
    effect on half-life 304
    effect on equilibrium reactions 214
    effect on rate of reactions 192, 195
    effect on solubility 142
    energy of reaction
    entropy 206 - 207
    heat flow 14
    heat calculations 15 – 17
    gas law calculations 22 – 26
    phase diagram 12
    phase equilibrium 209
    standard temperature 26
Thermometers 10
Tertiary alcohols 233
Thompson, JJ 49
    cathode ray experiment 50
Titrations 117
Tracers 314
Transition elements 39
Transmutations 291
    natural 295 – 298
    artificial 295, 299
Trihydroxy alcohols 234
Triple covalent bonds
    hydrocarbons 226, 229
    nitrogen 88

Unsaturated hydrocarbon 226, 228, 229
Unsaturated solutions 146, 149
    using solubility curves 150

Valance electrons 67 – 68
    of Groups 38 – 40
    in bonding 73
    Lewis electron-dot diagrams 86 – 87
    relation to ions 68
Vapor 157
Vapor pressure 157 – 158
    intermolecular forces 91 - 93, 157, 158
    solute effect on 159
Vaporization 9
    on phase change diagrams 13
    heat of 15 – 17
Voltaic cells 276, 278 – 280, 286
Volume
    kinetic molecular theory 19
    Avogadro's law 21
    gas law calculations 22 – 26

Water
    formula 1, 2
    properties 2, 27
    phase change diagrams 13
    freezing and boiling points 10
    heat constants 15
    bonding between atoms 25 – 27
    type of substance 79
    molecule of 81
    shape 83
    structure 82
    polarity 83, 84
    Lewis electron-dot diagrams 89
    Intermolecular forces 91
    hydrogen bonding 91, 93
    synthesis of 113
    molar (formula) mass 124
    hydrates 128
    in solutions 139
    molecule – ion attraction 140
    products of reaction 175, 254, 255
    heat of reaction of 200
    phase equilibrium 209
    electrolysis 286
    acids and bases 166
Wave mechanical model 49

CPSIA information can be obtained at www.ICGtesting.com
Printed in the USA
240580LV00001B/5/P